Achieving and Sustaining Institutional Excellence for the First Year of College

Achieving and Sustaining Institutional Excellence for the First Year of College

Betsy O. Barefoot

John N. Gardner

Marc Cutright

Libby V. Morris

Charles C. Schroeder

Stephen W. Schwartz

Michael J. Siegel

Randy L. Swing

JOSSEY-BASS
A Wiley Imprint
www.josseybass.com

Published by Jossey-Bass
A Wiley Imprint
989 Market Street, San Francisco, CA 94103-1741 www.josseybass.com

Jossey-Bass books and products are available through most bookstores. To contact Jossey-Bass directly call our Customer Care Department within the U.S. at 800-956-7739, outside the U.S. at 317-572-3986 or fax 317-572-4002.

Jossey-Bass also publishes its books in a variety of electronic formats. Some content that appears in print may not be available in electronic books.

Library of Congress Cataloging-in-Publication Data

Achieving and sustaining institutional excellence for the first year of college / Betsy O. Barefoot ... [et al.].— 1st ed.
p. cm.
Includes bibliographical references and index.
ISBN 0-7879-7151-0 (alk. paper)
1. College student development programs—United States—Case studies. 2. College freshmen—United States—Case studies. 3. Campus visits—United States—Case studies.
LB2343.4.A34 2005
378.1'98—dc22 2004026197

Printed in the United States of America
FIRST EDITION
HB Printing 10 9 8 7 6 5 4 3 2

The Jossey-Bass Higher and Adult Education Series

Contents

Foreword

The late Nevitt Sanford told a wonderful anecdote that contains the essence of why this book is so important for college educators who strive to improve the quality and impact of undergraduate education for their students, especially beginning with the first year. The anecdote was about the encounter between a dean at Brown University and a group of prospective parents.

The dean was explaining to the assembled audience the benefits that would result from a Brown University education for the lives of their young men and women if they decided to spend four years as undergraduate students at Brown. Since the institution had chosen carefully which of the deans would speak to audiences of prospective parents, the presentation was eloquent, thoughtful, and extended. At the end of the talk came time for questions. One obviously skeptical mother held up her hand for recognition and asked the truth-in-advertising question: "This sounds just wonderful, but how can we parents be assured that these changes will actually occur?" The dean's apocryphal reply was both vintage Sanford and why this book is so important: "Madam, we guarantee results or else we'll refund the child."

The long-sought-after holy grail of higher education is to bring together entering first-year students and institutions of higher education in a seamless transition toward an undergraduate experience with a lasting impact. The pitfalls along the way, however, are so very numerous: what the student is actually seeking is often not really what the institution can offer; what the institution really excels at teaching is sometimes not what the student can or wants to learn; or the tasks in the process of transformation from high school to upper-division status are neither sufficiently well presented by the institution nor sufficiently well understood by the entering student to make the transformation from high school to college as meaningful, stimulating, and transformative as it can be. All of these need to go exceedingly well before a college or university can metaphorically assure that it will not have to "refund the child." In terms of Sanford's classic anecdote, this book is about what a carefully chosen group of colleges and universities are already doing so that they can "guarantee results" to the very best of their abilities.

Chancellor Otto von Bismarck of Germany in the nineteenth century is reputed to have observed that one-third of German university students broke down from overwork, another one-third broke down from dissipation, and the final one-third went on to rule Germany. In the context of this book, two observations are in order. First, this is a terrible waste of human talent and societal resources. Second, at least in the nearly first half of the twentieth century, those who went on to rule Germany did not rule very well.

This book examines vital elements of empowering educational experience to achieve institutional objectives, maximizing the development of human talent, and using institutional resources to the fullest advantage toward goals shared by parents, students, faculty, staff, and administration. Unlike the German universities of Bismarck's day, there is a shared commitment among authors and participants in achieving and sustaining excellence in the first year of college.

The authors have stated their purpose in embarking on the research that is the foundation for this book: "We sought to identify campuses in which the first year has become a high priority and truly central to the collegiate experience." Thirteen campuses were selected for intensive case studies based on "their comprehensive attention to first-year students—attention that is embedded in or linked to the curriculum and cocurriculum and is coupled with evaluation and evidence of continuous improvement."

Steps in the Process: Borrowing from the British Detective Story

It is new and uncharted territory to use an intensive case study design to discern the ingredients of exemplary undergraduate education in the first year of college. Elements of the British procedural detective story will be employed to illuminate the steps the authors took in realizing the goals of the ambitious project reported in this book. Since the territory investigated by the authors is uncharted, this device will sharpen the methodological choices made that are so important to establishing the validity of the findings:

- *"Round up the usual suspects."* When actor Claude Raines instructed his policemen to "round up the usual suspects" in the movie *Casablanca* with Humphrey Bogart and Ingrid Bergman and a wonderful supporting cast, he already knew the identity of the perpetrator of the crime, and he really did not want him caught. But what do you do when there is a universe of nearly 4,000 potentially eligible possible "suspects" and the goal is a credible search for participants in a focused research project with finite participants (in this case, thirteen)? The authors were exceptionally clear about the processes they followed in sample selection. They wanted "to move beyond a random collection of good ideas for first-year programs" or a "rounding up of the usual suspects" to make a more systematic selection of colleges and universities that can serve as exemplars for achieving first-year excellence. While the authors note that there are many good ideas throughout the book on such facets of the first year as orientation, residence life, learning communities, first-year seminars, and advising structures, what they focused on finding were campuses where "the primary focus is on the totality of the first year—how these various components become embodied in a campus's overall approach to its new students."
- *Identifying the elements of the crime. How did the perpetrators go about their "nefarious business"?* How would an investigator go about the task of identifying "suspects"—or as the authors more eloquently phrased it, Where would you look for models? What would be your criteria? Would you simply know it when you saw it?
- *Where would you look for models?* The approach of the authors proceeded on several tracks. One track was to send an invitation to all chief academic officers of regionally accredited two- and four-year institutions of higher education in the United States. This invitation was to nominate their institution as an Institution of Excellence in the First College Year. Another track was to write to 2,000 college and university educators whose names appear on two electronic listservs of individuals with interests in the first year of college. This

self-nomination process resulted in 130 potential case studies, which were reduced first to 54 and then to the final thirteen.

For educators wanting a road map for thinking specifically about where to begin improving their own first-year structures and programs, Table 1.2 is a brief but exceptionally important part of the book. This table, as characterized by the authors, "provides a list of the most common first-year initiatives described by the thirteen institutions in the nomination portfolios." These initiatives were considered to be the most important by both the authors and the campuses that were the object of the case studies.

Table 1.2 identifies twenty initiatives that contribute to excellence in the first year:

- Advising
- Central advising center
- Common reading
- Convocations
- Core curriculum/general education
- Electronic portfolios
- Experiential learning
- Faculty development
- First-year seminars
- Leadership programs
- Learning centers
- Learning communities
- Liberal arts
- Mentoring
- Orientation
- Peer leaders/advisers
- Residence life
- Service initiatives
- Summer academic programs
- Supplemental Instruction

The power of the case study method in this context is that it allows readers and researchers to observe how these program initiatives interact in the context of an exemplary institutional approach to the first year. Each of the thirteen campuses has its own areas of emphasis within the twenty programmatic areas of emphasis, and no campus has all twenty. For example, only LaGuardia and the University of South Carolina use convocations, and only two (Kalamazoo College and LaGuardia) use electronic portfolios. Many institutions, in contrast, use some version of first-year seminars, learning communities, orientation, and peer advisers.

• *What would be your criteria?* Determining and applying the five criteria to the 130 nominees and fifty-four semifinalists was a procedure untaken by a panel of thirteen external evaluators and the staff of the Policy Center on the First Year of College. The five criteria, elaborated in Chapter One, were as follows:

Criterion 1: Evidence of an intentional, comprehensive approach to improving the first year that is appropriate to an institution's type of mission

Criterion 2: Evidence of assessment of the various initiatives that constitute this approach

Criterion 3: Broad impact on significant numbers of first-year students, including, but not limited to, special student subpopulations

Criterion 4: Strong administrative support for first-year initiatives, evidence of institutionalization, and durability over time

Criterion 5: Involvement of a wide range of faculty, student affairs professionals, academic administrators, and other constituent groups

• *Would you simply know it when you saw it?* As the authors put it, "We recognized that excellence would have to be identified within the framework of institutional size, type, and mission." With a case study format investigating first-year excellence in context, it was essential to include diverse institutions. Therefore, the authors studied community colleges, private liberal arts colleges, regional comprehensive universities, research universities, and one of the nation's military academies. As a commentary, they pose the question, "Was this selection process simply another ranking system in disguise?" They answered it emphatically, "No!" The research design issues are discussed in detail in Chapter Two.

Insights into Enhancing Quality and Impact

This commentary began with an anecdote of the late Nevitt Sanford, which underscored the importance of an institution's configuring its programs for students in an optimal manner, or as he put it more as a metaphor, so that the institution can "guarantee results." The broader context of the work is the importance of making the first year of college a source of strength for the realization of the broad purposes that unite parents, students, faculty, staff, and administration.

Within the higher education research and policy community, there are a number of quite viable and credible macro approaches to reforming education and improving quality. For example, in the 1970s, the late Frank Newman led a commission whose sharp criticisms of existing higher education practice were followed by systematic advocacy of reform. Another example is the more recent macro policy reform and efforts at transformation of the type undertaken by the National Collaborative for Postsecondary Education Policy, a joint project of the Education Commission of the States, the National Center for Higher Education Management Systems, and the National Center for Public Policy and Higher Education funded by The Pew Charitable Trusts. This latter approach aims to persuade, at the level of individual states, the adoption of major policy changes.

By contrast, the case study approach taken in this book aims at providing insights based on an approach to micro analysis—an approach in this application that focuses specifically on the interaction of discrete program and policy variables under the control of individual campuses. The broad contribution of this book is that improving the quality and impact of the first year of college goes beyond a collection of good ideas and programs and putting those into practice. Rather, the key to success is in the planned interrelationship and interaction in practice of the twenty plus program initiatives identified in Table 1.2.

And there is a hierarchy of what is catalytic of excellence in first-year programs. The key catalytic elements at the top of the hierarchy are intentionality, comprehensiveness, systematic assessment and feedback, broad impact of programs, strong campus support for comprehensive programs (the location of key campus support in a system of shared governance may vary from campus to campus, but the commitment of administration seems central across campuses), institutionalization of the broad initiative, and a wide and comprehensive involvement of students, faculty, staff, and administration.

Returning to the Major Theme

Another way to think about the broad purposes of this book was provided by that notable cultural philosopher Gary Trudeau in a memorable commencement ceremony where the commencement speaker endeavors to speak directly to a graduating class that he considers "prematurely professionalized" and "chillingly competitive." His poignant lament concerned the students' "obsessive concern for the future," an approach that has been "the salient shaping influence on your attitudes during a very critical four years." He then went on to state eloquently: "It could have been more than that. This college offered you a sanctuary, a place to experience PROCESS, to FEEL the present as you moved through it, to EMBRACE both the joys and sorrows of moral and intellectual maturation! It needn't have been just another way-station" (Trudeau, May 16, 1976).

Insights from all the case studies and the important variables identified in Table 1.2 offer ingredients for a college and university to use in constructing its own road map to make the college experience a genuine opportunity to experience educational process and, as Trudeau had his commencement speaker say so memorably, to "embrace both the joys and sorrows of moral and intellectual maturation."

University of California, Irvine — John M. Whiteley

In Memoriam
Omri Kenneth (O.K.) Webb (1926–2004)
Appalachian State University
and
Stephen Hanscom Good (1943–2004)
Drury University

We gratefully and respectfully acknowledge these two campus leaders. Their enormous contributions to and influence on their institutions' first-year experience helped make possible this achievement as Institutions of Excellence in the First College Year. We are also deeply appreciative of these campus leaders' personal participation in our research project and this resulting work.

Preface

If, in the 1970s, anyone had set out to discover and study colleges and universities in the United States at which the first year was a high priority, the journey would have been difficult. The campuses with any special focus on the first year were few and far between. Even as late as 1987, a survey conducted by the American Council on Education found that only 37 percent of institutions acknowledged taking steps to improve the first year (El-Khawas, 1987). Since that time, interest in the first year within U.S. colleges and universities has grown exponentially. Many campuses have joined the national conversation about the first year in an effort to improve student learning, personal development, and persistence to graduation. Faculty, administrators, and staff on campuses around the nation routinely develop and share highly innovative and effective educational practices through conference presentations, publishing, and other means. Nevertheless, through the years, we have observed that many, if not most, first-year efforts occur at the margins of campus life and have yet to be experienced as central to the core academic experience.

As we conceptualized the research study that is the foundation for this book, we sought to identify campuses in which the first year has become a high priority and truly central to the collegiate experience. Therefore, this book, while it provides many excellent examples of programs or activities, does something much more. It describes in detail thirteen campuses in the United States selected for their comprehensive attention to first-year students—attention that is embedded in or linked to the curriculum and cocurriculum and is coupled with evaluation and evidence of continuous improvement.

Chapter One provides study background and rationale as well as information in tabular form about the most common first-year programs and structures at these thirteen institutions. Chapter Two describes in detail the research methodology. But at the heart of this book are the thirteen case studies (Chapters Three through Fifteen) that detail what campuses of discrete types and sizes are doing, why they have selected their various first-year approaches, and how institutional history and leadership have inevitably affected commitment to first-year students. Finally, in Chapter Sixteen, we highlight themes common to all or most of the thirteen institutions and offer our recommendations based upon the findings.

We acknowledge our indebtedness to George Kuh, John Schuh, Elizabeth Whitt, and their colleagues who, in 1991, undertook a somewhat similar study to identify "involving colleges"—institutions that model involvement at all levels of campus life. The book *Involving Colleges* was the inspiration for our research design in its focus on individual campuses that illustrate certain core principles of excellence. Kuh and colleagues' portrayal of unique campus cultures led us to wish to do the same in capturing selected, but representative, examples of excellence in the first year of higher education.

The Policy Center on the First Year of College

Six of the eight authors of this book were or are staff members of the Policy Center on the First Year of College, a national higher education research center located in Brevard, North Carolina. Since its establishment in October 1999, the work of the Policy Center has been focused on first-year assessment. Funded initially by The Pew Charitable Trusts and later by The Atlantic Philanthropies and Lumina Foundation for Education, the Policy Center has encouraged and collaborated in the development of new assessment tools and methodologies and has conducted a number of national surveys to determine current curricular and cocurricular practices in the first year. This study was the natural outgrowth of our prior work, but it also set the stage for a subsequent Policy Center initiative—a project described in the Epilogue entitled Foundations of Excellence® in the First College Year. The Foundations of Excellence Project is designed to develop and measure achievement of first-year standards of excellence.

Study Parameters

This study focuses on a particular time period—the year 2002. Although each case study details historical antecedents to the efforts that are described, chapters do not consider changes beyond 2002 in each campus's approach to the first year. The study is limited to investigation of regionally accredited two- and four-year institutions in the United States and its territories, and it focuses on the first thirty semester hours (or the equivalent) of a student's experience in higher education, realizing that a "first-year student," especially at the nation's community colleges, may be so characterized for two, three, or even more years. The study does not include investigation of initiatives designed specifically for transfer students.

Audience

This book is intended for all educators who have an interest in the first year of college: faculty, administrators, those involved in directing first-year programs, institutional research or assessment personnel, trustees or state coordinating or governing officials, and members of other constituent groups. We have written this book so that it will be accessible to practitioners as well as researchers. We have done our best to identify terms, avoid the unnecessary use of educational jargon, and make the case studies engaging and interesting for readers of any disciplinary background. One of the distinguishing features of this book is that the case studies were written by a diverse group: an English professor, a former public relations official, professors of higher education, a historian, and an assessment professional. Although each chapter addresses central questions and themes as outlined in Chapter Two, each tells the institutional story in a distinctive way.

A Final Word to Readers

Although these case studies are descriptive of many institutional types, we strongly urge you to pay equal attention to those campuses outside, as well as inside, your own institutional sector. Many of the illustrations provided and lessons learned have broad potential application beyond the particular institutional type being represented in each case study.

And finally, we urge you to remember that the study on which this book is based is a snapshot, albeit we hope and trust a very in-depth snapshot, of thirteen institutions taken in the year 2002. These are dynamic places, and what they are now is not exactly what they were when we visited and wrote about them. Thus, we encourage you to determine how these campuses have evolved in their approach to the first year since the time period reflected in this research by visiting their Web sites, reviewing their catalogues, and communicating directly with those responsible for the first year in these respective settings.

Betsy O. Barefoot
John N. Gardner
Marc Cutright
Libby V. Morris
Charles C. Schroeder
Stephen W. Schwartz
Michael J. Siegel
Randy L. Swing

Acknowledgments

Without the support of The Pew Charitable Trusts, The Atlantic Philanthropies, and Lumina Foundation for Education, this research effort would not have been possible. We thank these foundations for their willingness to underwrite this effort to discover and describe excellence in the first college year.

Many individuals played an essential role in the research process. First, we acknowledge and thank project liaisons from each of the thirteen Institutions of Excellence who assisted us in arranging the site visits, answering myriad questions, and finally reviewing the text for the chapters:

Jeanie Allen, visiting assistant professor, Interdisciplinary Studies, Drury University

Paul Arcario, dean of academic affairs, LaGuardia Community College/City University of New York

Steve Braye, professor of English and director of general studies, Elon University

Dianne Cyr, director of high school and early college partnerships, Community College of Denver

Lisa D'Adamo-Weinstein, director of the Academic Excellence Program, Center for Enhanced Performance, U.S. Military Academy

Scott Evenbeck, dean of University College, Indiana University-Purdue University, Indianapolis

Sandra Harper, provost and vice president of academic affairs, Texas A&M-Corpus Christi

Suzan Harrison, professor of rhetoric, Eckerd College

M. Stuart Hunter, director, National Resource Center for The First-Year Experience and Students in Transition, University of South Carolina

B. Thomas Lowe, associate provost and dean, University College, Ball State University

Joni Petschauer, director of freshman learning communities, Appalachian State University

Zaide Pixley, assistant provost for the first-year experience and director of advising, Kalamazoo College

Steven Wyckoff, director, Coordinated Freshman Programs and English composition, Lehman College/City University of New York

We also are indebted to the team of external reviewers who assisted with the difficult process of institutional selection:

James Anderson, Texas A&M University, College Station

Trudy Bers, Oakland Community College, Illinois

Jay Chaskes, Rowan University, New Jersey

Joe Cuseo, Marymount College, California

Jean Henscheid, Managing Editor, *About Campus*

Jodi Levine Laufgraben, Temple University, Pennsylvania

Cecilia Lopez, Harold Washington College, City Colleges of Chicago

Kay McClenney, University of Texas at Austin

Karl Schilling, Miami University of Ohio

Charles Schroeder, Noel-Levitz

Stephen Schwartz, Marietta College, Ohio

Lee Ward, James Madison University, Virginia

Jean Yerian, Virginia Commonwealth University

Finally, our sincere thanks go to our Policy Center staff members, Samantha Landgrover and Angela Whiteside, for helping us with the difficult task of transcribing, organizing, and assembling the materials that made possible this research and writing.

About the Authors

Betsy O. Barefoot serves as codirector and senior scholar at the Policy Center on the First Year of College, funded by grants from the Lumina Foundation for Education and The Atlantic Philanthropies and located in Brevard, North Carolina. Prior to assuming this position in October 1999, Barefoot spent eleven years as codirector for research and publications at the University of South Carolina's National Resource Center for The First-Year Experience, where she conducted ongoing research on the first-year seminar in American higher education and edited a variety of publications on the first-year experience. She holds degrees from Duke University (B.A.) and the College of William and Mary (M.Ed. and Ed.D.). In her role with the Policy Center, she continues research and publishing on issues related to student retention and the design and delivery of first-year initiatives. She also consults with college campuses around the nation and rest of the world on the structure and assessment of first-year programs.

John N. Gardner is a Distinguished Professor Emeritus of Library and Information Science, Senior Fellow of the University of South Carolina's National Resource Center for The First-Year Experience and Students in Transition, and executive director of the Policy Center on the First Year of College. As a higher education change agent, his principal interest is calling more attention to the importance of the first year of college. Toward this end, he has led a twenty-year international reform movement to persuade colleges to change their approaches to working with their first-year students. He is the founder of two national centers, the National Resource Center for The First-Year Experience and Students in Transition at the University of South Carolina and the Policy Center on the First Year of College based in Brevard, North Carolina. His second and related professional passion is improving the student transition process out of college, what he has coined "the senior-year experience." Gardner holds a B.A. from Marietta College in Ohio, an M.A. from Purdue University, and seven honorary doctoral degrees from institutions in the United States and the United Kingdom.

Marc Cutright is an assistant professor of higher education at Ohio University, Athens, Ohio, and a research fellow of the Policy Center on the First Year of College. From 2000 to 2002, Cutright was a staff member of the Policy Center, where his work included the compilation and analysis of an extensive database of first-year-support programs at large research universities. A veteran of more than twenty years in the field of college and university public affairs, he was also associated with a research center at Johns Hopkins University. His research, teaching, and university service largely focus on engaged learning and institutional support of engaged learning. Cutright holds a B.A. in American studies from Lindenwood College, an M.Ed. from North Georgia College, and an Ed.D. from the University of Tennessee, Knoxville. He was also a Fulbright Scholar at the University of Calgary, where he undertook a general study of Canadian higher education and engaged in research on strategic planning.

Libby V. Morris is associate professor and graduate coordinator in the Institute of Higher Education at the University of Georgia. Morris holds a Ph.D. from the University of North Carolina at Chapel Hill. Her teaching and research interests include evaluation and assessment, academic programs, and distance education. She is currently the principal investigator for a multiyear grant to investigate teaching and learning on-line in collaboration with the Advanced Learning Technologies unit of the University System of Georgia Board of Regents. She is editor of *Innovative Higher Education,* a peer-reviewed, international journal focusing on innovations in postsecondary education. She has presented research or conducted workshops, or both, at meetings of the European Association for Institutional Research, American Association for Higher Education, Association for Institutional Research, Educause,

National Forum on First-Year Assessment, and Southern Association of Colleges and Schools.

Charles C. Schroeder received his B.A. and M.A. degrees from Austin College and his doctorate in education from Oregon State University. During the past twenty-two years, he has served as the chief student affairs officer at Mercer University, Saint Louis University, Georgia Institute of Technology, and the University of Missouri-Columbia. In 2001, he was appointed a professor of higher education at the University of Missouri. Schroeder became a senior executive with Noel-Levitz, a national higher education consulting firm, in 2004. He has assumed various leadership roles in the American College Personnel Association (ACPA). He is the founder and immediate past president of the ACPA Educational Leadership Foundation. In 1996, Schroeder was recognized by ACPA for his contributions to higher education by being honored as the recipient of the Esther Lloyd-Jones Professional Service Award.

Stephen W. Schwartz is visiting senior fellow at the Policy Center on the First Year of College. He came to the Policy Center from Marietta College in Ohio, where he spent thirty-nine years. A professor of English, he also served as director of the freshman year program, director of advising and career advising, and director of the Honors College before becoming associate dean of the college. From 1987 to 2003, he was dean of Marietta College's McDonough Center for Leadership and Business, a primarily undergraduate center devoted to the study of leadership and civic engagement. In 1999, he was asked to lead the merger of the student life division with the McDonough Center as vice president and dean of student life and leadership. Schwartz holds a B.A. from Wilkes College, an M.A. from New York University, and a Ph.D. from the University of Pennsylvania.

Michael J. Siegel serves as research fellow for the Policy Center on the First Year of College. He joined the Policy Center in March 2001 and is responsible for a wide range of projects and research initiatives aimed at improving the first college year, including the development and dissemination of assessment instruments, tools, and practices. He assists with survey instrument design, development, and analysis; aids in the collection and analysis of best practices data for first-year programming; and helps design and conduct workshops for educators and administrators. He received a B.A. from Wake Forest University, an M.S. from Georgia State University, and a Ph.D. in higher education from Indiana University. His research interests include the study of new college and university presidents, newcomer socialization, and the study of colleges and universities as culture-bearing organizations.

Randy L. Swing serves as codirector and senior scholar for the Policy Center on the First Year of College. Swing's work has focused on developing new tools and techniques for evaluating the efficacy of first-year programs and helping colleges improve the first year through data-driven decisions. Until 1999, he worked for twenty years in a range of first-year programs at Appalachian State University, most recently, as founding director of the Assessment Office. Earlier, he codeveloped the freshman seminar program, founded an academic advising center for first-year and sophomore students, and coordinated an Upward Bound program for low-income, first-generation students from rural Appalachia. Prior to earning a Ph.D. in higher education from the University of Georgia, he earned an M.A. from Appalachian State University and a B.A. from the University of North Carolina–Charlotte.

Achieving and Sustaining Institutional Excellence for the First Year of College

Chapter One

On Being Named an Institution of Excellence in the First College Year

The Process and the Places

Suppose you wanted to find a campus or campuses that had become truly excellent in delivering the first year of higher education. Where would you look for models? Would you know such a campus when you saw it? What would be your criteria? These questions guided a two-year research project begun in February 2002 by the Policy Center on the First Year of College and supported by The Pew Charitable Trusts, The Atlantic Philanthropies, and Lumina Foundation for Education. The project, called Institutions of Excellence in the First College Year, was designed to move beyond a random collection of good ideas for first-year programs to a more systematic selection of colleges and universities that can serve as exemplars for achieving first-year excellence. Although this book contains many examples of specific first-year programs—orientation, residence life, learning communities, first-year seminars, advising structures, and others—the primary focus is on the totality of the first year: how these various components become embodied in a campus's overall approach to its new students.

This book provides portraits of excellence in the first year in the form of case studies of each of the thirteen institutions selected for this recognition. Case studies were constructed following an intensive review of written materials submitted by each campus in nomination portfolios and a campus visit conducted by a two-person research team in the fall of 2002. These teams authored each of the thirteen case study chapters in the book. On campus visits, researchers met students, faculty, and administrators; heard their stories; and experienced firsthand the institutional environment. Each case study reveals a unique mix of institutional history, leadership, student characteristics, and programmatic initiatives that converge to create an exemplary first year. We believe that educators from any sector of higher education can learn from the experiences of these thirteen institutions—not only about their successes but about challenges, past and current, that frame the ultimate shape of what these campuses have been able to accomplish. Each institution has its own story to tell, and with the inevitable shifts in student characteristics, available funding, and administrative leadership, each continues on its own evolutionary path.

The research project, which culminated in this book, started with an invitation. This invitation, sent to all chief academic officers of regionally accredited two- and four-year institutions of higher education in the United States, requested that they consider nominating their institution as an Institution of Excellence in the First College Year. The call for nominations was also posted on two electronic listservs, First-Year Experience Listserv (FYE-List) and First-Year Assessment Listserv (FYA-List). Collectively, these listservs reach over 2,000 college and university educators. Institutions that chose not to respond to the invitation were never potential candidates for selection. But 130 institutions (listed in Appendix A) did respond by sending detailed descriptions of their first-year efforts along with evidence of effectiveness. From that initial cohort of 130, we narrowed our selection to fifty-four semifinalists (listed in Appendix C) and ultimately to the thirteen finalists whose compelling stories are chronicled here.

Was this selection process simply another ranking system in disguise? The answer to this important question is a resounding no. By offering descriptions of thirteen colleges and universities that model best practice in the first year, we do not mean to imply that these institutions have been somehow compared to all others and judged to be "the best." What we can say with some assurance, however, is that the colleges and universities highlighted in this book are representative of "the best" in their varied and innovative approaches to the first year.

From the project's beginning, we recognized that excellence would have to be identified within the framework of institutional size, type, and mission. Therefore, the finalists include community colleges, private liberal arts colleges, regional comprehensive universities, and research universities, in addition to one special-purpose institution, the U.S. Military Academy. Although each campus is different, we discovered many cross-cutting themes and lessons that we develop thoroughly in the concluding chapter.

Why the Policy Center on the First Year of College Conducted This Study

The Policy Center on the First Year of College opened its doors in October 1999 with initial grant support from The Pew Charitable Trusts. As an outgrowth of the University of South Carolina's National Resource Center for The First-Year Experience and Students in Transition, the Policy Center was founded to achieve a specific mission: to promote and conduct assessment of the first year. In the Policy Center's early years of operation, staff members engaged in the development of new first-year assessment instruments and methodologies. The Policy Center also convened educators from campuses in five southeastern states to conduct qualitative evaluations of the first year and conducted two national surveys, in 2000 and 2002, to collect information about current practices in the first year (http://www.brevard.edu/fyc/Survey/index.htm). These surveys of both curricular and cocurricular life produced valuable data about the way institutions, for better or worse, are organizing and delivering the first year. But these data did not purport to define excellence.

In 2000, as we prepared proposals for additional grant funding from Pew and The Atlantic Philanthropies, we requested support to take our investigation to the next level by engaging in a systematic research process to identify those campuses that we could legitimately call Institutions of Excellence in their approach to this critical period in the undergraduate experience. We subsequently received additional support from Lumina Foundation for Education to transform the research findings into a major book, which we believe will be an important addition to the literature of the first year. While the programs and policies at these particular campuses may change in the future, the innovative ideas and lessons learned from these examples will continue to be valuable to both researchers and practitioners for years to come.

Moving the First Year from the Periphery to the Center

A second driving motivation for undertaking this research study was our intention to advance the conversation about the first year of college from the periphery to the center of the collegiate experience. Higher education's focus on the first year is a three-decades-old movement that on many campuses has become known as the "freshman" or "first-year experience." In practical terms, this focus has often been realized through a menu of innovative but piecemeal programs. The most common of these are first-year seminars, the largest proportion of which are offered as one-credit-hour courses (National Resource Center for The First-Year Experience and Students in Transition, 2002). Other programs include preterm orientation, residence life activities, campus organizations designed for first-year students, volunteer service, and various mentoring initiatives, learning communities (linked or clustered courses), Supplemental Instruction, and service-learning (the inclusion of required service in courses across the curriculum). With the exception of efforts that have an inherent link to the curriculum, many of these efforts exist at the margins of institutional life—barely connected, if at all, to student learning and vulnerable to the whims and exigencies of campus change. In his 2003 book, *The Learning Paradigm College,* John Tagg quotes Kay McClenney as she argues that "innovation does not equal transformation, and multiple innovations do not add up to fundamental change. . . . The willingness [for higher education] to allow innovation on the margins is a way of containing it, preventing it from contaminating 'core functions.' Innovation on the margins relieves pressure on the institution to create more essential change" (p. 11).

Many faculty and administrators in American colleges and universities seem to labor under the false assumption that somehow students can be prepared for the realities of college through a single programmatic initiative. Therefore, many of these efforts, although well designed and sincerely executed, serve as only an antidote for the remaining core functions of the first year. Another false assumption is that by their very nature, first-year efforts lower standards or lessen students' accountability so that more students can meet institutional requirements.

An explicit agenda for this project was therefore to identify campuses that have moved beyond the notion of the first-year experience as a patched-on, isolated program to a much broader and inclusive recognition of the first college year as a critical time period—a fundamental unit of analysis—that can serve as a meaningful platform for the undergraduate years. The project was also intended to show that first-year efforts, carefully crafted, do not lower standards but maintain high expectations coupled with support, thereby laying the foundation on which a solid collegiate education is built.

Addressing the Challenge of Defining Excellence

A third intention for the Institutions of Excellence project was to confront the challenge of defining and measuring excellence in the first year. The diversity of American higher education provides both a good reason and a convenient excuse for our collective lack of clarity about excellence. The much-maligned institutional rankings produced annually by *US News & World Report* have produced one template for institutional excellence that relies primarily on campus resources and "input" characteristics. These characteristics include size of endowment and amount of alumni giving, qualifications of entering students and faculty, and a number of other attributes that have little to do with what actually happens to students. Beginning in 2002, *US News* added additional rankings for programmatic components of the collegiate experience, including the first-year experience ("America's Best Colleges," 2002). But those rankings were created by surveying chief academic officers about their *opinions* or *perceptions* of other institutions' performance in a number of key areas, not by gathering actual documentation or evidence of excellence.

Campus educators understandably do a good bit of grousing about external rankings—unless they happen to be at the top of those rankings. But they have also been extremely resistant to working with similar institutions to create their own internal definition of excellence. The familiar argument, even among colleges and universities sharing the same objective characteristics, is that campuses, courses, students, and faculty are just too different to impose standards from one institution to another. While we agree that standards development is difficult, we also find that educators are nevertheless hungry for information about models of excellence or best practices to which they can aspire. Hardly a day goes by when we are not asked to provide either a blueprint for first-year excellence or examples of institutions that have been successful in achieving higher levels of student learning and retention. This book takes a first step toward clarifying what we mean by excellence in the first year of college by presenting thirteen case studies representing institutions of all types and sizes. We recognize the need to take this notion of defining, measuring, and recognizing first-year excellence even further, and the Policy Center is currently engaged in efforts to do just that. The Epilogue at the conclusion of this book describes an ongoing project begun in 2003 that is designed to define and measure institutional achievement of first-year standards of excellence. These standards, still in draft form in spring 2004, are being developed collaboratively by the Policy Center, Penn State University's Center for the Study of Higher Education, and more than two hundred higher education institutions in the United States.

Selection Criteria

An obvious prerequisite to implementing a recognition process of this type is the determination of criteria by which an institution's approach to the first year might be evaluated. We began this project by drawing on available scholarly literature, in addition to the collective experiences of Policy Center staff, to determine a set of common criteria by which diverse approaches to the first year could be evaluated in two-year and four-year, public and private, large and small campuses. Five criteria resulted from our lengthy deliberations and provided the yardstick by which an eighteen-member panel—Policy Center staff and thirteen external reviewers—measured the efforts of the 130 nominees:

- *Criterion 1: Evidence of an intentional, comprehensive approach to improving the first year that is appropriate to an institution's type and mission.* Institutions of Excellence are characterized by an approach to the first year that spans the curriculum and cocurriculum. This approach is central and systemic rather than appended or patched on to the core institutional mission.

"Down with serendipity and up with intentionality!" This statement, often made in public settings by John Gardner, is at the heart of this first criterion. Throughout the history of higher education, Gardner would argue, we have relied too much on serendipity—those special chance meetings of students and faculty, or students and other students, that shape the educational experience. Through the years, we have found that serendipity is not sufficient; rather, being intentional about the way we engineer meaningful student-faculty and student-student interactions is a key to success. It is also important that campuses have a clear rationale for the first year—what the first year is intended to do that goes beyond a low-level functional purpose (for example, making money for the institution, weeding out undesirable students) to a first-year philosophy that serves as a platform for the achievement of institutional mission.

- *Criterion 2: Evidence of assessment of the various initiatives that constitute this approach.* Institutions of Excellence are committed to an assessment process that results in data-driven continuous improvement in the first year. They should be able to report what was studied, how assessment was conducted, and how results were used.

A bird's-eye view of first-year assessment discovers some disturbing trends—first, an overwhelming focus on measuring retention and the absence of evaluation of higher-level cognitive and affective outcomes. Of course, retention is important; but we believe most educators would agree that the purpose of the first year is more than simply keeping students at the institution where they began their undergraduate journey. A 2002 national survey of the nation's chief academic officers conducted by the Policy Center discovered a second troubling trend: 31 percent of two- and four-year institutions conduct no assessment of the first year using national or regional comparative data, and another 31 percent collect data but make no meaningful use of these data (http://www.brevard.edu/fyc/survey2002/findings.htm). Such data tend to languish unused—a waste of institutional energy and resources. An obvious key to achieving excellence is not only conducting assessment, but also using assessment findings for institutional improvement.

- *Criterion 3: Broad impact on significant numbers of first-year students, including, but not limited to, special student subpopulations.* First-year initiatives are characterized by high expectations and essential support for all students at all levels of academic ability.

What is a reasonable level of student participation in first-year initiatives? 100 percent? Less than 100 percent? This question has no one-size-fits-all answer. Rather, we argue that institutions should determine how they can realize maximum impact through a variety of first-year efforts and whether desired impact can be achieved if all students are not required to participate. We also maintain that a college or university's design of the first year should take into account both the special needs of students who may be underprepared or at the honors level, and the needs of students in between—those who on many campuses are considered just too average to require special attention. Our collective experience argues that all students are potentially at risk in one way or another for failing to realize maximum benefit from the first college year.

- *Criterion 4: Strong administrative support for first-year initiatives, evidence of institutionalization, and durability over time.* Institutions of Excellence have a demonstrable track record of support for first-year initiatives. First-year programs and policies enjoy high status and receive an equitable share of fiscal and personnel resources.

Among multiple competing institutional priorities, the achievement of high status is no small feat. And for many campuses, where attention to the first year is a peripheral responsibility managed by entry-level employees, a high-status first year is only a dream. But for others, the first year is supported in high places, has been institutionalized, and has become the centerpiece of campus marketing—the way the institution proudly presents itself to its various publics, including, but not limited to, incoming students. High status also implies a reasonable and equitable level of financial support for organizational structures that support the design of the first year.

- *Criterion 5: Involvement of a wide range of faculty, student affairs professionals, academic administrators, and other constituent groups.* Institutions of Excellence involve all campus constituent groups in the design, implementation, and maintenance of first-year initiatives. These institutions are characterized by partnerships in support of the first year across divisional lines.

"Why can't we get the faculty more involved in first-year initiatives?" This common question has many possible answers, but it is clear that first-year excellence cannot be achieved, much less sustained, without the involvement of an institution's faculty. Faculty ownership, however, is not enough. Achievement of first-year excellence requires meaningful partnerships among various campus constituent groups—faculty, administrators, student affairs professionals, and students. The first year is also a focal point around which such partnerships can be created and sustained.

The institutional stories as provided in this book breathe life into these five criteria and provide multiple examples of the way institutions of varying sizes, types, and missions have achieved excellence according to this model.

A Snapshot of the Institutions of Excellence

Although the institutions selected for this honor are described in depth in the thirteen case study chapters, what follows is a brief general description of each of the campuses presented in the order in which their case studies appear (see Table 1.1).

Two-Year Institutions

Community College of Denver

The Community College of Denver (CCD), the city's only community college, shares its main downtown Auraria Campus with Metropolitan State College of Denver and the University of Colorado at Denver. Together, the three institutions have a student population of approximately 44,000—13,000 of which are enrolled at CCD. CCD operates three additional branch campuses, all within an eleven-mile radius of the Auraria campus. It has received national recognition from the League for Innovation in Community Colleges as a Vanguard College for learner-centered educational excellence. The college offers degrees and certificates in more than 125 programs and is Colorado's most diverse higher education institution, with a 58 percent minority student population representing more than seventy countries. The average age of

Table 1.1. Institutions of Excellence

Institution	*Location*	*Student Population*
Community College of Denver	Denver, Colorado	13,000
LaGuardia Community College	Queens, New York	12,000
Eckerd College	St. Petersburg, Florida	1,600
Kalamazoo College	Kalamazoo, Michigan	1,300
Drury University	Springfield, Missouri	4,450
Elon University	Elon, North Carolina	4,500
United States Military Academy	West Point, New York	4,000
Lehman College of CUNY	Bronx, New York	9,700
Texas A & M University-Corpus Christi	Corpus Christi, Texas	7,700
Appalachian State University	Boone, North Carolina	14,000
Ball State University	Muncie, Indiana	18,000
Indiana University–Purdue University Indianapolis	Indianapolis, Indiana	28,000
University of South Carolina	Columbia, South Carolina	25,000

students is twenty-eight years old, and 59 percent of the student population is female (http://ccd.rightchoice.org).

LaGuardia Community College

LaGuardia Community College is one of the nineteen two- and four-year campuses that comprise the City University of New York (CUNY) System. LaGuardia, located in the borough of Queens, enrolled its first class of students in 1971 and now has a student enrollment of approximately 12,000, including students from approximately 170 countries. LaGuardia is CUNY's only cooperative education college, offering day students two mandatory work experiences as part of their associate degree program of study. Three on-campus high schools are acknowledged forerunners of similar college–high school collaborations elsewhere in the nation. LaGuardia is well known for its success in acquiring grants to support educational innovation and for its history in implementing learning communities for students at all levels of academic preparedness and English proficiency (http://www.lagcc.cuny.edu).

Four-Year Institutions with Fewer Than 2,000 Students

Eckerd College

Eckerd College is a private, coeducational, residential college of liberal arts and sciences located on the Gulf Coast in St. Petersburg, Florida, and is affiliated with the Presbyterian Church, USA. Since its founding in 1958, Eckerd has developed programs that have been adopted nationwide and have earned the college an international reputation for academic excellence. As a residential campus of about 1,600 students, Eckerd boasts a curriculum grounded in the liberal arts and committed to the integration of the liberal arts and career preparation. In 2003, Eckerd became one of the youngest colleges to receive a Phi Beta Kappa chapter. Eckerd is well known for its Autumn Term, a three-week period in late summer that functions as an early start to the academic curriculum for first-year students and includes traditional orientation activities as well (http://www.eckerd.edu).

Kalamazoo College

Kalamazoo College is a private, coeducational, residential college of liberal arts and sciences founded in 1833 and located in southwest Michigan in the city of Kalamazoo. Kalamazoo College is nationally recognized for its innovative Kalamazoo Plan, a program that combines optional off-campus career development internships and study abroad experiences with on-campus courses, a required electronic portfolio, and a senior individualized project. Kalamazoo's student population is approximately 1,300; 85 percent of students study and live in another country during their undergraduate experience, making Kalamazoo a language-rich and internationally oriented community. Students also have the opportunity to participate in LandSea, an optional eighteen-day wilderness orientation that takes place in Ontario's Killarney Provincial Park during the summer before the first year (http://www.kzoo.edu).

Four-Year Institutions with 2,000 to 5,000 Students

Drury University

Springfield, Missouri, is the home of Drury University, a residential, coeducational university founded as Drury College in 1873 by Congregational missionaries. Drury's enrollment is approximately

4,400 undergraduate and graduate students. Every Drury undergraduate earns a minor in global studies through Global Perspectives 21, a unique core curriculum that combines the sciences, social sciences, and humanities to enhance communication and problem-solving skills. Drury offers a comprehensive liberal arts curriculum. In addition, students can pursue degrees in the university's Breech School of Business Administration, Hammons School of Architecture, and the departments of education, science, mathematics and computer science, behavioral sciences, and exercise and sport science, to name a few. Drury was one of the first universities in Missouri to offer continuing education and evening classes to meet the needs of nontraditional students. The centerpiece of Drury's first year is the ALPHA seminar, a year-long required course for beginning students (http://www.drury.edu).

Elon University

Elon University is a private, residential, coeducational institution founded in 1889 by the Christian Church, now the United Church of Christ. Elon's student population is just over 4,500, and the campus is located in central North Carolina between the cities of Greensboro and Burlington. Elon's curriculum operates on a four-one-four academic calendar, which includes a three-week January term. First-year students take four core courses in common. Students may choose among forty-nine major fields of study leading to bachelor of arts, bachelor of fine arts, or bachelor of science degrees. Elon also offers a dual-degree engineering program that is affiliated with North Carolina State University, Virginia Tech, North Carolina A&T State University, and Washington University in St. Louis. The majority of Elon courses carry four credit hours and include an experiential component (http://www.elon.edu).

U.S. Military Academy

The U.S. Military Academy (West Point) is located on the banks of the Hudson River in eastern New York State. The academy is a coeducational institution with a cadet population of approximately 4,000. Founded in 1802 during the presidency of Thomas Jefferson, West Point is the nation's oldest engineering school. In recent years, greater numbers of minorities and women have been admitted to the academy and the Corps of Cadets. Academy graduates are awarded a bachelor of science degree and a commission as a second lieutenant in the U.S. Army and serve a minimum of five years on active duty. Since its founding more than two centuries ago, the military academy has accomplished its mission by developing cadets in four critical areas—intellectual, physical, military, and moral-ethical—a four-year process called the "West Point Experience" (http://www.usma.edu).

Four-Year Institutions with 5,000 to 10,000 Students

Lehman College of the City University of New York

Lehman College was founded in 1931 as the Bronx campus of Hunter College. In 1968, Lehman was established as an independent coeducational college and now serves more than 9,000 students, most of them residents of the Bronx. Lehman is a nonresidential campus located on thirty-seven acres along the Jerome Park Reservoir in the Bronx. The college offers more than ninety bachelor's and master's degrees. Its mission is to offer its students a liberal arts education and preparation for careers and advanced study. The college, committed to meeting the educational needs of its urban population, serves as a center for the continuing educational and cultural needs of the region through access to the college's facilities and expertise in the academic disciplines, professional fields, and the fine and performing arts (http://www.lehman.cuny.edu).

Texas A&M University-Corpus Christi

The 240-acre Ward Island site that is now the home for Texas A&M-Corpus Christi has been the location for other higher education institutions, both private and public, since 1947. From 1971 to 1993, the institution, consecutively part of Texas A&I, the University System of South Texas, and Texas A&M Universities, enrolled only juniors and seniors. Beginning in 1994, Texas A&M-Corpus Christi, enrolled first- and second-year students. The student population now numbers more than 7,600 students; approximately 1,500 live on campus. The institution is committed to serving the needs of the South Texas region and prides itself on its system of undergraduate education that includes a core curriculum and learning communities. Program offerings include sixty-one degrees at the bachelor's and master's levels (http://www.tamucc.edu).

Four-Year Institutions with 10,000 to 20,000 Students

Appalachian State University

Appalachian State University is a public, comprehensive, residential university located in the mountains of North Carolina in the town of Boone. Founded in 1899 as Watauga Academy, the coeducational campus now enrolls more than 14,000 students and offers ninety-five undergraduate and eighty-one graduate majors. Almost 90 percent of students are state residents. In its early history, Appalachian was a teachers' college designed primarily to serve the educational needs of citizens of the western North Carolina mountains. In the 1960s, the campus grew dramatically, becoming what it is today: a multipurpose regional university. Appalachian's mission, "the practice and propagation of scholarship," is accomplished particularly through instruction, but also through the research, creative, and service activities of the university community. Appalachian has won numerous awards for its innovative efforts, including its 2001 selection as *Time* magazine's College of the Year for the Freshman Year Experience (http://www.appstate.edu).

Ball State University

Ball State University, a residential, public, coeducational campus in Muncie, Indiana, enrolls about 18,000 students who complete undergraduate and graduate degrees in forty-eight academic departments. The university began in 1899 as a private normal school but was purchased by the Ball brothers, Muncie industrialists, and given to the state of Indiana in 1918. Currently, more than 90 percent of Ball State students are state residents. Ball State is known nationally for its attention to assessment, the infusion of technology into instruction, and its University College, which coordinates the university's core curriculum and provides various forms of academic support as well as academic advising to all first-year students, regardless of major (http://www.bsu.edu).

Four-Year Institutions with More Than 20,000 Students

Indiana University-Purdue University Indianapolis

Indiana University-Purdue University Indianapolis (IUPUI) is a metropolitan university, contiguous to the downtown area of Indianapolis, and enrolling more than 28,000 students. Although the overwhelming majority of students are commuters, IUPUI offers residential accommodations to about 300 students and is building additional residence halls. IUPUI was created in 1969 as a partnership between Indiana and Purdue universities with Indiana University as the managing partner. Thus IUPUI is a campus of Indiana University that grants degrees in some 185 programs from both Indiana and Purdue universities. IUPUI offers the broadest range of academic programs of any campus in Indiana and is the home for the Indiana University Medical Center. IUPUI's nationally recognized University College is the academic entry point for all first-year students, regardless of major (http://www.iupui.edu).

University of South Carolina

The University of South Carolina (USC), founded in 1801, is an urban institution located in Columbia, South Carolina. Seven additional campuses of the university offering both two- and four-year degrees are located around the state and are part of the university system. The Columbia campus enrolls more than 25,000 students. Minority students represent approximately 25 percent of the total student population. The campus features various types of residential accommodations, including a residential college, honors housing, housing focused on academic themes and interests, and first-year residence halls. The university offers more than 350 degree programs in sixteen colleges and schools. USC has become nationally known for its focus on the First-Year Experience through its widely replicated University 101 course and the National Resource Center for The First-Year Experience and Students in Transition (http://www.sc.edu).

A Snapshot of Programmatic Initiatives

Collectively, these thirteen institutions offer an amazing variety of opportunities and services for their first-year students. Table 1.2 provides a list of the most common first-year initiatives described by the thirteen institutions in the nomination portfolios submitted in spring 2002 and investigated during the site visits. Undoubtedly, each campus could create a much longer list of its first-year efforts, but the table lists those that we and the thirteen campuses judged

Table 1.2. Programmatic Areas of Emphasis, Institutions of Excellence

Advising	*Central Advising Center*	*Common Reading*	*Convocations*	*Core Curriculum/ General Education*	*Electronic*	*Portfolios Experiential Learning*	*Faculty Development*
Ball State	Appalachian	Appalachian	Appalachian	Appalachian	Kalamazoo	Appalachian	Ball State
CCD	Ball State	Ball State	Kalamazoo	Ball State	LaGuardia	Elon	CCD
Drury	CCD	Drury	LaGuardia	Drury		Kalamazoo	IUPUI
Eckerd	IUPUI	Elon	USC	Eckerd		USMA	LaGuardia
Kalamazoo		Kalamazoo		Elon			Lehman
USMA		LaGuardia		IUPUI			USC
		USMA		Kalamazoo			
		USC		TAMU-CC			
				USMA			

First-Year Seminars	*Leadership Programs*	*Learning Centers*	*Learning Communities*	*Liberal Arts*	*Mentoring*	*Orientation*	*Peer Leaders/ Advisers*
Appalachian	Appalachian	Appalachian	Appalachian	Drury	Drury	Appalachian	Ball State
Drury	Eckerd	IUPUI	Ball State	Eckerd	IUPUI	Drury	Drury
Elon	Elon	Kalamazoo	CCD	Elon	LaGuardia	Eckerd	Eckerd
IUPUI	USC	USMA	IUPUI	Kalamazoo	USMA	Elon	IUPUI
Kalamazoo			LaGuardia		USC	IUPUI	Kalamazoo
LaGuardia			Lehman			Kalamazoo	USMA
Lehman			TAMU-CC			LaGuardia	USC
TAMU-CC						TAMU-CC	
USMA						USMA	
USC							

Residence Life	*Service Initiatives*	*Academic Programs*	*Summer Supplemental Instruction*
Appalachian	Drury	CCD	Appalachian
Ball State	Eckerd	Eckerd	IUPUI
Univ of SC	Elon	LaGuardia	
	IUPUI		
	Kalamazoo		
	LaGuardia		
	Lehman		
	USMA		

Note. For specific contextual meanings of each area of emphasis, see the case study chapters. CCD = Community College of Denver; USC = University of South Carolina; IUPUI = Indiana University-Purdue University Indianapolis; USMA = U.S. Military Academy; TAMU-CC = Texas A&M University–Corpus Christi.

to be most important. Readers whose interests may focus on a particular first-year program or service will find that this table directs them to campus case studies in which specific first-year initiatives are described in detail.

Final Thoughts

If additional time and money were available to enable the Policy Center to undertake a broader and more sustained investigation, undoubtedly we could identify hundreds of colleges and universities that model first-year excellence. As campuses continue to interact in professional meetings and through a personal and technological exchange of ideas, the dissemination of innovative and effective first-year initiatives increases year by year.

We hope that this book will give additional credence to our belief that achieving excellence in the first year requires time, energy, and the willingness to invest in more than innovation on the margins. If the first year is to reach its potential, it must take center stage and involve all the actors who have roles to play in institutional life.

Chapter Two

Research Methods

The purpose of this study was to identify and describe Institutions of Excellence in the First Year of College. A case study approach was considered appropriate because it allowed the researchers to explore a particular phenomenon, such as a first-year course or program, in context to allow for rich description, discovery, and understanding (Merriam, 1988). Case studies ask questions of "how" and "why" and are useful to investigate contemporary events within context (Yin, 1994). Using a multiple case study method, the researchers identified, investigated, and described thirteen Institutions of Excellence in the First College Year. Each institution was considered a separate case for data collection, and institutions are presented as such in the chapters that follow. Using the institutional case studies included in this book, practitioners and researchers are encouraged to analyze the programs and processes for transferability and replication as seems appropriate and to refine and test the ideas and constructs found in the descriptions of these exemplary institutions.

This study was conducted during a fifteen-month period from November 2001 to January 2003. In phase one of the study, the challenge was to identify Institutions of Excellence in the First Year of College from the broad universe of colleges and universities nationwide. This task was accomplished through criterion-based or purposive sampling and evaluation of documentary evidence provided by the institutions and reviewed by a panel of experts. In phase two, in-depth analyses of the selected institutions were conducted through an extensive review of archival data and documents, site visits, and interviews. These are the primary methods of qualitative research and are important in developing a descriptive case study that has a detailed account of the phenomenon under consideration (Marshall & Rossman, 1999).

In both phases, excellence was measured against the achievement of five principal criteria developed by the Policy Center on the First Year of College. This chapter gives a brief overview of the criteria, the research methodology, and the chronology of research events.

Invitation to Participate and Identification of the Selection Criteria

The study began with a letter of invitation sent by e-mail in early February 2002, by John N. Gardner, executive director of the Policy Center on the First Year of College, to chief academic officers of all regionally accredited two- and four-year colleges and universities in the United States (approximately 2,400 institutions) inviting their participation in the research study (see Appendix B). The list of institutions and names for the mailing was purchased as a database, the Higher Education Directory, from Higher Education Publications. Approximately one-third of the messages were not delivered for a variety of reasons (for example, incorrect e-mail addresses, mailboxes that were full), but the invitation was received by just over 1,600 chief academic officers. The letter invited the recipients to be considered for recognition as an Institution of Excellence in the First Year by preparing a two-page (1,000 word) narrative describing the institution's first-year efforts by responding to five criteria.

In addition to direct invitations, the Policy Center staff members posted the invitation on two national electronic listservs (First-Year Experience List and First-Year Assessment List) with a combined subscriber base of over 2,000 individuals. The invitation was also extended in various conference presentations during January and February 2002. Using these three techniques to solicit participation, it is believed that those colleges and universities with major emphases in the first year were aware of the purpose of the study and process for participation.

Because the research aimed at identifying those institutions from which much could be learned about the first year, it was appropriate to use a criterion-based approach to participant selection (Goetz & LeCompte, 1984; Marshall & Rossman, 1999). In criterion-based sampling, the criteria are designated in advance, and participants (institutions in this case) matching the criteria are included for analyses.

There were a number of ways in which the Policy Center could have identified candidates for this award, including convening an expert panel to suggest a roster of potential nominees, that is, reputational-case selection (Merriam, 1988). We selected the open self-nomination method judged against predetermined criteria because we believed that neither the Policy Center staff nor an external panel of experts could be expected to have the level of comprehensive knowledge necessary to identify all institutions with high levels of achievement in the first year. We did not seek a randomized sample of participants, generally the practice in experimental and quasi-experimental designs. Randomization would not ensure the identification of exemplary cases needed to understand excellence in the first year. Rather, the goal in qualitative research with purposeful selection is to locate those cases from which the most can be learned about the problem or issue under study (Merriam, 1988). It should also be noted that it was not the goal to identify all of the highest-performing institutions in the first year; rather, a reasonable number of cases was sought from which a great deal could be learned through this process. In summary, the call was widely and effectively disseminated, and we generated a large pool of institutions that were engaging in a number of best practices in the first year.

The criteria to evaluate nominations were developed from a review of the literature on first-year programs (Upcraft & Gardner, 1989; Barefoot, 2000; Upcraft, Gardner, & Barefoot, 2005) and from the collective years of experience of the members of the Policy Center in administering first-year programs on a number of campuses. The criteria were used to structure the nomination process and to provide a common rubric through which to evaluate all of the nominees. The criteria were designed to be broad in scope and equally relevant across all types of institutions, and they were regarded as authentic markers for first-year excellence.

The criteria for selecting the institutional cases were as follows:

Criterion 1: Evidence of an intentional, comprehensive approach to the first year that is appropriate to the institution's type

Criterion 2: Evidence of assessment of the various initiatives that constitute this approach

Criterion 3: Evidence of broad impact on significant numbers of first-year students, including, but not limited to, special student subpopulations

Criterion 4: Strong administrative support for first-year initiatives, evidence of institutionalization, and durability over time

Criterion 5: Involvement of a wide range of faculty, student affairs professionals, academic administrators, and other constituent groups

The deadline for receipt of the two-page narrative summaries was March 15, 2002. The Policy Center received 130 nominations for this award; Appendix A provides a list of those institutions.

Selection of Semifinalists

In spring 2002, 130 institutions had completed nominations using the criteria and format specified in the call for participation. Based on the number of institutions that replied and the variety in institutional characteristics and missions, the researchers decided to review the institutional nominations using stratified purposeful sampling to facilitate comparisons within sectors and to illustrate first-year performance across subgroups (Marshall & Rossman, 1999).

The 130 nominations received were stratified by type and size of institution into six discrete cohorts:

Institutional Type and Size	*Number of Nominations*
Two-year institutions	12
Four-year institutions with fewer than 2,000 students	28
Four-year institutions with 2,000 to 5,000 students	28
Four-year institutions with 5,000 to 10,000 students	20
Four-year institutions with 10,000 to 20,000 students	19
Four-year institutions with more than 20,000 students	23

Policy Center staff members acted as initial reviewers and rated the two-page nomination narratives, comparing institutions within each cohort group. Narratives were rated by using a simple three-point scale: a rating of three indicated a high evidence of achievement of all or most criteria, a rating of two indicated a moderate or mixed evidence of achievement, and a rating of one indicated inadequate evidence of achievement.

The goal of this review was to select institutions meriting further analysis by applying the criteria for revealing excellence. We decided that this stage one review of brief narratives would eliminate only institutions that, according to the consensus of Policy Center staff, provided inadequate evidence of achievement as measured by the five criteria. Failure to address the first or second criterion was the primary reason some nominees were not advanced to semifinal status. A number of nominations were focused on a single, limited first-year program (criterion 1), and others provided no evidence of assessment (criterion 2). From the 130 nominees, we selected fifty-four semifinalists (see Appendix C). All semifinalists engaged in a variety of first-year efforts worthy of further attention and were invited to participate in further analyses. These institutions fell into the following stratifications:

Institutional Type and Size	*Number of Semifinalists*
Two-year institutions	7
Four-year institutions with fewer than 2,000 students	9
Four-year institutions with 2,000 to 5,000 students	11
Four-year institutions with 5,000 to 10,000 students	11
Four-year institutions with 10,000 to 20,000 students	6
Four-year institutions with more than 20,000 students	10

The semifinalists were notified of their selection in late April 2002 and were invited by letter to provide a more comprehensive narrative description of their first-year efforts by June 15, 2002 (see Appendix D). We asked that a second narrative be submitted in no more than five pages (2,500 words), again using the five criteria. This lengthier narrative provided campuses the opportunity to elaborate on their first-year approach. Semifinalists were also invited to append relevant supplementary materials to the five-page narrative.

Selection of Finalists

A panel of thirteen distinguished educators external to the Policy Center with both research knowledge about and practical experience in administering various first-year initiatives joined five Policy Center staff members in reviewing the semifinalists' portfolios. Materials submitted by institutions within each cohort group were read and ranked by three external evaluators and one Policy Center evaluator. (One external evaluator read and ranked all fifty-four institutional submissions.) All raters worked independently and were guaranteed confidentiality in connection with any particular institutional evaluation. Because of our concerns about potential bias in the evaluation process, no evaluator was involved in rating any institution with which he or she had a direct relationship in the present or the past. Each rater was thus asked about conflicts of interest and was instructed to remove himself or herself from the evaluation of any institution for which an interest could be determined or suggested. Credibility in the review process was thereby maintained.

Institutional narratives were evaluated according to achievement of each of the five criteria on a scale of 1 to 20. A score 1 to 5 indicated unclear/unacceptable achievement of a particular criterion; 5 to 10, acceptable achievement; 10 to 15, good achievement; and 15 to 20, outstanding achievement. The highest possible cumulative score for each institution was 100.

In addition to receiving institutional materials and the scoring forms on which to rate achievement of the five criteria, the Policy Center provided evaluators with examples of indicators of achievement of each criterion. We suggested that these indicators might help guide the review; however, evaluators were urged to consider indicators as possible, but not exclusive, evidence of achievement of the criteria. Criteria with relevant indicators of achievement are as follows:

Criterion 1: Evidence of an intentional, comprehensive approach to the first year that is appropriate to the institution's type

- A rationale for first-year programs linked to mission, student characteristics, or another factor
- Initiatives that include attention to or a rethinking of first-year curriculum content or structure
- Meaningful integration of program elements

Criterion 2: Evidence of assessment of the various initiatives that constitute this approach

- Assessment that includes attention to learning outcomes and other measures in addition to retention
- Assessment that is ongoing and informs decision making
- An appropriate level of sophistication
- A mix of assessment tools and methods. Availability and dissemination of findings

Criterion 3: Evidence of broad impact on significant numbers of first-year students, including, but not limited to, special student subpopulations

- A level of participation that is reasonable for the particular initiative or the type of institution
- Initiatives that address the needs of the average student as well as those on the top, the bottom, or in special subpopulations

Criterion 4: Strong administrative support for first-year initiatives, evidence of institutionalization, and durability over time

- Adequate administrative support necessary for long-term survival of initiatives
- High status of first-year initiatives
- Evidence of future commitment
- Organizational structure to support and coordinate first-year efforts

Criterion 5: Involvement of a wide range of faculty, student affairs professionals, academic administrators, and other constituent groups

- Involvement of important constituent groups in the design and delivery of the first year
- Evidence of meaningful partnerships rather than different groups working essentially in isolation

After the ratings were completed and submitted to the Policy Center, the scores for each institution were aggregated, and a total score was assigned to each of the fifty-four institutions. The two institutions with the highest score from each of the six cohort groups were selected as Institutions of Excellence. Based on its high overall score, the U.S. Military Academy, an institution that could not be reasonably compared with any of the other campuses in the semifinal pool, was chosen as the thirteenth Institution of Excellence.

A retrospective assessment of this two-stage selection process revealed that the use of five criteria and the indicators of achievement led to high inter-rater reliability on the institutional evaluations, and, according to the reviewers, the criteria provided a systematic and rigorous guide to select institutions from which much could be learned about excellence in the first year of college. We do not claim that these thirteen institutions are "the best" in their approach to the first year; however, each institution is representative of a high level of achievement in its first-year initiatives and is deserving of the designation.

Site Visits

Case study research relies on multiple sources of data to gain perspectives from a variety of vantage points (Yin, 1994). Three data sources were important for this study: documentary information, interviews, and on-site observations. The Policy Center notified each of the thirteen Institutions of Excellence of its selection by letter in late August 2002 (see Appendix E). As a condition of accepting the award, each institution was required to agree to a two-day campus visit by a two-person research team in the fall of 2002. Prior to the site visit, the team received extensive archival and other documentary evidence of the institution's achievement in its approach to the first year. These documents verified and elaborated conditions described in the abbreviated nominations.

The site visits were used to clarify issues in the nomination portfolios and gave the team access to places and people important in the institutional life of the first year. In correspondence with the thirteen award recipients, we stated that "satisfactory completion of the on-site visit is the final step in our selection of your campus as an Institution of Excellence in the First College Year and identification as such in our subsequent publishing and public dissemination activities." In this correspondence we added the provision that "the Policy Center reserves the right to withdraw any institution's selection in the highly unlikely event that we were to determine during the site visit that such selection would not be appropriate, given our stated criteria." Using multiple sources of evidence—observations, interviews, documents, focus groups—the researchers were able to investigate the validity of the original selection of cases for in-depth analysis (Merriam, 1988). No institution was withdrawn following the site visit. Five Policy Center staff members in addition to three external experts conducted the site visits. Various members of the eight-person research group, working in pairs, conducted as few as one or as many as five separate site visits.

Before site visits were made, the Policy Center requested additional materials from each of the thirteen campuses, and these materials were distributed to the review teams. A review of these documents prior to the campus visit also gave the team the familiarization necessary to make the site visits worthwhile, and they provided a context from which to select activities for observation and individuals for interviews. Although the review of documents is time-consuming, familiarization with the problem and culture prior to interviews and observations makes those activities most productive (McCracken, 1988).

The documentary materials included the campus mission and vision statements, strategic plan, bulletin or catalogue, view book sent to prospective students, campus fact book or fact sheet, existing institutional studies, copies of student newspapers, additional descriptive information about first-year initiatives, and evidence of external recognition or awards. Most institutions provided copious and useful documentation above and beyond that requested to confirm their nomination and the achievement of excellence. This information was used along with findings from the interviews and the site visits to create the descriptive case study summaries in the subsequent chapters.

Prior to the visits, the Policy Center also advised each of the thirteen campuses to gain institutional review board (IRB) approval for the center's general research protocol, if such approval was deemed necessary. The Policy Center obtained overall IRB approval for the research protocol and interview procedures in September 2002 from the Western Institutional Review Board. A copy of the consent form used during the on-site visits is included as Appendix F.

The guiding purposes of the site visits were to (1) investigate in greater depth how each institution achieved excellence according to the five criteria, (2) construct richer and more detailed case studies than would have been possible working from only written materials, and (3) determine whether the individual institutional studies would yield cross-case findings that were common for most, if not all, of the thirteen institutions. Specifically we sought information to respond to the following guiding research questions:

- *Basic information:* What has the institution chosen to do to improve the first year? How does the institution deliver its various initiatives? What are the intended outcomes? What does the institution know about the effectiveness of its initiatives in achieving desired outcomes?
- *History:* How did the institution's approach to the first year come to be? What was its evolutionary (or revolutionary) path? What were the relevant external or internal factors that influenced the institution's decisions? What were the inherent struggles, barriers, and successes?
- *Rationale:* Why did the institution decide on its particular first-year approach? How does this approach link to the institution's mission, and how does it meet the needs of the student body?
- *Leadership:* Whose leadership or influence has been and continues to be essential in the success of the campus's first-year initiatives? How are resources allocated and protected for the first year?
- *The "lived" first year.* What is the experience of first-year students on the campus—those who participate in various initiatives and those who do not? What do upper-level students have to say about the first year? How do students from various minority groups experience the first year?
- *The future:* Given the various uncertainties of campus life, what does the institution believe to be its greatest challenges in the future? What plans exist for refining an already excellent first year?

These questions were used to focus the efforts of the research teams across the multiple sites and served as a guide in developing the semistructured interview protocols for use with key leaders in the first year. Semistructured interviews are particularly useful for investigating issues about which some things are known, yet the perspectives of those interviewed and their worldview is most important for understanding (Merriam, 1988).

The Policy Center also asked each institution to sponsor an open forum during the site visit in order to make public the claims made in the nomination materials. The forums provided a general overview of first-year efforts not only for the benefit of the research team but also to make the information contained in the nominations community property to be discussed and interpreted by all interested members of the campus community.

To gain the widest perspective on the first year at the participating institutions, the Policy Center requested the scheduling of interviews with the following individuals and groups:

- Campus chief executive officer
- Chief and associate academic officers
- Chief student affairs officer
- Dean or director of the first year (if such position exists)
- Faculty and student affairs professionals
- Institutional research or assessment officers
- Students, including first-year and upper-level students (To respond to human subjects research protocol concerns, we stipulated that all interviewed students should be eighteen years or older.)
- Such additional individuals or groups as appeared important to the unique institutional circumstances

It is important to interview upper-level administrators, for these institutional elites often have access to "organizational policies, past histories, and future plans from a particular perspective" not shared or known by others (Marshall & Rossman, 1999, p. 113). In every case, the chief executive officer and other upper administrators were accessible and open in their interpretations of first-year successes and challenges.

Those faculty, student affairs administrators, and other staff involved directly with first-year efforts were regarded as key informants, providing not only factual information but also insights and corroborating evidence and access to such evidence for the study (Yin, 1994). Semistructured interviews were conducted with more than 100 key informants. In open forums, several hundred other faculty and staff presented their examples and interpretations of the first college year. Students were included in the research through focus groups, meetings around specific activities and programs, and serendipitous exchanges in walking across campus and at meals and in receptions. To verify the extent and impact of the first-year experience, it was important to interact with those specially selected for this purpose (for example, student leaders, first-year faculty, and staff leaders) and those students and faculty less involved in the cocurricular campus life. The convergence of multiple sources of information was believed to yield a more comprehensive perspective on the first-year experience (Yin, 1994).

During each visit, all interviewees were supplied with copies of an informed consent agreement. The agreement stated that only senior administrators would be identified by title and name; all others would be anonymous, designated simply as faculty, administrator, or student unless specific permission was granted to use an individual's name. (Where actual names or personally identifying information appear in the book beyond those in senior administrative positions, explicit permission from the interviewee has been secured.) Over 700 faculty, staff, and students were interviewed during the thirteen site visits. The campus site visits provided the data-rich opportunities for the team leaders to triangulate the data and to begin generating themes, categories, and patterns descriptive of institutions of excellence

Data Analysis and Case Study Development

Site visits were completed in December 2002. During 2003, the eight researchers who conducted site visits engaged in ongoing analyses of institutional materials and development of the case study chapters. Taped interviews were transcribed and prepared for analyses, field notes were reviewed, documents were reread, and ongoing contact with the institutions was maintained. These data sources supplied the full, thick descriptions for the individual case stories. Although the site visits were invaluable to this process, we found that additional work was needed after the visits to verify details, flesh out additional important elements of a story, and clarify an occasional misconception. This process of data collection and member checking is important in qualitative research to increase the credibility and validity of the findings (Merriam, 1988). In addition, for each case, an audit trail was created by the team members to allow others involved in the study to examine both the process and products of the research over time as needed (Lincoln & Guba, 1985). The audit trail was composed of raw data, including transcripts, documentary evidence, and field notes, as well as notes on emerging themes, categories, and the case stories. Finally, senior administrators from each institution were given the opportunity to read the final drafts of each case study chapter to correct errors in fact and misunderstandings as needed.

To build the cases, a decision was made by the teams to tell the story of the first-year experience within its institutional context as that story emerged in the site visits, the documents, and the descriptions and words of the participants. These in-depth descriptions allow readers to evaluate their usefulness and transferability to other situations (Merriam, 1988). Again, the interpretations of the cases were established through member checks and cross team review.

To analyze within and across cases, the investigators turned first to the criteria that guided the study. These might be considered the theoretical propositions on which the cases were evaluated. Through content analyses, the researchers looked for patterns that dominated the research, for recurring ideas or images that illustrated the criteria, and for examples that did not fit. Both convergence and divergence were important to examining the original categories and building new categories. One of the pitfalls of using theoretical propositions is that important data may be rejected because they do not fit into the previously decided analytical scheme (Yin, 1994). The researchers were sensitive to this condition and combed the data for categories and themes that did not fit the predetermined criteria. Finally, a goal of the research was to "build a general explanation that fits each of the individual cases, even though the cases will vary in their details" (Yin, 1994, p. 112). Another goal of this study is to launch the theory building that will support future advances in the practice and research into the first year of college. We trust that we have accomplished these goals in our final chapter.

Institutions are dynamic places, and cases capture a phenomenon at a particular point in time. Since the site visits were completed, a number of the thirteen institutions have made alterations to their first-year initiatives and have seen changes at senior administrative levels. The descriptions of each campus's approach to the first year have been limited to those activities in existence during 2002. However, where needed, we have noted changes in administrative leadership since 2002.

Summary

This research study relied primarily on qualitative methodology, specifically case study research, to provide an in-depth portrait of thirteen institutions that model excellence in the first year. Case studies describe each institution's efforts at a particular point in time—fall 2002—but also provide extensive information about the historical antecedents to current policies and practices. Research team members elicited the observations of faculty, students, staff, and administrators on how students themselves experience the first year. Finally, case studies provide a wealth of information about the many factors of campus life—culture, history, and leadership, for example—that may have either a correlative or causal relationship to first-year excellence. Although this information was gathered from thirteen specific institutions of different sizes, types, missions, and access to resources, we believe these findings are broadly applicable to other colleges and universities in the United States. Although no international campuses were involved, the researchers, the majority of whom have extensive knowledge about international education, believe that the results are easily extended to non-U.S. institutions of higher education as well.

Part One

Case Studies of Two-Year Institutions

Chapter Three

The Community College of Denver

A Second Family for the First-Year Student

Marc Cutright

Randy L. Swing

A widely embraced story is that families with low educational attainment value the goal and promise of a college education for their children. While many such families see higher education as the gateway to the American Dream, sadly, that is not always the case.

Mario (a pseudonym), a first-year student at the Community College of Denver (CCD), described his family circumstances. His parents were divorced and living in different states, his mother in Colorado. His father, depressed by the collapse of the marriage, descended emotionally to the point where he was of little support to Mario, and tempers tended to flare. Back with his mother, Mario decided that he needed to get an education that would allow him an independent future. His decision was met with little enthusiasm.

"Another bill?" his mother said. "Bill collectors are calling all the time. Why don't you just get a job?"

"And she really doesn't believe in me either," Mario said. "She thinks I'm dumb or something." With the exception of supportive grandparents, other friends and relatives are mocking of his ambitions to go into health care, perhaps one day to become a doctor.

But that is not the reaction he receives at CCD. "Here, my case manager, everybody, tells me I can do it." Discouraged at first by his family circumstances and the new academic demands, Mario stopped going to classes. He recalls that his case manager found out almost immediately and then found him. "She encouraged me, told me I could do it, but she also told me, 'Look, it's past drop day. You have to pay anyway.'" She told him to see his instructors—to tell them that he wanted to be back in class. To a person, they told him he had some catch-up work to do, but that he could do it, and they would help. As a result, he was catching up. Even as Mario told his story, other students added words of encouragement and support. One clasped a strong and supportive hand on his shoulder and gave it an optimistic and encouraging shake.

This story sounded like the philosophy that a large group of faculty had expressed to us as visiting researchers earlier that same day. "We hold their hands," one said, "and we do that proudly and without apology."

"Yes, but we know when to let them go," another added. Another said, "And we know when to give them a kick in the rear too," which drew appreciative and agreeing laughter.

On a more somber note, faculty recalled their reactions to the events of September 11, 2001, the news of which broke as many of them were arriving at the college. "I have to get to class. I have to be with my students," one recalled as her immediate reaction. The comment drew silent nods from other faculty members, and students remembered the comfort they drew that day from going to class. In other words, we found that the Community College of Denver, in a multitude of circumstances, gives the kind of support that a person can usually get only from a family.

We might be forgiven if we did not expect much from this college. There are twenty-eight public colleges and universities in Colorado. CCD, established by the Colorado legislature in 1967, now delivers one-third of all the developmental education offered at the postsecondary level in Colorado, and one-third of all the credit hours offered at CCD are for developmental education.

The college's demographic profile is not one commonly associated with high levels of student success. Two-thirds of the students are low income, and 72 percent attend part time. Two-thirds of the students are the first individuals in their families to attend postsecondary education of any kind. Nearly 10 percent of students deal with a physical or learning disability. For nearly 10 percent, English is their second language. Minority students—Latino, Native American, African American, and Asian American—comprise about 60 percent of the student body. The average age of students is twenty-eight, with only a third below twenty, suggesting competing demands of family responsibility.

But instead of a record of predictable failure, CCD exceeds commonly held expectations for community college outcomes, for student success. Consider these remarkable indicators. After steady progress toward ambitious goals, by the late 1990s, there were no significant differences in student success indicators—persistence, graduation, transfer, and others—based on race, ethnicity, age, or gender. By 1995, students who began their CCD experience in developmental studies were as likely to graduate as those who did not, and by 1999, enrollment in developmental education became a predictor of success. In 2001, CCD's first-to-second-year retention rate was over 50 percent for full-time degree-seeking students. Nine of every ten CCD graduates who seek admission to a four-year Colorado college are accepted, and these transfer students average a solid B grade average at their second institutions. Well over 90 percent of graduates and alumni of CCD report satisfaction with their instruction when surveyed, and employers who are surveyed show nearly universal satisfaction with the skills of CCD alumni.

A strong institutional philosophy and a variety of structures—many that primarily serve first-year students—create and support this success. The focus on the first year is no surprise, as about three-quarters of CCD students are classified by earned credit hours as first-year students. But as is true for virtually all community colleges, the lines between the first and second year are blurred, and many of the programs designed primarily for beginning students essentially serve all students, no matter what their official designation.

Keys to Success at CCD

What are the keys to success at CCD that account for its noteworthy achievements? This is the question that guided our site visit. We think the answers lie primarily in the following institutional characteristics:

- An array of innovative and successful educational practices that addresses the needs of the diverse students who attend. One size is not assumed to fit all at CCD.
- Steadfast and innovative leadership that spans much of the college's thirty-three-year history.
- Close cooperative relationships with four-year institutions on the Auraria campus.
- Success in acquiring external funds to support college initiatives.
- Commitment to accountability and continuous improvement.
- An intentional focus on student success as shown through a clear college mission, goal setting, and planning processes.

These characteristics, which include those within and beyond CCD's direct control, have been leveraged by the college to meet the challenges of serving first-year students.

Innovative and Successful Educational Practices

The educational practices used at CCD are the primary reason that this college has achieved success with students. CCD provides a wide array of services to meet the specific needs of different student subgroups as highlighted in the following examples.

Assessing and Placing Students

It is not unusual for campuses to use basic skills assessment instruments, but the scope of the task and the need for varied delivery mechanisms are examples of successful educational practice at CCD. Because many potential CCD students are unsure of their academic skills, uncomfortable being tested, and decide on short notice to enroll in college, it is particularly important that assessment be as accommodating as possible and provide quick results. One example of such service is the use of Accuplacer, a commercially available, standardized reading, writing, and math test designed to assess students and place them in appropriate-level classes. Unlike many other standardized tests, Accuplacer is conducted with a Web-based interface using artificial intelligence software to provide immediate results. Understanding that not every potentially successful new student enters with computing and keyboarding skills, CCD makes a paper-and-pencil version of the test available for those who are not comfortable with computer testing.

For more than a decade, CCD has required assessment of basic skills for all students unless they have a college degree or have taken college-level entrance examinations (SAT or ACT). In 2001, Colorado followed CCD's lead by making assessment and placement mandatory for all first-time, entering college students at state institutions. Because CCD is ahead of the curve, the new rule has little impact on it; the college was already assessing some 6,500 students each year. CCD's testing center staff members, however, are not willing to wait for students to come to them; they take Accuplacer into the Denver public schools, where they test more than 400 high school juniors and seniors annually in order to help them in their college planning decisions. CCD also delivers basic skills testing to students who are taking on-line classes from home or at any of the college's remote locations.

The results of testing and placement are clearly documented by institutional data. Students enrolled in developmental classes successfully complete those courses at a high rate (70 percent completion). First-time developmental students who finish one year have a 2.94 cumulative grade point average, indicating that they were successful in a variety of courses and are poised to complete a college degree. Seventy-two percent complete the first college-level course in English after finishing a developmental English course, and 76 percent complete college algebra after completing a developmental mathematics course.

Academic Advising

While academic advising is nearly ubiquitous in higher education, the scope and diversity of CCD's approaches to advising separate this college from other institutions. In its materials submitted in the nomination portfolio, CCD described a three-level integrated advising model that is administered by the Integrated Advising Committee. This model, which addresses students' needs from the first point of contact through graduation or transfer, includes general core advising, referral to support services, and premajor and major advising. Advisers can be professional advisers who work in the Educational Planning and Advising Center, faculty members, support services staff members, or an academic center educational case manager (ECM). (CCD's educational case management concept is described in detail later in the chapter.)

Level I Advising: Educational Planning and Advising Center

The Educational Planning and Advising Center (EPAC) is for many students their first contact with an academic adviser. Often this contact happens before a student is officially admitted. At least fifteen times a year, the college holds Red Carpet Days, when prospective students can tour the campus, participate in orientation, receive advice on financial aid, take the Accuplacer assessment and receive their scores, meet with an EPAC adviser to develop an educational plan, and register for courses—all in one day.

Level II Advising

After a student has been accepted, advising continues, with students in special populations receiving additional targeted advising in specific programs. These include the Student Support Services program (a part of TRIO Scholars, federal outreach programs designed to motivate and support students from disadvantaged backgrounds), the First Generation Student Success program (FGSS), the Title V Access and Success project, and the North Lincoln Campus of Learners (COL) partnership.

More than 200 associate degree-seeking students participate in Student Support Services (SSS), a U.S. Department of Education grant-funded TRIO project. Students receive assistance from a peer mentor, an ECM, and a tutor until they receive their associate degree. The SSS program is routinely evaluated by using student focus groups, surveys to determine student satisfaction, and tracking students' academic performance with a college-designed tracking database. The fall 2000–fall 2001 retention rate for SSS students was 85 percent, and nearly 90 percent maintained at least a 2.0 grade point average.

The FGSS Program, now funded by institutional funds, grew out of the La Familia Scholars Program (La Familia), funded in 1995 by a Title III Hispanic-Serving Institution (HSI) grant. (Federally designated HSIs are those in which the student population is at least 25 percent Hispanic/Latino.) La Familia recruited Latino first-generation students who held a high school diploma or GED, and low-income students were given priority for acceptance into the program. The program was so successful and popular that its scope and its title were changed in 1997 to reflect expanded service to first-generation students in general as a first-year, college-funded program. No Title V funds are used for FGSS.

Currently, about 600 first-generation students participate in FGSS. They represent a broad spectrum of first-generation, low-income students. FGSS is designed for students with fewer than twelve credits; when FGSS participants earn twelve college credits, they are transferred to one of the four college instructional centers, where they receive advising and other assistance. The FGSS program includes a combination of strategies to increase student learning and retention including educational case management, peer mentoring, learning communities, computerized instruction, and a focus on skills development, academic tracking, and intervention.

The quantitative indicators of the FGSS program are impressive. Although the case manager's student load is heavy—only two case managers are assigned to some 600 students in the program—the retention rate is high. Approximately 84 percent of students who complete the first year of college as a participant in the First Generation program are retained to the second year. Early indications of the program's success led to its expansion by 45 percent in the 2001–2002 school year.

Because of the FGSS program's successes with first-generation students, the U.S. Department of Education funded a new Title V project for 2000–2005 in the four College Instructional Centers. This project is designed to increase student success in the second year for CCD's first-generation students, who represent 64 percent of the total student population. In 2002–2003, the number of first-generation, low-income Title V graduates was 25 percent of the total number of CCD graduates for that academic year.

The North Lincoln Campus of Learners program serves adult learners who live in the North Lincoln Park area. This project, conducted in partnership with the Denver Housing Authority, enrolls nearly fifty students each year and receives support from the FGSS and Title V educational case management teams. The difference is that educational programming is taken into the community where students live, allowing greater involvement with family members and the community. The North Lincoln Campus of Learners program produced an 88 percent one-year retention rate, with nearly 50 percent of students enrolling in at least one honors course.

Of course, the institution does not accept unilateral responsibility for any student's progress. Upon acceptance, students participating in these targeted programs sign a program agreement. The document walks the first-year student through the critical points in the educational process, such as registration, review of academic progress, and the selection of a major—times when the student is responsible for meeting with the case manager. The student agrees to participate in at least one learning community of combined courses, a financial aid workshop, and a career exploration workshop or activity. If the student gets any grades other than A, B, or C, he or she is committed to follow an academic intervention plan that may include more intensive tutoring and advice from the ECM. Finally, the student waives such privacy rights as may be necessary to consolidate and examine his or her financial, personal, and academic circumstances holistically.

In today's legalistic environment, such a document and the arrangement it represents might be considered contractual: you do this, and in return, we will do that. But a contractual relationship is about each party's meeting minimal standards of outward performance or intention. The various special programs at CCD have characteristics that mirror something more—a family. The arrangement is not that of a contract but a covenant: you do all that you can, and we will do all we can. It is not about meeting minimal standards but about reaching maximum potential.

The college has documented the experiences of many students to show how La Familia, FGSS, and other first-year targeted programs have contributed to success. A multitude of stories is necessary, because no story and no individual is typical. For instance, after high school graduation, raising a family, and many years in the workforce, Antoinette (another pseudonym) wanted to fulfill more of her educational dreams. She confronted and dealt with fears normal to this situation—the balance of home and school responsibilities, the "rust" that might show from being out of school for years—but she had more particular challenges. An attack that happened years before in a workplace rest room left her extremely fearful of using them. CCD's counselors recognized that this fear was as significant as any academic issue and helped her confront and overcome it. Antoinette not only realized personal academic success—she was named to the Colorado All-Academic Team—but she also helped others achieve it through such service as the presidency of a student organization that implemented a college-preparedness program for teen mothers. Her long-term goals include a doctorate in nursing. She credits CCD for much of her confidence and accomplishment. "Now, I feel that I have a red cape and can fly."

Level III Advising: Title V HSI Access and Success Strengthening Institutions Project

This project, begun in 2000 and funded by a five-year Title V grant, is designed to improve the retention and success of degree-seeking students with a declared major who are also low-income, first-generation, and minority students. This program generally serves students who have completed thirty hours of course credit, but first-year students who are certain of their major may also be advised and monitored in this program. For these students, educational case management is centered in one of four academic centers: Center for Arts and Sciences, Center for Business and Technology, Center for Educational Advancement, and Center for Health Sciences. Participating students may also enroll in first-year experience and discipline-linked learning communities.

The Educational Case Management System

The ECM system, used at CCD for nearly twenty years in a number of special programs, is a model for holistic student services that borrows heavily from the field of social work. Case managers maintain one-to-one relationships with a cohort of students and manage a comprehensive portfolio of student support services, including academic advising and planning, career exploration and advising, financial aid application, time management coaching, connection to tutoring and other academic services, crisis intervention, and referral when appropriate to community-based assistance and programs. The case manager does not depend on the student to initiate contact or request help but rather monitors the student's progress on a regular basis through direct contact and an elaborate student tracking database system. Active intervention is often executed.

The ECM system began with two case management positions that were funded by a Title III HSI grant. That grant also allowed the college to select and train peer leaders, called student ambassadors, who work alongside the case manager to deliver services to students. Later, a Title V HSI grant provided the opportunity to add four additional case managers and expand the concept of ECM by adding other staff and faculty (a program chair or director, faculty advisers, and an office manager) to form cross-functional ECM teams. These teams meet on a regular basis and discuss each student, developing individual plans of action and support when called for.

Learning Communities and Professional Development

Learning communities, courses linked together by coenrollment, were also started at CCD as part of the First Generation Student Success program. Learning communities have been tied by research to such desirable outcomes as increased retention, more engaged learning experiences, higher content accomplishment, and even better lifestyles (Shapiro & Levine, 1999). CCD used federal grant monies to invest in the development and implementation of learning communities at the college. That investment included a stipend of $350 to each volunteer instructor for participation in twelve hours of faculty preparation and development of a learning community portfolio. The faculty workshop included examining successful models of learning communities, advice on merging class contents, learning the Blackboard electronic instruction system, and developing a learning community syllabus.

Although $350 is small compensation for the actual time investment, it is not the only compensation for instructors. There is also the satisfaction of increasing class retention, priority access to computer classrooms, learning new teaching techniques, and the opportunity to work with other instructors.

In fall 2002, the college sponsored twenty such first-year learning communities, typically involving two classes and six hours of academic credit. Some of the combinations are intuitive and linked by discipline, for example, Business Statistics and Principles of Macro Economics. Others are much less so: Sociology and English Composition, or College Algebra and Art History.

Faculty participants are enthusiastic about their experiences in learning communities, despite the extra effort necessitated by coordination with another instructor. Faculty comments included, "It's what keeps me here," "I love the camaraderie and cooperation," "It's why I got into teaching," and "It's an amazing way to draw on all of this college's resources." And the weaknesses? "We should be paid better," and "It's a shame that we don't do this for all students."

The learning communities initiative is just one of many faculty and professional development efforts concentrated in the Teaching/Learning Center, a unit that was founded in 1990 and has become core to the college's program development and improvements. The center issues grants of up to $1,500 for the internal development of new learning initiatives, with priority for those proposals that align with the college's strategic goals and have potential for ongoing support through other financial means. The center offers more than 100 workshops annually for faculty development; a particular focus is assisting faculty with using technology in instruction. The center has amassed and makes available a print and electronic library on a variety of pedagogical and college cultural topics. Frequent surveys of CCD instructors allow the center to develop new support mechanisms for emerging needs. The Teaching and Learning Center "operates as a nucleus for change and leads the College in its efforts to become a learning college" (Roueche, Ely, & Roueche, 2001, p. 61).

High Utilization of Technology

The Community College of Denver makes extensive use of technology, particularly personal computers, to support its learning objects. Its 1,700 instructional computers give it the highest ratio of machines to students among community colleges in Colorado. A statewide study also found that CCD ranked first in technology training for faculty.

Computers are at the center of activities and exercises in math and writing labs, among other instructional support functions. Computers are integral to the case management approach; making the student-tracking database an increasingly sophisticated and more comprehensive record of the student experience has been a driving goal. Case managers can track each student's specific interactions with college offices and even faculty members. CCD's inventive use of technology is exemplified by its development of a bilingual computer program, La Academia de Computacion (Computer Academy) in the Center for Business and Technology, to meet the needs of first-year Spanish-speaking students with an interest in computer technology.

But the high use of computers represents a resource choice as well. Many at CCD note that personnel are in short supply in some areas. More classes are taught by adjuncts than most faculty think desirable, and the compensation for those part-timers, in line with national circumstances, is low. The use of computers therefore represents a decision made about how the college will use its resources. Given the funding circumstances of public higher education nationally, and in particular in Colorado, it is representative of the many difficult choices that any two- or four-year college needs to make.

CCD's choice to invest in technology is supportive of the central articulation of learning outcomes, allowing closer monitoring and intervention in the first-year experience and self-paced student learning on a flexible schedule. The approach also enhances student facility with technology, an important skill in advanced education and career placement.

Steadfast and Innovative Leadership

Many individuals date the foundation of CCD's transformation to an address given in 1989 by former president Byron McClenney. In this address, "The Faces of Denver," he encouraged the faculty and staff to embrace the college's location and mission. "We don't look like Denver" was his message, and he championed more genuine outreach to the citizens of Denver whose lives could be most transformed by attendance at CCD. He asked the college to be more deliberately reflective of Denver's demographics and to commit to the philosophy and possibilities of developmental education.

Far from alienating his audience or creating dissent, the college seemed to rally to the cry. McClenney appeared to be tapping into ideas and motivations that existed in abundance at CCD but had not previously been gathered or fully articulated. "It resonated with me," one administrator recalled. "The faculty and staff had been personally engaged in much of this, but not as a group." McClenney also emphasized the development, use, and disclosure of accurate data to measure CCD's progress toward its goals and a strong and highly participatory planning model to get people focused on problems and opportunities in a meaningful, long-term sequence.

This leadership continues with McClenney's successor, President Christine Johnson, who took office in March 2001 and became the first Latina president in the history of Colorado higher education. "Byron was the president we needed then," one faculty member said, "and Christine is the president we need now."

Before taking the helm at CCD, Johnson was vice president for educational services at the Colorado Community College System, and before that director of urban initiatives with the Denver-based Education Commission of the States. Her background includes teaching and administration in secondary schools and appointment by the U.S. Secretary of Education to several national commissions charged with establishing standards for learning outcomes. Perhaps most significant, she was once a first-generation college student herself.

Johnson maintains McClenney's commitment to serving the Denver community, to information transparency, and to an annual participatory planning cycle. She has added to the mix her more personal outreach to the Denver community, particularly to its public school system, and a strong belief in meeting student needs through innovative educational approaches. A hallmark of her administration has been expansion of the college's branch campus operations, neighborhood-located centers where residents can start entry-level college courses on a virtually continuous calendar system.

While Johnson does have concerns that "we'll burn people out," she also says with pride that "we challenge ourselves to get ever closer to the Denver community and to the ideal of being a learner-centered college." That community commitment includes further expansion and strengthening of CCD's five branch campus locations, heavier recruitment in Denver's public schools, and the development of more relationships with business and industry. Becoming more centered on student learning relies on critical self-review and teamwork. "We're always ready to break data down to the next lower level to find opportunities for improvement."

While the leadership of Presidents McClenney and Johnson is not to be underestimated as a driving factor in CCD's development, leadership does not emanate solely from the top rung of institutional management. CCD was notable to us for the widely dispersed leadership we saw in first-year student programming, in the personal investment that individuals made in CCD and its students as a "cause," and for the strategies that the institution employed to acquire and develop such leadership.

A listing or description of the individuals who are leaders and champions of CCD's transformation by the nature of strong and diffuse leadership is certain to fail by omission. But perhaps two examples of individuals, one recruited to CCD and the other a home-grown leader, will illustrate.

Cindy Miles is the vice president for learning and academic affairs at CCD, having joined the staff in August 2002. Before coming to Denver, she was vice president and senior program officer with the League for Innovation in the Community College. She is the author or coauthor of a dozen books and articles and has served as a consultant to more than fifty colleges and organizations in higher education. Miles is a graduate of the renowned community college leadership program at the University of Texas-Austin. In fact, she served her doctoral internship at the Community College of Denver in 1995, working with President McClenney. She has taken on the challenge of insulating CCD's enrollments and program offerings, including first-year-student support, from peaks and valleys in the economic cycle and public funding.

She recalled the atmosphere that drew her to Denver: "The Community College of Denver is unique in its candor and willingness to be self-critical." She recalls the college's being very strategic in its search process, looking for someone who would contribute to a culture that says openly, "We're good, but we're not *that* good." She noted, "That appealed to the researcher in me."

Dianne Cyr, by contrast, is a home-grown leader. She was named dean of the Center for Learning Outreach in 1999, a role in which she is responsible for CCD's branch campus operations and nontraditional credit-bearing programs, and associate vice president for learning in 2001. But she has been at CCD since

1984, beginning her career as an instructor. In 1993, her faculty peers selected her as CCD Faculty of the Year; in 2000, she was similarly awarded Administrator of the Year. Her responsibilities include management of the Teaching/Learning Center, and her leadership of that center resulted in its being named as winner of the 2000 Theodore M. Hesburgh Award from TIAA-CREF for excellence in faculty development.

As with many others at CCD, Cyr works long hours and worries about what could be better. During our visit, a current concern was how to make class selection information friendlier to students. Currently class selection is a challenge because of the array of CCD variations on course offerings that include accelerated courses, courses that start late in the term, and courses connected to learning communities. She was also interested in ways to create more sophisticated outcomes assessments. In our meetings, she grilled us on solutions to those and other issues that we might have seen at other colleges.

But experts are not the sole source of input for her. "We take as much feedback from students as we can," she said. "You can never assume anything," she noted. "You can never assume that they know what to do next" in the educational and bureaucratic processes. Then she adds, "All socioeconomic stereotypes are meaningless at this college. . . . I've found that students see the light. We help them find their way to it."

Close Relationships with Four-Year Institutions: The Auraria Campus

One factor that has contributed to the CCD's success has been its colocation with Metropolitan State College of Denver and the University of Colorado at Denver. With CCD's over 13,000 students, Metro State's 19,000 students, and UC-Denver's enrollment of 12,000, one of every five Colorado residents in higher education is affiliated with this location, called the Auraria Higher Education Center. CCD first occupied its Auraria location in 1975 and was the first institution to open on the new campus. The Auraria campus was a significant improvement over CCD's first location, a renovated auto showroom close to Denver's Civic Center that served the college during its initial years of operation.

The Auraria Campus is a 124-acre complex. Construction and building expansion have been virtually continuous since the mid-1970s. The campus occupies what was once a neighborhood of the same name, Auraria (from the Latin for gold), that began as a mining camp in the nineteenth century. More than 150 families were displaced by the construction and urban renewal project of thirty years ago. Most of the residents were poor and came from families that had lived at that location for several generations. Before construction began, houses on the site were purchased for $15,000 or less. Twenty years after the dislocation, a group of former residents calling themselves the Displaced Aurarians received the further concession of a scholarship fund for families whose neighborhood had been destroyed for the campus construction—but only after campus officials guessed incorrectly that a demonstration was coming during a reunion of the old neighborhood. It was not a particularly promising start for CCD among the citizens it now so devotedly serves.

While the Auraria Campus has many assets and physical attractions, they are not particularly well concentrated at CCD. Its classroom facilities lack a genuine collegiate feeling; they seem far removed from the stereotypes of ivied walls and classic architecture. Hallways and public areas are often crowded and at peak times are packed. Lines to service providers such as the registrar frequently wind beyond office boundaries into the hallway. Faculty regularly share limited office space. The feeling of compression comes from more than architecture or scheduling, however. Between 2001 and 2002, CCD was the second-fastest-growing community college in the United States in the 5,000- to 10,000-student category, with an enrollment increase of almost 22 percent.

In spite of a general lack of space, CCD students benefit from the fact that the physical boundaries among the institutions on the Auraria Campus are virtually seamless. The schools share an impressive array of facilities, including a regional library, a state-of-the-art fitness center, and a student union with bookstore and dining facilities. The circumstances favor collaboration and cost efficiencies in such matters as parking, security, child care, printing, and advanced technologies. CCD students also have ready physical access to desirable transfer institutions and personal experience in the environment of the senior institutions.

Some challenges related to the campuses' physical proximity have arisen from predictable institutional rivalries and self-interest. For example, President Johnson, on close examination of financial records, noted that while CCD was delivering developmental education for other institutions, the fiscal benefits to the college were not commensurate. That inequity has been resolved through recent agreements. When it was perceived that the library was not adequately addressing the needs of CCD students and faculty, the prospect that Johnson raised of withholding funding to the library was enough to reopen consideration and get better tailoring of library facilities to meet the college's needs. Despite these occasional "enforcements" of collegiality, the physical and philosophical blending of various levels of higher education offers a number of advantages to CCD students.

CCD has sought to strengthen the transfer transition by having its students who transfer to the senior institutions return to act as mentors and formal advisers to students who have or could benefit from transfer aspirations. This mentoring has taken the form of telling CCD students what to expect when they transfer. The mentors let CCD students know that they too can succeed at higher levels. But the transfers acknowledge that the personal support students come to know and expect at the community college will not always be there for them. It is a double-edged message: you need to work on your own internal sources of support and motivation—and you can always come back to CCD to receive advice and encouragement. Indeed, many of the mentors say that they take as much out of their return visits to CCD as they bring.

Not every community college has at hand the same opportunity for connections with four-year colleges as does CCD. But CCD did not always exploit its physical circumstances, and physical proximity may be only one avenue to realization of a deeper institutional philosophy: use every opportunity to connect the college and its students to other higher education opportunities. Smooth the connections as much as possible. Expect the four-year institutions not only to benefit from the connection but also to invest in it. And keep the flow of students operating strongly in both directions, bringing successful transfers back to serve as mentors, role models, and cheerleaders for those who aspire to follow in their footsteps.

Commitment to Accountability and Continuous Improvement

The college's commitment to genuine continuous improvement is possible only because of its practices of gathering institutional performance data and ensuring a high level of transparency in data reporting. Consider CCD's annual climate survey. The college believes that students will be successful and will persist only in an environment where they feel supported, valued, and respected. Respondents are asked to evaluate, on a scale from "strongly agree" to "strongly disagree," such statements as: instructors treat students with respect; instructors do not treat men and women with equal respect; faculty and staff are sensitive to differences in sexual orientation; I know how to seek help if I am mistreated because of my gender; it's easy for individuals with physical disabilities to get around campus; and I would recommend CCD to my friends. The open reporting of annual results is a catalyst for conversations about means to improve and identifies target areas for improvement.

A similar survey is conducted among faculty and staff, assessing their impressions of the college's performance with and respect for students, as well as their own sense of the climate and support for faculty and staff. Alumni and employers are regularly surveyed as well; alumni report on their post-CCD circumstances and their satisfaction with CCD, while employers evaluate the preparedness and performance of CCD graduates.

The college regularly and openly reports its progress and goals to the greater Denver community through various means that include an annual report. Basic descriptive information is reported: enrollment, student statistical profiles, and donors, for example. The status of current planning priorities is reviewed, and new goals are articulated. But CCD also goes to considerable lengths to report data that reflect institutional effectiveness. Those data include summaries of constituent surveys, information on graduation and transfer rates, recognition and evaluations offered by external entities, and budget source and allocation information. It is what the college calls "excellence through accountability."

The capability to use information for continuous improvement is made possible in large part by the focus CCD has put on institutional research. Greg Smith served for 10 years as the vice president of institutional effectiveness, planning, and technology. Former president McClenney recruited him to come to CCD to fill a vacant position and upgraded it and its responsibilities to make it attractive to Smith. Few other community college institutional research directors have Smith's credentials and experience. He holds a Ph.D. in experimental social psychology, and he spent nine years at the University of Denver and then six years at the Community College of Colorado System before coming to CCD. (He recently left CCD to accept a vice presidency at Arizona Central Community College.)

Byron McClenney was not hesitant to invest in this position in order to attract Smith to CCD, knowing how important good, current information is to improvement efforts. "If Byron had not decided he wanted to be a community college president, he could have been one of the best IR [institutional research] guys in the nation," Smith said, noting the former president's ability to analyze data in new and creative ways. The job was made a vice presidency directly reporting to the president, and planning and other functions were added to it. Beyond that, Smith said, "I asked only that I be given more responsibility as I proved I could handle it." He added with a laugh, "Getting more work turned out not to be a problem."

The Community College of Denver has been on the leading edge of some information-driven changes in higher education. It was an early adapter of the Higher Learning Commission's Academic Quality Improvement Project (AQIP), an alternative to the conventional, once-a-decade-or-so reaccreditation process of institutional self-study, site visit by outside experts, and address of perceived deficiencies. Conventional reaccreditation has been criticized as a backward-looking, "gotcha" process, in which an institution can, should it choose, be less vigilant about the gathering of effectiveness information after reaccreditation is secured. The AQIP process, by contrast, is one in which the institution chooses a focus area for improvement and engages in continuous efforts toward that goal. The reviews by the commission are more detailed on an annual basis and do not require site visits. The emphasis is toward the future.

CCD, like every other public college and university in the state and most public institutions in the country, has been under increasing legislative mandate to prove effectiveness. The first such piece of legislation in Colorado was passed in the mid-1980s, and a number of revisions and mandates have been passed since then. While this creates new reporting responsibilities for CCD, it has not induced a sense of panic or a change in procedures. "I've told people that as long as we're fulfilling our role and mission and collecting data to support that," said Smith, "we won't have any trouble hitting the moving target of external review."

Smith characterized his colleagues as "extremely self-critical people. It's a dedicated group. They always want to do better. And there's a critical mass of them here who carry everyone else along. We take the learning college concept seriously."

In line with that self-critical attitude, Smith took time to point out what CCD is missing in its data collection: the next frontier of improvement through assessment. "We have very good information at the institutional and program levels," he said, "but we need to know more about student gains at the classroom and course level."

That kind of interest is atmospheric at CCD. The educators at this institution have easily and regularly justified their means and ends to accrediting agencies, legislators, and the Denver community at large. But these educators feel that their ultimate accountability is to students, particularly those who have few or any options for higher education other than the Community College of Denver.

Success in Acquiring External Funds

The Community College of Denver is not a wealthy institution, and as in much of public higher education around the country, budget trends have ranged from discouraging to dire. As recently as 2000, the college had a deficit of close to $1 million. Annual cuts in state appropriations have become regular. Improvements, new initiatives, and intensive monitoring of students cost money. How then are these efforts accomplished?

CCD begins by investing in what it believes. The budget cycle does not begin until the planning cycle yields new and renewed goals. Resource allocations must then follow a rationale of support for the plan and the college's goals.

But state-provided funds and tuition alone would be insufficient to pursue all of CCD's ambitions. It has therefore entered into the search for outside funds with gusto.

Certainly governmental funds have been key among these sources, particularly Title III and Title V grants. A Title III grant of $1.3 million, aimed at Latino students, allowed the college to launch La Familia. As that funding wound down, the college shifted the program into its regular budget and expanded it into the more general First Generation Student Success Program. A Title V grant of $1.9, running from 2000 to 2005, has allowed CCD to launch the case management program and move it into the regular college budget.

The college has successfully pursued private funding as well, once the virtually exclusive domain of four-year colleges. In 2001–2002, CCD had more than twenty donors who each contributed more than $5,000; four of the donors gave $30,000 or more. To support the acquisition of both government and private funding, the college has a strong, central grant-writing function. But it also offers education to faculty and staff so that they can initiate funding requests for their own ideas and classroom ambitions.

Grant-funded programs are helpful for the students who are their direct, programmatic recipients, but the impact of such soft money programs can be limited if the programs do not survive the grant period. CCD has pursued a strategy of transition for such programs, moving the percentage of external funding from 100 percent in the first year to perhaps 20 percent during the grant's terminal year. By such means, the college is prepared to absorb successful programs into regular operating budgets without large budgetary shock.

CCD's success at getting outside funds is both a benefit and a challenge. "I worry that we sometimes get too far out in front of the college, its capacity to deliver," said one administrator. "There's a danger of burnout," said another. "If we get too far out in front, we lose people's creativity. And creativity is basically what we bring to students." But so far, the college has always managed to catch up, and even to exceed the potential promised in grant proposals.

Intentional Focus on Student Success

The CCD mission and pledge is "to provide: transfer programs for the baccalaureate degree; occupational programs for job-entry skills or upgrading; general education courses; remedial instruction and

GED preparation; continuing education and community services; and cooperative inter-institutional programs." The scope of this mission might initially appear overwhelming and fragmented. But we found that the focus on student success brings unity to the discrete aspects of this mission.

Ambitions for greater service to students may mean little if there is no consensus on institutional goals, if reasonable targets are not identified, and if there are no predetermined means to measure success. The annual planning cycle at CCD is one way that the institution develops consensus about its goals and measures of success.

This planning process dates to 1986, when faculty and staff were asked by former president Byron McClenney to rate and prioritize a number of institutional goals. Those responses were compiled and reported back to all. The general consensus, without much formal discussion, was that CCD should be, first and foremost, a student-centered institution, where teamwork and collaboration would enhance this vision.

Subsequent annual exercises were strengthened by the naming and operation of a large and broadly representative Planning Council. Through extensive data gathering on current educational outcomes, environmental scanning (broad consideration of the college's local, state, and national environment in the broadest terms), and refining the processes for gathering individuals' opinions about the future of the institution, the Planning Council routinely develops a set of institutional priorities for the coming year.

Priorities in early years of the process concentrated on institutional and structural issues not directly connected to student outcomes. By the mid-1990s, however, central issues were holistic advising, celebrating diversity, building community, and improving instructional delivery. Goals for 2001–2002 included increasing student learning and success and changing the organizational culture to support learning.

Unit budgets are not prepared or submitted until after the college has developed its primary goals for the year and the president has approved them. Then budgets are expected to demonstrate how units will advance both the plan and evaluation of its success. The result is a planning process that is deeply embedded within the realities of life at CCD. Roueche, Ely, and Roueche, in a brief but notable book about CCD, *In Pursuit of Excellence: The Community College of Denver* (2001), wrote that individuals at every level of the college regarded the planning cycle as "the single most critical component" of the organization, and that it has "exceeded all expectations as a collaborative activity" (p. 74). This remarkable planning process keeps the college focused on its core value: service to students in the first two years of college.

A Model Community College Is Recognized

CCD's success has made it a model for other colleges, both four year and two year. It is one of only twelve community colleges nationwide, chosen from 94 applicants, to be named a Vanguard Learning College, a special initiative of the League for Innovation in the Community College. The Vanguard Learning College project, funded by a special grant, intends that the Community College of Denver and the other selected institutions become incubators and catalysts for more learner-centered practices and outcomes. The project is focused on five broad objectives: the development of institutional cultures that support learning as a priority, staff recruitment and development programs to support learning, use of technology to improve learning, the development and assessment of learning outcomes, and a focus on the success of underprepared students. The colleges have participated in an active exchange of ideas and program experiences and have subjected themselves to ongoing and rigorous external review. (See the Vanguard Learning College Web site, http://www.league.org/league/projects/lcp/index.htm, for more information.) Although this effort is not specific to the first year of college, such efforts are heavily invested in new student success by the very nature of community colleges and their level of focus.

Roueche and his colleagues (2001) have noted CCD's excellence with a story that strongly parallels and reinforces the Vanguard objectives. Internal and external authors have told the college's story in numerous other venues. Visitors wishing to observe CCD up close have become so numerous that the college has established special visit days to minimize the impact on its primary mission of education. The accolades sometimes seem endless.

This innovative and nationally recognized environment might lead to smugness and self-satisfaction, a relaxed attitude toward improvement. But that is not the case at CCD. "We're always ready to dig down into the next level of data to find ways to improve," said President Johnson. "There's an attitude here that we're good, but we're not that good. We can be better," said another administrator.

These efforts are not all self-referential, as suggested by the Vanguard participation. When the college hears about a program at another institution, an innovation that may benefit its students, it often puts together a team of faculty and administrators to visit the college and bring back ways that the innovation could be adapted to CCD. It subjects itself to higher levels of external review, as evidenced by its participation (and success) in external awards competitions.

The cumulative result of self-examination, self-improvement, looking outward for models, and subjection to external review has been substantial external recognition for the college. CCD's recognition as an Institution of Excellence is just the latest in a long list of awards and favorable notations. Many government officials, both state and national, have commended its work, and the literature of best practices in community colleges is replete with examples from CCD.

Doing your very best, trying to get better, looking for ways to improve: this is a level of commitment that exceeds what most of us might do for our job, but it certainly would not be too much to ask for your family. And that is the way the Community College of Denver has approached its relationship to Denver and its citizens, particularly those with the fewest resources and the biggest dreams.

Chapter Four

LaGuardia Community College

A Window on the World

Betsy O. Barefoot

Michael J. Siegel

Community colleges are, by their very nature, diverse environments. They embody the ideals of democracy by providing an environment where anyone of any age, racial or ethnic group, or socioeconomic level has a chance to obtain job skills and enter higher education. But it would be difficult, if not impossible, to find a community college in the United States that is more diverse than LaGuardia Community College. Currently, over 12,000 degree-seeking students and 30,000 continuing education students from approximately 170 countries choose this educational platform from which to launch their version of the American dream. The institution's third and current president, Gail Mellow, describes "the layered complexity of LaGuardia students' lives"—students who were born into one culture, moved, and assumed the identity of a second culture before making a final move to the United States. She maintains that although "community college students in general tend to be heroic, . . . these students are unlike any I've ever seen."

The site for "The World's Community College," as LaGuardia promotes itself in its marketing materials, is the foot of the Queensboro Bridge in the Borough of Queens, New York. The campus occupies several blocks in a neighborhood of concrete "boxes"—former factories that produced Sunshine Biscuits, shopping bags, gyroscopes, and even bombs. The story goes that early in the institution's history, faculty felt free to park their motorcycles inside the buildings. Since enrolling its first class in 1971, the campus has transformed itself into a bright, inviting web of buildings that includes student art work on every wall and even green space—a grass and cobblestone courtyard where a few trees are planted. Another unique campus feature is the Hall of Flags, where flags are displayed representing every country from which a LaGuardia student has come. And even the neighborhood is beginning to change. While its Manhattan facilities are being renovated, New York's prestigious Museum of Modern Art (MOMA) is the campus's newest neighbor.

But what makes this campus so special goes far beyond its industrial surroundings or its physical transformation. The LaGuardia story, as it relates to serving first-year students, is a story about faculty, administrative, and student commitment; about leadership at all levels; about high expectations; about innovation; and, to quote the president, about "an intersection of certain people at a certain time." The merging of these factors has created a special institution that has become an exemplar not only for other U.S. community colleges, but also for institutions of any type, location, or level of selectivity.

During the site visit that is the foundation for this chapter, we, as the research team, were inspired by what we learned. We heard moving testimonies from students, faculty, and staff members about the power of this institution to transform lives. And we learned of the college's experience of September 11, 2001, when the campus community watched in horror as the World Trade Center towers fell, when Muslim students stood tall in the face of anger and frustration, when the FBI arrived on campus demanding to know names and whereabouts of Muslim students, and when amazingly over half of all the students still returned for class the very next day.

Before we launch into a description of what makes LaGuardia Community College an Institution of Excellence, it is important to acknowledge the challenge of talking about the first year in a community college setting. In most community colleges, first-year students are not an easily identifiable cohort. Students who are new to LaGuardia may have begun a college experience on another campus, and it is the rare student who completes the first year of course work within a nine-month period. Over 90 percent of first-time, degree-seeking LaGuardia students also begin their academic work by taking one or more developmental courses. So first-year initiatives are designed to address the needs of all students who are new to LaGuardia, whatever their age or precise academic classification.

LaGuardia as a Unique Culture

A central question that guided our study of LaGuardia was that of its institutional culture: How did the spirit of innovation and empowerment that characterizes this campus come to be, and how is it maintained? One answer lies in the intersection of people and time. The college was born in the heady post–student activism days of the early 1970s. The initial cadre of faculty were themselves activists who, to quote the president, "believed that what they were doing was fundamental to democracy" and were committed to "teaching as an act of social justice." President Mellow continues, "The early faculty were young themselves, and there hasn't been much faculty turnover. A huge group of the initial hires have remained here, and they're still at the cutting edge."

Faculty speak reverentially of the first president, Joe Shenker, described as an innovative risk taker who enabled the early faculty to have a stake in the institution. Shenker became president in 1970 at the age of thirty and, in his eighteen-year tenure, oversaw the growth of the college from 500 to over 16,000 students. Shenker left LaGuardia in 1988 to become president of the innovative Bank Street College of Education in New York City. In a 2001 ceremony to present Shenker the LaGuardia President's Medal, Mellow stated, "What [Shenker] did was fill the College with a spirit and passion. And these forces are still present because he just did not build a building, he built an institution of higher learning that has profoundly affected the students who come through these doors and go on to wonderful and important work."

When faculty describe LaGuardia's relatively short history, they tend to talk about three distinct time periods. The first was the Shenker era, when the college was on the move not only in terms of growth but also in establishing its distinctive leadership role in American higher education. The second, a period of about ten years, is often described as a time in which the college became more stable but lost its spirit of innovation and became somewhat stagnant. A senior campus administrator believes the reason for this stagnation was that "creativity was not encouraged. Faculty were not allowed to have a sense of responsibility—a stake in the college's progress. When this college opened, we were bigger than just the college, it was our responsibility to change the lives of these students in significant ways." In the third phase, comprising the past five years, the college's fire has been rekindled, assessment has become a center-stage activity, and faculty are incredibly productive at obtaining grants and making good use of funds received. The vice president for academic affairs maintains that "this first-year stuff is a natural—it gave us the opportunity to get people involved in what was really important for the institution."

Although it is probably fair to say that many college campuses tend to be oases of liberalism in a conservative national landscape, LaGuardia may be among the most liberal. It is still a refuge for less traditional, activist faculty who "are not penalized by a focus on teaching." Whether faculty were hired in the early 1970s or as recently as a year ago, teaching at LaGuardia often represents a deliberate choice—a calling—even when faculty are offered more prestigious positions at four-year institutions. One instructor commented, "Academic freedom of the place is why I came here. I came from another CUNY four-year school where I only taught on Tuesdays and Thursdays. And some of my friends still ask me, 'Don't you wish you could teach regular students?'" Another newly hired faculty member remarked, "I was offered a job at Princeton, but I told them I was really interested in teaching. This was what I wanted. Friends say, 'Why in the hell didn't you take that Princeton job?' I have a friend who works at the United Nations, and she's always talking about this ambassador, that ambassador. I tell her, 'UN, Schmoo-in, come walk through our atrium—let me show you the real world. One of my students is an African prince!'"

Where Is Leadership Found?

Although leadership is a central theme for all thirteen Institutions of Excellence, the nature of that leadership may be somewhat different depending on the particular institutional environment. When exploring the influence of leadership on first-year efforts at LaGuardia, one can look in many directions. Leaders are everywhere at all levels of the institution. Every administrator with whom we spoke gave credit to someone else: the president, academic leaders including the vice president and dean for academic affairs, individual faculty, and students themselves.

The current president, Gail Mellow, models outstanding leadership and encourages its development among faculty, staff, and students. Her commitment to the first year is demonstrated not only through the allocation of financial support but also through her willingness to be available to entering students. Her own experience as a first-year student in a community college gives her a high level of credibility with students, many of whom are amazed to learn her personal story.

One important manifestation of Mellow's leadership is in the area of assessment. The current director of institutional research describes the institution's uneven assessment history, but states that today, every new initiative is required to have a built-in assessment component. The Institutional Research Office is now a place where faculty and administrators can go to get useful statistical information about topics that range from broad institutional issues to the effectiveness of classroom teaching. The president believes that data are essential in order to survive in the external political climate, and in collaboration with the City University of New York Central Office, she insists that institutional decisions about the allocation of resources be supported by evidence.

The LaGuardia environment has been and continues to be an incubator for all sorts of innovative first-year efforts initiated primarily by the faculty themselves (who include student affairs counselors with faculty rank). The dean of academic affairs maintains that "when faculty are interested in a project that they thought up, you don't have to pull teeth." Any good idea needs administrative support, funding, and time, and faculty find that the LaGuardia administrators are supportive of innovation, even when that innovation involves uncertainty and risk. Administrators assist faculty in seeking grant support through the City University of New York, state and federal governments, and private foundations, and faculty have been successful in obtaining grants for a number of initiatives. These include a variety of learning communities, a campuswide common reading experience, mentoring programs, presemester academic preparation workshops called "intensives," academic workshops for students who fail a basic skills course called Second Chance, and the integration of technology into the academic experience including the building of e-portfolios of student academic work. Even the college's Student Association has become an internal funder by contributing $10,000 collected from student fees to support the common readings and by providing additional monies for mentoring and study-abroad opportunities.

Faculty who generate new ideas become leaders for their dissemination and trainers in a variety of faculty development activities such as teaching in learning communities, writing across the curriculum, and using technology. It is the institution's practice to involve adjuncts in all professional development activities, as they comprise an increasing proportion of LaGuardia instructors.

Any time we raised the question of leadership, another name—in addition to President Mellow, Vice President John Bihn, and various faculty members—was mentioned: Paul Arcario, currently serving as dean of academic affairs and described as a "quiet, somewhat self-effacing leader who inspires the confidence and trust of all the faculty." Arcario brings to his position hands-on experience in teaching English as a Second Language (ESL). Therefore, this area of instruction, so much a part of the day-to-day work at the college, is not an abstraction to him but a field to which he devoted much of his academic life. Over and over again, we heard, "It was Paul's vision," "It was Paul's leadership," "Paul accepted my idea," "It's easy to be comfortable with Paul—there's no risk that if your ideas fail, you'll be penalized." Arcario recognizes that money is the "huge issue," and he has wisely used grant funds to support faculty. But he adds, "We don't have to support them for everything. When faculty know that we're supporting them, they're willing to jump in and do other things." Arcario not only serves as the primary administrator for the various first-year programs, he continues to teach in the freshman interest group program so that, in his words, he will "stay in touch with what's happening in the classroom."

One important decision made in 2000 by the interim president, Roberta Matthews, had the effect of creating a closer working partnership between academic and student affairs on behalf of first-year students and empowering faculty and staff to take on leadership roles. That decision was to ensure that off-campus professional development experiences be shared by both academic and student affairs. The case in point was the Year 2000 First-Year Experience Conference in Reading, England. As a condition of her attendance at this conference, the vice president for student affairs was required to take along representatives from academic affairs. Therefore, she was joined at this conference by the academic dean and a cadre of faculty. While far away from the campus at the conference, which team members describe as "so rich that there was a lot for us to look at," they had opportunities for extended conversation and brainstorming. Each team member attending the conference was given carte blanche to pick a project described at the conference and to implement that project at LaGuardia. Dean Arcario states, "We wanted to match people with their interests to encourage them to generate ideas about what they were interested in doing." From that single conference experience came the ideas for the new student convocation, mentoring, and common reading experience. Now it is the institution's policy "never to send only one person to a conference." According to Arcario, the Reading conference was the beginning of a revitalized partnership between academic and student affairs on behalf of first-year students that continues to this day. In fact, senior representatives from both the divisions of academic and student affairs continue to cochair LaGuardia's First-Year Committee.

The New Student Experience at LaGuardia

In designing its experience for new students, LaGuardia has kept in mind two central goals:

- Fostering academic success among developmental and ESL students. Over 90 percent of first-time, degree-seeking students at LaGuardia take at least one developmental course, and 34 percent of entering students are placed into ESL.

- Creating a sense of community and connectedness to the college among a highly diverse group of commuting students.

When compared to other community colleges around the nation, LaGuardia has been highly successful in meeting both of these goals through a remarkable range of special initiatives. We were struck by the power of LaGuardia's positive predictions for itself as an institution and for its students. The unwritten rule is, "If it can be done anywhere in higher education, it can be done at LaGuardia." It is fair to say that every student who enters a degree program at LaGuardia will benefit from at least one, if not multiple, special programs designed to foster academic success and connection to the institution. These special programs include learning communities taught in various formats, the New Student Seminar, Quick Start and other intensive programs, opening sessions, common readings, mentoring, honors programs, study-abroad programs, and the integration of technology.

Learning Communities

LaGuardia began its first-year efforts in the area of learning communities and has established a national reputation in this arena primarily through the efforts of two outstanding faculty members, Will Koolsbergen and Phyllis van Slyck. The campus offers a variety of fully integrated, learning community programs for both ESL and non-ESL students that include liberal arts and sciences clusters, New Student House, paired courses, and freshman interest groups.

Liberal Arts and Sciences Clusters

These clusters, first developed in 1976, are available for liberal arts and sciences majors. Clusters are thematically organized; all have two courses from the core liberal arts and science curriculum, English Composition, The Research Paper, and an integrated hour that is team-taught. Topics for the research paper course are interdisciplinary and based on materials in all the other courses. Each of these liberal arts clusters constitutes a full schedule for participating students. Examples of frequently offered liberal arts clusters are as follows:

Harlem on My Mind: American Music, The Art of Theatre, English Composition, The Research Paper, Integrated Hour (one team-taught hour to help with integration used in variety of ways)

Men Talk, Women Talk: Oral Communication, Art of Theater, English Composition, The Research Paper, Integrated Hour

Women's Lives; Women's Struggles: Introduction to Sociology, Women and Society, English Composition, The Research Paper, Integrated Hour

Sociology and Culture of the Family: English Composition, The Research Paper, Introduction to Sociology, Sociology of the Family, Integrated Hour

The Moral Thinking Cluster: Introduction to Philosophy, American Film, English Composition, The Research Paper, Integrated Hour

Movies and the City: Intercultural Images: American Film, Intercultural Communication, English Composition, The Research Paper

Media, Power and Justice: Introduction to Sociology: Introduction to Sociology, The Art of Theatre, English Composition, The Research Paper, Integrated Hour

New Student House

The New Student House program, begun in 1991, is offered for students with basic skills needs in at least three areas: reading, writing, and speech. The program follows a coordinated studies model. This means that the curriculum in reading, writing, and speech is coordinated and often organized around a theme, that activities and assignments are linked, and that classes are sometimes taught by a group of teachers.

New Student House is a full block of four courses: Basic Reading, Basic Writing, New Student Seminar, and a college-level content course. Recent New Student House clusters have included content courses in oral communication, critical thinking, business, and computer science. This is a highly integrated learning community, which includes joint readings, projects, field trips, and large group meetings (for debates and role-playing activities). A counselor, who teaches the New Student Seminar, meets weekly with faculty teaching in the New Student House to offer guidance and feedback especially for the most at-risk students. Recognizing that some faculty have neither the time nor the inclination to invest in the total collaboration required by teaching in New Student House, the college has implemented another variation of the learning community for basic skills students, the freshman interest group (FIG).

Freshman Interest Groups

In 2001, LaGuardia implemented the FIG, designed to expand the number of learning communities available for basic skills students. Each FIG comprises a small cohort of students who meet together weekly in an integrating seminar. These students also become part of larger class groups in two basic skills courses, a freshman seminar, and a college-level course. The integrative seminar is taught by a faculty member, who is termed a "master learner." This individual takes the responsibility for linking the content of the various courses. Recently, the integrative seminar has also been used as the venue for helping students develop electronic portfolios.

ESL Communities

Students who require extra assistance with ESL are offered an ESL version of the New Student House and ESL courses that are paired with regular content courses across the curriculum. The ESL New Student House has been designed around two themes: "Immigration" and "Women's Condition and Women's Rights Movement in the Early Nineteenth Century America." This cluster includes Basic Reading, ESL, Communication for the Non-Native Speaker, and a New Student Seminar.

ESL–Content Course Pairings

Since 1990, LaGuardia has paired courses across the curriculum with ESL courses. The original purpose of this pairing, according to Jack Gantzer, a long-time ESL professor, was not improving retention, overall grade point averages, or even generating a stronger sense of community, although these outcomes have been realized through the ESL pairs. The original goal was helping students learn the English language in new ways—ways that relate to their lives. The intent of ESL pairs is to prepare students for their "chosen communicative environments"—to give them the ability to read and write about what is most interesting to them and what relates most specifically to their educational and career goals. The number of pairs has grown with the help of external grants and currently is approximately forty-five. These include ESL pairings with such courses as Introduction to Business, Accounting, Biology, Computer Science, and Human Services. A ten-year longitudinal study of course grades, comparing students in ESL pairs and ESL New Student House with stand-alone courses, finds that students in paired courses earn statistically significant higher grades in both content and ESL courses than students who take the same courses in a stand-alone format

Impact of the Learning Communities Experience

LaGuardia's learning communities have redefined and heightened the expectations both faculty and students have for the learning experience. Not only does integrated learning improve the quality of teaching and learning, all of LaGuardia's longitudinal data indicate that students are more likely to pass courses taken in clusters than stand-alone courses.

As is the case with virtually all the innovations at LaGuardia, learning communities were born out of faculty interest in collaborative work. To quote a faculty member, "At LaGuardia, it is common for faculty to find their teammates and teach together over a period of years in a variety of formats. Faculty connections then help students connect." Faculty with whom we spoke were unanimous in their belief that they have had a remarkable impact not only on the students but also on the culture of the faculty experience. They believe the content of the learning community structure is rich, freeing, and invigorating.

We came to believe during our visit—and this was borne out by the statements of several individuals—that many of those involved in learning communities have a predisposition for the work. These faculty noted the importance of having the "ability to work collaboratively and closely with other members of the faculty." And they realize the benefit of being able to talk to other faculty and staff about students coenrolled in their classes and to address problems or issues that students face—problems that at times relate more to social and psychological concerns than academic. There was a common perception that faculty were able to deal with many problems before they became unmanageable. One faculty member offered a telling comment about his involvement in the learning communities: "The affective part is bigger than the pedagogical." In terms of benefits to the students, another faculty member summed it up by saying, "Students join a community of learners, which [is all about] extending the classroom."

Because learning communities provide ongoing interaction with a cohort of students as well as repetition of experience, participating students have the opportunity to develop their self-esteem and self-confidence. Many students spoke not only of the academic benefits they derived from being involved in learning communities, but also the social and psychological benefits. One student remarked that in the learning communities, students "always have someone to talk to." And several students commented on the "warm atmosphere" and the presence of "supportive faculty" on campus, due in large part to the structure of the learning communities.

Although learning communities are the centerpiece of LaGuardia's success with new students, the patterns of both student enrollment and progress through courses limit to some extent the level of student participation. Students who fail one course within a learning community repeat that course in a standalone mode. And because learning communities, by their very nature, require coenrollment in at least two and up to four courses, participation overwhelmingly tends to be of full-time rather than part-time students. (Currently about 60 percent of LaGuardia's students are enrolled full time and 40 percent part time.)

New Student Seminar

The New Student Seminar is a one-hour-per-week, noncredit course required of every degree-seeking student during his or her first term. Some sections of the seminar are designed for students in particular majors, and seminars may also be part of learning communities—clusters, FIGs, and paired courses. A special version of the seminar is offered for College Discovery students. College Discovery is a special program of the City of New York for students who need academic and financial support to complete college. Because so many LaGuardia students meet the qualifications for admission to College Discovery, enrollment is determined by lottery. College Discovery seminar instructors serve as their students' counselor for as long as the students are enrolled at LaGuardia.

New Student Seminar is administered through the Department of Counseling, which is an academic department at the college, and is taught by the counselors themselves, who have faculty status. The seminar covers such topics as adjusting to college life, high-stakes testing, study skills, career exploration, and academic advising. In fact, the seminar is the structure within which formal academic advising takes place, with the seminar instructor serving as academic adviser for students in his or her section. Because the seminar is required for all new LaGuardia students, each class is a rich and diverse mix of student backgrounds, prior experience, and familiarity with higher education. Although some students require help in basic academic skills, others have earned degrees in their own country. A counseling faculty member who is a New Student Seminar instructor stated that in her seminar, there is a mix of some poorly educated students but also a "dentist, doctor, and chemist" who earned their professional degrees before immigrating to the United States. The prior educational experience of some of these students results in sophisticated classroom discussions that keep faculty on their toes.

The New Student Seminar yields benefits for both students and the institution. These benefits include a greater sense of connection, improved confidence, and better academic preparation. However, the course faces a number of challenges common to first-year seminars on any campus. The first challenge is class size. Currently some seminar sections enroll as many as forty students, which counseling faculty acknowledge is far from ideal. Other issues are the limited amount of contact time allocated to the seminar—one hour per week—and the fact that the seminar, although required, carries no graduation credit. According to counseling faculty, one of the most serious difficulties in teaching the New Student Seminar is prioritizing among many critically important topics: complicated outside policies that must be discussed and translated, student skills, academic and career preparation, and preparing for advisement, for example. Because of the rigid structure of available credit hours and the increasing numbers of new students, the problems of class size and instructional time will not be easily resolved in the foreseeable future.

"Preps" and "Intensives"

As an external observer, one cannot help but be amazed at the number and quality of "prep," "second-chance," and other intensive courses available for LaGuardia students during the intersession periods and summer session. Steve Dauz and Vincent Bruno, director and codirector, respectively, of Academic Collaborative Programs and Services, administer these programs. Both have a long history with the college, working in both student affairs and academic affairs. Summer and intersession programs are supported through funds from the City University Central Office.

The prefreshman intensive program, called Quick Start, includes from one to three weeks of instruction in developmental math, reading, writing, and upper levels of ESL. One-to-one tutoring and individual counseling are also components of the program. Quick Start programs are targeted to all students needing basic skills and are required of College Discovery students as a condition of entry to the college. In the summer of 2002, the college added a component to the prefreshman program by offering short preterm, intense prep classes, lasting from three to five days, in critical thinking, precalculus, and other college-level courses.

Second-chance intersession programs—one-week courses for students who "nearly pass" a basic skills course in math, reading, ESL, or writing—are offered four times per year after each academic session. Although not all "nearly passing" students opt to take the second-chance option, approximately 60 to 65 percent of students who participate are able to pass so that they do not have to retake the semester-long basic skills course.

Collegewide Mentoring Program

LaGuardia's mentoring program is another result of the efforts of Steve Dauz and Vincent Bruno. Although mentoring is part of the College Discovery Program, it was Dauz who decided to take mentoring collegewide. He recalls that this was another idea gathered at the 2000 International First-Year Experience Conference and supported by Dean Paul Arcario. The mentoring program has as its goals supporting new students and increasing their sense of connection as well as their ultimate retention and graduation. Since its beginnings in spring 2001, the program has connected with 1,300 new students through the efforts of faculty, staff, and increasing numbers of student mentors. To prepare for being a mentor, LaGuardia students may take a three-credit mentoring course. Students who cannot take the course can opt for a four-session workshop followed by weekly meetings throughout the semester. Future plans call for putting mentor training on-line in order to accommodate prospective mentors who are unable to participate in either the credit course or the workshop.

Dauz and Bruno have designed an effective system to match mentors with mentees by means of questionnaires that ask lots of questions about interests, experiences, and background. And they communicate with mentors by means of the "Mentor Connection"—an electronic newsletter of sorts with short articles and links to Web resources and the Mentoring Program Web page (http://www.lagcc.cuny.edu/mentorprogram).

When the Mentoring Program was piloted in spring 2001, there were many more faculty and staff mentors than student mentors. However, every semester sees an increase in the numbers of student mentors, currently at forty-eight. Early research comparing one-year retention rates for students who select mentors and those who do not shows dramatic differences favoring the mentored students. Mentees also express higher levels of satisfaction with various aspects of their first-year experience and the college in general.

Opening Sessions and Common Reading

Many colleges and universities feature opening convocations or other large group ceremonies to welcome each entering cohort of students. And the past several years have seen a national rebirth of the preterm common reading, a book given to new students that becomes the topic for small group discussion during their first days on campus. But such events are extremely rare at community colleges because of the obvious difficulties of getting commuting students to commit extra time on campus before the official beginning of the term. However, once again, on the assumption that "if we build it, students will come," LaGuardia decided to defy the stereotype and create its own version of an opening convocation that would include a common reading.

LaGuardia first offered an opening session in fall 2001, and since that time, sessions have been scheduled at the beginning of each term. The overall goals for this event are to build connections between students, faculty, and staff; relieve students' anxiety; and provide them a dry run for the college experience. Both academic affairs and enrollment management–student development have taken joint responsibility for this day. A faculty committee selects the common reading, and an operations committee organizes the events. Student ambassadors are also involved to make sure that new students find the best (and most attractive) way around campus.

Opening sessions begin with a theater presentation that often includes music. Faculty and administrators remember the student who at the 2001 opening session musical theater production acted the part of Fiorello H. La Guardia, the former New York City mayor after whom the college is named. Word has it that the student actor bore some resemblance to La Guardia himself. Following the opening production, students join faculty in small discussion groups about the common reading. The closing event is another large group session in which students are invited to share their personal stories. Students also hear an inspirational message from the college president. Each opening session now draws about 700 participants, one-third of the entering student population at LaGuardia, and the event is given superior evaluations by student participants.

The selection of a common reading that will appeal to students and can be read by students at varying reading levels is never easy. But under the leadership of Professor Liz Clark, a series of common reading events are developed each year, including related films and an essay contest. To date, the college has selected three works that emphasize the theme of personal narrative. The first selections were *Having Our Say: The Delany Sisters' First Hundred Years,* and an excerpt from Fiorello H. La Guardia's autobiography. In 2002, students read *When I Was Puerto Rican,* by Esmeralda Santiago. In December 2002, Santiago made a visit to the college to read from her book and meet with students.

LaGuardia provides the common reading at no cost to every student who registers, even those who register at the last minute. The college has also developed a Web site that offers background information on the book and links to related sites, and some faculty use the book in their courses.

Honors Program

While the majority of LaGuardia students need one or more basic skills courses on entry, a growing number of students qualify for admission to the Honors Program and graduate with an honors diploma. In order to be admitted, entering students must have a B+ average in high school or twelve transfer credits with a 3.2 grade point average. LaGuardia's newly established Honors House is the home of the Honors Program and the Phi Theta Kappa International Honor Society Chapter. The LaGuardia Web site describes the Honors House as a "one-stop shop for the needs of honors students that provides an intellectual and social gathering place where honors student can engage in mentoring and tutoring, utilize the computers and the transfer/scholarships/research resources, view the Phi Theta Kappa Satellite Seminar Series on the Honors Study Topic, and become involved in other enriching activities."

To enrich the intellectual climate for the honors students at LaGuardia, the director of the Honors Program, Professor Reza Fakhari, has recently inaugurated the Dean's Reading Circle where students discuss a selected book and have dinner in the Assistant Deans' Complex. The book is provided free of charge to the first fifteen students who sign up for each Dean's Reading Circle event. Students are required to read the book and be prepared to have an intellectual conversation about its main themes, ideas, or arguments. Interested faculty and staff may also participate in the Dean's Reading Circle.

It is no surprise that many LaGuardia honors students go on to transfer to prestigious colleges, including Vassar, Columbia University, Mount Holyoke, and New York University. In fact, of all the students who earn associate degrees at LaGuardia, over 60 percent transfer to a senior institution.

Study Abroad

Throughout this chapter, we have tried to make the case that students entering LaGuardia Community College have opportunities that rival those available at most four-year institutions. One of those opportunities is study abroad. Students whom we met recalled their amazement at learning that this option was available to them and that it was fully funded by the college. Each year as many as ten second-year students travel to countries in Europe, Asia, and South America and earn six credits for academic work completed.

Integrating Technology

In 2001, with the support of a major Title V grant from the Department of Education and a technology fee paid by students, LaGuardia began a major initiative to infuse technology throughout the curriculum. Currently, technology is embedded in over 100 courses, in faculty development activities, and most recently in student life through the new e-portfolio project.

Grant funds have been used to support the creation of new computer labs in the tutorial areas of English, reading, math, and ESL. Perhaps the most innovative feature of the grant-funded project is the Design for Learning (DFL) seminar, a year-long professional development experience administered by LaGuardia's Center for Teaching and Learning under the direction of Bret Eynon. Faculty who participate in the DFL seminar draw on their own pedagogical expertise and experiment with intentional ways of enhancing course pedagogy through the use of technology.

One of our most stimulating meetings was with a group of faculty who have participated in the DSL seminar and are now spreading the word to others on campus. Over the period of a year, faculty not only experiment with integrating technology into their courses (the majority of which are first-year courses); they also participate in regular meetings to share ideas and give each other feedback. Eynon observes that faculty are both asking the questions about technology and developing the answers. To date, several hundred faculty, including adjuncts, have participated in introductory DFL workshops, and almost 100 faculty continue year-to-year in intensive, sustained programs. One faculty member summed it up this way: "Technology has changed my life as a teacher—it hasn't displaced me, but it certainly has enhanced my teaching and has enhanced student learning. Students are more likely to do their homework. I'm getting far more assignments done and far fewer excuses. Students can't say 'the dog ate my computer.' The quality of student work is better, and I even cover more material now with the inclusion of technology."

The grant also supports a cadre of technology mentors—students who are paired with faculty to develop course Web sites and assist other students in tutorial labs. Eynon states that this is a win-win situation for both student mentors and faculty themselves. Although this project is in its early stages, preliminary data indicate that students in classes taught by a faculty participant in the Design for Learning seminar report higher levels of connection to the campus, improvement in writing skills, and higher levels of course content knowledge than a control group. Faculty who are strong advocates for the DFL program and for the power of technology to enhance learning still struggle with the issues of balancing "humanity" with technology and viewing technology as a means to learning, not as an end in itself.

In 2002, with an additional Title V grant that was submitted collaboratively with the New York City College of Technology, LaGuardia launched the E-Portfolio Project, which is designed to accomplish two primary goals. First, the e-portfolio will add an assessment component to the technology-enhanced courses by the periodic posting of student writing. In addition, the e-portfolio allows students to represent themselves to others through a mix of pictures, personal narrative, academic work, and selected material that can include music, poetry, art, and other media. The FIG learning communities provided the structure within which the e-portfolios were piloted.

Ongoing Assessment

Through its Office of Institutional Research, LaGuardia is committed to an assessment process that leads to the improvement of first-year programs. This involves regular internal outcomes assessment using qualitative and quantitative approaches, as well as a comparison of the college to national benchmarks such as retention. During the five-year period from 1997 to 2002, persistence from the first to second year averaged 65 percent.

The college's decision to invest heavily in learning communities has resulted from their repeated evaluation. Studies in 1997 and 1999 found that both ESL and non-ESL learning community participants had higher pass rates than students in single courses. In 2002, the college conducted a massive quantitative study of ten years of data on ESL learning communities, analyzing over 90,000 course sections. Data showed a statistically significant positive difference in grade point averages for learning community participants.

Other first-year initiatives are also regularly evaluated for their effectiveness. Quick Start intensive courses have a 70 percent pass rate, and second-chance intensive courses typically have pass rates of approximately 90 percent. Early qualitative assessment of the campus's opening sessions and common readings shows a high level of student satisfaction with these activities.

Although LaGuardia's director of institutional research confesses to LaGuardia's "uneven history of assessment," she adds that President Mellow's influence has made program evaluation a required activity for every program administrator on campus. Although the director spends considerable time meeting the various reporting requirements of the CUNY central office, she is readily available to work with faculty and administrators to design meaningful assessments of LaGuardia's various course structures and out-of-class programs.

The Student Experience

It is virtually impossible to generalize about LaGuardia students. In our futile attempts to encourage faculty and administers to characterize them in one fashion or another, we were constantly reminded that there is no typical student. But it was clear to us through our meetings with the students themselves and other members of the college community that President Mellow's description of many of them as heroic was on the mark. It was also clear that college faculty and administrators respect the students. One faculty member recalled her experience in a meeting with educators from elite colleges and universities: "I was in a room listening to professors complain about students being underprepared. You don't hear that at LaGuardia. We're pragmatists. We don't have any hang-ups about students who have needs. Their search for the American dream melts any cynicism a professor might have. We're realists, but we're not pessimistic. But we're not in denial, and we're not pandering. There is so much purpose to what we do."

Another faculty member describes students at LaGuardia: "Students are hungry for this experience; this is an extraordinary chance for them—maybe their only chance. And the incredible diversity of students creates such an intellectual crucible here. For instance, in my Philosophy of Religion class, every religion we discuss is represented. Students may come just to get a job, but they begin to think outside their own box. So students select other courses. Students often graduate with more credits than they need."

But because the majority of LaGuardia students work off campus or have families (or both), they are very schedule driven so that they will take whatever classes they can fit into available time.

Another difficulty for many students is the cost of tuition. While still a bargain when compared to four-year public or private institutions in New York State, tuition is significant, especially for the many international students who do not qualify for any financial aid. In 2003, full-time New York State residents paid $1,250 for twelve to eighteen credit hours of course work at LaGuardia; for nonresidents, that amount was $1,538.

So how do students do it? What enables so many of them to succeed in an unfamiliar and challenging environment? For answers, we turned not only to the faculty and administrators but to the students themselves. As Dean Arcario made arrangements for our visit, he had expressed concern on several occasions that the students' academic, job, and family commitments might make it difficult for them to clear time to attend our focus group sessions. But the attendance at the student focus group sessions was really amazing. In our three separate group sessions, we met with approximately seventy-five LaGuardia students who represented a range of ages, nationalities, and academic experience. They told us that coming to LaGuardia was initially an anxiety-producing experience but also, in the words of a thirty-three-year-old female student with four daughters, "my dream come true." Although the vast majority of students live in the Borough of Queens, students tend not to know each other before arriving on campus. But friendships develop quickly, spurred by the myriad student clubs and organizations, most of which are organized by academic interest or ethnic group. An Ecuadorian student said, "There are people from all around the world—you feel comfortable, even if you have an accent." A student from Colombia added, "I was very scared—this was a whole new experience for me, and in English! But I'm not scared now." A student from the Dominican Republic continued, "It's one thing to speak, but I was scared to write in English. But I'm not scared now. Here it's like a big family. It may look like a factory on the outside, but it's light and bright on the inside."

The problems of juggling family responsibilities were expressed by one female student: "I have to help my mother in our business—it's a perfume store—that's my only problem. But education is so important. I wish I could stay here longer so that I could go to the library. But I have to go to work until 9:00 or 10:00 and then back home. It's not easy to concentrate."

Some students acknowledge the conflicts or difficulties that can arise with family members: "I have to take care of my little sister, and I think my mother has decided to go back to my country. I know I'll have to go with her, but I want to stay here and study."

We were struck by the high ambitions expressed by many students. Almost all the students we met were planning to transfer to a four-year institution, plans that were supported and encouraged by faculty and staff. A male student stated, "When I first came here, I could barely put a few words together. But I found a mentor and joined the International Business Club. Now I have so many friends."

Although LaGuardia's first-to-second-year retention at 65 percent far surpasses the national average for community colleges—which, according to other sources, is approximately 50 percent (American College Testing Program, 1999)—we wanted to know why some students drop out either during or after their first year. Students responded that the reasons were almost always external: "Some people have their own issues—kids to raise, work, they get in trouble, have to go in the military. I don't know anybody who's dropped out because they're unhappy with LaGuardia. For six months I was working in construction, but I didn't want to do that anymore. You meet really nice people, not just the neighborhood punks."

We asked students to comment on what they would change about the campus if they were president for a day. Responses were typical: better food, more student gathering space. One student stated emphatically, "I'd move the whole school to Brooklyn, where I live!" Another student expressed concerns about the campus climate, remarking that "September 11 brought us all together. I was talking to strangers—giving people rides wherever they needed to go. But now we're back to the same place we were before." In spite of this student's concern, empirical data from the ACT 2002 College Outcomes Survey, as reported by LaGuardia's Office of Institutional Research, found that "a significantly larger number of LaGuardia students, compared to their national peers, said they had experienced personal growth in their ability to interact well with people from cultures other than their own." The rating on this item is 4.1 on a scale of 5 (exceeding the national norm by 0.26).

While many of the students who attend LaGuardia clearly face multiple challenges in making the transition to college, the students with whom we spoke during our visit offered no excuses for their struggles. In the discussion groups, which consisted of students in various learning community clusters, the students spoke not to the difficult challenges they faced but the opportunities available to them on campus, academically as well as socially. Given that Queens, as 2000 census numbers indicate, is the most diverse county in the country, it is not surprising that LaGuardia Community College has capitalized on the broad range of human experiences and backgrounds of its faculty and staff to provide effective means for students of all walks of life to feel welcome on campus. One student poignantly noted in our discussion, "LaGuardia brings the world to us."

Additional LaGuardia Programs

In spite of all we learned, there were areas of campus life that we were not able to explore in depth, given the limits of time. The first was cooperative education. While not defined as a first-year program, it is an important component of a LaGuardia degree. All day students are required to successfully complete cooperative education courses or their equivalent. These courses include both a preparatory seminar and internship experience. Students can choose from internships at over 600 cooperating companies and organizations.

Another important area of campus life that is outside the primary focus of this chapter is adult and continuing education. Over 25,000 students per year participate in either noncredit continuing education activities or short courses leading to certification or licensure. These include programs for special populations such as children, youth, deaf adults, visually impaired adults, veterans, unemployed and underemployed men and women, homeless heads of households, and non-English-speaking adults. One of the largest of the continuing education licensure program is the program that prepares New York City's taxi drivers. Since 1984, the New York City Taxi Driver Institute at LaGuardia has successfully prepared over 45,000 people to qualify for a license to drive a medallion (yellow) taxicab.

Finally, we would be remiss if we did not mention LaGuardia's Middle College High School, started in the mid-1970s as an alternative to the traditional high school curriculum. This program, jointly administered by LaGuardia Community College and the New York City Board of Education, combines the last two years of high school with the first two years of college and provides students with intensive counseling, small classes, an interdisciplinary curriculum, and career guidance. The Middle College is designed for students who might not reach their full academic potential in a traditional high school setting. As an alternative high school, Middle College is a nationally recognized leader for its work with at-risk students. In 1992, the U.S. Department of Education recognized Middle College as an A+ "Break the Mold" School. In 1996, the New York State Education Department designated Middle College as a 21st Century School. Both of these designations attest to the high academic standards of Middle College High School and to the dedication of its faculty and staff.

Future Challenges

When asked about future challenges, the common response in every setting was "money." President Mellow observed that "community colleges are perennially underfunded" although their return on the public's investment is "incredible." The college has been very effective in grant funding, but administrators are concerned that there is never enough money to go around, to pay faculty an equitable wage, and to fund all the new ideas that emerge from the faculty and staff.

Related to concerns about money are the issues of faculty hiring and of space. This campus, like all other CUNY institutions, is hiring more and more part-time faculty, and currently part-timers outnumber full-timers over two to one. Administrators are making a concerted effort to draw more part-time faculty into faculty development opportunities and are finding that many part-timers are keenly interested in the faculty development activities made available to them. It is apparent that a number of long-term, part-time faculty play critical roles in the various educational innovations offered by the college, including learning communities and the New Student Seminar. Although LaGuardia has at its disposal significant space, much of it is empty waiting for sufficient funds to refurbish and furnish. Currently, space is a limiting factor for program growth.

Concluding Observations

While much of American higher education seems engaged in playing the ratings game and gaining a market edge through spending on more and more elaborate residential and recreational facilities, we found it refreshing and reassuring to visit a campus where those dynamics never come into play. Rather, LaGuardia Community College's faculty and administrators spend their energies finding ways to support new students and spend their money where it counts most: in direct support of student learning. Whatever stereotypes we, as members of the research team, had about the limits of community college education, those stereotypes vanished during our visit. As a true leader in American higher education, LaGuardia Community College attests to the power of human potential—not only student potential but also the potential of faculty and administrators who have spirit, passion, and a clear sense of purpose to shape an educational experience that is second to none.

Part Two

Case Studies of Four-Year Institutions with Fewer Than 2,000 Students

Chapter Five

The First Year at Eckerd College

Responsible Innovation

Stephen W. Schwartz

Michael J. Siegel

It is a commonplace in higher education that every curriculum is a compromise, a political statement that mediates between the past and the present as well as among the various stakeholders of the institution. What a luxury, then, not to be bound to the past or to stakeholders invested in specific and sometimes narrow points of view, to begin with nothing more than the dream of being a different kind of college. This was the luxury afforded to Florida Presbyterian College in 1958, the year it was chartered. The result was a curricular plan that was based less on compromise than on the convictions of the early planners, who went about the task of self-invention with a degree of fervor that transcends politics. And while details have no doubt changed over the past forty-six years, Eckerd remains faithful to the intentions of the founders.

Eckerd College is a small, private, liberal arts college in St. Petersburg, Florida, related by covenant to the Presbyterian church. Located in a beautiful setting on the Gulf Coast, it is a relatively young institution (the admissions director is quick to point out that it is only twice the age of its students) and, under the former Carnegie classifications, the only highly selective, private, national liberal arts college in the state. The college first bore the name Florida Presbyterian

College when it was chartered (after receiving a $10 million gift in 1972 from Florida philanthropist Jack Eckerd, the college was renamed Eckerd College in his honor), and it was in operation for five years when the city donated 267 acres of prime waterfront real estate. The current campus was completed and opened in 1963.

The words of one of the founders of the college capture the creative and innovative spirit that would characterize the college from its early beginnings to the present day: "What is envisioned here is not just another college that lives day to day on a routine, unimaginative basis. A new college requires a high degree of vision and creativity and should capture the imagination not only of Florida but of the American public."

That spirit exists today and explains the ease with which innovation occurs. James Annarelli, the dean of students, who arrived at Eckerd in 1990, says of its ethos of innovation:

> I am really struck by the notion of responsible innovation; that seems to be what charged the founding faculty members, and it's threaded throughout the brief history of this college. Today, there is latitude for people to feel experimental; innovation is an honored value. This is a place where one can always float a pilot project, and I must confess I've used that description many times because what it tends to do is relieve individuals of the fear that if they assent to a particular idea, we're stuck with it forever.

While what was once innovative and creative about Eckerd has been imitated by other colleges throughout the country, the spirit of innovation and differentiation remains. Even the campus looks different. Replacing red brick and ivy with pastel and palms, the architectural style of the campus is described humorously by some as Polynesian Gothic. In fact, some think it looks more like a condominium than a college, and the fact that it is so close to Boca Ciega Bay gives some credibility to the joke. Whatever its geography and architecture suggest, however, Eckerd College is serious about providing the proper climate for learning.

A New College, a New Opportunity: The 1960s

Although only 155 first-year students taught by twelve faculty members began class in 1963, the founders knew that if they created the innovative college they envisioned, enrollment would grow significantly to include students from across the country and around the world. Four commitments, described by Vice President for Academic Affairs Lloyd Chapin, guided the development of the college: "First, it was to be a college that would stand in the best of the liberal arts tradition. Second, it was to be a Christian college, meaningfully related to the Presbyterian Church. Third, it was to be dedicated to the highest standards of academic excellence. And fourth, it was to be a pacesetting institution that would demonstrate to other colleges ways to facilitate student learning" (Chapin, 2000, p. 97).

Today, that college is a reality, offering educational programs that are well suited to the students who come from forty-nine states and sixty-six countries. In fact, within its first ten years, the college grew to over 1,100 students with more than eighty faculty members, and today the enrollment holds at about 1,600.

According to the dean of admissions, Richard Hallin, Eckerd students are independent, confident risk takers interested in serving a needy world. As high school students, they have worked for Habitat for Humanity and taken mission trips to Mexico, Costa Rica, and Appalachia. Imbued with a strong work ethic, they are high achievers who are attracted by a college that has a clear sense of identity: Eckerd promises its students hard work in a caring community where professors serve as both traditional instructors and mentors. In Hallin's words, the emphasis at Eckerd is not on "making a living, but on making a life," and it is no surprise that student interest in performing community service increases over the course of their education. President Donald Eastman adds:

> Eckerd students come from all over the country and all over the world. They come expecting to be treated like adults, having access to just about any academic area that they're interested in. They're invariably people who think for themselves, who create their own swath. I don't want to say that they're all marching to different drummers, but there's something of that. They come looking for a different kind of nonregimented, non-crowd-oriented way of looking at the world and looking at their options. If you're marching to a different drummer, we can give you a different cadence.

Since its inception, Eckerd has changed with the times. Nonetheless, some of the original decisions about curriculum, pedagogy, and calendar continue to inform the contemporary college.

Early on, for example, the college decided that its liberal arts mission would best be realized through an interdisciplinary core curriculum extending over four years. One implication of this is that the curriculum is essentially developmental, not in the sense of offering remediation, but rather in attending first to the intellectual, moral, and spiritual needs of first-year students and then moving them along an intellectual and personal continuum so that as seniors, they are ready to embrace the commitments they are asked to make. These commitments include an acceptance of the liberal arts, not just as a theoretical construct, but also as a key to living in the world; acceptance of Christian values, especially related to the values of the Presbyterian Church; acceptance of the highest academic standards; thinking for oneself; taking risks for the sake of social and economic justice; and stewardship of the earth.

Rooted in values issues inherent in the most significant texts of the Western world, the core began with a course taken by all first-year students, Western Civilization and Its Christian Heritage. This course provided a common experience for students regardless of their proposed academic major and prepared them for the core courses of the next three years, culminating in the senior core course, Christian Faith and Great Issues.

In addition to the most obvious assumption of the core—that the first year should prepare students for the rest of their education—other assumptions underlay the first course—for example:

- Knowledge is unified and therefore students' academic experiences should also be unified.
- Students need to prepare themselves, through mastery of the great texts of the Western world, to form and articulate judgments of value.
- Such mastery involves not only grappling with difficult primary texts but also developing skills of analysis, argument, and communication.
- The core will be staffed by faculty from across the campus, regardless of discipline.

Stressing active learning through the promotion of group discussion, the course departed from the typical Western civilization course by taking a multidisciplinary approach and requiring that students develop critical thinking skills through analysis of difficult texts.

As innovative as the course content was, the staffing of the course was equally innovative. In the words of the founding dean of the faculty, Jack Bevan, Eckerd created a core curriculum that would include a course in Western civilization and would staff the course with faculty in all academic areas. Under the title "universal participation," the course (and other parts of the core) still draws its staff from the faculty at large.

Another example of educational innovation, Winter Term was developed to accommodate Eckerd's emphasis on independent learning and study abroad. Students had the opportunity to take classes designed by Eckerd professors or to develop a course concept of their own with the sponsorship of a professor. A specialized four-week period between the fall and spring semesters, Winter Term courses also allowed students—even first-year students—to have a short study-abroad experience. Although Winter Term has subsequently been adopted by many of the nation's more established colleges and universities, it is important to realize that it started at Eckerd.

Building on the Past: The 1970s

While the curriculum developed in the 1960s was largely successful, the world of the 1960s gave way to the 1970s. The United States was wracked by violent cultural changes, and education grappled with the demand that learning be made relevant and that its scope be enlarged to embrace cultural diversity. Just as society at large was being challenged, so were some of the basic assumptions about education, including the justification of a carefully structured core curriculum. In a world in which knowledge is created and pluralistic, it is impossible to make value judgments about which knowledge students should be required to acquire. Project '73 was Eckerd's response to those challenges.

Among other changes, including a rethinking of the first-year core course, Project '73 created a new calendar that remains in effect today, established a mechanism for strengthening the relationship between students and faculty, and reorganized the structure of the faculty itself. A calendar change brought forth another unique feature: a three-week orientation experience for first-year students that would prepare them for the rigors of the education to come, provide intellectual stimulation by allowing in-depth exploration of a topic of interest to them, and establish a mentoring relationship between themselves and a faculty member. This orientation period was called the Autumn Term, and to this day Eckerd's new students show up three weeks prior to the start of the fall semester to begin their college career. The centerpiece of Autumn Term was and continues to be a three-week course taught by a faculty member who has real enthusiasm for the subject and will serve as the students' mentor (academic adviser) for the first year.

Following Autumn Term, students continued to take the first-year core, but it changed to accommodate two needs: the student need for greater relevance and faculty need to reflect the postmodern view that knowledge is not simply inherited from the traditional canon but selected from texts that were previously considered marginal. Thus, the first course became a multidisciplinary inquiry into human nature and the second an exploration of spirituality with an emphasis on the diversity and individuality of spiritual experiences.

Finally, the faculty chose to reorganize themselves. The original three traditional academic divisions (arts and humanities, social sciences, and natural sciences and mathematics) gave way in 1973 to six collegia: Behavioral Sciences, Comparative Cultures, Creative Arts, Letters, Natural Sciences and Mathematics, and one known as the Foundations Collegium. According to the catalogue, collegia were designed, from a substantive point of view, to demonstrate the "interrelatedness of knowledge." From a structural point of view, they were intended to remove the artificial barriers that sometimes exist between academic departments.

While five of the collegia were groupings based on a shared method of intellectual inquiry, the Foundations Collegium brought together faculty united in their belief in the importance of interdisciplinarity and the need to provide students with strong mentoring. The expectation of universal participation continued: all members of the faculty were expected to participate periodically in the Foundations Collegium by teaching an Autumn Term course and serving as a discussion leader in the first-year core.

Content for Contemporary Life: The 1980s and 1990s

By 1979, the faculty began still another review of the liberal arts core. This review resulted in changes launched in 1980 that remained in effect for the next fifteen years. It is essential to note, however, that the revised curriculum retains links to its predecessors. The first-year core course continued to follow Autumn Term but was now named Western Heritage I and II and organized into three themes: self, community, and the transcendent. Mentors still served as discussion leaders, and skill development balanced knowledge acquisition. The course, however, now included a section on the natural sciences, a supplementary text on art history, and a series of primary texts by women and minorities.

In 1993, Eckerd's faculty undertook another review, this time to try to create a curriculum that would provide Eckerd graduates with the knowledge and skills needed to succeed in the twenty-first century. The curriculum that grew out of this review modified and strengthened the 1980 curriculum. "Western Heritage," renamed "Western Heritage in a Global Context," focuses on European-American civilization, but includes as well the important cultural contributions of other civilizations. It is a response to new communication technology as well as to the development of a globally interdependent world. Always active, the pedagogy of Western Heritage in a Global Context now makes use of e-mail, news groups, chatrooms, and the Internet. Organized into themes—the hero, justice, truth, the sacred, power, nature, freedom, and hope—the course continues to evoke debate among the faculty on such topics as which texts, which themes, and which voices.

Although the details of the Eckerd curriculum have changed, the meta-objectives remain in play. Although debate among the faculty results in a creative tension—"vigorous, productive debate among various perspectives and a constantly shifting consensus rather than stalemate and sharp division," according to Vice President Lloyd Chapin—the college boasts an outstanding faculty committed to the general education core curriculum as well as excellence in teaching and mentoring students. And if it is true that the proof of the pudding is in the eating, it is clear that Eckerd students are truly engaged in the academic enterprise and that they enjoy a supportive and collaborative relationship with the faculty.

The Foundations Collegium: The First College Year

The Foundations Collegium oversees several components that support comprehensive student learning outcomes and the success of first-year students. Primarily, the Foundations Collegium is composed of components:

- Autumn Term
- Mentorship
- Skills Development
- Orientation
- Western Heritage in a Global Context
- The Leadership and Self-Discovery Program

Autumn Term and Mentorship: The Cornerstone of the Eckerd College First-Year Experience

Starting in early August, three weeks before the official beginning of school each fall, Autumn Term requires that new students begin their matriculation at Eckerd at the same time their friends are still enjoying summer vacation. Other than a group of "activators"—student leaders who assist in the new students' transition to college—upper-class students have not yet returned to campus, so that the college's full attention is given to new students. This is a time to acculturate students to the demands of an Eckerd education by enrolling them in one of several three-week-long courses on a topic of interest to the instructor and related to his or her discipline, a course that would not ordinarily be offered during the fall or spring semesters. In 2002, for instance, the following broad array of topics was offered:

- Imagining America
- The Wonderful World of International Business
- Politics, People, and Imagination: Understanding Power, Violence, Freedom, and Justice
- A Journey into Contemporary French Culture and Society
- From Medicine to Mangroves: Exploring Careers in Biology
- Coming to America: Italian and Latin American Perspectives in Literature and Film
- Energy: Scientific, Social, and Environmental Perspectives

- Politics and Film
- Roots of Terrorism
- Philosophies of the Buddha
- The Science of Subjective Well-Being
- Dimensions of Self
- War on Film
- The Chemistry and Oceanography of Tampa Bay
- Imago Dei: Religion and Film
- Imagined Cities: Literature and the Grand Tour
- The Golden Age of Athens
- Stage Movement: The Body in Motion
- Mathematical Modeling
- The Art of Contemporary American Poetry

Prior to their arrival, new students indicate their top six preferences in an effort to get a course of real interest to them, and usually they get one of their first three choices. For the next three weeks, students (no more than twenty per section) are in class from 9:00 A.M. to noon Monday through Friday, studying with a professor who is also their mentor (that is, their academic adviser).

Eckerd's mentors are known on campus as "caring scholar-teachers," who encourage students to make the most of the learning opportunities provided. They help students set goals and plan a four-year curriculum, including study abroad and involvement in campus activities, and they encourage them to become reflective learners. Although the mentors establish the primary relationship with students, they collaborate with other professionals who are able to help students develop personally and academically. They also function as a clearinghouse for other professors teaching first-year students. Thus, when a first-year student is in trouble in another course, the instructor calls on the mentor to alert her or him to possible problems. In extreme cases, this triggers an intervention team designed to handle the most extreme cases. The team represents a first line of defense for responding to a call for intervention on behalf of students who are at risk. An e-mail message to the team indicates that a student is having academic or other difficulties and essentially puts the team on alert. The team's response is either in the form of an e-mail, a phone call, a requested visit, or a more drastic measure. This response uses the resources of the academic and student affairs leadership, as well as the firsthand knowledge of mentors who interact with students daily, to monitor students and respond in a positive way to their needs.

As students discover, the relationship with the professor-mentor does not end when the three weeks of Autumn Term are over. Rather, this is the beginning of a faculty-student relationship that is designed to grow and deepen throughout the first year. Just as mentors instruct their students in the Autumn Term course, so they will serve as the discussion leaders for the two semesters of Western Heritage in a Global Context that follow. Moreover, they will continue as mentors until the end of the spring term, when most students choose an adviser in their major. In fact, although the formal mentoring relationship dissolves at the end of the first year, it is not uncommon for students in a particular instructor's Autumn Term course to request that the same instructor serve as instructor of Quest for Meaning (the required senior Core Curriculum course) and for the same group of students.

Is mentoring a burden? According to the faculty who serve as mentors, it is an enormous burden, but one they would not give up. Consider the opening of Autumn Term. Mentors participate in a day and a half workshop on the Thursday and Friday before Autumn Term begins. Then they have the afternoon off; in the words of Suzan Harrison, associate dean of general education,

> These are the final hours of peace and quiet they're going to have all year, or at least until January. At 4:00 P.M. on Friday, the faculty meet not only with their group of students, but with whatever entourage the students have brought with them. So typically the faculty are meeting with the students, with parents, with siblings, with aunts and uncles. And faculty do a variety of things in the sessions. Some actually include a little mini-lesson for the parents as well as for the students about what is involved in the mentoring relationship. In some cases, they discover what's *not involved* in the mentoring relationship, and that, of course, is a lot of parental intervention in the relationship between the mentor and the students.

At 7:00 P.M. Friday evening, faculty gather for the Ceremony of Lights, a candlelight ceremony that officially welcomes new students to the College.

Skills Development

Obviously, students must master the content of their Autumn Term course, and the requirements are stringent. But the course requires more than content mastery. In addition, it provides students with their introduction to college-level writing, oral communication, and research. While the content of each section varies, requirements do not. All sections require that students write papers; take tests, including a comprehensive final; engage in discussion and oral presentations; and begin to use the library in more sophisticated ways than they did in high school. (It should be noted that since faculty in Autumn Term and Western Heritage in a Global Context come from all academic departments, the college provides workshops in a variety of relevant areas to prepare them to teach the required skills.)

Writing

Given the orientation function of Autumn Term, the emphasis on writing is understandable. Not only will students have to write in Autumn Term and throughout the next four years, but they will have to complete a writing portfolio successfully in order to graduate. (Eckerd does not require a course in composition except in the event that a student's portfolio does not meet the standards for graduation.) Early in Autumn Term, students receive a folder that describes the portfolio requirement. In a word, the portfolio is an anthology of each student's best writing. The standard for passing is the equivalent of C-level writing in a senior course within the student's major.

To prepare students to pass the portfolio requirement, Autumn Term instructors emphasize not only principles of good writing, but also the need to develop skills for self-assessment of one's own writing. In a May workshop taught by the director of the Writing Center, instructors receive guidance in such topics as the roles, values, and kinds of writing; design of assignments; and evaluation of writing and constructive feedback. Thus, in Autumn Term, they are prepared not just to assign writing topics to students, but also to provide for students an initial assessment of their writing. On the basis of this assessment, they are in a position to recommend that some students register for composition courses and others attend sessions at the Writing Center.

Oral Communication

Faculty are also trained by the director of the Communication Lab to help students develop the skills of oral presentation and group discussion because oral communication, like writing, is a requirement for graduation. Based on research that demonstrates a relationship between speaking, active listening, and enhanced student learning, the requirement involves communication across the collegia; that is, all departments work with students on improving communication skills (and thus learning). The May workshop also prepares faculty to teach communications. It introduces them to types of oral communication related to learning styles (speaking, listening, effective group discussion, debate, and role playing) and to the techniques involved in helping students excel at each type. Faculty in Autumn Term are trained as well in evaluating and providing feedback on students' oral communication abilities. When they discover a student with excessive stage fright, problems in group discussion, or listening and following directions, they make one of several possible recommendations to the students: to take another lower-level course that gives them practice in oral communication, to see the director of communication for help in an independent study, or to attend the communication lab, which is staffed by trained student tutors. Much of what needs to be done is to disabuse students of some erroneous notions about speaking in class. For example, "We try to deemphasize that class participation, good class participation, is about quantity," says the director of communication. "It is about quality and insight. And very often that comes from excellent listening skills. When people are listening well, they then are able to participate in a meaningful way, and even when a student doesn't say anything for several times and then comes up with a comment that shows major insight and helpfulness in the group, this is beneficial to everyone."

Whether in writing or orally, Eckerd students are expected to be able to formulate and articulate value judgments about particular topics and issues and be able to communicate them clearly in class. Autumn Term helps students develop the necessary skills to meet these expectations.

Library

The final learning component of Autumn Term involves use of the library, and librarians work throughout the three-week term and first semester to prepare students to walk the fine line between information literacy and traditional library research as a way of helping them complete the college's technology requirement. That requirement involves four areas of proficiency: word processing, use of e-mail and listservs, use of library systems, and use of the Internet for academic research. Although the librarians are aware that their challenge, as they say, is to "make it interesting to seventeen- to eighteen-year-old freshmen who see library research as just as interesting as resoling your shoes," they are committed to teaching students how to collect and review material and then formulate a reasonable thesis. To this end, the librarians visit the twenty to twenty-two Autumn Term classes. They tailor their presentations to the specific topic of each class, giving students fairly sophisticated library assignments that relate thematically to course material and that the students must complete by the end of Autumn Term. These visits are followed by one-hour work sessions in the library during which students are asked to find books, journal articles, and supplemental literature. While these assignments may seem inconsequential to some, many students come from high schools with libraries that were not technologically advanced. They are accustomed to Yahoo! and Google search engines, but not to the many electronic databases of the contemporary library.

To sum up, Autumn Term is a highly comprehensive collection of academic experiences, and its centrality to the academic success of first-year students cannot be overstated. It is intended to engage students early on in the culture of the college's intellectual enterprise and socialize students to the academic expectations of college. Furthermore, it is at once an orientation to college and a significant academic experience.

Orientation

Autumn Term is also a period for the more traditional first-year orientation. All the typical transition activities that take place at colleges and universities around the country—placement testing, advising, registration, substance abuse sessions, and community service—take place at Eckerd during this three-week period. In fact, as Associate Dean of General Education Suzan Harrison puts it, "We orient those students within an inch of their lives! My chief concern with Autumn Term is the overscheduling, and this year I wanted study time in the printed schedule. I wanted study time explicitly stated in there because otherwise we have students feeling as though it's all about having fun, not understanding that they'll need to make choices."

Jim Annarelli, the dean of students, was happy to provide that study time; in fact, that advanced his particular agenda, which was to reduce the dichotomy that had grown up between academic affairs and student life. When he accepted his current position, he believed that the dichotomy made no sense in terms of the innovative ethos of the campus or of Eckerd's mission and values. "Those dichotomies," he said, "fly in the face of the founders' vision and of the founding faculty who felt as comfortable hanging around the residence halls and teaching classes in lounges over there as they did in their classrooms. Over the years, however, a bit of a wall developed, an invisible wall, and for the past year we have been dismantling the wall in the style in which they dismantled the Berlin Wall."

Annarelli began his work at the organizational level. Rather than assuming the vacated position of vice president for student affairs and dean of students, he and the president agreed on the title of associate vice president for academic affairs and dean of students, reporting to the vice president for academic affairs. This structure, he felt, "underscores the fact that student affairs is an important dimension and source of resources and support for the academic program and that the students who sleep in the residence halls are the same students who work on campus in our labs and in our classrooms. So we wanted to ensure that our organizational structure reflected our philosophy." He also integrated faculty into a number of important tasks, like establishing campuswide cocurricular programming, revising the alcohol policy, and sitting on student conduct boards. "I felt," he said, "that if you're going to take a holistic approach, you need to involve all mentors and appropriate faculty." Nowhere else has the partnership of academic and student affairs been more important than in the restructuring of the Autumn Term orientation.

To begin the restructuring, the student life staff gathered all the principals—both inside and outside the division—to decide how this orientation should be different from past orientations. The first response was from student affairs, and it was predictable for this group of professionals who view themselves as educators truly dedicated to Eckerd's academic mission: the staff needed to ensure that the proper relationship existed between the formal academic component in the morning and the student affairs programming in the afternoons, evenings, and weekend. They faced the classic conundrum of working with the tight structure of a three-week intensive program and trying to maintain a balance of intellectual and social fare. In examining brochures from previous orientations, they concluded that a dichotomy did exist, that the programming was recreational and entertaining. "Which is not a bad thing," said Rebecca Jacobson, assistant dean for campus activities. "And we had no intention of abandoning that kind of programming, but what we decided was this. We decided, first of all, to double the amount of money appropriated to give students a broader choice. We decided that we would enhance some of the cultural offerings, that we would add dimensions to recreational activities, . . . so a trip to Fort DeSoto Park, which is a major public beach here, included eco tours so that students could become somewhat familiar with the local ecosystem so they're not merely, you know, lying on the beach slathering on the oil. They can walk through a salt marsh that's on the bay side of the barrier island."

The second major revision was the development of the Autumn Term portfolio and "survival guide." The orientation planning group decided that their attempts to socialize students would be enhanced if they could encourage students to reflect on their experiences. Thus, they developed a calendar of required and elective events and a form that linked the events with possible learning outcomes. They invited students to talk about how a particular learning outcome related to the event by writing brief, reflective statements. Although no one assignment was very long, when all of the responses were put together, they ended up being a substantial number of pages. In spite of some of the student complaints about the new orientation requirement, the staff considered it important to offer an opportunity for all students to start thinking about how to dissect or deconstruct an experience as a learning experience. As the assistant dean says, "I saw the form, however mechanistic it might be, as a set of training wheels for the process of reflection. I can't expect them to do that right out of high school, but this will model the kind of thing they'll be expected to do later on."

Orientation events are gathered in the survival guide, a calendar that divides each day into four columns: one for time of day, one for required events, one for cocurricular events, and one for notes. The guide reminds students of many things, ranging from taking a towel and sunscreen to the beach to such tips as, "Remember—you should be devoting at least four hours per day to preparing for your Autumn Term class." Little is left to the imagination of students who are trying to learn their way around Eckerd.

Western Heritage in a Global Context

Following Autumn Term, students are required to enroll in a yearlong, two semester, interdisciplinary core curriculum course, Western Heritage in a Global Context. The central objective of the course is to use the written word to introduce students to the influential thinkers, ideas, and worldviews of the ancient and contemporary worlds. While the majority of the writings represent Western thought, the course takes seriously the phrase from its title, "Global Context." Thus, Western writings are discussed in terms of a worldview that embraces diversity of peoples and their most basic beliefs as communicated in the cultures' greatest documents.

According to Associate Dean Suzan Harrison, who wrote the introduction to the Western Heritage textbook, students participate in this course in the enduring conversations of humankind, regardless of the geographical, racial, or ethnic origins of the speakers. In the first semester, these conversations are about heroic journeys, justice, truth, and the sacred, and they cast students' eyes and ears backward. In the second semester, they are about power, freedom, and nature, the dynamics of human behavior and human society, and they open their eyes and ears to the conversations of the recent past, present, and future. In the first semester, students read from the great texts of ancient cultures (from the Bible to the epic of *Gilgamesh* to Sophocles' *Antigone*). In the second, they read from works of modern physics (Stephen Hawking) to works that explore the darkest human moments (Wiesel's *Night* and Achebe's *Things Fall Apart*). Whatever the readings, the course introduces students to the most important of humankind's global conversations through important works in the canons of the Western and non-Western tradition. It is the hope of the faculty that students will develop an understanding of and appreciation for major historical, intellectual, political, psychological, social, and artistic paradigm shifts and, through these, an understanding of social relationships. And although the readings and conversations are rooted in the here and now, they launch students' thinking about the sacred, spiritual, and transcendent. It should also be noted that Western Heritage in a Global Context continues the skill building students need to complete general education requirements in writing, oral communication, and technology.

The effectiveness of Western Heritage in a Global Context was confirmed by external evaluation as recently as 1999–2000. The executive director for core texts and courses, J. Scott Lee, serving as an evaluator in the college's assessment process, reached the following conclusion as cited in an internal assessment report:

> The students [in Western Heritage in a Global Context] are reaching an understanding and appreciation of ideas and works within the course. That understanding should form a groundwork for students to build their bachelor's education with much better confidence about what sort of questions to ask of what they read and learn as they mature through their four years' stay. The course, also, provides assurance that Eckerd students are exposed to important works, to introductions and overviews, to ideas which span fields and which are part of every baccalaureate student's legitimate claim to be literate and educated. No disciplinary structure of courses can guarantee this kind of broad overview which is so necessary in helping our citizenry relate one field to another. Eckerd, indeed, is to be justly commended and proud of the curricular accomplishment and content and of the student achievement in Western Heritage in a Global Context [Brunello, 2000, n.p.].

The Leadership and Self-Discovery Program

Of the five components of the Foundation Collegium, the Leadership and Self-Discovery Program (LSDP) is the only one that is optional. Essentially, this component is delivered as a winter term (January) course designed especially for first-year students. A substitute for one of the thirty-two core courses required for graduation, LSDP combines experiential learning and the development of skills and knowledge in a uniquely designed arrangement.

Participants receive training in leadership, teamwork, goal setting, time management, communications, presentations, and the use of technology. Because the program is a practicum, they learn by doing, not through lectures, and, according to students who take LSDP, nonstop fun activities (with a purpose) make this program a great alternative to being home for six weeks between semesters. Imagine, for example, improving teamwork skills by crewing on a sailboat.

Working in five-person teams, students select an interesting topic to research through both traditional means and community service projects. In the process, they learn about the college and community, about each other, and about themselves. Both games and more serious activities teach them how to work effectively with others and how to communicate ideas in both formal presentations and informal discussions. They write personal mission statements and think about what is most important in their lives. Through a series of self-discovery activities, they conduct a self-assessment of their own personal style preferences as midyear students and think strategically about the many opportunities to achieve their goals at Eckerd College.

In general, this activity-based program engages first-year students in ways that challenge them and provide new insights into themselves. On completing the program, they report beginning the spring semester with new abilities, new confidence, and a new sense of direction.

Not Without Its Critics: Pros and Cons of Eckerd's First Year

Involvement in the first-year curriculum, including the Autumn Term and the Western Heritage in a Global Context course, is not without its critics. Vice President Chapin indicated that some faculty in the program struggle with integrity issues—with "going outside their discipline to teach." They wonder if their involvement in interdisciplinary activity will lessen their exposure to the scholarship of their disciplines and their perceived commitment to those disciplines. Some faculty, especially the young and untenured, are fearful of breaking out of the role of the expert in order to teach in an interdisciplinary program. Within their disciplines, they are confident of their expertise; outside their disciplines, they risk foundering and consequently receiving negative evaluations. There is another side to that coin: some students have similar concerns. They pay a significant amount of money to attend the college, and some assert that when they enroll in such a generalized first-year curriculum, they are not getting an "expert" for the money they paid. According to Chapin, open and honest communication with students about the purpose of the program and descriptions of the intensive faculty development have been the key to the ongoing success of the program and to allaying student doubts.

Of some concern at Eckerd are the implications of this conflict for the future of the Foundation Collegium and specific courses like Autumn Term and the Western Heritage in a Global Context. Will the younger faculty take up the mantle of the core curriculum and nurture it as did the early supporters? That remains to be seen. In the meantime, the Eckerd community of professors and scholars deliberates frequently about the challenges to the first-year programs, the Autumn Term, and the first-year curriculum. Regarding this debate, the president articulates an interesting irony: "At a college like this, one that prides itself on innovation and that takes its pulse frequently to see that it has not fallen into more routine educational patterns, even first principles are not taken for granted. They're something that people are committed to going over and over and over again just to make sure we are not falling into step with normal practices at other places." The result is that first principles are never entirely secure, even those that lend the college its distinctiveness.

And so there is healthy creative tension at Eckerd, and many stakeholders weigh in. Younger faculty, concerned with stepping outside the boundaries of their expertise, question the effect of their participation in the core on their ability to deliver a quality major. They also question the time commitment required by mentoring. In a zero-sum system, time given to mentoring is time taken from scholarship. Older faculty support the interdisciplinary core and argue that at a liberal arts college, general education is certainly as important as disciplinary expertise. Alumni, many of whom maintain close ties with the college, value the education delivered by the core curriculum and by faculty mentors, and since a large number of trustees are alumni, they lobby hard for continuance of what they call "the Eckerd Experience."

On the whole, there is overwhelming support from the majority of faculty as well as students. Moreover, as President Eastman has told some faculty members, "You guys get to debate this, but you don't decide; decisions of such a critical nature require inclusion of a broad group of stakeholders." This puts the role of the faculty regarding the curriculum in an interesting and unusual light. Chapin, however, does not worry too much about the continuation of the core. Rather, he thinks about issues of quality: Does Eckerd have the best Autumn Term and core curriculum it can possibly offer? When asked what he believes remains to be accomplished, he talks about securing more interaction between academic affairs and student affairs in order to attend more specifically to the needs of first-year students who are making the transition from high school to college. Perhaps a seminar could be developed that would be both interdisciplinary and focused on side issues of the students' personal development. Chapin says,

> I think the format would be very much like what we have now where there could be a series of interdisciplinary lectures and presentations that you would go to, and then the mentor groups that formed during Autumn Term could meet as discussion groups around the subject of the lectures. You might pick universal myths, for example, and see how different cultures and different generations have dealt with key issues. This could lead to discussions on a more personal level, where students share their experiences. I think our students could benefit from such a course. Many of them come from families that have moved all over the place. Their parents have divorced and remarried several times, and there really is a lot of stuff swirling around in their heads. I think it would be interesting to organize that course.

Another of the issues facing the core curriculum is universal participation, a system involving all faculty in teaching the interdisciplinary core. The justification for universal participation is twofold: the community agreed that the core curriculum would derive its greatest impact from both universal participation and boundary crossing. To these ends, it is expected that all faculty will teach core courses, especially the highly innovative Autumn Term with its emphasis on nontraditional subject matter, and when the college advertises for new faculty, the requirement of teaching in the core is always prominently displayed. During campus visits, candidates are asked to affirm their commitment to the core and their willingness—even their eagerness—to teach in it. Suzan Harrison relates this story:

> One of my jobs as associate dean is that I also interview every candidate for a teaching position here, and I interview them specifically to get a sense of their fit for our general education program, and I was interviewing a chemist whose undergraduate minor was philosophy. And he was in here asking me, "Well, if I were doing an Autumn Term, would I have to do chemistry? Could I do something that had more to do with philosophy?" And the answer is, "Of course, you can; of course, you can." So he was speaking about the interrelationship between philosophy and science and in particular chemistry and what he might do with that for an Autumn Term. And faculty do all kinds of things; it's their creativity, and they are very creative, so we get wonderful, wonderful Autumn Terms.

In addition, faculty from a variety of disciplines meet one another in preparatory workshops and weekly staff meetings, and both they and their disciplines rub against one another. In the words of one faculty member, "It sets up our collegial structure so that there is interaction clearly between disciplines that may not exist in the same ways at other institutions, and faculty in the natural sciences and letters and behavioral sciences are getting together and working toward a common goal. It creates good connections and really strengthens a lot of the interactions and leads to some wonderful multidisciplinary projects."

Another faculty member and former director of the first year views universal participation on a more personal level: "People become acquainted with one another who would not normally become acquainted. They cross boundaries. Some of my dearest friends are people with whom I became acquainted when I was either teaching in Western Heritage in a Global Context or leading the course."

President Eastman, a product of research-extensive universities, also praises universal participation: "In previous institutions, the faculty were always a collective—some biochemists, some veterinarians, some English profs—a group of individual people. But here, it's a singular noun. It's a faculty that focuses, that works together. It's an integrated force for educating students, and that kind of integration of educational purpose you just don't find that at big, public research universities." The president continues on the subject of the influence of universal participation: "In some ways, teaching at Eckerd is a career choice. I don't care where your Ph.D. is from; here you're going to focus more on teaching students than on physics, and you're going to wind up teaching students the history of Western culture from the earliest physicist, Demosthenes, to Picasso, when you participate in Western Heritage. That's going to make you a different kind of faculty member."

The benefit of the arrangement and the nature by which faculty teach out of their own discipline, particularly with regard to the Western Heritage in a Global Context course, is that students get to see the faculty struggle throughout the program much as the students themselves struggle. This humanizes and personalizes the role of the instructor, a phenomenon that strengthens the mentor and student relationship.

The Impress of Leadership at Eckerd College

In many small, private, liberal arts colleges, the culture of the institution is inextricably linked to the personality of the senior leadership, primarily that of the president. At Eckerd, President Eastman is in his second year; thus, he has yet to leave his mark on the institution. Nonetheless, he is a keen observer of the faculty, students, and alumni of the college, and he understands the support of most constituents for the Eckerd experience. He has an appreciation for the college's dedication to the first year and to the work of the faculty and staff to improve the first year of college through programs like Autumn Term, Western Heritage, and mentorship. In particular, he speaks enthusiastically about the socializing aspect of the Autumn Term for first-year students and comments about the importance of the three-week course in helping to connect, even bond, students to one another. He celebrates the multicultural and multinational aspects of the Autumn Term and appreciates the fact that it is "free of distraction" from upperclass students. First-year students essentially have free rein of the campus for three weeks before upperclass students arrive, and they are able to enjoy their status as sole proprietors of the college for that time.

Although literally decades separate the new president's tenure from that of the vice president for academic affairs, there is remarkable synergy between the two, and they have a shared understanding of the powerful and important role of a successful first year as a springboard to an enhanced academic experience in the upper-level classes.

Embedded Assessment for First-Year Improvement

The culture at Eckerd is data driven, and according to the director of institutional research (IR), "The IR function is involved in everything." As one person explained, "The college does not have tradition to go on, and so needs assessment data to be the guide." Whatever the explanation, President Eastman believes in making informed decisions and makes extensive use of assessment for improvement and strategic planning. Thus, he encourages the director of IR to assess from top to bottom.

What kinds of things has institutional research uncovered? One is the reasons students choose to attend Eckerd. Entering students report, for instance, that they come for "the Eckerd experience": they are treated as adults, they have open and extensive access to faculty members, they feel they have a great deal of independence, and the college is responsive to their academic needs.

As for the faculty, the director reports that they feel energized by Autumn Term. They feel it is liberating and allows them the opportunity to explore, learn, and teach in innovative ways. At least one of the major goals of assessment has been to find a way to evaluate and articulate the spirit of the place, and first-year assessment is the primary means to that goal.

Students report that they feel like individuals; they are allowed and encouraged at the college to think for themselves at the same time that they are supported by a nurturing, flexible environment, and many report that "Eckerd changed my life." In our focus group toward the end of the two-day site visit, students corroborated this description by comments about the first year. One said, "I think it embraces the students, it embraces people and that is what really drew me here. That and the variety and flexibility." Another said, "I realized that I could make a difference in my own education. I could do an independent study, or I could study abroad during January Term. Like there's so many options for everybody."

Chief among the subjects of assessment is Autumn Term itself. There are certain risks associated with conducting Autumn Term in Florida. Students have to cut their summer short, and they come to campus in early August amid sweltering heat. Given the challenges to the college in conducting a meaningful and useful three-week intensive academic term when students are sacrificing nearly a month of their summer to come to college, assessment is a critical component for the Autumn Term planners to evaluate the student experience. They need to get it right, and, according to the students, they do. One said,

> Halfway through September, some of my friends were still at home. One asked me what college was like and said, "I hate living at home still. I'm sick of it"! But I wasn't sick of it. By that time, I was into the fall semester. I felt like a college student. Autumn Term was great, and I really liked explaining the concept of coming early to school. I was really happy with it [Autumn Term] and people would think about it as I explained it, and they would say, "Oh, that's a really great idea!"

Asked whether Autumn Term did accustom them to the work load, there was universal assent. One said,

> I was reading and doing stuff every night, but that got me used to it. Like Bradley [the instructor] said, he gave us the amount of work you would have on a normal night, which was actually true. `Cause once I started having four classes, I had the same amount of reading that I had per night during Autumn Term. So I had gotten used to that much work and then you learn where the bathrooms are and where the classrooms are and where to go on Friday nights.

What We Learned from Eckerd College

Colleges are culture-bearing institutions that develop significant norms, values, and beliefs. These forces govern institutional behavior, determining how individuals understand the institution. Although a young institution by comparative standards, Eckerd College has a rich culture that serves as both anchor and compass—keeping the college firmly rooted and providing guidance in planning for change. The goals, values, and beliefs of Eckerd College are well documented on campus and public in nature. They are evoked in faculty meetings, campus retreats, convocations, graduations, orientations, and other celebratory occasions on campus. At the heart of this culture is Eckerd's long history of innovation and progressive thinking.

One such innovation—as old as the college itself—is the first-year core and Autumn Term, and perpetuation of this innovation requires a sense of purpose and intention rooted in the past. Policy formulation, decision making, curriculum change, and programming at the academic and social levels are all conducted within the context of this commitment.

Universal participation is the mechanism that implements the commitment, and all faculty are required by contract to fulfill the obligation of staffing the first-year core. Because of this values-based hiring policy, faculty are committed not only to the craft of their discipline, but also to Eckerd's philosophy of general education. The faculty model the liberally educated person who engages with his or her students in the process of learning, whether discussing classic texts or engaging in a unique mentoring relationship. Students are referred to not as "advisees" but as "associates," and faculty are not "advisers" but "mentors."

Success depends on more than faculty. Thus, both faculty and staff report a sense of shared responsibility for the learning experiences of first-year students, both inside and outside the classroom, and academic and student affairs collaborate for student success. For these two divisions, student success begins with the intention to socialize first-year students into the academic culture as early as possible. The result is that students develop realistic expectations about the first year of college and what they must do to be successful. In short, Eckerd does not leave student learning to chance, but rather creates realistic expectations so that students will understand the challenges of being at Eckerd.

Like any other college or university, Eckerd has undergone significant changes in its history: curriculum changes, budgeting concerns, leadership transitions, and program additions and deletions. Throughout, Eckerd has remained loyal to a set of core values and beliefs that inform decision making, programming, and policy formulation. Though highly innovative and unafraid of change, the college does not stray from its core identity in its programming and policy formulation. In fact, the identity of being the only highly selective, private, liberal arts college in Florida governs the actions and behavior of the college. It is an institution that understands its mission and role and strongly adheres to both in conducting its business.

Chapter Six

Kalamazoo College

No Stone Left Unturned

Stephen W. Schwartz

Randy L. Swing

Our first view of Kalamazoo College in mid-afternoon reveals gently rolling hills and a patchwork of new and old buildings—mostly old. It is a typical liberal arts college; if you were producing a movie about a small college, you could certainly film it here. Kalamazoo looks just like a college. The campus is set in a residential district. In fact, it is hard to tell where one ends and the other begins, and thereby hangs a tale, or at least a metaphor, for Kalamazoo College, located in southwestern Michigan, has, from its inception, blurred distinctions: between the college and the city, between faculty and students, between the life of the intellect and the values by which one conducts his or her life, between the needs of the campus and the larger needs of a young America. The habit of blurring distinctions has been continuously reinforced since 1833, when the college received its charter, and the values of the institution have, over time, been modified by the emerging needs of the nation and, ultimately, by the recognition that today's students will live their lives in a globally interdependent world.

In the early twentieth century, the traditional separation between professor and student blended at Kalamazoo into a "Fellowship in Learning," in which faculty and students became collaborators in the enterprise of educating and being educated. Consider the description of Kalamazoo College as it appears in a

"Ritual of Recognition for New Students," written by President Allan Hoben during his presidency (1922–1935):

> Kalamazoo College is a Fellowship in Learning. It is not land and buildings. These are but the shell of a congenial group life that has persisted here for more than a century. Through interplay of minds both past and present and in friendly contact with faculty members, students evolve their best selves and therefore their charters of service to mankind. To this fellowship, this self-discovery, with its attendant joy of purposeful living, Kalamazoo College welcomes succeeding generations of students and sends them out into the "wide, wide world," possessing something of the likeness and life of their Alma Mater—the scholar's spirit dedicated to human welfare [Kalamazoo College, n.d., p. 1].

The contemporary realization of this philosophy and this spirit is the K-Plan, which created, in the last third of the twentieth century, the ultimate blurring by turning Kalamazoo College into a global campus.

For these reasons, among many others, Kalamazoo College is distinguished from a large number of other liberal arts colleges by the intentionality with which it conducts its business. Mission is paramount, known and taken seriously by the entire college community. The college is unapologetic in the outward focus of that mission: "to prepare its graduates to better understand, live successfully within, and provide enlightened leadership to a richly diverse and increasingly complex world." Today, the college describes its educational schema as one that "calls upon community members to make informed judgments and to take responsibility for translating learning into life—an education that produces confidence in approaching the complexity and plurality of a changing nation and a global society."

The K-Plan

The vehicle for implementing the mission is the K-Plan, which delivers a rigorous undergraduate program through traditional scholarship and experiential education at home and abroad. The K-Plan is unabashed in articulating a holistic educational scheme intent on the development in its students of the intellectual and personal, the cognitive and the affective. The K-Plan is intended to cultivate five dimensions of intellectual and personal growth: lifelong learning, career readiness, intercultural understanding, social responsibility, and leadership. Phrases from both the mission and the K-Plan are often heard from members of all college constituencies. If it can ever be said that a college mission statement is a living document, the mission is certainly alive at Kalamazoo. This mission provides a sense of direction, a source of pride, and distinctiveness in a cohort of colleges in which it is very easy to look like everyone else.

The View Book

To describe the mission with the metaphor of a living document is to direct attention to the written forms in which mission is manifest. None is more important than the view book, the means by which Kalamazoo tells prospective students about itself so that they and their families can make an informed choice. One look at the cover reveals that the college prides itself on being different from its competitors. The cover is not a photograph but a stylized drawing. The central feature is a tree, and the leaves depict symbols that reveal Kalamazoo's values: a Native American, an ancient Chinese statue surrounded by calligraphy, the Eiffel Tower emblazoned on international postmarks. Some leaves depict students—two riding a camel, others receiving individual attention from a faculty member. Surrounding the tree, the background is filled with code and scientific symbols, images suggesting space, exploration, and scientific discovery. Most important perhaps is the ground out of which the tree grows. The tree's roots are the K-Plan itself, and they derive their sustenance from the arts, humanities, and sciences. From the world itself—past and present, real and imaginary—the K-Plan enriches and guides the growth of Kalamazoo students.

The organic metaphor adumbrated on the cover—the suggestion that Kalamazoo nurtures the growth of its students from before matriculation to graduation and beyond—is so pervasive that it drives the organization of this first document that establishes students' expectations. This is a college that is very deliberate about what it does, and the view book discloses Kalamazoo's uniqueness. Kalamazoo is a special place: a liberal arts college that measures its uniqueness in terms of its students' uniqueness. Thus, the K-Plan is described as different for every student, the result of collaboration between students and their advisers, a special and complex relationship that bonds students and faculty professionally and interpersonally.

And yet it is also the same for every student, at least in its general outlines. Students who choose Kalamazoo do so because it offers, along with small, challenging classes in the liberal arts and sciences, a variety of opportunities to study abroad, perform service, complete the highly intellectual senior individualized project (SIP), test career options through internships, and keep track of and reflect on intellectual and personal growth in a portfolio that begins before matriculation and links on- and off-campus experiences to the selection of a major and the choice of a career path.

The opportunities for students are far more international than at many other places, as is the behavior of the faculty. Students experience the world not just through study-abroad opportunities, but also through internships and SIPs that take them to other countries. Moreover, faculty members signal the importance of a global education by traveling with students—for example, to Costa Rica to study the egg-laying habits of leatherback turtles as part of an Earthwatch team.

Alongside the internationalization of this campus, however, is another commitment—to active learning, for Kalamazoo is a college at which faculty have made a commitment to supplement the traditional mode of teaching and learning, the lecture, with more experiential modes. Between the first year, in which they learn to use the library and write effectively, and the senior year, when they complete the SIPs, students prepare for independent learning, for it is not enough at Kalamazoo to learn facts and ideas. Students also learn how to learn—by doing research and by extending the learning in a Visions of America seminar to the direct learning that comes from collaborative service projects in the community.

Kalamazoo is no ivory tower. Career advising begins early, and students are helped to see the connection between academic study and occupations. But connections are not just emphasized between study and occupations. Kalamazoo stresses preparation for leadership, the need to turn thought into effective action, in order to encourage students to enter the world ready to make a difference.

In short, Kalamazoo stresses the connection between academic study and the values that drive everyday life.

The Reality

Does the reality of Kalamazoo live up to the promises? It appears so. Known as an academically demanding institution, Kalamazoo attracts students capable of profiting from its unique curriculum. In 2001, students had a mean high school GPA of 3.67; some 82 percent were from the top 25 percent of their class. In the same year, the mean ACT score was 27.8, and the mean SAT 633 (Verbal) and 624 (Math). Moreover, Kalamazoo students are unusually motivated in an intellectual sense. In responding to questions on the Cooperative Institutional Research Program (CIRP) survey (administered by UCLA's Higher Education Research Institute) about why they decided to attend college, 80 percent reportedly answered "to gain a general education and appreciation of ideas" and 70 percent also checked "to make me a more cultured person." Also, 64 percent of Kalamazoo students said that the chances are very good that they will communicate regularly with their professors, and 59 percent indicated that they consider the development of "a meaningful philosophy of life" to be essential or very important. (Kalamazoo administrators state that these responses are significantly higher than those of the appropriate comparison group.) CIRP results indicate as well that Kalamazoo students chose the college because of its "very good academic reputation" and because its "graduates gain admission to top graduate/professional schools." These are students who have an unusually strong scholarly bent and the ambition to succeed in high-level professional careers. Finally, Kalamazoo students are aware of the benefits of the K-Plan and its special elements, especially study abroad and experiential education. The majority of Kalamazoo students describe themselves on the CIRP survey (again disproportionately) as political liberals, and they consider promoting racial understanding, cleaning up the environment, and participating in community action programs to be essential or very important.

According to a self-study document, Kalamazoo's "combination of rigorous academic courses, on the one hand, and experiential engagement with and service to the larger world, on the other, seems entirely consistent with the abilities, expectations and goals common among our entering students. Further, our good record of sending students on to postgraduate programs, an achievement probably facilitated in part by the independent research our students carry out as undergraduates, clearly is in line with the longer-term educational and career plans of the majority of our entering students" (Kalamazoo College, 2003, p. 7).

The reality is apparent as well in campus conversations. Listen carefully to the faculty and staff at Kalamazoo College, as well as to the students themselves, and you discern a leitmotiv, a pattern of words and phrases repeated often enough—and with enough conviction—to make you take notice. The most common is *intentional,* which is often followed by mention of the college mission. Listen longer and you are certain to hear someone talk about "the right start," and "collaboration," and "budget sharing," and "innovation," and "rigidly academic campus." At a more idiosyncratic level, students and faculty talk about the "K-Bubble," a phrase that has shared meaning at Kalamazoo.

Consider what one staff member says about "getting students off to the right start." The phrase is used primarily to describe the approach taken to the first year and its students, and it is followed quite often by the sentence, "This is a rigidly academic campus." From this, you might conclude that the institution is intentional about preparing students for the rigorous academic path they are about to traverse, and you would be right. What is so interesting, however, is that those words are spoken by members of the student life staff—professionals who on other campuses might be talking about the need for students to gain a degree of comfort with the college in their first weeks at the institution. At Kalamazoo, student life professionals understand the rigors students will face, and thus their design of the required first-year orientation attends to the students' adjustment to the academic life as much as to the residential side of the institution. In the words of the dean of students, Danny Sledge, "What we are about is the development of students, of assisting students in meeting the college's mission. Thus, we have changed the name of the division to student development."

This is not the whole story, for it is as common to hear faculty members talking about their need to learn more about student development theory. Faculty convey real excitement, for instance, when they describe the 2002 Fall Faculty Colloquium, at which noted higher education scholar Lee Knepfelkamp discussed learning as a developmental process. Building on earlier colloquia that featured David's Kolb's Experiential Learning Circle and William Perry's Scheme of Intellectual and Ethical Development, Knepfelkamp addressed the needs of a changing population of students and highlighted the differences between teaching a first-year seminar and a course in computer science or chemistry. Not all faculty were receptive. A few responded negatively: "That's not what I'm about. I'm comfortable with where I'm focused, and it works for me." But many others responded positively: "Oh! Now I understand why, in a discussion about affirmative action and its historical context in my political science class, the discussion blew up. It had everything to do with how students approach and resolve conflict." Where other faculties might dismiss developmental approaches to teaching and learning as soft, schemes that divert attention from course content, the Kalamazoo faculty listens carefully to anything that will get students off to the right start. In fact, although the colloquium was designed for instructors of the first-year seminar, so many other faculty regularly attend the annual event that the provost has rewritten faculty contracts to start the academic year with the colloquium.

The depth of Kalamazoo's commitment to its students and "the right start" is reflected in the structures and policies the institution has put in place in the first year, for these reveal Kalamazoo's attempt to weave a seamless environment. The senior associate dean of students, Vaughn Maatman, states, "Once first-year students step onto campus they will encounter people—whether they are in student development or athletics or on the faculty—who speak the same language. They know what sort of experience we're trying to create here. There's a broader commitment to helping students make the adjustment they need in getting off to a good start." This same dean, a staff member at Kalamazoo for some sixteen years, boasts with obvious pride about the faculty: "I often hear faculty members saying things like: 'If we're serious about educating the whole student, we will [fill in the blank]'; or 'What an incredible place this is! I have colleagues who [fill in the blank]. They really care about what they do'; or 'I'm here to make sure that my students grow and do well.' "

These are faculty members who are so committed to their students and the mission of the institution that they are willing to try new things. Zaide Pixley, the assistant provost for the first-year experience, maintains, "One of the keys to our success has been the willingness of the faculty to innovate. Faculty are willing to try new ideas, and the administration is willing to support new ideas and take chances. If you want to try something and can make a case for it, faculty would be more likely than not to do it."

The First Year

At Kalamazoo, the first year is composed of the following components: orientation, summer common reading, first-year seminar, first-year advising, first-year forums, student mentors, portfolio, Fall Faculty Colloquium, and an emphasis on study abroad and career development. The list, while impressive in its breadth, is certainly not unique in higher education. Many colleges and universities reporting on their first year would no doubt report similar components. What is significant at Kalamazoo, if not unique, is the extent to which these components articulate with one another. While seamlessness may be an impossible dream in this rag-tag world, the degree of alignment at Kalamazoo is remarkable.

First-Year Seminar

While each component plays an important role, the first-year seminar (FYS) is the cornerstone of this foundational year. Begun in 1990 as a writing course owned by the English department, the FYS is now a special topics course and has evolved to a requirement taught by faculty across the campus. Although it is the vehicle by which students complete their writing requirement, it serves a larger function in the curriculum. As the single common academic experience of first-year students, it is the gateway to Kalamazoo College.

The roots of the FYS can be found in a 1986 writing-across-the-campus project intended to strengthen the writing and critical thinking skills of first-year students as preparation for the work in all college courses as well as the SIP. To this end, Kalamazoo hired a director of writing, and by 1990, the writing course had become the means by which students satisfied the college's writing requirement.

For faculty, the seminar provided not just the opportunity to help first-year students get off to the right start, but also opportunities to teach at the margins, that is, to teach something different, new, cutting edge, and to do so with a small group of students. Faculty are motivated by a sense of mission as well as a sense of personal benefit, and there is widespread agreement that faculty who teach the FYS take true pride in the good they believe they do.

Until 1996, FYS instructors continued to focus on writing and critical thinking skills in the context of a theme-based discussion course. In 1996, the seminar took a giant step forward as a result of a Mellon Foundation grant. Interestingly, the purpose of the grant was totally unrelated to the seminar, although the objectives of the grant were relevant to the first year.

The Mellon Foundation had provided funding to modify an innovative yet disjointed calendar. Because of this calendar, students were typically off campus during their sophomore spring quarter for career development, back on campus for their sophomore summer, off campus participating in study abroad during their fall and winter junior quarters, back on campus for spring and summer of their junior year, and off campus for their SIPs during the fall or winter of their senior year. Although distinctive and replete with numerous benefits, the calendar inhibited the development of community and disrupted student organizations, faculty committees, and departmental administration. Moreover, learning could become fragmented; students had few uninterrupted opportunities for intellectual reflection and integration. The grant would correct these problems by changing the calendar to a more traditional quarter system, using the summer quarters to work on SIPs and to test career interests through externships (defined by Kalamazoo as short internships).

That this totally unrelated change in calendar had such a beneficial effect on the FYS, however, should not suggest evolution by serendipity. Rather, change resulted from a keen insight on the part of the dean of students and a coalition she had been gradually building: a period in which a major change is being effected often offers the opportunity to make other major changes. Acting on this insight, the dean and others helped initiate a number of changes.

According to some, the most significant was the creation of a new part-time position, director of the first-year experience, and the appointment to that position of a faculty member in music then in her eleventh year at Kalamazoo, Zaide Pixley. Other changes included additions to the seminar of elements that were missing, but that many considered essential to a more fully realized first year. This group of change agents knew that the faculty would never accept a seminar styled after the University of South Carolina's University 101 orientation model. However, they also knew that more Kalamazoo students were withdrawing from the college in the first year than should have been at such a selective college. The time was right to make significant changes.

With the cooperation of a group of key faculty members and administrators convened to study student attrition, the assistant provost and the dean "worked several angles at once." One result was the amalgamation of the FYS and advising. This did not change the content of the course, but it did enhance the quality of the instructor-student relationship. Within the context of the course topic, instructors could help first-year students look at the big issues: the nature of an academic life, the nature of a socially responsible life, the unusual curricular opportunities Kalamazoo offers students. Advisers helped advisees become not just independent but also interdependent. As one adviser articulated it, "Advising within the context of the FYS helps students understand that in discovering academic interests and an academic identity, students form a contract for service to humanity."

FYS, however, afforded an opportunity for only twenty-two faculty members. The question that remained was how to ease the entire faculty into the first year so that all faculty share the responsibility of getting students off to the right start. The answer was coadvising, a program that allows faculty not teaching the FYS to share advising duties. Since most of the FYS sections are taught by nonscience faculty (because it is difficult to release the science faculty from their normal course structure), coadvising provides the science faculty with the opportunity to work with first-year students. Thus, every FYS section has access not just to the adviser who teaches the class, but also to one or two coadvisers who are familiar with the demands of the curriculum and trained to engage in big issue advising. Together, advisers, coadvisers, and student mentors—

the advising team—help students deal with the big issues of clarifying goals, understanding the curriculum and degree requirements, selecting courses, and identifying college resources. From the moment the team meets students and parents at orientation, the message is clear: "We're there for you." And from that moment, the team creates a highly supportive environment for socializing entering students to the new rules, the heightened expectations of Kalamazoo College.

In an environment of widespread change, other additions consistent with the values of the college and reflecting a sense of student need at the end of the millennium were made. These included oral presentations, a focus on the development of intercultural understanding, and the creation of the habit of reflecting on experience through the medium of the portfolio.

Today, the FYS is highly developed and structured to achieve the following purposes: improving fundamental academic skills in writing, oral communication, collaboration, and research; exploring a compelling theme that will trigger engaged class discussion and writing; beginning the development of intercultural understanding; incorporating student work into the portfolio; integrating academic advising into the first quarter on campus; and building bonds between students and advisers. The seminars are not introductions to disciplines, but are more often interdisciplinary explorations of events, ideas, or topics located at the edges of a discipline, the locus of some of the most interesting questions and connections. Employing a variety of active learning instructional strategies, faculty use texts, films, speakers, and traditional and action-based research to help students gain an expansive, multicultural view of the topic.

Topics are offered in stand-alone seminars or as part of a cluster of courses. In 2002, for example, of the twenty-two sections offered, nineteen stood alone and three were clustered. Stand-alone sections included such topics as:

- Civility and Kindness in America
- American Images of Asian-Americans
- Young Adults in Film and Literature
- Justice and the Just Society
- Impressionistic Art
- Religious Experiences and the Nature of Religion/Spirituality

- The Literature of Home and Leaving Home
- Applied Ethics in Everyday Encounters
- Reading and Writing as the Twin Skills of Self-Understanding and Self-Creation
- Using Intellect, Creativity, and Spirituality to Move Beyond the Borderlands of One's Life
- American Culture, Then and Now
- The Implications of Nineteenth- and Twentieth-Century Colonialization/Imperialism
- The Impact of Media on Education
- The Arthurian Myth in History and Literature

Three sections were clustered under the heading "Visions of America":

- First Person, an examination of American autobiography through the lens of four determinants of social identity (race, class, gender, and sexual orientation)
- On Page, a discussion of novels that highlight the relationship of race, gender, and class to everyday life
- By Ear, an examination of race, gender, and class in American music

A brief excerpt from the syllabus of "Visions of America: First Person" captures the spirit of the seminars, as does "The Border-Crossing Project," an action-based research project required of all students in the Visions cluster. Students add to the knowledge they gain through traditional library research by investigating in person areas relevant to their topics. For example, students researching homelessness actually visit and work in homeless shelters to gain an understanding of homelessness.

> What does it mean to say, "I"? To write in the "First Person"? To tell the story of your "self"? How many tributaries combine to produce the river that you are? If we are like plants, growing from the earth in which we are rooted, what elements of that earth combine uniquely to make us who we are?
>
> What does it mean to say, "I am an American"? What impact does our national history of struggle, difference, conflict, and contradiction have on the identity of first-year college students in 2002? How

does one tell one's own story within the larger story of multicultural America? Is America a "given," or is it a continually evolving idea, open to the creative visions of its diverse participants?

These questions and many others that flow from them will be at the center of our journey together over the next eleven weeks.

The objectives of The Border-Crossing Project are multiple:

1. For every student to cross a major boundary created by a social identity that deeply affects people's experience: gender, race, class, physical ability, religion, ethnicity, nationality, etc.
2. For every student to reflect on the risks of border crossing, the skills and attitudes that make such a journey successful, and the learning gained in the experience.
3. For every student to reflect on our commonalities and our differences as human beings.

In light of the fact that FYS is the one course all first-year students have in common, it is important to know what students say about the course and its impact. While not all students have an intellectual and psychosocial experience that tops the scale, students report that most do. In most cases, the seminar pushes the experiential envelope for students, many of whom have never before considered issues of race, class, gender, and sexual orientation with the degree of seriousness and personal revelation characteristic of the seminars. One student describes the experience as "mind-boggling." Another said,

> We had lots of groups represented in one classroom, and we would write down racial issues, gender differences, sexual preferences, and it was almost as though everyone was bringing a part of themselves to that whole classroom. . . . People would leave exhausted sometimes, but you knew you had learned something. It wasn't just about writing. I mean my writing skills improved immensely, but for me it was about learning *for me*. It was the first class I ever had that focused on, "What can we teach you that you can carry with you for the rest of your life?"

Another student, a male, characterized the seminar as follows:

> Better than the best thing that ever happened to me before I got here. I had [name of instructor], and [s/he] brightened our lives.

> I was the only African American in the class, but everybody had different geographical origins and everything, and it was like a lot of differences coming into one class, and we all just talked about our experiences growing up and we read books, and all the different perspectives on the book depended on how you grew up, and there were classes where people cried. People would tell their life stories, and the whole class would be bawling together. Like just sitting there leaning on somebody you had just met three weeks ago. And then every time I see somebody from seminar, I am just like, "Hey, how you doin' there?"

This should not suggest that the seminar is little more than a sensitivity session, for the emphasis on reading (eight books in some sections), writing papers, giving oral reports, and doing service and action-based research is too great to ignore. What is clear, both from assessments and self-reporting, is that for most students, FYS more than achieves its goals.

Orientation

Prior to 1996, the watershed year prompted by the Mellon grant, orientation was not a requirement for first-year students, and the administration was concerned about the number of first-year students withdrawing from this selective college. But concern for new students extended beyond issues of attrition. Members of the student life staff were well aware of both the positive and negative sides of the transition from home and high school to a residential college. In their words, "Relationships must be forged anew; sudden independence feels both exhilarating and frightening; academic challenges escalate; and a complex pattern of requirements, policies, and opportunities needs to be mastered. Orientation thus means far more than learning where buildings are located or when meals are served; it is a critical and often sustained time of coming to terms with a whole new social system and one's place and identity within that system."

The task that fell to Marilyn LaPlante, the former dean of students (now retired as vice president for experiential education, emerita), was not just to find solutions to the problems of attrition and transition, but to find solutions that would work within an environment of academic rigor. LaPlante, a former member of the faculty, maintained excellent relations with her faculty colleagues, and she began to build alliances with supportive faculty and fellow administrators. It was up to them to attack the problems.

Working with this band of innovators, LaPlante promoted a view that has since become commonplace: students in transition need a period in which to gain a realistic view of college and faculty expectations. With this in mind, she and her "co-conspirators" proposed a week-long orientation for all new students as well as a corollary: every faculty member should advise first-year students. And in the milieu of the calendar change, the required orientation was born, its goal, in her words, "to acculturate new students to the fine K College tradition of bugging your profs. You know, most of the students are very well behaved, outwardly respectful, Midwestern kids, and the profs, the faculty are Dr. This and Dr. That. We need to give them the skills, the technique, the comfort level to knock on someone's door all by themselves if they, the stars in their high schools, need academic help. 'How do I ask this doctor, this Ph.D., for help without feeling stupid, awkward, and you know?'"

Realizing the goals of the orientation is the responsibility of Zaide Pixley, the assistant provost for the first-year experience, who reports to the current dean of students on matters related to orientation and to the provost on academic matters. She is responsible for developing and coordinating the many parts of orientation, and she does this in cooperation with the student development staff. The approach to orientation is based on a holistic model of student development. Thus, the program pays attention to both academic and nonacademic matters.

From the moment students step on campus, they meet a large number of people who are devoted to first-year students. Opening day reveals athletes, identified by their jerseys, busily transporting the possessions of new students from car to room. Their goal is to have everything moved into a room in under ten minutes—a task that serves not just the practical function of moving in but also breaks the ice by creating an atmosphere of frantic endeavor involving new and upperclass students in a common enterprise. The residence life staff also ensures that students find a welcoming environment in the halls by arranging mixers at which students meet other students as well as faculty members.

Other activities take place at orientation. The summer common reading, for example, is highlighted. Having been assigned a reading prior to their arrival, new students attend a symposium in which the author of the book is the featured speaker, and some get to continue their discussion with the author at lunch. The reading typically focuses on intercultural or identity issues, and new students, in conjunction with their FYS instructors, advisers, student mentors (in the words of the president of the college, "guides" and "truth-tellers"), and fellow students, attend the author's symposium and form discussion groups in which to consider key themes. In recent years, visiting authors have included Richard Ford (*Independence Day*), Chang-rae Lee (*A Gesture Life*), and Ha Jin (*Waiting*). Within their FYS/advising groups, students discuss majors and choose classes, participate in community service projects, and consider the goals and values of a Kalamazoo education. In lighter moments, they share their talents as poets, prose writers, and musicians. This is the renewal of "A Fellowship of Learning."

Orientation also introduces students to the first-year forums, a series of programs intended to help entering students learn the history and traditions of the college, consider critical interpersonal issues, and continue academic and personal growth. The forums are deliberately structured around the five dimensions: intercultural understanding, leadership, social responsibility, career readiness, and lifelong learning. Although the forums are begun during orientation, they continue throughout the fall term, and students are expected to attend five programs (many students attend more than five). Interestingly, while this "rigidly academic campus" would never tolerate a credit-bearing orientation course, instructors of the FYS are more than willing to include attendance at forums in determining students' grades, and students who attend fewer than five forums find themselves losing points.

The forum topics for the week of orientation are instructive of the Kalamazoo ethos. Whereas other institutions create orientations intended strictly to enhance the comfort level of the entering students in this transitional period, Kalamazoo tackles thornier issues: "Enlightened Leadership for a Diverse and Complex World"; "Sex After Seven"; "Tough Guise: For Men Only"; "Finding Your Voice: For Women Only." These programs are followed throughout the fall term by similarly provocative topics: the possibility of global ethics; America's cultural values; the nature of ecstasy (not the drug); alcohol, drugs, and sexual assault. Alongside these topics are workshops on choosing a major and a career, understanding the benefits of a liberal arts education, and learning from returning students about their study-abroad experiences.

While the focus of orientation is the students, parents are not left out. A number of administrators meet with parents; chief among them are the president and dean of students, who coordinate their message to parents. In the words of President James F. Jones, Jr., the theme is "tough love." "Together," he says, "the dean and I invite parents to join the college in making students not just independent, but also interdependent." (In Fall 2004, James F. Jones stepped down to assume the presidency of Trinity College in Hartford, Connecticut.)

Kalamazoo also offers another orientation, optional and scheduled several weeks before the required orientation, the famous "LandSea." Each year since the early 1970s, approximately eighty new students join fifteen to twenty upperclass students and several staff members (sometimes including the president himself) at Killarney Provincial Park in Ontario, Canada, to begin a demanding orienteering program including hiking, canoeing, sailing, rock climbing, rappelling, and "going solo." Learning by doing, participants teach one another as they experience living in the wilderness or sailing a brigantine. While this is a lesson in collaboration and leadership (that is, different students assume different leadership positions depending on the task at hand and their individual talents regarding these tasks), "going solo" is also critical. Participants spend two days alone in an area bordering a lake; there they reflect on what they have learned and which new behaviors they want to take back to the college.

The benefits of LandSea to the eighty entering students who participate are obvious enough. They learn something about themselves, they experience the kind of interdependency that Kalamazoo values, they gain confidence, and they bond with new and older students and staff. As one woman participant said,

> LandSea was one of the most amazing life-altering experiences I've had. It forced me to accomplish obstacles that I never thought I would ever be able to overcome. I canoed for eight days, I rappelled

> down a rock face, I rock climbed, I spent two days alone in the pouring rain—only to sleep in a puddle and without food, I survived an infected pinky finger, I learned about 9/11, and then I hiked for four days through some of the most beautiful mountain terrain I have ever seen. I came away from my LandSea experience feeling like I could accomplish anything and everything that I set my mind to do.

Portfolio

The K-Plan also requires first-year students to keep track of and reflect on intellectual and personal growth, and the medium for this is the portfolio, completion of which is a graduation requirement. The portfolio actually begins prior to matriculation and continues through the spring semester of the senior year, when it is submitted for the last time to the portfolio office, major department, or assessment committee.

For first-year students, the portfolio is the repository of their foundations essay, one of the requirements for orientation. Prior to their arrival, entering students write an essay in which they examine their pre-Kalamazoo experience in terms of any two of the five dimensions, as well as the intellectual skills considered essential for academic success (information literacy, quantitative reasoning, writing, and oral communication). Students are instructed to support their analysis with specific reference to academic work, community service, employment, travel, or other influential experiences. They discuss the influence of their activities and commitments in shaping them and their academic and career interests. Prior to the conclusion of the essay, in which they set goals for the first year, they select and discuss a third dimension that they would like to develop at Kalamazoo. Before orientation begins, students send in two copies of this essay, which advisers, coadvisers, and student mentors read and comment on. The essay becomes the basis for a relationship between entering students and those who will guide their entry into the college.

The foundations essay is the first of several components of the first-year portfolio. As the year progresses, students create an electronic home page that will contain a number of self-assessment writing assignments. These include what has come to be called the "best seminar paper." That is, students are asked to link their best FYS paper or papers from other Kalamazoo courses to the electronic portfolio, which are read by the FYS faculty and other faculty members who serve as portfolio consultants.

By the time of senior year submission, the portfolio is a record of a student's life at Kalamazoo. Entries can include the senior connections essay, department assignments, letters of intent for graduate school or a job application, application essays for student leadership positions, and self-assessments by athletes (with input from their coaches).

The senior connections essay, the final entry in the portfolio, brings closure to the process of reflection begun in the first year. It offers seniors the opportunity to audit and reflect on their accomplishments; to see the interrelatedness of their experiences, both academic and otherwise; to account for the intersection of their academic programs with career development, study abroad, and volunteer, leadership, and work experiences. And it asks that these reflections be tied to the five dimensions that are at the heart of the Kalamazoo experience

Support Services

The progress that students record in their portfolios is the result of a deliberate academic scheme that is both comprehensive and well coordinated, offering an array of services designed to promote success. Given the centrality of the first year to student success, many, though not all, of these services radiate from the seminar.

Library

The library, not normally considered a support service, plays an important role in the life of students enrolled in FYS and an even more important role later. This role is related to the SIP, for which students begin their preparation in the seminar. Although orientation to the library is standard fare across the country, it sometimes serves up empty calories. But at Kalamazoo, librarians have cooked up an exercise known as "Survivor in the Library: College Information Literacy Skills." Librarians work with seminar instructors on a series of topics related to the topic of each seminar. Following individual work sessions by seminar section, librarians create student teams and assign each the task of gathering information from a book, an article, an on-line article, and a Web site. The point is for students to become adept at searching through both print and electronic sources.

Academic Resource Center

First-year students receive academic support from the Academic Resource Center (ARC), the source of tutoring in writing and mathematics as well as the site for Supplemental Instruction. Student tutors are trained in both areas to provide one-on-one consultations to students seeking help and to do so efficiently and tactfully. Writing tutors, for instance, help students first with the larger issues of writing, such as thesis, organization, and the development of an argument, and second with the sentence-level concerns of grammar, punctuation, and spelling. Based on the tutor's evaluation of an essay, students write an action plan for improving the essay, and the tutor e-mails faculty to inform them of who came in for help. To ensure high-quality tutoring, the ARC asks all students seeking help to fill out evaluation forms on the overall experience.

Writing tutors are also assigned to two first-year seminars each, and they visit the seminars during the first week of classes to explain what the Writing Center does. They collect and read syllabi so that they are aware of seminar content and the schedule of writing assignments. Throughout the semester, they visit instructors to pick up assignment sheets, and in order to encourage use of the Writing Center, they visit classes again before assignments are due.

Tutors in mathematics follow a similar procedure. Working with individuals or groups of students to help in courses ranging from precalculus and calculus to linear algebra and probability, tutors guide students rather than tell them how to do problems. They follow a format of asking students to identify the starting point of solving a problem, then ask that students work on problems individually and in pairs to generate a sense of the many ways in which mathematical problems can be approached. Emphasis in the Math Center is on developing problem-solving skills, an area that many professors do not always have time to present in class.

In both the Writing and Math Centers, tutors are trained carefully in the pedagogy of tutoring, not just the content. Because writing and mathematics tutoring both lend themselves to group work, much of the training is in the area of collaborative learning, and tutors are encouraged to hold group discussions, assign work in clusters, divide tasks into "jigsaw-sized pieces," and help clients put the puzzle together.

Early Alert Committee

In an age in which it may be no longer fashionable for a college or university to act in loco parentis, Kalamazoo has put into place a number of systems to ensure student success. On some campuses, these systems might be viewed as intrusive violations of a student's freedom to fail. One of these is the early alert committee, designed to secure from faculty the names of students who are struggling or disengaged. Composed of faculty and administrators from across the campus, the committee meets once a week to discuss students whose names and problems are reported and described on a spreadsheet. Students in difficulty—those missing classes, failing examinations, not submitting assignments, or having severe family problems that might affect performance—are assigned to a member of the committee, who might choose to initiate an intervention, anything from notifying an adviser to meeting with a student. The effectiveness of early alert is indicated in the fact that 50 percent of the faculty report cases to the task force, and the remaining 50 percent simply do not have to use the system.

Center for Career Development

Although career counseling professionals often debate the merits of including career advising in the first year of college, Kalamazoo has come down on the affirmative side of the argument, as usual with a unique spin. Its Center for Career Development plays a role in the first year, as early as orientation and the FYS.

The spin is informed by the understanding that, in the first quarter, students are bombarded with all manner of information. Nonetheless, because the center plays such an important role in the K-Plan, students have to be informed about the resources that will influence their lives. In orientation, then, peer leaders who are paraprofessionals in the center provide a brief introduction, emphasizing the importance of the center in facilitating the choice of a major and finding internships that help confirm that choice. Following orientation, these peer leaders also visit each FYS, where they take five minutes to describe three programs. The goal is to begin a process that asks students to be aware of the unusual opportunities Kalamazoo has for them.

According to the director and dean for experiential education, first-year students view the question of a major as one of the most significant facing them. The job of the center is not to minimize its importance but to convince them that it is not "earth shattering." Consequently, they ask undecided students to create a short list of viable options as a first step. Once they have taken this step, the center offers several programs that allow them to test their preliminary choices.

The grants program is designed specifically for testing interests and aptitude by bringing students into communities as part of the workforce. Students apply and compete for grant funds ($600 to $2,000) to defray the expense of summer employment that often takes them away from their homes. Students are responsible for meeting 20 percent of their expenses.

The fellows program gives stipends of $3,000 to students predisposed to do volunteer service in order to explore a new location, perform service, and learn about professional life in that location. It is expected, and explained to students, that recipients of these fellowships will, as alumni, give the money back.

Finally, the new externship program allows students to spend up to four weeks observing and participating in an organization at which an alumnus or alumna works. Students live with the alum so that, in addition to the work itself, students get "porch time" with their hosts—time for dialogue between alum and student.

Although most of the opportunities provided by the Career Center come after the first year, the center plays an important role in laying the foundation for what is to come later. This is yet another example of the intentionality of a Kalamazoo education.

Underwood Stryker Institute for Service-Learning

Given the importance of the dimensions of a Kalamazoo education, it is no surprise that community service begins as early as first-year orientation and the FYS. While there are many ways to bring about social responsibility and intercultural understanding, direct experience is certainly one of them. Students visit one of nine service sites during orientation, and they begin the practice of reflection, so important to the portfolio submitted in the senior year. Within the context of the FYS, students also perform service and learn experientially. In a seminar on autism, for example, each team of three students connects with a family, where they observe autism firsthand. Observation is enhanced by reading and writing, and, in tandem, they contribute to learning. At least one role of the director of the institute and the service-learning committee is not just to line up service experiences, but also—and perhaps more important—to teach students to learn experientially, something they will have to do when they study abroad and do their SIPs. In short, community service is still another link in Kalamazoo's integrated curriculum.

The Campus Speaks

Both quantitative and qualitative data provide insight into Kalamazoo's success in the first year. These data come from student responses to nationally and locally developed assessment tools and from the words of faculty, administrators, and the students themselves.

Assessment

Over the past several years, Kalamazoo has begun to use a variety of assessment tools to measure success and modify programs, and the assessment committee has encouraged use of both in-house efforts and national surveys. In-house assessment of the first year begins with the foundations essay written prior to matriculation. This essay, which focuses on two of the five dimensions, establishes a benchmark against which a student's growth and development are later measured. The portfolio becomes the means to judge that growth. In addition, course evaluations are used in the FYS itself to measure course and instructor effectiveness. More significant is that instructors evaluate student achievement in writing and critical thinking skills through class papers and assignments, and students themselves engage in self-assessment. As a result, students choose their best seminar paper for inclusion in the portfolio. Another form of in-house assessment occurs in faculty development workshops for the FYS, where instructors assess their previous sections of the seminar to determine best teaching practices. This leads to constant fine-tuning of the seminar.

Kalamazoo also uses national instruments for purposes of assessment. The annual Cooperative Institution Research Program (CIRP) survey, for example, provides a snapshot of each year's class, and the national survey, Your First College Year (YFCY), provides a follow-up to CIRP. In the light of their interest in the quality of instruction in the FYS, engagement in campus life, use of time, and student satisfaction, Kalamazoo also continues to participate in the First-Year Initiative (FYI), a national benchmarking survey of first-year seminars.

The data collected are meaningful only when they are used for decision making, and in this area Kalamazoo has developed an interesting approach. The syllabus of the FYS faculty workshop asks the question, "Who Are Our Students?" and uses new data from CIRP, YFCY, and FYI to provide answers. The remainder of the workshop then follows up with topics including how academic advisers can best respond to changing students, the specific role of academic advisers at Kalamazoo, and the expectations of parents. The point is that Kalamazoo uses the data derived from national and in-house data collection as they continue to improve the first year.

Voices

Ask Marilyn LaPlante, vice president for experiential education, emerita, to account for the success of Kalamazoo's first year, and she will cite the Mellon Grant, which paved the way for all manner of changes; her good relations with the faculty; and the current president, who is "very savvy about student life." Ask Zaide Pixley, the assistant provost for the first-year experience, and she will describe the pride of the faculty in the first year and their role in student success. "This is a faculty that doesn't mind exploring new ideas and taking chances," she says. In addition, she cites the willingness to share budgets as a source of real achievement in the first year: "No one can do this alone. We all rely on one another."

Ask President Jones the same question, and he will cite the appointment of the assistant provost for the first-year experience. "It was brilliant," he says of her appointment, "a wonderful example of this institution's intentionality," and he goes on to boast of her success in convincing the faculty to teach all FYS in the fall semester; of the advising program's ability to focus student attention on the relationship of the academic program to their developmental needs; of the forums, which acculturate students to Kalamazoo traditions and acquaint them with the social and personal issues that await them; and of the portfolio, not just a computerized résumé, but an electronic anthology of a total educational experience—from foundations essay to senior essay.

Ask the faculty members of the committee on teaching, for instance, and they will say that the success of the first year is due in part to the academic leadership they themselves provide as they communicate to the rest of the faculty the nature of some of the most interesting teaching coming out of the seminar; as they sponsor faculty development workshops, such as "Writing Beyond the Seminars," intended to teach how to use evidence to construct and revise an argument and how to cite sources properly; as they plan the Fall Colloquium in order to promote good teaching; as they hold Teach Lunches (the provost pays) every other week to discuss such topics as "the problem students" or "what to do when the class attacks"; and as they sift through the nominees for the biannual teaching awards they sponsor.

Finally, ask the students about the Kalamazoo experience and the first year. Students can explain quite articulately what brought them to Kalamazoo: a kind of mystique because the campus extends to the entire world; a diverse, multicultural atmosphere where the sense of community is palpable; an educational scheme that pushes each of them to the limits of their abilities, but makes the journey feel safe and personal (upperclass students assert that Kalamazoo is a Volvo: it gets you wherever you want to go, it goes as fast as you want, and you always feel safe). "The K-Bubble," they shout. "We're really protected here"!

As high school seniors, these students were made aware of the details of a Kalamazoo education: the K-Plan, SIP, portfolio, study abroad, service-learning opportunities, and internships. One student explained how prospective students knew so much about Kalamazoo: "Chalk it up to the admissions counselors. As soon as you ask them a question, they see to it that you get an answer, often several answers from administrators, faculty, and students.

One Friday morning, I sent in five questions. That Saturday night, the head of a department e-mailed me. He had a wife and a three-month-old kid, and yet he took the time to e-mail me."

"And the counselors don't drop you once you sign up," another said. "I've become really good friends with my counselor. I'm going to her house for Thanksgiving. It's like a whole network of community."

Most students agree that Kalamazoo follows through on its promises. Most faculty have incredibly high expectations for students, and students have equally high expectations for faculty and for themselves. According to the students, faculty push students hard. Yet, while pushing, "they [the faculty] also provide this incredible amount of support and resources for us so that we know we can push ourselves outside of the box and still be supported in some fashion."

"But it's more than high expectations," another student said. "Like when I was a sophomore, and the head of my department e-mailed members of a class we were in to tell us that he was thinking of changing the time when the following semester's class would be offered. He wanted to know if the proposed time would work for everyone; otherwise, he wouldn't make the change. I just think that kind of stuff is kind of neat."

The same student said she had her gripes, and others agreed. One said, "I don't think it's all, you know, lovey-dovey, but the truth is I'm in love with my college." Another followed up with, "I have my frustrations with it, but never enough that I think I should leave." "Yeah, you get really bummed out, but the next day a professor you hardly know sees you and says, 'Hey, I heard you're applying for a Fulbright. Can I help?' and well, I don't know. There's always something amazing happening."

As for the K-Bubble, "Well, it's a nice myth. But when you find yourself tutoring at Woodward School, face to face with poverty and social conditions that are so different from what you've come from, those experiences prick the bubble." "Same with the internship I had," says another. "K makes sure you understand the real world." One first-year student in a FYS on the topic of American apartheid, who found herself teaching at an alternative high school, said, "And just kinda, you know, standing next to or sitting next to someone who grew up so differently, and just three blocks away. I think it was a really good experience for me."

Student response to the FYS depends to a large extent on the seminar topic and the instructor. In some cases, students viewed the seminar as "just okay," "no better than what I had in high school." Even when students found their section pedestrian, however, two benefits emerged: skill building and community building. "Mine wasn't stellar," said one student, "but it was the first time my writing was challenged to a level I never imagined possible. It really sharpens your communication skills."

Just as students agree that the seminars enhance their writing and thinking skills, they value the feeling of family that develops in the seminar: "That seminar was something that really helped me through that first year because everybody in that seminar was like family. It was like a new family, and that's something of tremendous value." For students in the "Visions of America" sections, the sense of family was even greater because, once a week, the three fifteen-person sections would meet together: "It was forty-five now, and we were sharing these experiences, and, I don't know, I felt close to all of them as the different classes told what they were learning." One student reported that the seminar was what kept her in school: "I was very, very, very homesick, and I needed someone to get to know me and to take me under their wing and talk to me, and my professor did that for me." Another student said, "I had [name of instructor] also, and she really helped me through my first quarter because it came to the point where I was really struggling just keeping my sanity because I was playing soccer and things weren't going as I was hoping they would go in soccer. I was staying out way into the wee hours of the morning. I wasn't getting sleep. You could just like look at me, at least in her class, and she'd notice that I just didn't seem the same as the weeks progressed. She would take me aside and really ask how I was doing, and she would write me e-mails and make sure I was doing okay. It was *very* helpful."

Conclusion

It is twilight. Classes for the day are mostly over. But the campus teems with a communal life, rare in these days of students who hole up in their residence halls. Athletes walk together, returning from practice; bell-ringers walk to the chapel to practice change ringing on the English bells. In an academic building, student tutors make coffee and put out plates of cookies in anticipation of their evening appointments. Inside the student center, students move back and forth—from the mailboxes to the dining room, from one club meeting to another. In the middle of the lobby, a protest is being planned. Sprawled on the floor around a huge bed sheet, students sign their names with permanent markers: a group of students are preparing to go to a national student demonstration protesting the School for the Americas. As the self-study reveals, this is a student body that is more liberal than one might expect at a private college in southwestern Michigan.

In a residence hall up the hill from the student center, the dean of students is showing *The Full Monty* as part of a residence hall program called "Dialogue with Danny" (his name). Laughter fills the room throughout the movie, but subsides noticeably as Dean Danny begins the dialogue: "Okay, what I want you to do is not look at this movie strictly as entertainment, but what are some of the cultural things that you perceive from this? What if these men had been women? What's acceptable for men and what for women?" As twilight gives way to darkness, brightness fills the room as the intellect of one educator kindles the minds of new students just beginning their intellectual awakening. "Our goal is to move students from looking at the world from their own cultural ends to at least being exposed to and aware of others and then to gain an appreciation and understand the collective benefits of all views."

The dean sums it all up:

> In our attempt to prepare students to succeed in this rigidly rigorous environment, we start from the assumption that students need to be socialized to the values of the institution. And we are very intentional about providing programming that will structure students' experiences appropriately. The intentional structures ease students into the social environment. Linkages are created to fellow students, to the instructor as instructor and as adviser and to the coadviser. In residence halls, programming is about what we want students to think about. Residence hall programs, like "Dialogue with Danny," are even structured to help students develop their critical thinking skills and to think carefully about diversity issues.

> We are educators, not service providers, and we are very intentional about what we do. That's why we changed our name to student development. What we are about is the development of students, of assisting students in meeting the college's mission. We help students see that much of what they learn is out of class, for example, peer relationships, making good decisions about health. Students have begun to view our division as part and parcel of the educational package.

In themselves, these words are impressive. But these words are not one voice. Rather, they reflect the sense of partnership that pervades this campus. In partnership, in collaboration, in community, faculty and staff and students compose the Fellowship of Learning that is the lifeblood of this mission-driven college.

Part Three

Case Studies of Four-Year Institutions with 2,000 to 5,000 Students

Chapter Seven

Drury University

Balancing Intellectual Rigor with Intrusive Personal Support in the First Year

Charles C. Schroeder

Randy L. Swing

Drury University seems perfectly at home in Springfield, a modern city reflecting the values of middle America and shaped by its location in southwest Missouri. Just fifteen years before the founding of Drury College in 1873, Springfield was still an isolated Ozark town remarkable mainly for the Civil War battle at Wilson's Creek and being a stop on the Butterfield-Overland stagecoach passage to California. Drury was founded at a time when Springfield was experiencing tremendous growth spurred on because it was a stop for the "Frisco"—the St. Louis to San Francisco Railroad. Transportation continued to play a role in shaping Springfield as it later became the birthplace of the famous Route 66, the first paved transcontinental highway in America.

Congregational home missionaries founded Drury in the "New England Liberal Arts Model" to provide students with a broad-based, liberal arts education, a mission completely in keeping with the needs of a growing city at the crossroads of America. The original campus, only one and a half acres and a single building, evolved into the current eighty-acre urban campus of architecturally

Stephen Good, vice president for academic affairs and dean of the Drury College, passed away on February 16, 2004.

attractive buildings and mature hardwood trees. The physical expansion of the campus reflects the purposeful and conservative evolution of the original institution into a modern campus of excellence. Just as advances in transportation brought new challenges and opportunities to the city of Springfield, Drury College has successfully managed to become Drury University (the name was officially changed on January 1, 2000), an institution that prepares students for professions while still embracing a strong liberal arts foundation.

Drury is a traditional residential campus of approximately 1,500 undergraduates as part of a total enrollment of 4,450 students, and the university admits the vast majority of its above-average students immediately after high school. About 70 percent of Drury students are Missouri residents. Over a third of the students are members of a fraternity or sorority, 70 percent are residential, and 90 percent are white. Nearly 40 percent have graduated in the top 10 percent of their high school class, and most of the rest graduated in at least the top 25 percent. Drury seems to be successful in recruiting bright students who seek involvement in both the academic and cocurricular aspects of campus life.

Drury prides itself on close attention to students, small classes, and a caring, responsive faculty and staff. It is very rare for any class to have an enrollment over fifty students. But even then, as it does occasionally happen in an introductory chemistry lecture, the larger class is followed with a lab of only fifteen students.

The focus of this chapter is the current success of Drury University: how it serves first-year students and how it developed into an exemplary campus. This level of excellence was not always the case. In the 1970s, Drury experienced a series of short-term presidential tenures that made the future of the institution quite tenuous. With declining student enrollment, tuition revenue, and the lack of stable or visionary leadership, the institution was clearly approaching a crisis. The worst was avoided, largely due to administrative changes that occurred in 1983. In February of that year, Stephen Good accepted the position of vice president for academic affairs and dean of the college. Good brought experience as a faculty member, scholar of utopian literature, and former vice president of academic affairs and dean at Westmar College. Only six months later John Moore Jr. was named president. This presidential appointment was a bold move by the trustees, as Moore had no prior experience as a college or university president. Before assuming this position at Drury, he had served as assistant commissioner of education for Missouri.

Good's contributions to the leadership team are praised by the president and a wide array of faculty members. We found the combination of his academic credentials and early interest in the impact of nonclassroom experiences to be especially remarkable. As Good recalled, he came to Drury as a faculty member who had learned about student development theory. In his new administrative role, he began to explore the advantages of combining in-class and out-of-class experiences to create a more seamless and coherent experience for students. He determined that engaging students and faculty both in and out of the classroom were foundational elements of the kind of institution he wanted Drury to become.

It was a natural extension of Good's interests that led him to arrange a visit to Drury by John N. Gardner to help the campus launch a first-year seminar modeled after the University 101 class at the University of South Carolina. Although the seminar was successfully initiated, many individuals felt that it lacked adequate coherence and attachment to the institution's core curriculum goals. After only two years, the seminar was abandoned.

By 1987, five years after the appointment of the new president and academic vice president, Drury was still struggling to find the right core curriculum and plan for first-year students. Facing a review by the North Central Association in 1990, the institution spent nearly two years developing a new mission statement. The resulting statement, which follows, was approved by the faculty and the board of trustees in spring 1989:

> Drury is an independent university, church-related, grounded in the liberal arts tradition, and committed to personalized education in a community of scholars who value the arts of teaching and learning.
>
> Education at Drury seeks:
>
> - To cultivate spiritual sensibilities and imaginative faculties as well as ethical insight and critical thought;
> - To foster the integration of theoretical and practical knowledge;
> - To liberate persons to participate responsibly in and contribute to life in a global community.

A curricular reform plan was implemented in 1994–95 based on this mission statement, and especially the concept of life in a global community. This new curriculum integrated disciplinary courses into a coherent first-year core known as the Global Perspectives 21 curriculum. The reform plan was hotly debated and did not win unanimous approval of the faculty. In retrospect, it is now widely acknowledged that the considerable faculty debate, discussion, and analysis that preceded the adoption of Global Perspectives 21 shaped the new courses as a grassroots faculty effort.

The reform effort grew as a partnership between administrative and faculty leadership emerged. One faculty member said, and several others voiced agreement, that a key turning point was the vice president's decision to appoint a faculty member as the full-time director of the new curriculum. That person would be responsible for faculty development, assessing program outcomes, and monitoring the implementation of the curriculum year after year, allowing experimentation and change to continue to shape the effort over time. Ted Vaggalis, a philosophy professor, became the first director of the newly created Interdisciplinary Center, home of the Global Perspectives 21 curriculum. Continued collaboration between faculty, administrators, and several student affairs educators resulted in the creation of a course designed to anchor the Global Perspectives 21 curriculum and the first-year experience of Drury students: ALPHA Seminar.

ALPHA Seminar is a two-semester required course with a shared theme that connects out-of-class and classroom experiences. The course begins with the American experience and encourages students to engage the issue of "what it means to be an American in an increasingly diverse global community." The course develops students' writing, critical thinking, and communications skills, all of which are needed for success in college. The seminar, taken in each student's first year, is the initial step in the general education curriculum at Drury. In the second year, students continue their study with a course in global awareness and values analysis. In the second and third years, they study minorities and indigenous cultures. And in the third and fourth years, they continue with a "global futures" class and senior seminar research. As one faculty member stated, the ALPHA Seminar is a deliberate process: as students progress, they see how things "fit together," and they make significant "intellectual connections" along the way.

ALPHA Seminar: The Heart of the First Year

We found widespread support for the ALPHA Seminar, a course described by one faculty member as the "heart of the intellectual community" for all first-year students at Drury. The current director of ALPHA Seminar said that by using faculty, staff, and student peers, the course "intentionally integrates first-year students into the Drury community." All first-year students are assigned to one of twenty ALPHA sections, generally composed of approximately eighteen students who meet for two semesters with the same faculty member. Because seminar instructors develop close connections with students by serving as adviser, orientation leader, and teacher, they are commonly referred to as ALPHA mentors, signaling the importance of their role in students' total college experience. The first year at Drury is designed to connect students to the intellectual community, the student community, the faculty and staff community, the Springfield community, and the global community. These broad-based aims are accomplished almost exclusively through ALPHA Seminar, thereby making it truly the gateway to the Global Studies 21 curriculum.

Currently, the twenty faculty members teaching ALPHA come from a broad range of departments, including math, English, foreign language, history, theater, communications, philosophy, and the Interdisciplinary Studies Center. ALPHA students work with their instructor-mentor to examine the historical and cultural heritage of America in ways that enhance their critical thinking, writing, and oral communication skills. All ALPHA sections share an interdisciplinary common reader compiled by the faculty, thus creating a learning community atmosphere for the entire class of first-year students. The reader encompasses four broad themes: the individual versus the community, identity and difference, private interest versus public welfare, and life and work. Each section examines the tensions created by these opposing concepts. Each instructor-mentor also maintains the freedom to create case studies, as well as to use innovative pedagogics (active, collaborative, or cooperative learning) that connect class content and current events.

Right from the Start

The ALPHA experience begins in June, when all first-year students spend a day at Drury registering for their first semester, meeting their ALPHA class, and receiving a common summer reading assignment. In past years, first-year students have read Norman Maclean's *A River Runs Through It,* Jon Krakauer's *Into the Wild,* and Annie Dillard's *An American Childhood.* Students leave this first meeting of their ALPHA class with a set of guided reading prompts that form the basis of class discussions and their first writing assignment in the fall term. Most important, they leave the June session with a set of common experiences that connect each student with all other first-year students on campus, which becomes the start of meaningful relationships with peers and their ALPHA mentor.

Just prior to the first day of class, all first-year students return again to campus for a mandatory four-day orientation. The goals of this orientation are to encourage students to meet one another, provide them with an understanding of the academic expectations at Drury, and increase their knowledge regarding the services available as they begin college. ALPHA Seminar is again the center of this orientation process. In these classes, students engage in icebreakers and other social activities, an intellectual discussion designed around the summer reading and the assigned paper, a community service project, and a session led by upper-division students focused on the institution's academic expectations and resources. In addition, all first-year students are required to attend a special convocation that addresses "best practices of successful college students." This convocation is integrated into the academic discussions throughout the year in each ALPHA Seminar.

Of particular note is that during orientation, each ALPHA Seminar section participates in a community service project that connects them to the Springfield community. Numerous students commented that this activity was the most powerful, and even transformational, experience that they had not only throughout their first year, but more important, throughout their four years at Drury. As one student remarked, "Everyone really came together . . . dorm kids and commuters. . . . Everyone was focused on the same thing." Clearly, this activity was the primary bonding experience for students. Because the ALPHA Seminar is at the core of the distinctive Drury first-year experience, bonds between students are so tight that many seminar sections attend reunions, informally organized by students themselves, throughout their college careers.

Leveraging the Power of Student-to-Student Interaction

Another important dimension of the first year at Drury is the role of orientation leaders, a select group that serves as the bridge between new students and the broader student community. Orientation leaders are assigned to specific ALPHA sections and participate in the June registration day, the four-day preterm orientation, and ALPHA classes periodically during the year. Based on faculty and student evaluations of the orientation leaders, a new category of peer assistant has recently been created, the ALPHA leader. This student leader serves as the primary contact person for students, faculty, and the first-year experience office. The ALPHA leader can also enroll in a special course for credit and serve as a peer tutor in the class. The use of peer tutors in ALPHA was piloted in 2001, and the assessment results suggest that using a peer tutor enhances student learning.

Strong Faculty-Student Connections

Another primary objective of the first-year experience is to create meaningful and powerful connections between students, faculty, and staff to build a greater sense of community and enhance the overall college experience. The first faculty connection that all first-year students make is with their ALPHA mentor, who serves as teacher and adviser for the entire first year. During orientation, faculty members who are not serving as ALPHA mentors host a dinner in their homes for students in one ALPHA section, the mentor, the orientation leaders, and a small group of other faculty members. This occasion enables first-year students to meet a variety of faculty other than their ALPHA mentor in an informal setting. This chance to meet faculty outside the classroom—in a faculty member's home—was referenced consistently by students as one of the most important aspects of their first year at Drury. As one student remarked, "Going to the professor's house for dinner really made me feel special. . . . It also helped me understand that faculty were interested in me and my success." Also during orientation, each department holds an open house during a specified time, and first-year students attend these events in order to meet professors in all disciplines.

Faculty members who are tapped for service as ALPHA mentors are widely acknowledged as outstanding teachers and informed in advance that teaching the course is both challenging and rewarding. One faculty member reported that ALPHA mentors regularly say that "the ALPHA Seminar is the most rewarding course you will ever teach." Another faculty member described four primary assumptions that undergird his teaching. His assumptions flow from a central question, "What does it mean to live well?" He considers this question and the related assumptions to be at the core of his course and his efforts to serve as a mentor to new students. These assumptions, which have become the focal point of various faculty development seminars, are as follows:

- The teacher must look at both process and product, not only providing appropriate college-level material but also being mindful of the conditions in the classroom throughout the year.
- The teacher must meet students where they are and build on what they know by using such resources as contemporary films and short readings as a starting place.
- The teacher must be committed to student-centered learning to reflect continuously on what students are doing and why they are doing it as part of the classroom experience.
- The teacher must understand the necessity of blurring the boundaries between the course and the rest of the student's life.

Unlike other institutions that sponsor centers for faculty development, Drury embeds faculty development in the Global Perspectives curriculum. This is judged to be highly successful because, as one faculty member said, "we like each other." Faculty at Drury interact frequently in a variety of settings for a variety of purposes, and this interaction appears to be not only collegial but often collaborative. For example, faculty regularly exchange course assignments. They attend a training session before beginning to teach ALPHA Seminar. They meet as needed and use e-mail, in addition to a host of informal channels, to communicate about students and about the course. One faculty member summarized the faculty-to-faculty connection as "a fluid conversation." There is plentiful evidence that this is a reality on the Drury campus and not simply a platitude. For example, each Friday, over half of the faculty gathers in a reserved room for a faculty luncheon. Faculty reported that conversations around those tables often lead to new initiatives and to a rejuvenation of their commitment to teaching and to students. It is easy to envision the weekly luncheons as an ongoing series of celebrations of student learning and commitment to the institution.

Student-faculty connections are also ensured through academic advising. During the first year, the ALPHA mentor serves as the student's academic adviser. It is hard for advisees to fall between the cracks when they are in class with their instructor-adviser at least two times each week. Advising at Drury is not limited to schedule planning for the first several terms. A key charge for first-year advisers is to help students select a major and find an adviser in that major. Each ALPHA Seminar uses at least one class period for students to explore majors and connect with academic departments. The majors fair, conducted each spring as a campuswide event, makes it easy for teachers to plug a unit on career and major decisions into their syllabus. During the majors fair, students visit academic departments where they learn about majors firsthand. Most students declare a major by the end of the first year and select a new adviser to complete the transition out of ALPHA Seminar and into the second college year. Students who are not ready to declare a major either elect to continue being advised by their ALPHA mentor until they are ready to declare a major or they elect to be advised by the director of advising, Jeanie Allen.

Drury's use of academic advising ensures that students have a home base throughout the undergraduate experience. The institution is intentional in helping students connect with major departments and advisers but provides the necessary safety net of specialized advising for students who are not yet ready to declare a major at the end of the first year.

Connecting the Class to the Campus and the World

Another important aspect of the first college year at Drury is the long-standing tradition of providing high-quality convocations. As the result of a project funded by the National Science Foundation, Drury has provided a series of convocation speakers around an annual theme. During 2001–2002, the theme was "origins" and the speakers were authors, historians, researchers, philosophers, and scientists who challenged and inspired students to explore the "web of knowledge," the "theory of everything," and "Lucy." Themes for 2002–2003 were "gender and sexuality" and for 2003–2004 "Discovery, Exploration, and creativity." These biweekly convocations were described by a faculty member as "the common thread for all first-year students which connects them to the intellectual community of the campus."

The intentional and formalized Drury first year also connects student learning with the university's mission to "liberate persons to participate responsibly in and contribute to life in a global community." Community service projects, convocation speakers, study-abroad opportunities, and activities for international students create multiple connections for Drury students to the wider world.

Another important element is the focus on community service. During orientation, each ALPHA Seminar participates in a community service project. For many students, participation in that experience whets their appetite for ongoing volunteer experiences during the college years. Drury's commitment to community service is so strong that the institution has established a full-time position for coordinating and promoting community service. The effort has worked exceedingly well in that a large proportion of first-year students participate in voluntary community service during the year. The largest service initiative places students in local elementary schools that enroll a high proportion of low-income students. Drury volunteers provide personal attention and encouragement to the elementary school students through tutoring and participation in reading groups. A second initiative, associated with the local Boys and Girls Club, involves a large number of Drury volunteers who become mentors and tutors for youngsters in fifth to ninth grades. These activities, from playing basketball to tutoring, were developed to serve local youth and help Drury students connect in a personal way with the themes of the ALPHA Seminar.

Although these efforts spring from formal course structures, they are truly voluntary during the year. But like much of the Drury first year, community service is not left to chance after the initial exposure during orientation. Each spring, ALPHA Seminar instructors use service-learning to reconnect students with the community around course questions such as, "What does it mean to live?" and "What does it mean to be a member of a 'good' community?" The service-learning component includes direct service to the community during the spring term, selected course readings, and student self-reflection papers, all built into the structure of the ALPHA Seminar.

Drury's Approach to Excellence

Drury's development of excellence in the first college year resulted from a series of institutional decisions, skillful personnel management, creative thinking, and hard work by faculty, staff, and administrators. Five key themes undergrid the evolution of the campus: (1) patience, (2) leadership, (3) clarity and constancy of purpose, (4) faculty involvement, influence, and investment, and (5) assessment-based, data-driven decisions.

Patience

In the words of the vice president for academic affairs, Stephen Good, the Drury approach to the first year was a "decade in the making." Faculty members involved in the process also report that it was a ten-year effort that started with Good himself "planting seeds and patiently waiting for them to take root." It also involved a grassroots approach that was combined with top-down support. Clearly, ALPHA Seminar and the Global Studies curriculum were faculty driven from the start, and this fact, beyond all others, has resulted in incredible faculty investment in the overall first-year experience. Finally, over three years were devoted to getting interested faculty from core disciplines to meet frequently and discuss ways of building a more coherent, integrated first year.

Leadership

One of the most remarkable aspects of Drury University is the unusual continuity in its administrative leadership. Drury's twelve-member administrative team has an average tenure of nearly nineteen years. These twelve senior team members work together effectively and share a strong commitment to the institution's progress. Clearly, the driving force behind ALPHA Seminar, as well as the integrated, coherent first year, was the vice president for academic affairs and dean of the college, Stephen Good. We found Good to be a quiet, humble, and relatively unassuming man who provided masterful leadership for creating a climate and context that encourages and rewards innovation. His more than twenty years as the chief academic officer was the key to the development of the first-year experience. It is also apparent that President Moore has, for over twenty years, provided a common sense of purpose, encouraged collegial relationships with internal and external constituencies, and instilled a spirit of forward momentum—all signs of a dynamically successful college. The partnership, and indeed synergy, exhibited between Moore and Good resulted in a stimulating, vibrant, and effective learning environment, not only for students but for faculty as well.

Although her tenure is not as long as others, a key player in the first-year experience of all students is Jeanie Allen, the first-year experience director, a member of the student affairs staff, and an incredible dynamo. Allen's enthusiasm and commitment to the program are contagious. A strong and dedicated student advocate, she coordinates, with a minimal amount of staff support, advising, orientation, and many other common elements shared by ALPHA Seminars. She is currently devoting more time to connecting ALPHA Seminar and other dimensions of the first year with the cocurricular life of students by building and strengthening bridges between academic affairs and student affairs. The personal attention and advocacy she demonstrates is most apparent to students, who often refer to her as the "savior" of all first-year students who are in trouble.

Allen delivers a significant amount of direct service to students, but she also is a key coordinator of an array of faculty and student affairs professionals. She is in close contact with faculty, especially those teaching ALPHA Seminars, and she trains and guides the residence hall assistants (RAs). Both groups refer students to Allen when special needs arise, from intervening with tutoring help to letting a student use her office for some "quiet time away from my roommate." Several students mentioned her homesickness remedy: a stuffed "homesickness bear" that waits on the sofa in her office for students "who need a hug."

Much of her work to support first-year initiatives occurs out of sight. She personally assigns each student to an ALPHA Seminar rather than leave the composition of the sections to chance. To accomplish that task, she reads the application essays for every first-year student to learn about their experiences and their dreams. She uses admissions data in combination with information gleaned from the admissions essays to balance each ALPHA section in terms of gender, academic ability, and prior experiences. Admittedly the process is not scientific, but her professional judgment and instincts guide her in arranging each class to create a diverse, compatible group of students. The admissions applications often provide important clues that certain students will need special attention during the first year, and she takes that into consideration as she assigns them to an ALPHA Seminar. Allen's work in the summer to manage the student composition of ALPHA Seminars is yet another example of the intentional design process used at Drury to create a powerfully challenging and supportive first year of college.

Drury is fortunate to have a number of long-serving administrators, but that is only part of the story. This institution works to build collegial structures. For a number of years, the president has selected an aspirational institution for Drury administrators to visit. The president's office coordinates travel for a team of key faculty and administrators to visit another institution that is implementing one or more best practices. In the past, campus leaders have visited campuses such as the University of Missouri-Columbia and Elon University, another of the thirteen Institutions of Excellence. Over the two-day visits, team members interview administrative staff and students on the campus and spend evenings analyzing and discussing what they have learned.

These trips have reportedly been a successful method for administrative development and for bringing new ideas back to

Drury. They also stand symbolically for the same learning conditions that Drury purports to give to new students: the creation of sustained relationships as part of the learning process; the taking of people out of their comfort zones and exposing them to new ideas that encourage them to determine their own worldview; and the provision of common experiences that can be shared and can serve as a common language for discussions in future years. We believe that perhaps, most important, activities such as this highlight another distinctive feature of the Drury culture: a continuous quest for excellence that entails a fervent search for best practices. By identifying and studying best practices, Drury leaders are constantly seeking to improve the undergraduate experience in an intentional and systematic fashion. This overarching focus on institutional excellence can be seen in the well-developed five-year strategic plan that Drury has developed to move the institution to the next level of excellence. Like the current first-year plan, this one also grew out of the clear mission statement developed in 1989 that continues to guide the institution.

Clarity and Constancy of Purpose

A primary reason that the first year is so powerful at Drury is clarity and constancy of purpose. There are clear, measurable, and mutually understood goals for the first-year curriculum that are communicated frequently and reinforced in multiple ways. Faculty, staff, and students can explain the design of the Drury first year and why the designed goals are important. Most important, there is a sense that the whole academic enterprise is working together to achieve the desired outcomes of the Drury first year.

One anecdote told about Jeanie Allen highlights Drury's clarity and constancy of purpose. When an athletic practice ran into scheduled orientation events, Allen marched onto the practice field dressed in her business suit to "assure the coach" that academics have priority over athletic practice. According to the story, after only a brief exchange with the coach, the student athletes were quickly lined up to follow Allen off the field and to the appointed orientation session. It is easy to imagine the shocked faces of these young athletes as the values of the institution were made clear to them and the coach that academics really do come first.

Faculty Involvement, Influence, and Investment

Faculty are at the center of every aspect of the first year at Drury. This reality is the result of extensive faculty involvement and influence in conceptualizing a new core curriculum and a set of core experiences for helping students make appropriate intellectual connections. The continuous process of involvement and influence has led to a tremendous amount of faculty investment in the first year—investment that reflects a sense of collective ownership for the initiative. Clearly, a critical mass of faculty generally agrees on the purpose and direction of Drury's approach to the first year, and faculty members are committed, primarily through experimentation and risk taking, to improving this approach continuously. This attitude results primarily from an unusual level of trust, steadfast but gentle leadership from senior academic leaders, and consistently communicated high expectations for student and for faculty performance.

The trust level is very high throughout the campus, and we found it to be particularly noteworthy among the faculty. An ethic of caring about the students, each other, and the institution pervades the campus. The overall atmosphere is very welcoming, and students know the institution cares about them.

There is a remarkable amount of faculty interaction, both formal and informal. Approximately half of the entire faculty meets for lunch every Friday; these lunches are not spontaneous. Administrative support provides space and time to ensure that this community has the opportunity to gather together.

The selection of the right faculty is a key component. The vice president for academic affairs ensures that every potential new faculty member is introduced to the mission of Drury and interviewed about his or her belief in the institution's curriculum, which involves a student affairs and academic affairs partnerships. It is not by chance that one side of the vice president's office has two chairs facing an antique fireplace over which hangs a framed copy of the Drury mission statement. It is easy to envision the vice president and a potential faculty member sitting in front of the fireplace and discussing the mission of Drury as a part of the interview process. This emphasis on the intentional recruitment of faculty who buy into the teaching and learning mission and the emphasis on the first-year experience is another reason for Drury's success.

Based on student comments, it is clear that Drury faculty members are effective and consistent in their communication of high expectations for student performance. Students report that they know Drury will be both demanding of academic excellence and supportive of their attempts to demonstrate it. Faculty members prove that it is possible to hold high standards and also mentor first-year students. They have defined the role of professor as a unique blend of challenge and support, both in and out of the classroom, which faculty and students understand and appreciate. The level of faculty involvement and investment in first-year student success is easily recognized and frequently commented on by Drury students. As one student said, "There is a great deal of personal attention here. From the minute you walk on campus until you graduate, you know that faculty and staff really care about you." The strong emphasis on personal attention and support is balanced by high expectations and intellectually challenging experiences. This was highlighted by another student who remarked, "My ALPHA class was really hard, but I have no regrets. I was constantly forced to think outside the box, and as a result, I have a totally new perspective on how I view the world."

Assessment-Based, Data-Driven Decisions

A critical ingredient in the success of Drury is reflective, evidence-oriented practice—practice that responds to the question, "How do we know that what we are doing is achieving the results we desire?" At Drury, well-developed and comprehensive assessment of skills and knowledge drives innovations in the ALPHA Seminar. The founding director of the Interdisciplinary Center, Ted Vaggalis, reports that he came to appreciate the central role that assessment plays in program improvement even though he was originally skeptical.

Assessment, just as is true with the delivery of the seminar, has evolved. The assessment committee first focused on the creation of a critical thinking test that would assist them in measuring students' cognitive development in that area, a stated learning goal of the seminar. Eventually the committee's emphasis shifted from a test to using writing and communication samples to understanding critical thinking better.

Writing has been assessed in the ALPHA Seminar for the past seven years. The first essay is a common essay that is submitted to a faculty committee assigned to examine the baseline writing skills of all entering first-year students. During the year, a common in-class writing assignment is also submitted to this assessment group. This baseline information allows faculty to engage in creating what they describe as "writing assessments that meet students where they are in terms of their writing abilities." In addition, these papers are compared to papers submitted by all seniors as they complete their senior seminars. Faculty state that attention is then given to those areas that appear to "remain writing weaknesses throughout the average student's tenure at Drury." Each ALPHA mentor also uses these essays to advise certain students to take a variety of courses designed to improve writing skills. Finally, nine external evaluators from Southwest Missouri State University (located in Springfield) review ALPHA students' essays to provide an external validation to the process. Assessment data from multiple sources such as these not only help to enhance student performance, but these data also assist in the early identification of at-risk students, particularly during the first six weeks of the fall semester. Campus administrators believe that strategies such as these contributed to increasing first- to second-year retention from 80 to 83 percent in the years following the initiation of the ALPHA Seminar.

Oral communication skills are also assessed. Students in each ALPHA section deliver formal presentations during both semesters, and these are audiotaped. These tapes are then submitted to an assessment committee to establish a baseline and to examine progress in first-year students' presentation skills. Similar to the writing assessment protocol, these tapes are compared to senior presentations and used by faculty to advise individual students to complete courses designed to enhance oral communication skills. The assessment of these communication skills has led to the creation of a Writing Center and the Oral Communication Center, where students receive additional help on papers and presentations.

The results of assessments in these three areas—writing, communication, and critical thinking—are used in a systematic, consistent, and sustained way to improve the ALPHA Seminar experience for all students. In addition, recent data generated by the National Survey of Student Engagement (NSSE) clearly indicate that Drury students exhibit a considerably higher level of engagement in academic and intellectual experiences than students at peer institutions. Similar gains are noted in the following NSSE categories as well: mental activity, reading and writing, quality of advising, enriching educational experiences, time use, and educational and personal growth.

The faculty assessment team also used a general survey instrument to gauge students' ratings of their progress on relevant objectives in the ALPHA Seminar. Six of the twelve learning objectives received, on average, a score of 3.5 or higher on a 5-point scale from at least 80 percent of the students. These scales included the following:

- Developing skill in expressing myself orally or in writing
- Learning how to find and use resources for answering questions or solving problems
- Learning to analyze and critically evaluate ideas, arguments, and points of view
- Developing creative capacities (writing, inventing, designing, etc.)
- Learning to apply course material (to improve thinking, problem solving, and decisions)
- Developing a clearer understanding of, and commitment to, personal values

Clearly, one of the most distinctive features of the Drury first-year experience is the degree to which faculty and academic administrators use data from systematic assessments consistently to improve their programs.

Overall, the assessment effort has confirmed current practice more than informed change. The strong planning process that led to the development of the ALPHA Seminar created an instructional unit that was largely effective from the start. Over time, certain course elements such as service-learning have been added, and faculty have been able to systematically evaluate student opinion of the course and related learning gains. As one faculty member said, "If a student asks, 'Why should I take this course?' we should be able to answer that question." Assessment findings have confirmed local views that students may complain about the seminar—specifically, that it is hard and not uniformly delivered across multiple sections. But later assessments indicate that students who complete the seminar see it as "one of their favorites." As an example, one student commented, "My ALPHA class was hard, and I didn't always like being challenged; however, I have no regrets. I now have a totally new perspective on the way I view the world." Comments like these confirm that the long-term, combined with short-term, assessment provides a much richer picture of the seminar and its impact on students.

Efforts to improve the first-year experience are clear, consistent, sustained, and systemic. Linking and aligning parts with the whole is a hallmark of the Drury first-year experience. The evidence is clear: Drury is goal and data driven. The faculty's appreciation for and use of assessment data is highly unusual and one reason for the effectiveness of the overall program.

Future Challenges

Although Drury has an exceptionally effective and integrated first-year experience, challenges remain. For example, the core of the program is the well-developed ALPHA Seminar, which is very successful in enhancing students' incorporation into the institution and facilitating their academic success. Opportunities still exist, however, for strengthening connections with the cocurricular lives of students, particularly in residence halls, academic advising, leadership initiatives, service-learning opportunities, and even Greek life. ALPHA Seminar has achieved significant success in communicating high academic expectations; however, it has an opportunity to expand on and strengthen communication about institutional values and social responsibilities of students. In addition, there is a need for more assessment evidence of the impact of the cocurricular experience on the desired outcomes of the program.

Another challenge is ensuring continued ownership across campus, particularly in view of predicted significant changes in the central administration in the near future. Historically, momentum for the seminar program has been sustained by a highly committed group. And although the program is a clear reflection of the institution's mission, keeping its centrality in everyone's mind is a continuing concern. Finally, some students and faculty mentioned the "significant degree of variability" between sections of the ALPHA Seminar. Student comments included remarks such as these: "Some teachers give loads of work, others don't"; "Some faculty are really demanding, while others are less so"; and "No two faculty teach it the same." Although these comments may reflect perceptions more than reality, they should nevertheless be examined and addressed if need be.

Conclusion

Small colleges are often characterized by clear missions, academically capable students, caring and competent faculty, and a sense of community. In this regard, Drury University fits the image. However, Drury's success in developing an exemplary first year cannot be explained by these characteristics alone; indeed there is much more to the story.

The 375 new students who matriculate each year find an organized welcome to the campus that ensures personal attention from the beginning. By the time classes begin, students have already met a faculty mentor and an undergraduate student mentor and had dinner at a faculty member's home. During orientation, they are introduced to Global Perspectives 21, the Drury general education curriculum. The creative and comprehensive steps to welcome students and introduce them to Global Perspectives 21 are clearly congruent with the intentional mission of Drury.

ALPHA Seminar, so central to the success of Drury, has a profound impact on the experiences of first-year students in the following ways:

- The seminar helps promote a sense of community by proving a human-scale, family-like setting for students.
- The small seminar experience facilitates a smooth transition for students by serving as the primary socialization process.
- Students experience a sense of connectedness to the curriculum, the faculty, their peers, and the campus and surrounding communities.
- Innovative pedagogies challenge students to leave their comfort zones and become more introspective.

- Students increasingly become more thoughtful and responsible learners, growing intellectually to the point that they create their own personal philosophy and worldview.

Of course, a truly successful first year cannot be built on a single course or set of structures to welcome new students. Multiple efforts and a shared commitment by Drury faculty, administrators, and staff support and challenge first-year students to use campus resources in educationally purposeful ways to create an integrated and coherent first year. Clearly, the emphasis is on connecting course content, the campus, the local community, and the world—a process that produces integrated learning by connecting, in an intentional fashion, the core curriculum with core experiences. This approach to undergraduate education incorporates a number of best practices: clarity and constancy of purpose; formal methods for incorporating new students, faculty, and staff into the institutional culture; the centrality of teaching and learning broadly defined; the use of systematic assessment of stated learning outcomes; high levels of faculty involvement, influence, and investment in facilitating the success of first-year students; an openness to experimentation and risk taking; senior leadership that is focused, encouraging, and steadfast but gentle; and a culture of collaboration that encourages cross-disciplinary interaction.

The Drury story does not end here, for it continues to evolve. Nonetheless, the Drury experience has demonstrated critical characteristics, processes, and elements that must be brought to bear in creating an effective first year for all students—elements that other institutions can employ to create similar successes. Indeed, the lessons learned from the Drury journey are worth learning.

Chapter Eight

Elon University

Transforming Education Through a Community of Inquiry and Engagement

Libby V. Morris

Randy L. Swing

Elon University is a private liberal arts university set in the rolling hills of the piedmont area of North Carolina. Founded in 1889 as Elon College by the Christian Church, now the United Church of Christ, the founders had a clear vision for their new college. They saw it as "an academic community that transforms mind, body, and spirit and encourages freedom of thought and liberty of conscience." With clarity of purpose, the university leadership has built a nationally recognized program of undergraduate education that attracts students from forty-eight states and forty-one foreign countries. Confirming its national audience, 70 percent of the 4,270 undergraduates in fall 2002 came from out of state. With the expansion of its undergraduate programs coupled with existing graduate degrees, Elon College assumed university status and changed its name on June 1, 2001.

Elon University is set on 502 acres of green lawns amid a canopy of trees; apropos, the word *elon* is Hebrew for "oak." This pastoral setting, however, conceals its urban proximity: Greensboro is only twenty minutes away, and Chapel Hill a thirty-minute drive. On first entering the campus, the visitor is struck by both the traditional architecture and the monumental scope of new development. In 1998, the $17.2 million Dalton L. McMichael Senior

Science Center, designed around the themes of discovery-based learning and interdisciplinary collaboration, opened with seventeen teaching labs, fourteen student research labs, and specialized computer capabilities. Soon after, the $14 million Carol Grotnes Belk Library opened with more than 200,000 volumes, 150 computers, and a variety of networked classrooms and collaborative spaces. In 2001, the R. N. Ellington Health and Counseling Center opened along with Rhodes Stadium, a $13 million campus athletics facility seating over 8,000. In August 2002, living and learning space was completed with the opening of the Isabella Cannon International Studies Pavilion and the Kenan Honors Pavilion, two of five buildings planned for the new Academic Village.

Former president Fred Young is credited with launching the campus's architectural revival. In 1984, he replaced the parking lot in front of a centrally located academic building with a large fountain; thus was the beginning of a plan to build the ideal campus environment featuring Fonville Fountain at the center. Current administrators call Young visionary and strategic in his actions, and they point to increased applications and admissions to Elon beginning with the creation of the fountain as the psychological and physical core of the campus. Whether causation can be established is certainly a point of debate, but Young's leadership in building the campus and student body is without question.

As described by a current administrator, Young's administration was noted for "centering on the way the place looks and feels. . . . It laid the groundwork for a lot of other good things to happen." It was noted that Young understood marketing and understood admissions. According to those interviewed, he knew that you had to "get them out of the car" before you could tell students and parents about the academic program. Today, under the leadership of President Leo Lambert and committed senior administrators, the building plan continues, intertwined with a climbing academic reputation and enhanced academic programs, which begin with each student during the first year.

Elon is more than a bucolic setting of tree-lined walkways, soaring oaks, pristine facilities, and an ever-bubbling fountain; the physical improvements are synergistic with curricular changes over the past two decades. Elon's reputation is reflected in the honors and records recently claimed by the university. *US News & World Report* ranked Elon eighth overall out of 131 southern colleges and universities in the 2003 edition of *America's Best Colleges.* In the category of "first-year experience," Elon tied for fourteenth among all colleges and universities, only slightly behind Harvard, UNC-Chapel Hill, University of Maryland, and Indiana University-Bloomington. The *Kaplan College Guide* (2003) of "320 most interesting colleges" listed Elon as one of thirty "hidden treasures" where students live their knowledge through experiential learning. In illustration of this assertion, Elon ranked first nationwide among comparable colleges and universities for the number of students who study abroad.

Elon University's mission statement, approved by the board of trustees on March 14, 2000, grounded in the forefathers' vision, is the guiding force for the programs and activities that today create the total Elon experience:

- We nurture a rich intellectual community characterized by active student engagement with a faculty dedicated to excellent teaching and scholarly accomplishment.
- We provide a dynamic and challenging undergraduate curriculum grounded in the traditional liberal arts and sciences and complemented by distinctive professional and graduate programs.
- We integrate learning across the disciplines and put knowledge into practice, thus preparing students to be global citizens and informed leaders motivated by concern for the common good.
- We foster respect for human differences, passion for a life of learning, personal integrity, and an ethic of work and service.

As the story of Elon unfolds, observable connections between activities and the Elon vision are apparent. It is as though the mission statement gave literal birth to the first-year core, service-learning, and study abroad. The phrases "student engagement," "integrated learning," "work and service," and "respect for human differences" resonate in publications, activities, community dialogue, and personal interactions. Teaching and learning are primary in Elon's mission statement, and the close coupling of this expectation for faculty and student interaction with first-year programming allows for clarity in direction, synchronicity of action, and integrity in the process that has brought Elon's first-year program to premier status.

How did Elon get to this point of accomplishment? What changes have been made? How will they be maintained? Elon University's approach to the first-year experience is created by five substantive programs extending across seventeen months: spring orientation, summer experiences, fall orientation, Elon 101, and the first-year core curriculum. The goals and objectives for student learning and engagement, which reflect the university's mission statement, are explicitly woven into each of the programs, and collectively they represent an intentional and comprehensive approach to the first-year experience.

The Precollege Connection

Students' exposure to the Elon ethos starts when potential students first learn about Elon University. As described by the provost, Gerald Francis, the message from the president is that everyone is responsible for admissions and retention and the vision of the first year starts with the admissions staff on the road. Explaining the Elon vision and programs is easy for university recruiters because all of them are Elon graduates. These alumni can speak firsthand about the opportunities, benefits, and challenges of college life at Elon, and because of the coordinated, multifaceted approach to the first year, the recruitment staff has a substantive story to tell.

The contagious enthusiasm for Elon was captured from several students in comments about their first campus visit:

> After touring here . . . everyone made me feel so comfortable . . . especially the staff in the admissions office. So it made me really want to come here, knowing that I would be a person, and get . . . attention.
>
> When I came here, the international admissions officer, he really treated me like he wanted me here, and I just felt like I was at home. I had visited other universities as well, and it was . . . the sense of comfort that I felt here; [it] made me really want to come here.

Spring Orientation

The first-year experience at Elon University is actually seventeen months in length because it officially begins with orientation in the spring. On Fridays and Saturdays in March and April, before beginning the first term, accepted students along with their parents and siblings are introduced to the academic and social climate of Elon. The sense of community begins to emerge as faculty advisers and returning students share information about housing, campus recreation, core curricula, and the "Elon Experiences," five exceptional cocurricular programs that extend classroom knowledge through active learning. During orientation, students are immersed in Elon values, Elon culture, and the opportunities and expectations for student growth and engagement. According to students we interviewed, orientation created a sense of belonging and confirmed the decision to attend Elon. For others, it "tipped the balance" and solidified the decision to enroll.

The special attention given to students during orientation does not end with the passing of the weekend; rather, it is only the beginning. For example, for minority students, Hand-to-Hand matches faculty mentors with ethnic minority first-year students to ease adjustments during the first year, and the S.M.A.R.T. peer mentoring program (Student Mentors Advising Rising Talent) pairs upper-level minority students with entering minority students. Following spring orientation, all students receive a CD entitled *Destination Elon*. Communicating by CD with teenagers who were the first generation to grow up on-line sends a substantive and subliminal message about connecting with first-year life at Elon and is a natural communication strategy for a campus with more than 500 computer workstations, twelve computer labs, and fully wired residence halls.

In multiple ways—face-to-face, Web site, and CD—Elon tells and reinforces its mission, vision, and activities. Importantly, during our visit, none of the students with whom we spoke complained of expectations set by promotional materials and orientation sessions that were not being met after enrollment. Through interviews with faculty and staff, it was clear that creating expectations and then fulfilling the promise represent an act of integrity and importance to Elon faculty and administration.

Engaging Summer Experiences

Experiential activities that emphasize learning beyond the classroom are important to delivering the holistic Elon experience. The first opportunity for student engagement in the highly touted ethic of work and service occurs in the summer prior to the first year. Students may choose to participate in a variety of summer programs. For example, in the Pre-SERVE Program, incoming students focus on collaborative learning, ethical decision making, and leadership. Adventures in Leadership serves approximately eighty students with adventure activities that emphasize team building and leadership, two goals of the General Studies program. Adventures in the Environment takes a small group of students to the Appalachian Trail to study the environment and experience teamwork. These summer activities are objective-driven programs that are congruent with Elon's mission and serve as a stepping-stone to student integration into campus life.

Beginning with the first contact and extending through the summer, Elon maintains regular contact with potential students using e-mail, telephone, publications, and host city receptions in locations with large numbers of Elon-bound students. This strategy to build connectedness is important considering the geographical diversity of the student body and the investment in time and resources needed to visit and enroll at this institution.

Fall Orientation

Fall orientation is a campuswide activity as student orientation leaders, faculty, and staff arrive in droves to welcome the first-year students and their families. Extending over four days, orientation begins on Friday with a moving-in extravaganza. To the Elon community, moving in is both psychological and physical. To address the physical demands, the campus has developed a novel method of encouraging faculty and staff to lend a hand. During the spring semester, first-year students are asked to nominate a favorite faculty or staff member to help new first-year students move into the residence halls. On moving day, the parking lots are lined with administrators, faculty, and staff performing various functions for incoming students, from unpacking cars, to carrying boxes, to assembling lofts. It is considered an honor to be nominated for move-in day, and across campus faculty and staff could recount how many times they had been nominated for assisting with this important act of making the transition to college. Many former nominees and others show up year after year.

During orientation, incoming students are placed in small groups led by faculty advisers and returning students who are orientation leaders. Conversations about leaving home and fears about coming to college are mixed with discussions of academic goals, the honor code, and course work. Even before classes begin, faculty advisers and student leaders introduce the academic goals of thinking critically, exploring ways of knowing, and respecting diversity—all themes that are important to the courses in the first-year core.

To maintain the continuity of personal relationships forged in orientation, the fall orientation groups remain intact during fall term in class sections of Elon 101, the first-year seminar. The bonding and student attitude toward the faculty advisers, whom students first meet in small groups during fall orientation, can be summed up by one student's comment: "I think my adviser is the best on campus. She gives me her home phone number. . . . I can approach her any time. She's really on top of everything."

Fall orientation also includes a presidential address during the new student convocation. In this address, the president clearly states the standards for participation in life at Elon. In a ceremony rich with tradition, first-year students enter and leave the convocation through lines of faculty dressed in full academic regalia. Held "Under the Oaks" at the center of campus, this ceremony is filled with symbolism. In giving each student an acorn, symbolizing the seed of learning, the expectation for future growth supported by the Elon community is planted. In May, when seniors return to this site for graduation, the circle is closed as they receive an oak sapling to take out into the world.

Lest students get lost in the pageantry of the moment, immediately following convocation advisers meet with their new students and then their parents. The signal is given that the academic life for first-year students is programmed and now under way.

First-Year Experience: Integrated and Individualized

Programs and activities central to the first year at Elon include Elon 101, the common reading, and the first-year core.

Fall Semester: Elon 101

Elon 101 demonstrates the university's long-standing commitment to first-year students. Elon 101 is a one-credit-hour, semester-long extended orientation course offered each fall. Orientation groups become Elon 101 groups with the beginning of fall semester. Initiated and sponsored by the Academic Advising Center, Elon 101 was launched more than twenty years ago when the first director and other colleagues attended a conference on the first year organized by the University of South Carolina's National Resource Center for The First-Year Experience. Termed a grassroots effort from the outset, the driving force behind Elon 101 was better advising and an attempt for faculty to develop closer relationships with students.

Elon 101 was first taught by ten faculty members who were identified and recruited without extra compensation as 101 instructors because of their demonstrated interest in students as evidenced by their commitment to the college's advising center. And from the beginning, the advising function of 101 and the continuity of purpose "to help students adjust to college life" have never been broken. The central purpose of Elon 101 is to provide a place for academic and cocurricular advisement and a forum for discussion of the honor code and what it means to be an Elon student.

Over the years, the content of Elon 101 has been altered; changes, however, are carefully considered and are based on student evaluations and feedback from advisers and peer assistants. Recent evaluations pointed to an interest in thematic sections in addition to generic sessions; consequently, in fall 2002, nine thematic sections were piloted. In 2003, eighteen theme-based sections were offered. Themes centered on journalism and communications, civic engagement, and "Beginning Your College Journey with Poetry."

Elon 101 section enrollment is limited to sixteen students, and the seminar is taught by advisers (either faculty or administrative staff) and student assistants. Following the successful introduction of Elon 101 many years ago, a beneficial, but unplanned, outcome for the college was increased student retention; therefore, the administration wanted to make the seminar required of all students. But the developers resisted, thinking the "climate" would be affected, and the course has never been required. Obviously, for Elon, this was the right decision. Currently, Elon 101 has grown to eighty-five sections enrolling almost all first-year students each fall. The success of Elon 101 is likely due to the close coupling of orientation sections and Elon 101 enrollment (that is, the groups stay together from orientation into Elon 101). In addition, the course enjoys a good reputation, as shared by student word-of-mouth.

The broad-based support for Elon 101 is shown by extensive faculty and administrative involvement in this course. The dean of arts and sciences was scheduled to teach Elon 101 in 2003. Across the years, all deans, as well as a large number of other administrators, have taught Elon 101. Only a small stipend is paid to the instructor of each section, and each has a paid student assistant. The students spoke extensively about the bonds built with faculty starting in Elon 101 and extending to other courses and programs. They talked of e-mailing faculty members, going to their homes, and being invited for dinner. Overall, the students were positive about Elon 101, with comments such as these:

> Our Elon 101 group, during the first week, I had dinner with mine. And we went out and got pizza and that was really good to get to know the faculty away from the classroom, and learn about her family, a way to bond.

> From the beginning you have a group. I see my Elon 101 class all over the place. . . . You have a TA [teaching assistant], and they bring people to the group. . . . You have all their numbers if you need to call anyone. It is my favorite part of Elon.

In talking with the students, it is clear that the success of Elon 101 resides with the faculty advisers in addition to the course content; consequently, the selection and training of advisers is crucial to the success of this course. Understanding the critical roles played by the faculty advisers, the advising office trains new faculty in the spring term over several sessions and holds a three-hour workshop in the fall for all Elon 101 faculty and staff advisers.

Only two directors have administered Elon 101 since its inception; the current director has been in place now for ten years. This long-standing leadership and connection to the purpose, history, and life of the course has served the university and the first-year students well. But nothing stays the same forever, and goals for the future include staffing all 101 sections with faculty members to build the academic component of the course. The dean of the College of Arts and Sciences, seeing an opportunity for wider exposure for the basic disciplines, would like all Elon 101 instructors to be faculty in his college. His ideas include changing the course credit hours to two hours and making the instruction part of the faculty member's regular academic load.

In summary, Elon 101 started as a grassroots activity, still enjoys broad-based support, and has as instructors only faculty and staff who are interested in teaching the course. No student or faculty member is required to participate. The course benefits from continuous, long-term leadership, a focused mission, and extensive student involvement. In the short term, Elon 101 assists in successful integration into college; in the long run, many students form tightly knit groups and friendships that extend across the college years and beyond.

Common Reading Program

In 1994, in concert with other academic changes, Elon began the common reading program, another unifying activity for the campus community. Each year, a committee of faculty, staff, and students selects a book to be read by all incoming students. Faculty members incorporate the book into Global Studies and College Writing, two of the four courses in the first-year core curriculum. Elon's mission, "to integrate learning across the disciplines," is reflected in the selection of the reading and the commitment by faculty to a theme and dialogue that transcend individual first-year courses. Often the book author is invited to campus to participate in a campuswide colloquium. Selections in recent years have included James McBride's *The Color of Water,* a novel that reveals the life of an interracial family; Alex Kotlowitz's *There Are No Children Here,* which chronicles the lives of two brothers growing up in an inner-city Chicago housing project; and Gita Mehta's *Snakes and Ladders,* a book about India's folkways and history.

General Studies and the First-Year Core

Elon University's general studies curriculum is a deliberate academic program that includes the first-year core, liberal studies, advanced studies, and an experiential learning requirement. A total of fifty-eight out of 132 credit hours are earned in the general studies curriculum. The new general studies mission, established September 3, 2002, states, "The General Studies Program provides an interdisciplinary framework for learning, designed to cultivate a spirit of inquiry and a respect for human differences." The General Studies mission from May 7, 1993, summarizes the components of general studies as follows:

> The General Studies program at Elon College nurtures an academic community by developing in students, faculty and staff the habits of mind and actions that characterize liberal education.
>
> 1. Scholarship: critical, creative and connected thinking
> 2. Leadership: informed values and actions
> 3. Wholeness: development of the whole person
> 4. Diversity: respect for diverse ideas and approaches
> 5. Independence: experiential and self-directed learning
> 6. Foundations: writing and speaking, quantitative and computing abilities

The director of the General Studies program, Steve Braye, is a committed, long-term faculty member who, during our visit, seemed to know every student on campus by name, as they did him. General Studies is housed in the same office as the associate provost, Nancy Midgette, an advocate of the first-year experience and a long-term leader in the efforts that have created Elon's culture of student engagement. Our first interviews on campus were with these two energetic, strategic, and pragmatic leaders.

The first-year core is a plan that was hammered out by the faculty in the mid-1990s and is still undergoing change; the core comprises three four-credit-hour courses (Global Experience, College Writing, and Mathematics) and a two-credit-hour wellness course. As described by Braye and Midgette, Elon adopted the four-credit-hour courses in 1992–1993 during a reevaluation of general studies and at a time of great dissatisfaction with teaching loads and the number of students in each class section. The change from the traditional three-credit-hour course structure to the four-credit-hour course system not only reduced the number of courses and students in each class; it also provided a "fourth hour" for more in-depth course content, working in teams, and integrating out-of-class learning with course goals and objectives. As described in several interviews, the faculty took an "intentional risk" to do something different. At the time, all faculty members were not convinced of the value of four-credit-hour courses, and the credit hour change came after a narrow vote of fifty-five to forty-five. Yet in what was described as "Elon tradition," the faculty pulled together after the vote to make the new system work.

The adoption of the four-credit-hour course launched a year of workshops and discussions for rebuilding general studies and working out the details of the change from three- to four-hour courses. Ultimately, it was determined that these courses could have greater depth and could include an experiential component. The credit hour change is also reported to work well with Elon's four-one-four calendar of a fifteen-week fall semester, a three-week winter term, and a fifteen-week spring semester.

The importance of Elon's first-year core is difficult to overstate; it is embedded in a deliberate plan of general education, and it provides a cohesive, coherent, objective-driven program of study for students in the first year. During student interviews, we discovered that students could describe the core, knew its objectives, and saw it as an integrating force across the first year, even when they were dissatisfied with a single course or section. Through this core, Elon has largely escaped the Achilles heel of general education: too many courses, loosely connected, unfocused in purpose, and difficult to assess. The first-year core extends over the first year, and students are encouraged to take two of the four prescribed courses each term. However, because of the intensity of the Global Experience and College Writing courses, students are not permitted to take those two courses during the same term.

Building on Elon's faculty-to-student ratio of one to sixteen, all of the classes are small, averaging twenty-three students. The general studies courses are no exception. The accessibility of faculty and the small class sizes were endorsed by a number of students:

> She never shuts me off. She never gets tired of seeing me. She is always there. I really appreciate that. [This was in reference to help needed in a course.]

> Professors are really accessible. Like I have e-mailed with Professor [name] a lot and he is always like, he will always responds to my e-mail within twelve hours. And all of my professors are like that. Like any questions I have. I don't have any TAs or anything.

> When I think of Elon I think of how pretty it is. And, how small it is, and I take comfort in that when I am away from home. And the small class sizes really help. . . . And she [the faculty member] is willing to stay after any time, and you can e-mail her any time for help. Things like that really help a lot.

Elon's president, Leo Lambert, describes the required Global Experience course as the signature for the first year: "It is the best of what we believe . . . engaging, interdisciplinary, challenging." The Global Experience course (GST 110) is taught by faculty from across the disciplines. Faculty have latitude in the selection of resources, content, and activities, and occasionally the variety in course content and activities across sections creates concern for some students. But in spite of some differences in approach, the Global Experience courses have two primary features in common: the course focus must be global, and the students must attend to the six course goals.

GST 110 is an interdisciplinary course that mixes pedagogical methods, disciplinary perspectives, and wide-ranging content. The intention of the course is to move students from a dualistic view of the world to recognizing cultural, economic, social, and religious complexity surrounding global understanding. The common reading before the first year begins sets this educational exploration for global understanding into motion. In describing the course, one first-year student said, "It gets you thinking outside the box, and I know that is one of the goals. That is one of the main purposes. All of the materials may be really extreme, to one side, but that is to get you thinking; they want to open your horizons to why you come to college."

Faculty members teaching GST 110 are energized by the challenge. Because our visit to Elon coincided with the weekly global faculty lunch sponsored by the administration, we were able to view closely the commitment to teaching and learning represented by faculty members. They discussed pedagogical challenges, instructional resources, and various issues related to course design, delivery, and assessment. The Global Experience course aims to build a global perspective and whet the student's appetite for learning beyond the disciplines, for service work, and study abroad. The faculty were engrossed in these topics. Global Experience is the showpiece of the first-year core.

English 110, a course capped at twenty students per section, is the primary writing course in the core. The development of writing skills is a primary goal for Elon students, emphasized not only in English 110 but also across general education. In the pursuit to engage students at all levels in leadership, sophomores serve as writing fellows in the writing tutorial laboratory. A review of documents and other assessments shows that writing is central to both the first-year core and the general studies curriculum. A general statistics course and a wellness course are the other two components of the general studies core.

Throughout Elon's core, there is evidence of multiple levels of faculty involvement and interactions around courses and cocurricular activities. The goals for Elon's core are clearly communicated, and the responsibility for implementation of the core is shared and linked in important ways. To make the core work, the four required courses for all first-year students are overseen by faculty coordinators, who receive release time to monitor the content and quality of the courses and to work with the faculty teaching the various sections.

In contrast to the prescribed first-year core, students are given wide latitude in course selection in the liberal studies portion of general studies; nevertheless, students must complete eight credit hours in each of four areas: expression, civilization, society, and science/analysis. In advanced studies, students complete eight credit hours in advanced courses and one general studies interdisciplinary seminar.

Experiential Learning Requirement

A final component of general studies is the completion of experiential learning activities. Although these activities do not carry academic credit, they are required of all students and are recorded on the academic transcript. Through this requirement, students become active participants through involvement with what is being studied. Students must plan, implement, and draft a reflection paper exploring the experience. Each step is completed in collaboration with an adviser. Students may satisfy this forty-hour requirement through field-based courses like study abroad and internships, service or volunteer activities, leadership on campus, and independent activities that allow for observation, engagement, and reflection.

Elon Experiences: First Year and Beyond

While the required core is at the heart of the first year, the cocurricular program, known as the "Elon Experiences," provides the test-bed for experiential learning.

Elon Experiences comprise five cocurricular programs that provide the applied learning and experiential vitality of the undergraduate program. These programs include study abroad, service learning, leadership development, internships and co-ops, and undergraduate research. Clearly, not every student will participate in these experiences during the first year. Nevertheless, they are carefully woven into the academic life of Elon and are intended to create seamless educational opportunities across the college years. The anticipation of participation in Elon Experiences focuses the first-year student on returning each year to Elon and on deliberately charting a path of academic and cocurricular activities until graduation.

The Elon Experiences are coordinated by the faculty and supported by the Office of Student Life under the leadership of Smith Jackson, the vice president for student life and dean of students. Jackson is an administrator who came to Elon in 1994. Consequently, he has participated in developing student life programs from the ground up. A key to the success of the experiences is the awarding of academic credit for study abroad, academic service programs, and undergraduate research. Together, both credit and noncredit experiences were deliberately crafted to reflect the important values of the university and of the Elon student:

An ethic of service to others
An appreciation for cultural diversity

A productive work ethic

A commitment to civic responsibility

A desire to learn independently [Elon University, Elon Experiences, Year-end report, 2001–2002]

The discussion of these values begins in the first year in the core curriculum, and the values are experienced across the college career in the programs that are briefly described below.

Study Abroad

Elon University is first in the nation among comprehensive institutions in the percentage of students studying abroad. In 2001–2002, 58 percent of seniors had at least one study-abroad experience, and 643 students studied in twenty-seven countries. The majority of these students, 501, traveled and studied during the popular winter term, but study abroad may also occur over a semester or entire year. Students may choose from more than a dozen study-abroad courses, which typically carry four hours of credit.

Continuing the tradition of total campus involvement in curricular and cocurricular activities, secretaries, junior staff, and others in traditionally nonacademic units are brought annually into planning and participating in study abroad. President Lambert was quick to point out the advantage of staff involvement in study abroad, noting an enhancement of their commitment to the students and university mission and goals.

Study abroad is not programmed into the first year, but it is at this point that the expectations for global study and exploration are set. As students explore curricular and cocurricular opportunities in Elon 101 and learn about the world in Global Studies 110, student interest in study abroad escalates. The question between students moves from, "Will you go on study abroad?" to "Where will you go for study abroad?"

Service-Learning

Programs that emphasize service to others are foundational to Elon's leadership goals for students: ethical decision making, respecting diversity, and developing leadership and team-building skills. In Elon 101, first-year students learn of the Elon expectation for service and the opportunities to serve. This early introduction to service has a lasting impact across the undergraduate experience; more than 80 percent of seniors in 2002 had participated in some form of service. The Kernodle Center for Service Learning connects students to service opportunities through service programs, organizations, events, agencies, and courses. The center also offers first-year students a chance to live together, conduct monthly service-learning projects, and reflect on those in a group setting. Approximately thirty first-year students are selected for this service-learning community in Chandler Residence Hall.

In 2001–2002, Elon students completed more than 58,800 hours of service. Over 20,000 hours were generated by over 1,100 students who participated in service programs and organizations (for example, Habitat for Humanity). Course-linked service-learning generated over 10,000 hours of service by over 500 students. Twenty-six courses across the curriculum include a service-learning component as part of the course requirements.

Leadership Development

The leadership program at Elon started in 1992 and, along with the service program, was originally housed in academic affairs. The leadership program is currently administrated by the Division of Student Life through the Center for Leadership and Organization Development. The leadership program has strong connections to both academics and student services, connections that foster close communication and shared goals for student growth and engagement. The student affairs staff member who directs the Center for Leadership and Organization Development stressed the close relationship between student life and the faculty: "The workshops and activities we would have our students participate in are typically led by faculty or students and/or staff members. . . . One of our premier professors just did a personal mastery workshop for our emerging leaders. The dean of the School of Business just did our ethical leadership piece for our new students. So we've really tried to integrate that with their academics."

The process of leadership development at Elon is highly organized and is largely run by students for students. The Center for Leadership and Organization Development oversees the collection and validation of each student's leadership role for the Elon Experiences transcript.

At the heart of the center's activities is the Isabella Cannon Leadership Program (ICLP) named for this 1924 Elon graduate who became the first female mayor of a capital city in the United States, Raleigh, North Carolina. The complete ICLP is planned as a four-year program, but students may participate in the first year only or may come into the program in subsequent years. Students who complete all four phases are designated Isabella Cannon Leadership Fellows.

During the interviews, one staff person noted the quality of these programs and their influence on her decision to apply to work at Elon: "I'm at Elon because I met people who graduated from Elon when I was working somewhere else, and they would graduate and come to this national nonprofit. And I thought, these people have really good skills that I don't see in a lot of other students when they graduate. They just come out a lot more prepared. I thought, they must be doing something right there, these people are fantastic! I thought I better come find out."

First-year students indicated that they were well aware of the leadership opportunities and expectations for leadership development at Elon, and for many this was influential in the decision to attend this university.

Internships and Undergraduate Research

The final two of the five Elon Experiences, internships and undergraduate research, are aimed at upperclass students, opportunities that are introduced in Elon 101. In 2001–2002, over 600 junior and senior students participated in co-op or internship experiences at 587 sites. In 2000–2001, in collaboration with Elon faculty, approximately 150 upper-level students participated in over 100 research presentations at the Student Undergraduate Research Forum, and in 2001–2002, twenty-one students presented their work at the National Conference on Undergraduate Research.

Fellows Programs

In addition to the first-year core and the Elon Experiences, the university offers several "fellows" programs for selected populations of first-year and upperclass students. The programs include Elon College Fellows, North Carolina Teaching Fellows, Honors Fellows, Isabella Cannon Leadership Fellows, Jefferson Pilot Business Fellows, and Journalism and Communications Fellows. These cohorts of fellows share special courses, guaranteed internships, paid research assistantships, faculty mentoring, grants for study abroad, and scholarships of various values. These programs typically begin in the first year, and students may be eligible for participation across four years.

Documenting the Elon Experiences

In summary, the programs that comprise the Elon Experiences are important avenues for students to engage in seamless, cocurricular learning throughout the undergraduate years that is experiential, holistic, and purposeful. In recognition of these important outcomes, students record their experiences on an Elon Experiences transcript, a companion document to the Elon academic transcript. Faculty advisers use the Elon Experiences transcript in combination with the academic transcript during preregistration to advise students about curricular and cocurricular alternatives to achieve academic and career goals. As seen in our visit, first-year students seem eager to engage in and record the Elon experiences.

Culture of Assessment

The direction of Elon's first-year experience was set by a vision and adherence to a well-articulated mission, but improvements have largely been built on benchmarks established by assessment and evaluation. Beginning with the first Elon 101 course over twenty years ago, the faculty and staff asked, "What went right? What went wrong? And how can we improve?" Today, extensive assessment occurs around not only Elon 101 but also the overall first year and general studies. National instruments in regular use include the Cooperative Institutional Research Program's (CIRP) *Freshman Survey* (administered by UCLA's Higher Education Research Institute), the *Your First College Year* (YFCY) end-of-first-year survey, and the *College Student Report* from the National Survey of Student Engagement (NSSE).

Elon University collects and uses data. For example, findings from years of administering CIRP were instrumental in revising Elon's experiential activities, resulting in greatly expanded study-abroad and internship opportunities. CIRP testing is done during new student orientation in the fall, and in the spring, Elon administers YFCY in the English and Global Experience core courses, thereby reaching a majority of first-year students. YFCY was first administered in 2002–2003, and it serves as a companion to the CIRP freshman survey. Findings from YFCY confirm the high levels of student-faculty interaction and program quality. Elon students are satisfied or very satisfied with the amount of contact with faculty (86 percent), the overall educational experience (84 percent), and the overall quality of instruction (84 percent), to name only three items. From the results of an administration of the Core Survey on Alcohol and Drug Use, Elon also built an alcohol information program, which was ultimately incorporated into the core course on wellness.

Based on its long-standing commitment to assessment, Elon was one of 276 institutions participating in the first administration of NSSE. Findings from NSSE and other evaluation instruments led Elon faculty to redesign the first-year core course in mathematics as an introduction to statistics.

In addition to nationally normed instruments, Elon systematically assesses specific first-year programs and activities with locally designed approaches. In April each year, classes are suspended for Assessment Day, when first- and second-year students participate in holistic assessments of their experience at Elon. First-year students return to their Elon 101 groups and meet with the advisers and student assistants to discuss the first year. Data are collected from both student participants and student leaders. Summaries of these meetings are merged to provide an overall assessment of the first year to the assistant director of academic advising. A report available to the campus is generated from the merged data. Elon's first-year survey, in its tenth year of administration, also provides valuable data on faculty-student interaction, undergraduate research, intellectual and cultural programming, and program satisfaction. This survey monitors Elon's progress and has proven helpful in providing internal feedback and telling the university's story of success to parents, prospective students, and other external constituencies.

Elon also surveys faculty on a three-year cycle. The University of California, Los Angeles (UCLA) Higher Education Research Institute Faculty Survey, administered in 1998 and 2001, provided a glimpse into faculty attitudes about the college, commitment to students, the first-year experience, and Elon's experiential cocurriculum. Ninety-six percent of those faculty responding said that faculty are interested in students' personal problems, 70 percent had taught an interdisciplinary course, and 69 percent had participated in a teaching development workshop. These data, along with other student and faculty data, provide a broad perspective on the activities and outcomes of the first year.

Based on findings from national and local assessments, several changes are in progress. Because Elon is now attracting students with stronger academic backgrounds and precollege curricular preparation, orientation weekends are becoming more academic in direction, undergraduate research opportunities are increasing, and general studies curricula are tweaked to align goals, experiences, and outcomes more closely.

Assessment is part of the culture of Elon University. The director of institutional research praised the university's senior staff for their willingness to seek and use data for improvement purposes. Recently, the institutional research office decided to reduce the number of reports to focus more on the quality of analysis and to be more strategic in analysis and reporting. Reports are routinely shared with senior staff, the dean's council, and department heads.

Elon's Keys to Success

The keys to Elon's success lie in assessment; presidential, administrative, and faculty leadership; commitment to community and academic excellence; and an organizational structure that supports shared decision making and responsibility. It was leadership from trustees and a president that brought the campus facilities at Elon to the stature they enjoy today. Without former President Fred Young's vision for the physical plant and landscape, it is possible that Elon might not have achieved its current status. Yet without substantive and quality programs, colleges cannot excel. The success of Elon is in the marriage of both.

Administrative Commitment

Elon has a collegial, mission-driven, and experienced upper-level administration. While the position of associate provost was created only three years ago and the position of director of general studies ten years ago, these key positions are filled with leaders who have been at Elon for two decades. The associate dean of academic support, Lela Faye Rich, who launched Elon 101 over twenty years ago, is still at Elon providing leadership to the Office of Academic Advising. Similarly, Smith Jackson, the vice president for student life and dean of students, is a long-term administrator involved in developing programs of service, leadership, and the Elon Experiences. Gerald Francis, the provost/vice president for academic affairs, a central figure in supporting, both financially and philosophically, the ideas that bubble up from the faculty and staff, has been a faculty member at Elon for thirty years and has served in administration for twenty years. Elon University knows how to combine tradition with innovation, and this skill is evidenced in the recruitment of new campus leaders. Steven House, dean of Elon College (the College of Arts and Sciences), has been on campus less than two years, but he fully supports Elon's tradition and mission and is an advocate for Elon 101.

The highest-risk act in collegiate hiring is the selection of a new president and the energy or disruption brought to a campus by that decision. Leo Lambert is a dynamic president who came to Elon on January 1, 1999. His management and leadership style is backed by hands-on experience at multiple levels at prior institutions. For example, he has been director of a living-learning center, founder of an award-winning program for preparing future professors, overseer for a school-to-college academic program, instructor in first-year seminars, founder of an undergraduate research program, and catalyst for programs of international student and faculty exchanges. He has written extensively on university teaching and participated in several national projects focused on the improvement of and preparation for faculty careers. He is a past board member of the American Association of Higher Education. Elon needed and wanted someone whose principles and experience were aligned with the Elon mission, but whose vision and leadership skills could carry the institution to higher levels of excellence and national prominence in the first year of college and beyond. Lambert fit that bill.

Presidential Vision

One of our first campus interviews took place with Lambert. We found him to be energetic, open to ideas, assessment oriented, and collaborative. He readily gave credit to the faculty, other administrators, and the "let's make it work" model that is the foundation for management. He cited the most important word at Elon as *community*. He spoke of civility and not letting the human issues fall by the wayside. During the three-day visit, various descriptions of Elon emerged from multiple sources and documents, and these personal stories of Elon gave substance and confirmation to the president's words.

When asked to identify the central message to other institutions striving for excellence in the first year, Lambert said, "Very simple. Walk the talk about being student centered. The central question for decision making is, 'What is the best for students?'" He described a team approach to decision making whereby student affairs and academic affairs work closely together. He encourages "playing in the other person's sandbox. No walls." He notes, however, that the changes at Elon did not come overnight and in many ways were two decades in development.

Innovation at Elon is fueled not only by the enthusiasm and energy of the administrators and faculty: the president established a fund to leverage change. In the open session with faculty, several of them gave examples of individual projects for improvement and the funding they received through this competitive process. Awards in the range of $2,000 were often the springboard for larger accomplishments.

In paraphrasing the president, in the end, it is all about people. It is about fostering communication, creating community on campus, and hiring those who share an awareness of the important mission of Elon and the role of general education. During our visit, Lambert emphasized faculty participation in decision making, a philosophy of "come let us reason together." In teaching the skills of teamwork and collaboration to students, it appears that the president, the faculty, and the administration have internalized and practiced these skills in their relationships with each other.

Shared Decision Making and Responsibility

Clearly, leadership by the president and upper-level administrators is important to the success of Elon's first-year initiatives; of equal importance is the faculty's commitment to the first year and the practice of faculty participation in decision making and shared governance. The administration and the faculty, working in collaboration, have created a community of inquiry and engagement. The exchange of ideas is encouraged, and committees are intentional, focused around fulfilling the mission, and organized around putting students first. Reporting lines on campus support routine collaboration and communication between academic and student affairs units; the chief student affairs officer reports to the provost, who takes the lead in focusing on student learning. The dean of arts and sciences, although new to the campus, observed that the strength of Elon is in long-range planning and building and sustaining community. As a specific example of planning, Student Life Vice President Smith Jackson stated that the campus administration made a strategic decision to prioritize the development of educational programs and up-to-date facilities over the giving of scholarships and reduced tuition. And as another administrator described the decision: "We increased tuition, got better students, and grew in numbers! Some said it couldn't be done; and Elon has done it!"

Enhancing and Maintaining Community

Community is a word heard often at Elon. The leadership of Elon builds community through being accessible and being committed. As we toured the campus, we noted that every student seemed to be able to call faculty and administrators by their names, and the administrators or faculty members could reply in turn. "College Coffee," held on Tuesday mornings around Fonville Fountain, symbolizes the close connections the community members feel for each other. Whether it is coffee, cake, ice cream, or pie, the campus—including large numbers of faculty, administrators, and students—stops, takes a break, and communicates. Held inside during our campus visit because of threatening rain, there was elbow room only in the large hall on this typical Tuesday in the fall.

Prior to the beginning of each fall semester, Elon University holds a week-long faculty and staff planning session. This is a signal event that supports the building of community and faculty planning to ensure effectiveness. The planning conference begins with the president's address, the awarding of medallions for meritorious service, and introduction of new faculty and staff. During the week, deans meet with department chairs, and new faculty are inducted into the Elon system and substrata. Orientation for new faculty is extensive; it begins with the new faculty mentor lunch and continues throughout the year with regular meetings to introduce faculty to the Elon culture and to support faculty when help is needed.

While numerous sessions are organized for new faculty, equally impressive is the schedule of meetings that focus on courses and activities featured in the first year. Workshops are held for faculty teaching the core courses: Math 112, English 110, Global Studies 110, and Wellness Issues. New and returning faculty meet to discuss Elon 101, and other workshops are designed for faculty and staff working with special populations (such as mentors of undergraduate research and advisers for international students) and special issues (for example, technology and computing, library).

In a fine stroke of coordination, the end of the faculty and staff planning conference overlaps the beginning of fall orientation for new students. Thus, faculty members are on campus and ready to participate in this important welcoming and orientation event. Several administrators expressed concern about maintaining community as the university grows in number of students and faculty.This dedication, not to lose community, resonates throughout the university community.

Guiding the Future: New Century@Elon

Building on its current strength and planning for the future, Elon University has developed a blueprint for excellence: the New Century@Elon. This strategic plan names three primary goals for advancing to the next stage of achievement: to enhance academic excellence, provide facilities to support excellence, and provide resources to support excellence. A look at the current leadership, achievements, and strategic decisions leads one to believe that these and more will be accomplished for the first year and beyond.

Chapter Nine

West Point and the Plebe-Year Experience

The Long Gray Line

Michael J. Siegel

John N. Gardner

Many educators might be surprised to learn that one of the nation's most elite institutions of higher education—a military academy with a highly structured and historically rigid environment—is deeply concerned about the success of its entering students. The very name of the institution, the United States Military Academy, conjures up any number of images: unrelenting pressure on cadets to perform and succeed; the dogged pursuit of precision in military training exercises; the development of the warrior ethos; and perhaps the hard-nosed treatment that new cadets, or plebes, endure.

Justified or not, these images have dominated the public's perception of the academy throughout its long history. But a major change has occurred over the years at the academy, and an institution that once embodied a survival-of-the-fittest mentality now prides itself on building a success-oriented community of cadets with increased attention to peer responsibility and the well-being of fellow cadets.

The U.S. Military Academy, or West Point, is located fifty miles from New York City on the banks of the Hudson River. As the nation's oldest engineering school, West Point has been in operation for over 200 years. In addition to serving the country as an elite military academy, it is considered one of the nation's premier institutions of higher education. Founded on March 16, 1802, West Point has grown considerably in size, stature, and function, but it has adhered to the primary task of producing commissioned leaders for the U.S. Army. Chief among the goals of the academy is to develop the warrior ethos in its future leaders, and the current level of conflict around the world suggests that many officers who leave the academy will experience war at some point in their careers. The student body, known as the Corps of Cadets, numbers approximately 4,150; 15 percent are women.

West Point's campus is both awe inspiring and arresting. Immediately on entering the front gate area of the academy, which doubles as a military police checkpoint, visitors undergo a rigorous security screening process that seems more appropriately suited for a high-security government building or prison than a college campus. It is a daunting experience, particularly in a post-9/11 environment in which overwhelming attention is focused on the military and related security measures. The arrival procedure at West Point was unlike any other that our team members experienced at any other campus during the course of this study. In lieu of the proverbial pleasant waves received from faculty members and fresh-faced students as we passed through entrance gates on many other campuses, we encountered at West Point the waving arms of serious security guards with automatic rifles and waiting to question visitors and dignitaries alike about the nature of their visit and the contents of their automobiles.

After being cleared through security, we took a scenic drive onto the campus that revealed an imposing array of gray-colored granite buildings, intramural and military exercise fields, chapels, cannons and other armaments, and statues of former West Point cadets and soldiers whose names are synonymous with past American military conflicts. The culture of the academy, with its rich history, traditions, and norms of behavior, is instantly palpable. It is evident in the mess halls, in the classrooms, and on the many fields that serve as training grounds for future officers in the U.S. Army. Everything within the academy's walls has a place and a purpose.

The academy graduates more than 900 new officers annually; this represents approximately 25 percent of the new lieutenants required by the U.S. Army each year. The West Point application and admissions process is much different from that at traditional civilian colleges and universities in that applicants are nominated from states and congressional districts by either a congressman or senator. Each of the 435 representatives and 100 senators is allowed to nominate two individuals. Those nominated then have to undergo a complete medical exam and pass a rigorous physical aptitude test. With respect to its admissions criteria, West Point weights three characteristics according to the following percentages: academic ability, 60 percent; leadership potential, 30 percent; and physical aptitude, 10 percent. The formula for balancing the enrollment process and selecting students from each of the country's congressional districts makes West Point, along with the other U.S. service academies, unique among America's elite colleges and universities. Because students hail from all regions of the country, and thus from high schools of varying degrees of quality, there is a wide range of academic abilities, academic preparation, and other important skills represented in the cadet population. Therefore, West Point's inclusion as one of thirteen Institutions of Excellence is in large part related to its attention to developing civilian students, who represent a diverse range of abilities, into future leaders in the army and its ongoing commitment to assessment and evaluation of the first year.

Cadets may major in a wide range of disciplines, including behavioral sciences and leadership, civil and mechanical engineering, chemistry and life science, electrical engineering and computer sciences, foreign languages, English, geography and environmental engineering, history, law, mathematical sciences, systems engineering, physics, and social sciences. All graduates earn a bachelor of science degree in addition to being commissioned as a second lieutenant in the army. Following graduation from West Point, cadets are required to perform a minimum of five years of active-duty service in exchange for the free education that has been provided for them. Over 50,000 cadets have graduated from West Point since its founding in 1802 to become part of what is proudly referred to as "The Long Gray Line."

A caveat about the language and nomenclature used at the academy is necessary. Among the materials we received prior to our site visit was a glossary of terms that are commonly used at the academy. One of us had previously served in the military, and both of us had previously studied about the academy and knew colleagues who had either attended the institution as students or had taught there as instructors. Therefore, we were familiar with some of the terms. Nonetheless, there was a plethora of additional academy-specific words and phrases we needed to know and understand, not only to conduct our interviews but also to be able to match those terms with equivalent terms that are predominantly used in the higher education lexicon.

For instance, institutions refer to entering students as freshmen or first-year students; West Point refers to entering students as plebes. As we learned from Lieutenant Colonel Bill Adams, the director of the Center for Enhanced Performance and one of our hosts for the visit, first-year students at the academy are called plebes or fourth-class cadets, sophomores are yearlings or third-class cadets, juniors are cows or second-class cadets, and seniors are firsties or first-class cadets. To be expelled from the academy is referred to as "separation" or "being separated" from the academy. These are just some of the examples that suggest differences, at least linguistically, between the academy and other institutions of higher education.

The West Point Mission

The West Point mission, as recorded on the academy's Web site, is "to educate, train, and inspire the Corps of Cadets so that each graduate is a commissioned leader of character committed to the values of Duty, Honor, Country; professional growth throughout a career as an officer in the United States Army; and a lifetime of selfless service to the nation."

In addition, as the director of admissions, Colonel Michael Jones, indicated during our site visit, West Point's mission is "to be the Army's undergraduate institution." Furthermore, he stressed the idea that the academy is interested in nurturing its cadets from application through graduation, a fact mentioned by multiple individuals during our visit. In fact, the academy, as Jones stated, starts buying lists of information about students at the eighth-grade level. After interested students respond to the academy, they are put into what is called a "nurturing database." It is evident the recruitment and admissions process for future cadets begins well before plebes arrive on campus.

The Core Tenets of the Academy

The three underlying tenets of the academy, as spelled out in the promotional and admissions materials that are sent out to prospective cadets, are duty, honor, and country.

The information given to prospective cadets outlines all policies, practices, and procedures that affect the first-year cadet experience, including travel to the academy, drug and alcohol policies, clothing and personal grooming considerations, finances, and what is expected of cadets in their first year. Candidates who are officially accepted and enter West Point, for instance, are reimbursed for their direct travel to the academy from their home at the beginning of their plebe year.

While all colleges have certain strictures and standards to which first-year students must adhere, West Point's standards are unique among the colleges and universities in the Institutions of Excellence study, especially rules related to personal items, clothing, and grooming. There are restrictions on the amount of money, clothing, furniture, and other items that cadets may bring with them to the academy. For instance, cadets are instructed to have no more than $40 in bills and $1 in pocket change, and any money over that amount will be turned in to the treasurer of the academy and deposited into the cadet's account for future use. In addition, there is a set of stipulations about new cadet grooming. Although these stipulations are primarily unique to military academy life, they are worth mentioning because they offer a glimpse into the standardization of behaviors that underscore the cadet first-year experience. And they provide a context as well. According to "Instruction for Candidates Offered Admissions":

> All New Cadets will be required to maintain their hair in accordance with standard operating procedure for the United States Corps of Cadets. Male candidates should arrive clean shaven, since beards and mustaches are not authorized as a cadet. Male candidates SHOULD NOT arrive with a shaved head. . . . During CBT [cadet basic training], New Cadet women must maintain a hairstyle that is easy to maintain and requires only minimal time to prepare for training.

As life for all West Point cadets is extremely demanding physically, minimum standards of performance for push-ups, sit-ups, and multimile runs are required for entering cadets. They are advised to begin a formal program of running and other exercise prior to their arrival on campus. Finally, the only civilian clothes new cadets are allowed to bring with them are the ones they are wearing when they arrive at the academy at the beginning of the year.

The Core Tenets of the Plebe Year Experience

The West Point community is organized to support and assist cadets in excelling in the "three pillars of cadet life": academic, military, and physical development. This is a balanced and comprehensive approach to developing the whole student. The moral-ethical development of cadets, the overarching goal of a West Point education, is integrated across the three areas and permeates the plebe experience as well as the full four-year cadet experience, known euphemistically in the West Point lexicon as the "47-Month Journey." (This number reflects the nearly four full years a cadet will spend at West Point. With few exceptions, the academy requires cadets to complete the academic program within eight semesters and four years.) The mantra of the 47-month journey is widely used, and it is a reflection of an institution with a well-developed sense of purpose. As the associate dean for academic affairs, Bruce Keith, remarked, "We have developed a 47-month experience to integrate purpose. We are very clear on mission and purpose. . . . We believe we have the correct balance to achieve our goals."

There is some congruence between how West Point trains cadets to become soldiers in the military and how other colleges and universities prepare students to enter the workforce. Business, civic, and other community leaders convey information, tacitly or otherwise, about the types of skills and qualifications they would like to see in future employees. In the same manner, commanders in the field and leaders of various military units have a mental picture of the ideal officer, and that information informs what the academy does to produce that type of cadet. For that reason, the military program at West Point has as its goal the development of what is called "the warrior ethos," which is the "will to win, not to quit," according to Lieutenant Colonel Casey Neff, the special assistant to the commandant for strategic planning. As he said, "The goal is not to produce a Patton, but a leader with a common set of skills for use in any of the sixteen branches of the army, a skill set that is the foundation for further education within that branch."

The academy's commandant is responsible for both the military and the physical instruction, and the dean is responsible for the academic curriculum of the academy. The commandant and the dean, both brigadier generals, report to the superintendent, who is the equivalent of a college president on a civilian college campus. The vice dean, who conducted a briefing-like open forum during our site visit, reports to the dean.

Support Services at the Academy: Leaving No Plebe Behind

To help cadets succeed in this environment, the academy offers a sophisticated network of support services, training experiences, tutoring opportunities, and sponsorship programs for plebes. The following components are organized for the successful administration of the plebe year:

- Cadet basic training
- Core academic curriculum, additional instruction, and faculty mentoring
- Center for Enhanced Performance, Tutor Program, Student Success Course, and the Student Behavior Inventory
- Cadet leadership development and mentorship
- Fourth-class sponsorship program

Cadet Basic Training

Many American college students consider it challenging to make the transition from high school to college only three months after they graduate from high school. The same can be said of new West Point cadets, who have to make a transition not only from high school to college but also from citizen to soldier. To prepare them for that transition, West Point requires every plebe to complete cadet basic training (CBT), an intensive six-week period of orientation to the military with requisite drills, training exercises, and physical development that begin at 5:30 A.M. and end at 10:00 P.M. each day. During this period, all plebes sign an oath of allegiance that outlines cadets' responsibilities to the army and indicates their willingness "to bear allegiance to the National Government and defend the sovereignty of the United States." By signing the oath, cadets also agree to complete the course of instruction at the academy, and if tendered an appointment as a commissioned officer in one of the armed services, to serve on active duty for no fewer than five consecutive years immediately after the appointment.

As the cornerstone of the West Point experience for entering plebes, CBT is the first orientation to the academy's leadership development system. Approximately 1,200 cadets enter West Point each year and spend six weeks learning the basics of soldiering, military standards and operations, and cadet discipline. CBT is a rigorous and physically challenging experience, and it is intentionally designed to be stressful so that emotional stability and physical endurance under pressure can be adequately measured and developed. It is more than simply a physical boot camp; new cadets are also introduced to the academy's academic program through a series of placement tests and assessments. To understand what life is like during CBT, it is best to turn to the words of a cadet:

> July 2. I will never forget that day. CBT = Beast = six weeks. The objective of that is to introduce [you] to the military. . . . They break you down before they build you up. They adapt you to a new society. You have to be on top of a high school totem pole to get in [to the academy]. When you have those who are two years older—juniors and seniors—yelling at you, [you are] no longer at the top. I realize I have things to learn, and I have to follow others to understand the academy. It puts everyone on an equal playing field.

The emphasis of CBT is on military and physical development. During these six weeks, all new cadets complete a class characteristics inventory, which documents demographic information and provides measures of cadet attitudes, goals, and the level of preparation they bring to their experience. Data from the survey are designed to provide West Point personnel baseline information about entering students' characteristics. Following the successful completion of CBT, cadets begin the plebe year and the academic program. One lieutenant colonel's assessment of CBT reflects the sense of responsibility West Point personnel have in ensuring that cadets make it through the system; it also underscores the rigorous nature of cadet life and the responsibility the cadets have to stay on task and perform at an optimal level. Brigadier General Leo Brooks, the academy's second African American commandant of cadets, described CBT as follows:

> If a cadet does not meet the standards, then we provide the remediation. Juniors are involved and they supervise nine to twelve new cadets. CBT has 4 percent to 6 percent attrition—we took in 1,203 last year, sixty-one did not complete, nineteen were medicals. Back in 1970, we had 10 percent built-in assumption for attrition. This attitude has changed significantly. We expect anyone who enters has the potential to graduate, and we want them to graduate.

The CBT experience culminates at the end of six weeks with a long march to a reservoir, a week-long bivouac, and then a fifteen-mile hike back to the academy. This hike has been an annual ritual and tradition for many years, and it represents a rite of passage for entering cadets. Lieutenant Colonel Neff remarked, "The old grads come back to march back with them—as old as seventy. Ceremony is very important to us." With its ceremonial nature, the march experience gives the cadets a sense of pride and accomplishment before they begin classes, and it announces that a new group of cadets has arrived on campus. The march is yet one more example of teaching cadets to rely on themselves and perform at their fullest potential.

Core Academic Curriculum, Additional Instruction, and Faculty Mentoring

The academic program at West Point is under the purview of the dean of the academic board. The program consists of core courses designed to provide cadets with a broad-based education in the humanities and sciences. The curriculum is continually under review and is informed by a detailed academic program goals plan. All first-year students take similar courses—called the common core—and there is little intellectual isolation. That is, cadets are encouraged to study and work collaboratively with their fellow classmates rather than be isolated in their studies. There is a balance in the core between basic science, math, engineering, and social sciences, and the core runs across all four years. Plebes share a common experience that is intended to be a support mechanism. To ensure the common experience, each core course has standardized content as well as lesson objectives. In addition, the pedagogy in use at the academy is based on an active learning model whereby students are significantly engaged in classroom discussion and participation.

Comprising the plebe core are courses in composition and literature, American and world history, military science, physical education, computer science, psychology, and chemistry. Core course directors meet frequently to discuss and coordinate the delivery of the academic program and explore various classroom strategies, group projects, and other academic class assignments for plebe students. The faculty report to the dean, and approximately half of the military faculty are themselves West Point graduates.

Class sizes are small, with no more than eighteen cadets per class. This arrangement is intentionally maintained in the belief that small class instruction offers a more effective means to develop cadet confidence in the classroom and allows cadets to refine their academic skills. Each cadet receives a great deal of personal attention from the instructor not only in the classroom but outside the classroom if the cadet should need it. Cadets can also receive what is called additional instruction (AI) from their instructors. Similar to a professor's keeping office hours at a civilian college or university, AI is administered according to the needs of the cadet, and it allows students to get extra assistance with specific lesson plans and other assignments. According to Lisa D'Adamo-Weinstein, assistant director of West Point's Center for Enhanced Performance, students are proactive in getting assistance from instructors. The cadets themselves tell the same story; in fact, one cadet with whom we spoke talked appreciatively about having open access to instructors and being able to approach not only her instructors, but others in other subject areas as well. She said, "The AI is great—he gives out home and cell numbers. I have called him at 12:00 o'clock at night. . . . You can approach any teacher in the subject area; it does not have to be your teacher." Another cadet echoed the same sentiment: "Teachers look forward to hearing from the cadets. They tell us, 'If you need help, call me.'"

All majors are considered equal in the eyes of West Point. In past years, cadets predominantly majored in science and engineering, but with the advent of the liberal arts curriculum before World War II under Superintendent General Douglas MacArthur, there has been a significant increase of cadets selecting the humanities and social sciences. In fact, according to one official we met on our visit, some 55 percent of cadets major in the humanities and social sciences. But according to the vice dean for education, Colonel Barney Forsythe, "Ultimately the army is about 'boots on the ground.' The primary goal of a West Point education is to prepare young men and women for leadership positions in the army who can apply their expertise to solve the world's problems." Furthermore, Forsythe noted, "The challenge is to integrate the academic, the military, and the physical. . . . The army is our constituent. We have to connect our curriculum to the army's needs. We cannot train our graduates; we have to educate them broadly for a changing world. We have structured and organized the faculty into goal teams for the purposes of assessment."

West Point employs a special classroom pedagogy called the Thayer Method of teaching, which was developed by a reforming superintendent in the early days of the institution. The method is employed in the academy's small classes, where chairs are arranged in a horseshoe configuration so that every cadet ostensibly has a front row seat. As the assistant director of the Center for Enhanced Performance suggested, "Using the Thayer Method, the students are expected to have read the material the night before. In class, the instructor is not going to go over the reading. Instead, the instructor will apply the material. Students have a course guide that tells them what they are to be held responsible for, so there are no surprises."

During our visit, key West Point administrators and staff members conducted an open forum to describe in detail the components of the first-year experience and the ways in which various units and departments work together on campus. This presentation was designed to familiarize us with the policies and procedures that govern daily operations at the academy; it was also intended to give us an orientation to the culture, traditions, values, and norms of behavior. During the open forum, we were told that many instructors are selected from the field army because of their excellence as officers and practical knowledge in the field, and then are sent to graduate school for two years. They follow that experience with a minimum of three years of teaching, so faculty are fresh from rotating tours and graduate schools. The average number of students faculty teach per semester is approximately sixty, and given the personal attention that comes with these numbers, there is a strong need for, and desire to have, a robust faculty development program. As Vice Dean Forsythe indicated: "Teaching is job number one. Everything else feeds into that. Scholarship is . . . in . . . service to our teaching mission. We have a master teacher certification process. [And] faculty members also work with athletic teams and clubs so all faculty are involved in cadet development outside of the class. . . . We monitor grades—we monitor performance at the company level. Most faculty attracted here are interested in the student development end of things."

The words of one of the cadets with whom we talked indicates that students are aware that teaching is a priority at the academy: "The academy does not expect its teachers to have any other focus or responsibility except teaching. There are no research expectations."

One of the presenters at the open forum shared PowerPoint slides of some of the West Point faculty who were on assignment with the Tenth Mountain Division that went into Afghanistan. Upon their return, the faculty brought back what they had learned from the field into the classroom, an instance of practical teaching.

All students take placement exams during CBT. Cadets may be excused from (validate) certain core courses if they can demonstrate sufficient knowledge of a subject and can meet the appropriate department's standards. Credits earned at other colleges and scores on advanced placement exams are taken into consideration in validation decisions. All cadets must have a minimum of forty academic courses over their four-year experience in the academy. And since all first-year students take essentially the same courses, there is an embedded support structure that can readily be called on for assistance in academic courses. As one of our hosts noted, "We stress the importance of the common experience. . . . We do very extensive advising and counseling."

Center for Enhanced Performance, Tutor Program, Student Success Course, and the Student Behavior Inventory

The primary support network for the plebes and the catalyst through which the academy's first year is addressed is the Center for Enhanced Performance (CEP). The center, which is designed as a service to empower cadets and assist them in the three pillars of cadet life, consists of two programs: the reading and study skills program and the performance enhancement program. The center also provides professional development for the cadet chain of command—individuals who are responsible for support and development of cadets. This professional development includes tutor training, administrative support for the tutor program, and academic resources.

Plebes can also receive academic assistance from the company tutor program, a vast network of approximately 450 tutors from all of the thirty-two cadet companies. These tutor programs are organized at the company level by upperclass cadets, who are responsible for monitoring the academic progress of the entire company. As Lisa D'Adamo-Weinstein indicated during our visit, the tutors work primarily within their own companies, and with the high level of administrative organization, the companies become de facto communities of learning. The CEP provides administrative support to the company tutor program and the academic staff in each of the companies.

Cadets are given an overview and are exposed to the various academy programs during CBT, and they have the opportunity to request enrollment in one of three Center for Enhanced Performance courses: Student Success, Reading Efficiency, or Information Literacy and Critical Thinking. During the fall term, CEP courses are offered only to plebes, which further suggests more focused attention by the CEP on plebes during this critical time.

One of the courses that has become a staple at the academy is the Student Success Course, an elective course taken by many plebes and the most popular course of the three offered by CEP. Primarily it focuses on academic and cognitive skills for success. Approximately 450 plebes, or 37.5 percent of the entering class, take this course each fall. According to D'Adamo-Weinstein, assessment data indicate the course has a significant and positive impact on cadets' performance. In the narrative report submitted by West Point to the Policy Center on the First Year of College for the Institutions of Excellence project, the following assessment data described the effectiveness of the Student Success Course:

> Taking the Student Success Course increases cadets' academic GPA to 9.3 percent beyond predicted levels ($p = .002$) whereas those who do not take the course under-perform by 4.2 percent; increases graduation rates by 1 percent; and improves attitudes and behaviors towards learning ($p = .002$) as measured by the Study Behavior Inventory (SBI). Every plebe takes the SBI, which yields self-reported data on short-term and long-term study behaviors as well as academic confidence scales.

To facilitate the feedback process—vitally important when dealing with first-year students, let alone plebes at a military academy—plebes receive a customized report of the SBI based on their individual profile. Comprising the profile are the skills, behavior, and attitudes as measured by the SBI. The report allows cadets to assess their own attitudes and choices about how they spend their time and how they are performing as a cadet.

Cadet Leadership Development and Mentorship

Two of the primary components of plebe life at the academy are leadership development and plebe mentorship. The presence of these two elements is a clear indication that the academy is highly concerned with the successful assimilation of cadets. Team leaders provide individualized mentor-like relationships and leadership development opportunities to first-year students through what the academy refers to as the cadet chain of command, a complex command structure that informs the military ranking system and the units by which the military structure is subdivided. Expected behaviors and responsibilities for those in the chain are a function of where one is in the chain.

The team leader is part of the West Point command structure, which looks like this: one brigade comprises 4,000 cadets; each brigade includes four regiments, which have eight companies, for a total of thirty-two companies; each company has 125 cadets; within the company are three platoons, and within the platoon are three squads; finally, there are two teams per squad.

All plebes are assigned a team leader, a sophomore cadet from their company who is primarily responsible for plebe guidance. Team leaders are effective in helping entering cadets learn the cadet system and stay on track during their plebe year. After CBT, during the week before classes begin on campus, team leaders meet with plebes in their company and orient them to the basic tenets of the academy and cadet life, including the three pillars, the location of facilities and resources, campus technology, and company duties.

The importance of the chain-of-command structure, including team leaders, cannot be overstated. The notion of the peer leader model at West Point is different from what is found at civilian institutions. Although some educators may dismiss the chain of command or senior-subordinate responsibility idea as not adaptable to other institutions of higher education, we argue that the concept should at least be considered. The basic idea of the chain-of-command structure as related to the team leader concept is that each person in the command structure has some degree of responsibility to the person directly above and directly below him or her. So if a plebe is having extreme academic or behavioral difficulties, the team leader is part of the responsibility chain. In essence, poor performance reflects not only on the plebe but also on his or her team leader. If a cadet fails to meet performance standards, both that cadet and the team leader are held responsible. Cadets understand this responsibility, and it is ingrained in their education. Consider the following words of one of the cadets with whom we spoke: "[There is a] . . . theme of accountability. If you flunk, the chain of command will question why you didn't get help. There is an intense sense of accountability. Everybody here matters . . . everybody must succeed. A lot of teachers are alumni, so they can relate to us."

This concept of collective accountability for fellow students permeates the chain of command at all levels of the command structure; that is, accountability for others, both above and below one's own position in the chain of command, is stressed with administrators and faculty as well as students. We can only imagine the implications for civilian higher education if colleges and universities were to attempt to replicate this concept for teaching responsibilities, department evaluation and assessment, and other areas of college life.

Fourth Class-Sponsorship Program

In addition to the team leadership program, West Point has what is called a sponsorship program. Less formal in nature but equally as effective in terms of bringing a sense of community to the plebe experience, the sponsorship program is considered another entry point into the cadet socialization process. Plebes are assigned sponsors from the faculty and staff ranks, and sponsors are encouraged to get together with plebes on a voluntary basis. Essentially, each sponsor serves as a guide and mentor by talking to plebes about their experiences and offering them an outlet to decompress from the daily rigors of cadet life. Many at the academy with whom we spoke referred to the success of this program, indicating that it has a profound effect on plebes during their first year at West Point.

Sponsors commonly invite plebes to their homes (a significant number of faculty and staff live on campus), giving plebes an opportunity to relax for a brief time in a comfortable environment. Although the gatherings are informal in nature, plebes know they are to adhere to academy norms, values, and rules that govern behavior on and off campus. Plebes have to adhere to army standards twenty-four hours a day.

Assessment occurs even in the domain of the sponsorship program. Plebes are surveyed twice about their experiences with the program—once at the beginning of the year and once at the end—to ascertain if the sponsorship relationship is working out well. If it is not, plebes are assigned a new sponsor. The average faculty or staff member is responsible for sponsoring approximately four plebes. Both the team leadership and the sponsorship programs provide an intentional means by which plebes are introduced to the culture of the academy and offer an opportunity for entering students to interact with their peers as well as faculty and staff.

The West Point Honor Code

Undergirding the academic tradition at West Point is the cadet honor code to which every cadet must adhere. The honor code says simply: "A cadet will not lie, cheat, steal, or tolerate those who do." This is a prominent feature and a staple of the West Point experience, and as one administrator during our visit indicated, the honor code "helps maintain balance." All those associated with the academy live by this honor code, and it is impressed on first-year students the minute they arrive on the grounds as the guiding principle of the academy.

The academy distributes to all new plebes before they come to the academy a short video that outlines the tenets of the honor code and explores various plebe violations and the ramifications of committing violations. Academy administrators believe this intentional introduction is extremely important, given a cheating scandal that rocked the institution in the 1970s and affected a significant portion of West Point students.

The arrival of new plebes each year takes place at what is called Reception Day, or R-Day, where the nontoleration tenet is spelled out. Of particular note is the emphasis on the second part of the phrase: "or tolerate those who do." This statement underscores the importance of cadets' responsibility for one another and ensures there is a significant deterrent for one cadet's protection of another cadet who has violated any aspect of the code.

The Culture of Assessment at West Point

"From the minute they arrive at West Point until the day they graduate and receive their commission, cadets are constantly assessed and evaluated along multiple dimensions of their development" (United States Military Academy, 2002, p. 51). This quotation underscores the importance and centrality of assessment at West Point. Assessment and evaluation, not only of the cadets, but also the faculty, staff, programs, and services offered at the academy, are highly structured and deeply embedded in the West Point culture.

The culture of the academy, as befits a military institution, is one that supports constant assessment. Because of the need over the past two centuries in the life of the American military to provide assessments and evaluations of the dynamics of battlefield behavior—so-called after-action reviews—and the need to constantly improve the effectiveness of its troops, the U.S. Army has instilled in West Point the importance of assessment as being central to its mission. It is therefore intentionally designed and consistent throughout the entire academy.

Cadets take a battery of placement tests referred to as academic validation and testing. In addition, there are student grade reports at six, ten, and fifteen weeks, and there is a strong culture of open access for the rank-and-file employees, cadet leaders, and instructors at the academy to grades and other student academic information.

Students come to the academy realizing they must relinquish some of the privacy they might otherwise be afforded if they were at another institution.

The battery of tests and surveys that students complete on entry to the academy creates a profile of cadet needs, attitudes, and abilities and provides West Point leaders a baseline understanding of each entering class, allowing them to plan and implement the military and academic program accordingly. Each plebe class also completes a survey at the end of the first year, which is called the fourth-class survey. The survey asks cadets to reflect on their experience and evaluate the quality of their first year, including an appraisal of their work and efforts during the first year, an assessment of their experience with the three pillars of cadet life, and their impression of their interactions with their fellow cadets. This survey serves as a bookend to the first-class survey, which is administered to cadets when they graduate from West Point. Taken together, the surveys provide a comprehensive profile of the cadet experience and chart the physical, moral, cognitive, and social development of cadets as they move from plebe to graduate. As Associate Dean Bruce Keith indicated, "The most important piece is to use assessment primarily for improvement. We also use assessment for accountability purposes. We are accountable to the board of visitors, to Congress, to the accreditors. We start with the army's needs. Our perception of those needs leads to our vision and mission. We have articulated ten academic program goals and have a learning model for each."

The department on campus responsible for the collection of data on students is the Office of Policy, Planning and Assessment (OPPA). The OPPA uses aggregate data on the cadets to identify areas in the plebe year experience that need to be addressed by the academy and domains where resources and personnel can be more effectively used on campus. The data also give the academy tacit information about the nature of cadet life and the way in which plebes navigate their first year at West Point.

As a method of self-assessment, cadets are required to keep a personal officer development portfolio throughout their careers at the academy in order to develop and reinforce the value of reflection. These portfolios contain documents, reflective essays, and performance reports in all aspects of cadet development. In the end, the entire plebe class is assessed through surveys, personal reflection, course examinations and assignments, physical and military tests and competitions, cadet and officer observation reports, peer evaluations, and tactical exercises. Cadets receive evaluation of their performance formally through program scores in academics (similar to GPA), military development, and physical development.

Although at West Point, like nearly all other institutions of higher education, assessment is used for accountability purposes, what distinguishes the academy from many other colleges and universities is the number of external constituents to which the institution is accountable. In addition to the common stable of interest groups—boards of visitors, state and federal government interests, and accrediting agencies, to name a few—West Point is accountable to two other unique bodies: Congress and the U.S. Army. The academy starts with the army's needs, in terms of matters of physical and military programming, and the most important thrust of assessment is to use findings primarily for improvement. Assessment is the catalyst for measuring those program goals and the lever by which the goals will be continuously improved.

West Point Leadership: The Concept of Officership

The experience for new cadets is grounded in leadership development, the primary function of which is to prepare citizens for officership in the U.S. Army. The concept of officership is deeply embedded in the ethos of the institution, and the success of first-year cadets is a function of their ability to understand the role of and train for officership. Colonel Forsythe sets out here what it means to be an officer and outlines the philosophy related to the academy's role in the officer training process:

> What does it mean to be an officer? This is parsed into four overlapping roles and identities. Ultimately, it is about preparing, and when called upon, fighting and winning wars. War fighting is our profession. This is our body of expertise. After graduation, cadets have six to twelve months of specialty training in their branch, but this is the foundation. What they get here is the body of expertise. This is all about life-and-death issues. As officers, they are fundamentally servants. They are serving the client, and the client is the nation. The commission [as an officer] is the professional license

> to practice. We must know what responsibilities are attendant to legal status. The first fundamental professional value is duty. This is what officers do. We also must understand they are members of a profession. This is the corporate responsibility. A profession that has professional expertise, history, and tradition. [This is] a code of ethics, a set of values that guide the members of the profession.

The Future of the Academy and the Plebe Year Experience

During the past few decades, there has been a fundamental paradigm shift in West Point's philosophical and actual approach to military instruction, plebe education, and the training of cadets to become military personnel and soldiers. The current model of education, according to Brigadier General Daniel Kaufman, the dean of the academic board, is one that is developmental in nature, as opposed to a model of attrition that shaped the experiences of previous generations of West Point cadets. The dean, who ostensibly oversees all facets of the cadet academic program and is the equivalent of a vice president for academic affairs, shared thoughts about the changing goals and philosophy at the academy—from that of weeding out cadets to the intentional development of cadets. According to the dean, the philosophy and goal of the academic and military experience at West Point is "to close the gap between potential and performance." And as Vice Dean Forsythe indicated:

> We are preparing our grads to lead an army in the twenty-first century. We must be able to plan a mission, lead soldiers. No longer is the army saying, "We only do the big ones." We operate in 130 countries. We do everything from humanitarian relief, peace keeping, to preparing for significant armed conflict right now in Iraq. We are no longer focused on the cold war. It is no longer a bipolar world. Sometimes we are making this up as we go along. It requires that we be flexible, adaptive, creative leaders.

The success of the U.S. Military Academy is built around effective long-range planning. The various missions the army undertakes today are unique, and, as a result, the academy, according to Colonel Forsythe, needs to have a certain degree of flexibility and adaptability to meet the requirements of the army mission. So West Point has a basic goal to educate broadly, with the notion, shared by the vice dean, that it "must be sophisticated enough to operate in a global context." He indicated further, "Thus, we have to be capable of using advanced technology, and we have to envision the technology of the future. The first-year experience is nested in this conversation."

A current challenge for the academy is to be able to adjust for differences in the developmental needs of entering cadets. This is not unlike other colleges and universities around the country that have to be increasingly responsive to the vast array of backgrounds and behaviors students bring to their college experience. The common belief is that the typical cadet is highly motivated, bright, self-assured, and well rounded in both academics and athletics. While this may be true for many cadets, others enter the institution with varying degrees of developmental and academic deficiencies, and the academy is cognizant of the need to address those deficiencies.

The commandant, Brigadier General Brooks, who is responsible for the military and physical elements of the West Point experience, has, according to several administrators, "narrowed down the mission statement." The commandant currently emphasizes physical toughness and attention to high standards of excellence in the military arena. We learned that the commandant's focus is on the ability to adapt to different missions and environments and a lifetime of service to the nation. Many individuals share his views. As Lieutenant Colonel Neff said, "We are not just looking for graduates; the commandant wants twenty years out of these graduates."

In talking with cadets and administrators alike, we learned firsthand about the changing nature of the academy. While there is fundamental support for much of the change that is occurring at West Point, the process is not without detractors. The voices of dissent are largely outside the academy, but cadets hear them loud and clear. As one cadet remarked, "Some of the former cadets think the corps has slipped. [They say] it is much easier now—they get that from upperclassmen. The opportunity for failure gets slimmer. Every class thinks they had it the hardest; every year it is changing, constantly new." A female cadet also weighed in on her support of the significant changes in the culture of the academy: "This place is not afraid of change. The goal of change is to increase the probability of success. The army wants us to stay as lifers [stay in the army for life]. The world situation is changing, and so is the army. They need leaders who are good at adapting, so we have to change our own academic programs. [And that means] cadets helping other cadets."

Finally, the following quotation sums up the thoughts many in the West Point leadership have about the changing role and nature of the academy and the responsibility the academy bears in ensuring its own success and continued viability. And this has tremendous implications for the cadet experience. Vice Dean Forsythe ponders:

> There is a new conversation [here]—officers not only lead a complex bureaucracy, but they are leading the profession. How is leading a profession different from leading a bureaucracy in a complex organization? If these officers fail to accept responsibility for disciplining the profession, people outside the profession will take responsibility from us. . . . This is why the nontoleration clause of the honor code is so important. Finally, officers are leaders. The concept of officer is broader—it is more holistic. . . . These must be men and women in whom the American people can place their trust. They place us in charge of the lives of American sons and daughters.

Given their academic pedigree, background, and level of pride, many entering plebes find it difficult to admit they need help. As the director of the reading and study skills program at West Point indicated, "Ego is sometimes involved in students not being able to say they need help." Yet plebes soon discover there is an intentional support network that respects and rewards asking for help. In fact, the director said, students indicate they sometimes feel they are "overhelped."

We heard several times during the course of our visit that the coin of the realm in the academy is "cadet time"; that is, the most important thing to a cadet is time. There are far more time constraints on military cadets than on the average American college student, and they succeed or fail based on time management. As the registrar emphasized during the open forum—or "briefing" as it was called—the academy schedule "allocates time 24/7 at the micro level."

With a rigorously scheduled daily life at the academy, cadets are constantly striving to make good use of their time. They can be rewarded by being given more leave and personal time for activities (for example, cadets are awarded more personal leave time each subsequent year); they can also be penalized by having reward time taken away or by having free time blocks filled with other required activities. The following passage, shared by Lieutenant Colonel Casey Neff, who works with the academy's military program, illustrates the importance and value of time and the strategic nature of its use: "Every hour in the 47 months is allocated with specificity [by West Point] to the program [director] to accomplish their mission. One important rule is any time not explicitly used by the program director, who owns the time, automatically belongs to the cadet. People are our most valuable resource; time is the second most valuable resource."

There are high standards at West Point that are clearly and explicitly delineated, and the key to cadet success is to meet the standards, as the commandant of cadets indicated. The academy seeks to have a marriage of the academic and the military in each cadet so that cadets will become immersed in and part of the academy's culture. To aid cadets, West Point has what the commandant refers to as enriched support services. If students fail to meet standards in the physical program administered by the commandant's office, they must undergo "physical remediation." Early warning indicators identify when a cadet has entered into a "zone of concern," and appropriate measures are taken to put the cadet back on track.

When thinking about the life of the cadet at West Point, the concept of "a sound mind in a sound body," the ancient Greek ideal, comes to mind. Cadets are expected to engage in an extensive number of activities in addition to undertaking a rigorous academic curriculum. Activities are strategically designed to build confidence. Every cadet has to participate in at least one sport per week, which is another way team building and leadership are developed.

Important Findings and Lessons Learned

A telling comment by one of the officers during our visit suggested that West Point has a strong determination to succeed. How much of this determination stems from institutional pride or from the belief that success at West Point is in the best national interest, militarily speaking, is unclear. But there is an attitude at the academy that much is at stake in terms of its success, and therefore there is widespread dedication to achieving it. As the officer said, "The academy is built for success—it would almost have to shut down to fail." Much can be learned from that institutional commitment, and to that end we outline several of the major lessons we learned from the academy:

- *Work is conducted in all areas of the academy with extraordinary intentionality.* While intentionality of effort is a common finding across all thirteen Institutions of Excellence, there is a distinctive level of intentionality that characterizes the work of the faculty, staff, and administration at West Point, and it is prominent throughout all ranks, including the corps of cadets. Structures, policies, procedures, and other elements that affect the first year of college are implemented according to a well-developed design and plan. Given the tightly constructed cadet experience and the predilection for order and structure at the academy, conducting business in a highly intentional manner is not surprising. Much of the success of the plebe year experience at West Point can be attributed to the remarkable attention to systems thinking and planning; that is, units and departments are seen as inherently interconnected, and work flows accordingly. Because time management is so vital to the success of all cadets—and factors perhaps most prominently in the daily lives of plebes—the academy is keenly aware of the importance of planning and coordination among units. There is a tightly coupled relationship between the various facets of the cadet experience, including the academic, military, physical, and social domains.
- *History, traditions, culture, and mission are central to the socialization process of new cadets.* West Point is an institution that values its stories, especially those stories that figure prominently in American history. It follows that some of the most imposing features of West Point are the cultural elements that characterize life at the institution. The rich traditions that punctuate the cadet experience are deeply ingrained in the institutional ethos and are very visible throughout the college environment. The institution uses these cultural elements—history, traditions, mission, stories, rituals, and others—to socialize new cadets into the institution and convey values and norms of behavior.
- *Assessment takes on a special role and is vital to improvement and change.* Throughout its history, the American military has taken evaluation and assessment very seriously as a means for improvement as well as strategic planning. Whether it is the use of after-action reports from officers to analyze battlefield operations and move-

ments or the routine evaluation of officer training, assessment has always played a significant role in military operations. By virtue of its relationship to the army and the training of its future officers, West Point elevates assessment to a high priority. As one individual on campus asserted, "Improvement is what we are all about." It is evident assessment plays a central role in the change and improvement process on campus. The ongoing and ever-present assessment and evaluation program at the academy ultimately ensures a balanced, regulated, and ordered experience for first-year cadets.

- *Peer leadership and mentoring are key elements in the success and well-being of first-year cadets.* While many campuses use upper-level student leaders, at no other campus is peer leadership taken as seriously as at West Point. From the top of the chain of command at West Point down through all levels of work and functioning, individuals have a deep sense of shared responsibility for its successes as well as its failures. In short, members of the academy succeed together and fail together. To that end, peer leadership and mentoring are vitally important components of entering cadets' daily lives. New cadets are instilled with the belief that peer-to-peer learning and leadership build teamwork and camaraderie and strengthen relationships among cadets. In like manner, the mentoring program flourishing at the academy helps cadets feel more supported and encouraged and is intended to promote success in the first year and beyond.
- *West Point is concerned with the development of the whole person.* There is an evident commitment at West Point to developing cadets into highly educated, morally responsible, and physically fit citizen-soldiers. The typical experience of a West Point cadet consists of a balanced regimen of academic preparation, personal refinement, military training, and physical fitness pursuits, all reinforced daily in the curriculum as well as the cocurriculum. As a senior officer indicated, "We provide development experiences plus readiness, plus reflection—meaningful developmental experiences combined with appropriate challenge, support, and feedback."

Conclusion

During our visit, there were significant references to the notion of the "family of the army." The role of the academy in the lives of the cadets who pass through every year can be summed up in three action verbs referenced by Colonel Forsythe during our visit: "To educate, train, and inspire."

West Point is unique among the Institutions of Excellence in that it is a military institution whose first-year students go through rigorous academic, physical, and military training as part of their daily regimen. To many in academe, it might seem difficult to translate the unique West Point experience to other institutional contexts. To others, it may be tempting to conclude that West Point cadets are highly successful in college because they are students who enter the institution with a track record of successful accomplishments. The fact remains, however, that entering plebes at the academy face the same academic, social, psychological, and physical challenges that first-year students around the country face every year. And they enter an institution that, in order to be successful, must understand and respond to those challenges.

West Point has been concerned with changing its image for many years, and this change appears to have taken root most prominently in the transformation of the plebe year experience. The institution has long been viewed by the public, as well as the higher education community, as a daunting and impressive place, well known for its rigorous and harsh training in a callused, and sometimes unforgiving, environment.

Talking to veteran administrators and officers who have been involved with the academy for many years, we came to view the environment as one that is much more collaborative and supportive than it has been described in the past. In fact, as one individual suggested, the academy offers "a helping hand rather than leering eyes." Whereas it once embodied a culture in which attrition of the less successful cadets was both expected and acceptable and where the notion of the survival of the fittest reigned supreme, the academy is today an institution engaged in an evolutionary process that is focused on the improvement of the entire first year and the success of all cadets. Goals and expectations are clear, standards are high, and programs are structured to help cadets achieve excellence. The academy requires it, the army demands it, and the nation yearns for it.

Part Four

Case Studies of Four-Year Institutions with 5,000 to 10,000 Students

Chapter Ten

Lehman College of the City University of New York

Excellence in the Bronx

John N. Gardner

Betsy O. Barefoot

For the participating researchers, one of the most gratifying aspects of a study such as the Institutions of Excellence project is the opportunity to discover institutions that because of their location or demographic profile might not have been predicted to rise to the top of this review process. But to quote the old adage, "You can't always judge a book by its cover." Surely the same adage must apply to many campuses committed to the success of new students.

Lehman College of the City University of New York is a non-residential campus where most of the students are first generation and economically disadvantaged. By its own admission, Lehman takes graduates from what many of its employees describe as "the worst-performing high schools in the whole New York City School System, the Bronx." The very words "the Bronx" evoke cultural stereotypes of Grade B movies like *Fort Apache: The Bronx* and scenes of crowded, crime-ridden neighborhoods and urban decay. But this borough of the City of New York nevertheless produces high school graduates, who, in spite of many barriers, want to pursue the American dream of upward social mobility, which is accessible primarily by means of a college education. As the research team, we found Lehman College to be extraordinarily intentional about a vigorous pursuit of its mission to promote access and excellence for the students it serves. Let us reemphasize *intentional,* for it is truly key.

The site visit to Lehman College was the last each of us made as part of this study, and by that time we had become vigilant to special themes suggesting the central characteristics of Institutions of Excellence. We immediately found most of those characteristics at Lehman: great respect for the students served for what and who they are; unique leadership accomplishments of individual faculty and administrators; extraordinary mission focus and intentionality; longevity and stability of institutional senior leadership and program administration; and emphasis on partnerships between academic and student affairs administrators working with faculty to deliver an expanded vision of where and how successful learning can take place. At Lehman these characteristics are coupled with a grand effort to deliver a meaningfully connected, integrated curriculum in a uniquely cohesive structure: the Coordinated Freshman Program (CFP).

Our study of Lehman focuses primarily on this CFP and all its programmatic and human components—its origins; prime movers; long-term institutional and program leaders; faculty, staff, and student participants; accomplishments; and its still incomplete agenda. But before describing the details of the CFP, let us start with a few basics about the institution.

Lehman College: An Overview from Past to Present

Lehman College is one of the nineteen campuses of the City University of New York, established by CUNY in 1968 as a comprehensive, senior institution. The university took over a campus that had been operating since 1931 as the Bronx branch of Hunter College. For the decade prior to World War II, this branch campus served only women students for their first two years prior to their transferring to Hunter's Manhattan campus. During the war, the Bronx campus was vacated and turned over to the U.S. Navy as a training station for the WAVES (Women Accepted for Volunteer Emergency Service). To commemorate this period, the navy later installed a ship's bell, which remains on the campus today. Immediately after the war, the campus assumed another unique, temporary role as the site of the first meetings of the United Nations Security Council in New York City, held from March to August 1946. Visitors to the campus today can observe the commemorative plaque outside the gymnasium building where these first UN meetings were convened. More traditional collegiate activities resumed in 1946, but this time with the admission of men, and in particular male veterans, who studied in separate classes from the women. This policy lasted until 1951, when the college became fully coeducational with a four-year curriculum through Hunter College.

In 1968, when the college became an independent unit of CUNY, it was renamed for Herbert H. Lehman, as the college catalogue states, "in recognition of the commitment to public service exemplified by the four-time governor of New York State who became a US Senator and was the first Director General of the United Nations Relief and Rehabilitation Administration. The College was first dedicated on March 28, 1969, the ninety-first anniversary of Lehman's birth."

Lehman College's architecturally distinctive, tree-lined campus, which *The New York Times* has called "the most attractive of the CUNY colleges," is located immediately contiguous to the historic Jerome Park Reservoir, and enrolls just over 9,500 students who are pursuing bachelor's and master's degrees in nearly ninety majors. About 73 percent of the undergraduate students are female, and 92 percent are members of minority groups. Although the students are overwhelmingly from the Bronx (62 percent), Manhattan (12 percent), and Westchester County, New York (12 percent), they nevertheless represent some ninety countries of origin. As is the case for all other CUNY campuses, the college relies more and more on adjunct faculty; in 2002, Lehman had a full-time faculty of 294 and an adjunct teaching faculty of 321.

Over the past decade, enrollment trends have seen an increase in percentages of minority students and students attending full time. But from 1995 until fall 2002, Lehman experienced an overall decrease in the number of entering first-year students. During this period, enrollment patterns were negatively influenced by both a systemwide tuition increase and an increase in admissions standards at CUNY four-year campuses, both put in place during the tenure of Mayor Rudolph Giuliani. These changes were coupled with major shifts in the federal welfare policies administered by the city, which moved students who were welfare recipients out of the college classroom and into work programs. The net impact of these changes on the whole CUNY system was enormous. The City University as a whole lost approximately 22,000 students, most of them women, and Lehman College itself lost about 1,000 students. In fall 2002, however, enrollment figures began a turnaround: first-year enrollment increased by 14 percent and transfer enrollment by 30 percent.

Why Lehman Made Radical Changes in the First Year

What chain of events led to the creation of Lehman's unique and intentional approach to the first year? We have seen many motivations for change at other campuses in and out of this study: the arrival of a new chief executive officer; the desire to revitalize the curriculum; the urgency to address declining retention and graduation rates; the influence of external governmental mandates to do this or that better or differently; appropriate pressure and "encouragement" from regional accrediting bodies to improve quality, educational effectiveness, and assessment; a tragedy, including loss of student lives, that might have been prevented; and even in one case, a major student riot that resulted in institutional soul searching to understand and prevent such occurrences in the future. At Lehman, the story goes back to an interplay of key human variables, issues, and opportunities. The Coordinated Freshman Program began in 1991; however, it had its origins in summer and intersession interventions implemented in the 1980s. Although these earlier efforts were not intentionally connected, they laid the groundwork for progression to a much more cohesive integration of multiple initiatives.

In 1991, the City University of New York made available through its chancellor, Ann Reynolds, a competitive grants initiative focused on the first year. Campuses were invited to submit proposals describing weaknesses in the first year and suggesting innovative ways to address those weaknesses. In 1991, Lehman's president had been in office only one year, and he encouraged a response to the chancellor's invitation. The request for proposal ultimately found its way to an English professor who, with many colleagues, had long given thought to the most acute problems facing Lehman's first year and especially its students. One critical problem was student dropout. In 1991, attrition rates were at a totally alarming and unacceptable 50 percent into the third semester, and the primary culprit was perceived to be the student pattern of "tenuous movement" through a first year that was being experienced as "fragmented . . . without a sense of connection, without a cohesive structure that explained how x is related to y—or more to the point, how x and y are related to the students themselves."

This English professor-turned-administrator, Steven Wyckoff, who is the founding father of Lehman's approach to the first year, authored a proposal to design what is Lehman's Coordinated Freshman program (CFP), a twelve-month continuum of academic and support activities. The CFP was conceptualized as a cohesive, connected, and integrated curricular and cocurricular learning experience that would ensure student passage from basic skills to sophomore-year readiness and would have a positive effect on learning, satisfaction, and retention. Program goals would be accomplished through a partnership of faculty, academic administrators, and student affairs administrators with strong administrative and financial support from the most senior institutional levels. The chancellor's office responded by funding the Lehman proposal as well as proposals from four other CUNY campuses.

Coordinated Freshman Program

The CFP includes the following components: the Freshman Year Initiative, the summer immersion program, and the winter immersion program.

Freshman Year Initiative

The programmatic center of the CFP is the Freshman Year Initiative (FYI), clustered learning communities, or blocks, that are required of all first-time, full-time entering students. As program administrators readily admit, what is unique about Lehman's structure is not the learning community concept per se, which is now in place at over 60 percent of American colleges and universities (Policy Center on the First Year of College, 2002), but the dynamic whole of its execution. FYI is a year-long (two-term) structure, which sets it apart from first-year efforts that commonly focus solely on the first term. In the academic year 2002—2003, about 800 first-year students participated in thirty blocks of five courses (four academic courses plus a freshman seminar) in the fall semester. During the spring term, these full-time blocks were followed by part-time blocks of two linked courses. Each year, the blocks are taught by approximately 125 faculty (from almost all disciplines), in addition to student affairs professionals, academic advisers, counselors, academic support staff, peer counselors, and administrators. Blocks are interdisciplinary and thematically linked, and they include many liberal arts clusters as well as clusters for students in biology, pre-med, economics, accounting, nursing, health care, and teacher education.

At the time of our campus visit, the mandatory freshman seminar carried no credit, but was one of five courses in each block taught by faculty, student affairs professionals, and counselors. As of fall 2003, in response to student feedback, the seminar was being proposed as a two-semester-hour, credit-bearing course. Freshman seminar provides a vehicle for addressing the various issues that relate to the transition from high school to college, the challenges of student adjustment, multiple opportunities for cocurricular participation, problem solving, and consideration of the goals of a liberal arts education.

Connection to Lincoln Center

By virtue of its location in New York City, Lehman College has been able to take advantage of a unique partnership with the world-famous Lincoln Center for the Performing Arts and specifically its Institute for the Arts in Education. Since the mid-1990s, students minoring in education have the option of participating in blocks that include an overlay of collaboration with Lincoln Center teaching artists. These professionals visit the campus several times during the semester, and students themselves visit Lincoln Center twice a semester and frequently take part in performances. The goal of both Lincoln Center and Lehman College is to help these prospective classroom teachers recognize the relationship of all disciplines to the arts and to provide them an opportunity for rich experiential learning.

Summer and Winter Immersion Programs

Recent and ongoing changes in admissions requirements for all CUNY four-year institutions stipulate that entering students must pass placement tests in mathematics, writing, and reading. For high school students, these tests are given during the last semester of their senior year; adults, returning students, and transfers may take the exams at any time in testing offices at the various campuses. Students with high SAT or New York State Regents Examination scores may be exempt from testing, but other students must take and pass each test.

Any student applying to Lehman as either a first-year or a transfer student who fails one or more of these placement tests must participate in either a summer or a winter immersion program. Summer Immersion is offered in six-week, three-week, two-week, and even one-week formats and is designed to prepare students for testing or retesting. The two-week and one-week sessions, offered at the end of the summer, also function as a second chance for students who may have failed a test after the longer six-week session. The program uses a modified version of the block courses, which allows customized placement and homogeneous tracks for skill development in writing, reading, and mathematics. Testing requirements that are the focus for Summer Immersion create what the campus realizes is a tense high-stakes environment. Intentional faculty collaboration and interaction with students are intended to ease this tension to some extent.

Summer Immersion has been highly successful in meeting its primary goal. For example, in summer 2001, the program—with some 1,000 students enrolled who were a mix of first-year, transfer, and continuing students—achieved a 90 percent success rate in terms of students being admissible to senior college status, an outcome that according to senior administrators had "a considerable positive effect on fall enrollment." In a similar manner, a winter immersion program is offered in a more compressed time frame to address the needs of students who wish to matriculate in the spring term.

In recent years, the campus has analyzed data comparing the academic performance of students who participated in Summer Immersion and those who were not required to do so by virtue of higher entering test scores. Results have shown that participants in Summer Immersion had higher levels of subsequent academic performance than the ostensibly better-prepared nonparticipants. Faculty and staff hypothesize that the summer experience provides a bridge from high school that helps students maintain their learning momentum while simultaneously enabling them to make friends and develop campus connections. Because of those findings, the campus offered two sections of English 135, The Experience of Literature, to regularly admitted students in the summer of 2003. English 135 is a basic literature course that reinforces writing and reading skills as well as a critical thinking approach to literature. The summer offering was a huge success: applications far exceeded spaces available, no student failed to complete the course, and course grades averaged 3.2 on a 4.0 scale. Follow-up research will track retention and grade point averages of the summer 2003 students in English 135, comparing them to students who completed the same course in the fall 2002 semester. Because of the overwhelming response, the campus plans to increase the number of summer course offerings in years to come.

The SEEK Program

Four-year campuses in the CUNY System offer a special higher education opportunity program designed for students who need academic and financial support in order to compete successfully in college. Search for Education, Elevation, and Knowledge (SEEK), as well as the Higher Education Opportunity Program and Educational Opportunity Program. EOP programs throughout New York State, provide concentrated and specialized counseling as well as financial assistance. Currently about 40 percent of first-year students overall participate in SEEK, but 60 percent of each Summer or Winter Immersion cohort is composed of SEEK students. While non-SEEK students must pass reading, writing, and math exams before matriculating, SEEK students have an additional year to pass these tests, including Summer and Winter Immersion sessions.

The Founding Father's Influence: Key Program Rationale

As researchers in this project, we acquired valuable information from a number of primary sources. But frequently during our campus visits, we gathered some of our richest impressions and information from the interviews we conducted with the actual participants in designing the first year. In the case of Lehman, the lead storyteller is Steven Wyckoff, a creative English professor who has survived the many ups and downs of CUNY's rocky history, including the various political footballs lobbed at the college by both state and city politicians. Wyckoff has served Lehman College for twenty years, first as an English professor and now as an administrator of the CFP who also continues to teach and administer English composition. He is a reflective man who knows what both he and the college value and what he believes students value as well. We listened to his story, and thus Lehman's story, in an introductory session in his inviting office, which seemed a contrast with the rather grim appearance of the "aesthetically challenged" 1960s-era classroom building where the office was located. This setting, with its welcoming ambiance of a sofa and conference table, was constantly being visited by students seeking advice or simply wanting to talk. They ambled in and politely interrupted with the predictable assurance that they could and would immediately get what they needed from the freshman program director.

We were led to understand that the organizing principle of the CFP, and especially the FYI blocks, was to address and combat the fragmentation in students' lives both on and off campus. Perhaps the understatement of the visit was the program director's observation that "our students lead complicated lives." He went on to say, "Before the development of the CFP, we thrust these students, who are mostly first generation, into a very complex university system—not just Lehman College but a whole university system. We required them to take a series of unconnected, discrete academic courses taught by faculty who had no connection to each other, and those same students weren't connected in any intentional ways either." The result of this fragmented experience was that fundamentally, the students perceived the curriculum to be neither meaningful nor engaging. Lehman officials maintained that for their students, this kind of experience often results in attrition. So one of the goals of the CFP was to integrate classes, faculty, and students with each other: intellectually, thematically, and personally. Another goal was to integrate the classroom experience with tutoring, Supplemental Instruction, advising, and ultimately even cocurricular experiences (not noted for being an area of emphasis in urban commuter institutions). Currently, peer tutors are assigned to each English composition class, and one-hour weekly Supplemental Instruction sessions, facilitated by graduate students, are linked to a wide variety of courses and required for all students.

Lehman essentially took an existing curriculum and reshaped it into a new form. That new form "relied powerfully on logistics," and it is these logistics that often frighten off many admirers of the learning community model who say, "Oh, but that could never be done here." As researchers, we would respectfully argue that if it can be done at Lehman, a dramatically underresourced institution with many built-in structural and cultural obstacles to community, it can be done almost anywhere.

An enormous amount of faculty development and planning underlies the delivery of each block of courses. Faculty plan and integrate their individual course content and assignments collectively. The students are made aware of this, and hence they can assume that each of their professors understands both the content and requirements of all the other courses in which they are enrolled that term. We were told by the program director and we would see for ourselves that "students see the connections between the courses and the disciplines . . . the relationships in a learning process and how this mirrors life. This block program is part of the culture. . . . Everyone is familiar with and committed to this program. . . . We are trying to create an ecosystem that is connected, not despairing."

A number of the educators who deliver the FYI blocks speak of their work as a journey, one in which they and the students are growing and constantly discovering. Program participants seemed acutely aware of the original departure points for the journey, as well as the intended destinations. However, much about the journey's outcomes was perceived as not yet complete: faculty and administrators expressed their desire to take the journey beyond the first year to greater levels of intentionality and impact in subsequent years of the students' experience.

Another consistent theme we gathered from all academic and students affairs support staff was, "We work very closely with 'Steve' or with 'Steve's program,'" illustrating a sincere commitment to the CFP and how inextricably it is connected with its founder and leader.

Faculty Development for the FYI Program

The FYI block program depends for its success on communication and collaboration among teaching faculty and hence on intentional faculty development. Faculty who are teaching in each block receive their assignments in late spring, and summer gives them the opportunity to meet together to start devising ways to link content and activities across course boundaries. A focused faculty development workshop is scheduled for late summer. This event, attended each year by the president and provost, offers block faculty an intensive two days to put the finishing touches on course plans for the fall. But faculty development does not end when the semester begins. Faculty meet biweekly throughout the semester to share ideas and resolve problems in each of the blocks.

Each year a culminating activity is the preparation of a resource manual to which each block faculty member contributes. This manual is filled with innovative but practical ideas about how different academic topics can be linked into broader thematic concepts. The program director writes that "because faculty teach the same students in the set of courses that constitute each learning community, the prospect for creative and engaging curricula . . . across disciplinary lines is limited only by the ends of professional curiosity. Curricular juxtaposition is an active, even passionate enterprise, and provides students with a coherent interdisciplinary experience that may promote a deeper kind of learning than is likely to be found in courses that stand alone."

It is important to note that the majority of instructors in Lehman's FYI program are part-timers; many of them, however, have taught at the college for a number of years and have a high level of commitment and dedication to the institution and its students. The notion that successful educational innovations can be realized only with a cadre of full-time or tenured faculty is not supported by the Lehman experience.

In reflecting on their experience in the FYI block program, the instructors talked of its impact on both the students and themselves as faculty:

> I was petrified when I first had to teach in the block. I was used to being isolated. It was safer in my own environment; but block teaching simplifies my work as an English professor. I can get the

> students to write in my class based on the content of their other classes [in the block]. I use that content as a basis for discussion and writing in my class. Students contribute more and discuss more. The program has given me theory of what can be done plus the practice.

Block faculty also spoke extensively about the demands placed on them for high amounts of interaction with each other: "We have block meetings, three or four of them a term, to discuss student performance, exchange syllabi, point out the skills that the students need that are being taught in other classes." Faculty also gave testimony to the processes they experience of their own intellectual discovery when they can see for themselves how their subjects "connect . . . they are not isolated." And echoing the students, the faculty praise the block structure for giving students "the opportunity to get to know each other."

We queried the discipline-based faculty on their perceptions of the freshman seminar, which is required of students in the blocks but taught for the most part by nonfaculty. Faculty whom we interviewed were unanimous in their praise of the seminar "because there is so much that students don't know about the university that they learn in the seminar." Faculty spoke respectfully and appreciatively of the role student affairs plays in close coordination of the seminar: "You need to remember the differences on a commuter campus. Freshman seminar tries to get students involved." In summary, an even more comprehensive and holistic perspective was provided by one faculty member: "The first year initiative—and especially the freshman seminar—are about doing things we have to do without dormitory life."

A number of these faculty also teach courses in their disciplines but outside the block structure. One faculty member noted the contrast: "There is much more of a sense of bonding in my FYI course than non-FYI courses. Students feel the same way."

One prominent academic department head spoke of the attractiveness of the block as a teaching environment for the delivery of introductory courses: "In the block, the goal is to take care of a small group of students. Students know this, and they are surprised by it. They sense that we are all in this together—as a true community of learners. The block gives them a comfort zone." As researchers, we had to conclude that although the block provides the structure, faculty themselves are the key agents for providing that comfort zone.

Lehman Student Voices: What Makes a Difference for Them

How do Lehman students describe their experience in the FYI blocks and their overall perceptions about Lehman College? We were favorably surprised by the degree to which students used the same language and concepts as faculty and administrators to describe their FYI experience. Students reflected on the objectives of cohesion and connectedness, and it was quite apparent they were learning the Lehman culture. Here is what one student told us:

> The block has helped me develop tight bonds and study habits. I can interrelate things from one class to another. For example, the English professor is always willing to take time out to help us with our research and bibliography for another one of our courses. Two of our courses, sociology and philosophy, did a joint project. We found materials on the Internet in sociology, and we related this to the philosophy class. I had a prior college experience where I made no friends. Here we are all on the same e-mail list, and we all can call each other at night (and we do). Originally, I had only planned to go to class for two days a week and the block system forced me to go to class four days a week, but it now feels good to go every day.

Students spoke to the academic and disciplinary connections they were making: "I like the way the classes interrelate. We always know if we miss an assignment and get it from a friend by e-mail." "The block opened up so many opportunities for me. The block included music appreciation, and now I listen to Bach."

As we listened to the students describe the impact of their experience in the block structure, we were attentive to how they might describe the roles and behaviors of their faculty. Here is what they had to say:

> The teachers ask about the content and the assignments of other courses. We have to meet with the professors for a one-on-one

> interview in each class. This helped me out a lot. I would never have thought in a big college like this professors would have made this time available.
>
> The block is also good because the professors talk to each other.
>
> I wanted professors in college to know me by name, to have small classes and get that attention.
>
> I like teachers who really prepare. It shows they actually care, because we students are expected to really prepare too.

Students commented on the inextricable connection of academic, social, and out-of-class experiences in successful college learning:

> One of the best things is the students take all of their classes together. I had taken a math class outside the block with no friends. I felt like an orphan there, but in the block I made really good friends.
>
> I really like Lehman. I came in narrow-minded. I picked the honors block and got a scholarship. I like the Lehman services, for example, career services. I learned how to do a résumé, and I didn't think a college this large could extend these kinds of services. I didn't feel lost at all here. Because of the block system, we get informed. Everything here connects.

Both students and researchers could reasonably ask, Is this much togetherness a good thing? A successful second-year student told us:

> The freshman program is a good program, but it limits you because you only know twenty-five students. The second semester we have only two classes blocked and two totally new classes. This gives you more freedom to find things out on your own. Students should get more involved. With the block, we get more like a family; we get loose with people. I think more of the blocks should be combined.

Another upperclassman recommended an option to the one block of four academic courses. He would have preferred enrolling in two blocks of two courses each but combining the two blocks for "working together so you would have one group of twenty-five which would interact with another group of twenty-five. Knowing only one group of twenty-five limits you." This same student also reflected that looking back on his first year, "most of my fellow students are not here any more. . . . It is not easy to live in the city. Students tend to fall into deep responsibilities to their families, and plus you have to focus completely on working a full-time job."

In reflecting on the FYI experience, one student also looked ahead to life beyond and without the block: "I am happy we are all in the same block, but sometimes I get tired of seeing the same people. When this semester is over, I'll be so attached to people in this block I will feel awkward again."

As such students make the progression from the first term of a full-time block to a second semester of a part-time block, this is one possible reaction: "I was so accustomed to having everyone become so comfortable that some of my friends tried to sign up again for the two classes together in the spring block."

One of the central components of the CFP is participation in a noncredit freshman seminar. Students spoke candidly about the pros and cons of this experience:

> Freshman seminar is helping us get more involved and join activities. It helps you know what to do and how to succeed in college.
>
> The freshman seminar taught me about time management. We need time management because we work and go to school and live on our own.
>
> I would take the freshman seminar more seriously if it had credit. Without it, it is a joke. Even our instructor thinks it is a joke. If it had credit, I would turn my work in on time. I realize the course is good for us. We've learned to use long-term planners. The pass-fail grade doesn't really mean anything.

The perception of the freshman seminar may be very different for one cohort of students: those admitted through the SEEK program. For example, one SEEK student reported to us: "In the SEEK program the freshman seminar is totally different. Our [freshman seminar] instructor is really on top of us. The SEEK sections of the freshman seminar are not taken as a joke." One possible explanation for this more positive perception may be that SEEK students, who are considered the institution's most at-risk population, are the recipients of more intrusive, more intentional oversight and assistance than other "average" or "above-average" students.

And finally, from the voices of students, we circle back to what is always there: what Steve Wyckoff described as the complexity of the students' lives. How could it be captured more poignantly than this?

> I go home to a lot of problems. The Student Life Building is really a great place to be before I go home to these problems. It helps me to relieve a lot of stress.

> I live by myself in the projects. I am used to struggling. Counselors here are great. In high school nobody cared. I didn't trust anybody in high school. Here the counselors hear you out, and it's confidential. The activities are great. The student life people are so nice. I am in two clubs, and I am not by myself any longer. Everybody wants to help. I have a job on campus, and I have learned how to be polite. I am learning discipline. I am also learning to cope with people who want things fast!

An Inside View of a Learning Communities Classroom

During our visit to Lehman, we visited a number of classes. One class that was representative of what we saw was Women in Literature, taught by a professor who described her students as "wonderfully bright." She made similar positive descriptive comments about them in their presence during class time, thereby communicating basic respect for the students. About twenty students were present, but only one of them was male. The professor made reference in her presentation to learning skills required in another class students were taking in the FYI block and how those same skills would be desirable and reinforced in this class. She also made specific references to an assignment being read for another class in the block. All the students we observed gave the professor good eye contact, and many contributed verbally, both when called on and on their own initiative. The professor made intentional links between this and other courses in the block by asking students to define concepts being taught in other block courses and explained their relevance to the class she was teaching. She called all students by name and regularly complimented them in response to their contributions. When students spoke, she never interrupted them; thus, they were allowed to complete their statements. It was obvious that the students had prepared by doing the outside reading, and all seemed ready and eager to discuss the material. The professor sent a nonjudgmental message to the students who had not yet turned in their papers to the effect that she would look forward very much to reading them shortly. We noted that some students did not have their own copies of the text, and a number were looking on and sharing with others. One student came to class quite late but was warmly greeted by the professor with no hint of implied criticism. Overall, there was a great deal of student discussion and participation throughout the entire class period.

Noting the single male student in this particular class, we asked faculty why this gender imbalance is the dominant demographic characteristic of the campus. They explained to us that there is massive, disproportionate attrition of males in the Bronx high schools and that this trickles down to the colleges. And for male students who actually enroll, it was the consensus of the faculty that they were less likely to attend class regularly and more reluctant to engage in the intellectual, interactive give-and-take that we observed in the predominantly female first-year classes. There also was consensus that the female students "are more mature, because they are heads of households or mothers. It makes them different from men. Men don't have the same degree of seriousness and maturity."

How Support Staff and Campus Facilities Help Lehman Students

Professional support staff in student affairs and academic affairs speak proudly of their role in helping students achieve immediate bonding with the institution and the pride that students feel in Lehman. One staff member spoke for many we heard: "We are in their [the students'] culture. We know our students and their problems, and we can address them. This place was home for me, and I want to get the students to see this place as their home. We have very few student discipline problems. You won't find graffiti and garbage on our campus. Students are very mindful of the reasons they are here."

There are a number of ways that various support units on campus work directly with the CFP. Currently with the support of a three-year Title V grant, the director of academic standards is completing development of a new student tracking, intervention, and advising system, called the student development model. The model includes an electronic tracking system available to faculty advisers that enables them to monitor student progress and intervene when necessary. Faculty are participating in workshops designed to train them in using this system.

Another component of the model is a long-range academic plan (LRAP). This plan was begun in 2001 and originally implemented in the freshman seminar. But in 2003–2004, the college planned to introduce the technology-enhanced LRAP to students in English composition classes. Students will also spend out-of-class time working with both peer and faculty advisers to develop an academic plan for the entire undergraduate experience. This LRAP is maintained electronically, and both students and advisers have access to it. Academic advisers hope that by implementing this long-range model, students will be less likely to waste time taking courses that do not fit their overall major goals. Students who have not declared a major choose a hypothetical one so that they can begin to "navigate the terrain." An academic adviser stated, "We want to demystify the academic world for students."

A third component of the student development model is a survey that measures levels of student satisfaction in the first year. This research is helping to build a more accurate picture of students who leave Lehman for other than academic reasons. Upper-level peers are employed to make early contact with students whose survey results indicate likely college dropout.

Academic Support Center for Excellence

The Academic Support Center for Excellence offers services designed to support classroom learning. ACE provides instructional support for a wide range of academic subjects and skills. Literacy tutors are available to help students with the Writing and Reading Assessment Tests (ACT) preparation, proficiency exam preparation, and general writing and reading skills. Discipline tutors are able to assist students with particular courses in addition to study skills and test preparation. Students are encouraged to sign up early in the semester and come to the support center weekly. In addition to the individualized tutoring, there are many programs available for students at the support center designed to help them achieve academic excellence. These include writing seminars—group sessions that deal with different aspects of writing from basic compositional skills to writing research papers; writing enhancement workshops for English as a Second Language students; and weekly seminars designed for students to discuss informally a variety of topics ranging from globalism to poetry. During these seminars, students read particular articles, essays, or texts and discuss the readings.

Personal Academic Career Counseling Team

Title V funding (available to Hispanic-serving institutions) has enabled Lehman College to design a comprehensive approach to using upper-level students as academic peer advisers, career counselors, and personal counselors. Students with at least a 2.5 grade point average who have accumulated from twenty-four to seventy-five credit hours can apply to become a member of a personal academic career counseling team (PACCT). These students work throughout the year (including Summer and Winter Immersion) for six to ten hours per week in a variety of settings. They receive training for their responsibilities and compensation through Title V monies.

Special Facilities for Recreation and Child Care

The entire Lehman community speaks with pride about a special campus facility, APEX, a $57 million recreation and sports complex that supports Lehman's many academic, recreation, intramural, and community-outreach activities, as well as its NCAA Division III athletic teams. Membership in APEX is automatic for all currently registered Lehman students and is available, on a fee basis, for community residents. Its facilities, which are open seven days a week, are excellent and include two gymnasiums, four racquetball courts, a free weight room, a cardiovascular fitness center, an indoor running track, saunas, and other features.

A major issue for many first-year college students, especially women, is child care. Lehman responds to that need through the college's Child Care Center, which has both day and evening hours. Although the existing center cannot meet the demand, the college is renovating an adjoining facility that will approximately triple the capacity. This is an accredited child care facility, and the college has developed such expertise in this domain that it provides technical assistance to other CUNY campuses in implementing child care.

The View from the Top: Senior Administrators' Perspectives

One of the key themes of this study is the role that senior administrators play in successful first-year innovation. At Lehman College, Ricardo R. Fernandez, who joined the college as its president in 1990, was the leader who charged his institution to respond to a CUNY grants initiative to improve student success in the first year. In order to gain the background and perspective of senior administrators, we met with the president and the new provost, Anthony Garro, who assumed his responsibilities at Lehman in July 2001. Garro had already been described to us as someone who "came here and listened to the students—a jock, an iron man competitor who is really liked by the students." We learned that he brings to his position significant experience in working with the K-12 sector in a variety of pipeline programs aimed at producing more successful college students.

We asked both the president and provost to reflect on the CFP and its history. President Fernandez recalled that in the early years, the program operated on a shoestring budget. But since that time, both the president and provost have sought and funneled additional resources to both the CFP and academic support initiatives. Fernandez takes great pride in the CFP and supports the program through his annual participation in the CFP Faculty Development Workshop. He gives primary credit for the program's success to "leadership at many levels," especially the long-serving faculty administrator, Steven Wyckoff.

Garro stated that as soon as he arrived on campus, he became aware of the regard with which the CFP was held throughout the

CUNY system, and he has encouraged program leaders and faculty to disseminate their experiences and findings through publications and conference presentations. Both the provost and president spoke about the need to improve the pipeline through various collaborative initiatives with feeder schools in the Bronx, both high schools and community colleges.

In the summer of 2002, Lehman offered a special arts academy for local high school students. The provost commented, "Other CUNY campuses have run similar programs in math and sciences. We have such an excellent program and resources in theater and music, we thought it was wise to use this expertise to run a different summer academy, and we were pleased to have a large group of participants including eight students from the Bronx High School of Science."

Lehman's interaction with the public school system is part of a larger CUNY effort to link colleges and schools. President Fernandez described the CUNY and city board of education collaboration on a high school support program, College Now. With support from both the university and board of education, this program designed to prepare students for college has filtered down to the junior high schools.

Both of these leaders agree that to some extent, Lehman College is a prisoner to the history of CUNY and New York City politics. While the president credited former Chancellor Ann Reynolds with launching the 1991 grants initiative that started Lehman on its road to developing a more coherent approach to the first year, he also maintained that there are many problems remaining from the legacy of CUNY's travails with funding and major public controversy about remediation. In addition, CUNY's numerous fixed policies make some changes difficult, if not impossible. One example is the CUNY Central Office constraint to maintain the baccalaureate degree at a maximum of 120 hours. This arbitrary credit hour limit has, until this year, served as a disincentive for awarding degree-applicable credit for the first year seminar. In spite of these larger external constraints, however, these leaders seem determined to take as much as possible of the college's destiny into their own hands. In addition to his comments about the CFP, the president spoke of the college's support of first-year students through an active career center, the health center—

which provides "not just shots and pills, but education"—and the counseling center, which helps students address the various problems that are part of their "complex lives." The president is pleased that through the CFP, "advising becomes continuous, not 'arena-based' or episodic."

In fall 2001, the college created a new position to oversee all functions related to enrollment management. Currently, Anne Prisco, associate provost and assistant vice president for enrollment management, oversees all special first-year initiatives, including FYI, Summer and Winter Immersion, services to SEEK students, and advising and tutoring. Prisco stated that she accepted the position because it included far more than "enrollment services." Her oversight of academic programs makes it possible for her to influence the academic aspects of the first year that she believes are central to improving student retention. Prisco is proud and supportive of the current first-year FYI learning communities structure, but she foresees a possible evolution to a block comprising four, rather than five, discrete courses as general education requirements change across the entire CUNY system.

When senior administrators were asked, "What's next?" in the already well-developed set of first-year initiatives, they stressed the need to push for "an encore" with increased attention to and action on advisement. They would like to see more mentoring relationships develop between faculty and new students, which they agreed could potentially be effected through the freshman seminar or other courses in the block. Provost Garro also noted the need to improve the organization and levels of participation in orientation: "Currently new student orientation is only a few hours. So lots of information that, in my opinion, should be addressed in orientation gets shifted into the freshman seminar." Another envisioned encore area for new emphasis ahead reverts back to the interrelated areas of pipeline development and service by the college to the larger Bronx community. This would be more emphasis on the role of the college in cultural and arts enrichment as in the college's current partnerships with the Lincoln Center Institute and the Bronx Zoo, now known as the Wildlife Conservation Society. All senior officers see opportunities for enriching the student experience by linking with the many educational resources in the New York City metropolitan area.

Evidence of Effectiveness

Since the CFP began in the early 1990s, the Office of Institutional Research at Lehman College has studied its impact on academic achievement and on rates of first-to-second-year retention and graduation. Over the life of the CFP, average grade point averages have risen from 2.1 to the 2002 average of 2.9. Lehman's 50 percent retention rate has risen to 78 percent, and its five-year graduation rates have more than doubled.

Assessment data have also been used to bring about programmatic change. For example, in fall 2002, data analyses of the fall 2001 cohort resulted in a decision to bring about customized placement of students in block configurations. Beginning in fall 2003, students are placed in four different types of learning communities:

- Honors blocks
- Regular blocks for SEEK and non-SEEK freshmen who have passed or are exempt from the CUNY ACT test in writing and reading
- Blocks for SEEK and non-SEEK students who satisfied ACT requirements but are still determined to be at risk
- Blocks for SEEK students who have not satisfied ACT requirements and cannot place into English Composition

The program director and faculty believe that this redesign, brought about by assessment, will strengthen the FYI learning communities program.

What We Learned

In addition to findings that are common across all or most Institutions of Excellence and reviewed in Chapter Sixteen, several unique variables are at play to create this intentional environment in which many first-year students are thriving—for example:

- Although Lehman faculty, staff, and administrators have always known that the odds were against them in terms of getting nonresidential students involved in campus life, they never allowed that challenge to become a self-fulfilling prophecy. The campus has succeeded in getting students more involved by using the curriculum (that is, the FYI) as the primary vehicle for involvement.

• Lehman's approach to the first year couples an intimate knowledge of who students are with a well-thought-out philosophy and rationale for how they may best be served. Lehman's rationale for the design of its first year is the students' need for greater coherency, integration, connectedness, community, and support.

• In its approach to the first year that is based on learning communities, Lehman has achieved 100 percent participation of full-time students, the ultimate level of critical mass. Many campuses offer learning communities, but few are able or willing to deliver this structure to their entire full-time, first-year student body. In addition, the faculty who deliver these linked courses engage in a level of collaboration and coordination that is highly unusual and can serve as a model for other campuses.

In recognizing the obvious strengths of this campus, we also acknowledge one specific issue that the campus continues to address: the increasing proportion of part-time as compared to full-time faculty who are delivering the FYI program. Granted, this particular group of part-time faculty is very committed and dedicated to the goals of the FYI block program. But Steve Wyckoff shared with us his concern that the campus's full-time faculty need to be encouraged to participate more widely in the FYI learning communities. While we affirm the excellent contributions part-time faculty are making to this campus, we join with the program director in hoping that a better balance can be achieved so that more full-time and senior faculty are also involved in this important effort. It should also be noted that the significant and increasing use of part-time faculty is an issue for all campuses of the City University of New York, not just Lehman College.

We came away from Lehman with unique and confirming experiences. Nowhere else has this team observed more intentional connectedness across the first-year curriculum and a greater shared set of perceptions and values, owned by both faculty and students, about what makes for effective educational practice in the first year of college.

Chapter Eleven

The First Year at Texas A&M University-Corpus Christi

Starting with a Clean Slate

Michael J. Siegel

Marc Cutright

There is a saying in the real estate industry that the value of land is a function of "location, location, location." Texas A&M University-Corpus Christi (TAMU-CC) has an enviable location; the university quite literally sits on an island and proclaims itself to be, appropriately so, "The Island Campus." Driving southeast on Ocean Drive out of the city, Corpus Christi Bay is on the left and the Gulf of Mexico directly ahead on the horizon. Approximately halfway between the city and the Gulf, the coastline drive approaches a thin strip of highway best described as a causeway. Just off the road sits a small piece of land known as Ward Island, a 240-acre tract that is home to the TAMU-CC campus.

Given its relatively short history serving first-year students—just a decade—it is remarkable that TAMU-CC was named as one of the Institutions of Excellence in the First Year of College. But the intentional work the institution has done with first-year students in a relatively short period of time is truly extraordinary. The university's success in structuring the first-year curriculum to accomplish both economy of scale and personal attention is only one of the reasons that Texas A&M-Corpus Christi is unique among the thirteen selected institutions.

The Institution's Setting and History

Sitting just off the Texas Gulf Coast, TAMU-CC enjoys a balmy year-around climate. Palm trees dot the campus, and the buildings are uniform in color and structure—white or off-white in color and expansive, but basic, in an architectural sense. To fully appreciate the location of the campus on this relatively small island and the challenge the institution will likely face in coming years in terms of physical growth, one should probably see the campus from the air. Any number of publications, Web-based virtual tours, and view books provide striking aerial views.

Ward Island was first the home of the University of Corpus Christi, a private institution founded in 1947 and affiliated with the Baptist General Convention of Texas. Perhaps the most significant event in this institution's history occurred in 1970 when the campus was severely damaged by Hurricane Celia, one of the most destructive weather-related disasters in the history of the state. The destruction gave the institution impetus for rebuilding and renovation. The following year, in 1971, the university and the Baptist Convention took steps to end their affiliation, and after a coalition of local and state leaders lent their support to convert the school to a public institution, the Texas legislature authorized the creation of a state-supported institution of higher education. The campus was renamed Texas A&I University at Corpus Christi and served as an upper-level state university, or senior college, enrolling only juniors, seniors, and master's students. The institution went through another name change in 1977 when it became Corpus Christi State University. The campus's merger with the Texas A&M University System occurred in 1989, by act of the Texas legislature. The university officially changed its name from Corpus Christi State University to Texas A&M University-Corpus Christi in 1993 and admitted first-year students and sophomores for the first time in 1994. In 2002, student enrollment was approximately 7,600 students, and program offerings included sixty-one degree programs, thirty-four of which are undergraduate and twenty-seven graduate.

A Mission Espoused and Enacted

Texas A&M University-Corpus Christi is a comprehensive, urban, Hispanic-serving institution (HSI). According to federal guidelines, HSIs are those in which at least 25 percent of the students are Hispanic. The university serves primarily the state of Texas, and more specifically the needs of the vast South Texas region. The sense of responsibility to people of South Texas cannot be overstated; it is best summed up in the words of the dean of enrollment, Manual Lujan:

> People on campus need to remind themselves and their colleagues about the needs of South Texas. We get a lot of students from high schools where [a typical] class size is twenty-five people—so it's a different culture when you bring in that type of perspective. So for those people who step on this campus and are not used to the culture, it is our job to make sure when we bring that student aboard that we not just recruit that student and forget about that student—[it is our job to] make sure that we help that student [and] try and get that student into the culture of the campus to make them successful.

The institution focuses on coastal and urban issues, with special emphasis on allied health, teacher education, environmental studies, arts and humanities, business administration, and applied technology. The university has undergone a tremendous transformation during the past few decades in terms of both the expansion of campus programs and the diversification of the student body. In a typical year, more than forty-five percent of the institution's first-year students will have graduated in the top quarter of their high school class. And yet the university is also committed to support students who lack sufficient academic preparation. Great strides have also been made in the revision of the academic curriculum and the growth of degree programs on campus.

Like most other regional comprehensive institutions, TAMU-CC has as a primary goal the pursuit of excellence in teaching and learning. And like many other campuses in its sector, research and other forms of scholarly activity are becoming increasingly important as well. Complementing its commitment to excellence in teaching is a major goal to serve groups that have been historically underrepresented in higher education. Taken together, these goals and aspirations form the core of the campus mission statement:

> Texas A&M University-Corpus Christi is devoted to discovering, communicating, and applying knowledge in a complex and changing world. The university identifies, attracts, and graduates students

> of high potential, especially those from groups who have been historically under-represented in Texas higher education. Through a commitment to excellence in teaching, research, and service, Texas A&M University-Corpus Christi prepares students for lifelong learning and responsible participation in the global community.

The ongoing university mission is inextricably linked to racial and demographic variables, both locally as well as at the state level. The work and role of TAMU-CC reflect the needs of the region and the institution and, according to the president, "provides a real mechanism for Hispanic students to get a college degree." Changes in the demographic profile and needs of the local area ultimately have an impact on the work of the campus. For that reason, the president, who is involved personally in the life of the community, encourages his colleagues at the university to become involved as well. He not only wants to make external connections but also wants to model certain behaviors on campus that encourage others to do the same.

The arrival in 1998 of the current provost and vice president for academic affairs, Sandra Harper, who served as our liaison for the campus visit and study, brought a renewed interest in an existing learning communities program, especially in the way the first-year seminar course was embedded in TAMU-CC's unique learning communities structure. Prior to Harper's arrival, the first-year seminar was, to quote a campus administrator, "decontextualized"; it had no clear relationship to other courses in the learning communities. As a testament to her leadership and the importance she places on the academic success of first-year students—and in light of faculty feedback and data from students' evaluations—the one-credit seminar now serves as a linchpin for each learning community and has become more academically rigorous. To be sure, the basic staples of the typical first-year seminar—orientation, study skills, career information, time management, introduction to the library, and the like—are still in place, but they are addressed primarily through strategically scheduled presentations by the student affairs and library staffs on an as-needed basis.

The university's membership in the Texas A&M University System affords it all the benefits of association with a nationally reputable system of education. Given the powerful statewide presence, substantial resources, and diversity of programs and services within the system, the relationship the Corpus Christi campus has with its fellow system institutions provides significant opportunities for further growth and development in terms of human, financial, and academic resources. Like many other campuses that are part of large state systems of higher education, TAMU-CC's identity is characteristically derived from that of system's main campus, which is in College Station. With a great deal of pride and ownership, the individuals on the Corpus Christi campus say that although they appreciate and have benefited from the relationship with the College Station campus, they are interested in carving their own niche in the region and state. It is evident they are carving that niche in their work on the first year.

The First Year as a Clean Slate

Texas A&M University-Corpus Christi faced an uncertain future in the early 1990s when it embarked on the transition from a two-year, upper-division institution to a regional comprehensive four-year university. Prior to that time, the institution had focused on educating juniors, seniors, and graduate students (who had an average age of thirty-three) and preparing them to enter the workforce; it was now being challenged to educate primarily traditional-age college students and help them make the transition into and through the entire undergraduate experience.

That TAMU-CC did not have a long tradition of serving first-year students was something of a blessing in disguise, according to many individuals we met during our campus visit. Efforts over ten years to develop and implement a strong and effective first year have proceeded without the typical historical constraints and baggage that can have a negative impact on an institution's ability to be flexible and creative. Starting with a clean slate in 1994, TAMU-CC seized the opportunity to build the first year with a grassroots movement that relied on broad support and input from the campus community. Whereas some individuals predicted a clash between traditionalists and innovators, two distinctly different academic cultures, President Robert Furgason was more optimistic. He viewed this as a special opportunity to promote a campus culture and environment where the freedom to experiment and develop the first two years of the undergraduate experience without significant encumbrances would be possible. Consider his comments during this transition period:

> Our unique opportunity involves the ability to construct our freshman and sophomore years using a clean sheet of paper without the encumbrances of long-standing traditions and in-place curricula. . . . Our primary objective is to be viewed as a high quality institution providing innovative and motivating courses and curricula for students as they progress throughout their degree program. Perhaps the University could serve as a major demonstration site to implement many of the good ideas . . . related to new and better ways in which we can motivate and teach students [cited in Ramirez, 2002, p. 184.]

With those comments, the president signaled his desire to create an academic environment—a laboratory of sorts—where planning and programming might be conducted in experimental, creative, and innovative ways. The president expressed that pride often during our visit, most notably during the Open Forum, a public event to welcome us to the university, conducted by various faculty and staff and attended by university personnel from across the campus. He conveyed his appreciation for the opportunity to celebrate the success of the university in general and the first year in particular, and he was genuinely pleased that such a young first-year program had made a significant impact not only at the local level but nationally as well.

Through his leadership and specific attention to the first year, President Furgason has set an example for his colleagues and made it clear that his support for the first year is unequivocal. He encourages his campus colleagues to "take risks, but not be reckless," as he put it. He realizes, though, that emphasizing experimentation might be unconventional and further notes that some individuals believe that the "flip side of risk is punishment."

Seeding the Pot Early and Often: Orientation and Advising

At TAMU-CC, the twin themes of connection and community flow through the curriculum and the cocurriculum, the seeds of which are planted very early in the student-institution relationship. Before they officially become fellow "Islanders," prospective students become familiar with the welcoming and inviting culture of the campus. For many students, it all begins at Island Day, a visitation day for prospective students who descend on the campus en masse to learn more about the university, take campus tours, and hear from representatives of admissions, housing, financial assistance, and student services. The all-day event, which takes place on three different dates in the spring and one in the fall, brings out the campus community in full force, including professors, administrators, staff from various campus units, deans, student leaders, and student ambassadors, know as Island Ambassadors. It is a celebratory event, replete with a pep band, lively activities and conversations, and South Texas–style barbecue.

Another program designed to lay the foundation and cement the bond between the student and the institution is Aloha Days, an optional, summer camp–like, weekend-long program that helps students establish friendships and become familiar with TAMU-CC traditions in a relaxed environment. Following Aloha Days is the official campus orientation; all incoming first-year students are required to attend one of the new student orientation sessions. (An orientation session is required for any student, whether first-time-in-college or transfer student with fewer than thirty credit hours.) Optional, specially designed transfer transition workshops are also provided for transfer students with more than thirty credit hours. Finally, each summer, a one-day orientation is offered to the families of new students; conducted separately from the student program, the family orientation program focuses on a topics of interest to parents, particularly residence life, financial aid, health services, and safety issues.

While orientation in the traditional sense is considered an event or a time period at the beginning of an academic year in which welcoming events occur and students take placement tests and register for classes, it is more of a state of being at TAMU-CC. That is, the institution—while conducting orientation in the traditional sense—seems to be in a perpetual state of orienting and welcoming students to campus throughout the first year.

While the first days and weeks on campus can be overwhelming for any new student, this period can be especially so for first-generation students. Members of the faculty, staff, and administration are acutely aware of the need to design and implement programs and structures that address the needs of the first-generation student population and make their transition more manageable and comfortable. There is nuance in their work with students; they know their students well because many of them come from a similar background. As Dean Lujan reveals: "I don't know if you noticed this while you have been here, but a lot of the faculty are first-generation students as well—and a lot of the administration—so they can relate."

Knowing that the idea of groups and group involvement is especially important to Hispanic students, staff members seek to provide a scaled-down experience during orientation and advising that is conducive to group formation. Although some of the general orientation sessions are very large, breakout sessions in small groups of no more than twenty-five students are common. Students are typically able to have one-on-one sessions with their orientation leader and, most important, with their advisers. During our visit and conversation with the campus support staff, which included the directors of orientation and advising and the dean of enrollment, we learned how effective these small group and one-on-one interactions with the students can be. In what one individual referred to as a "micro-advising session," students are able to talk to their faculty advisers, alone, for forty-five minutes during orientation (the advising staff actually trains faculty to register students during the session on a laptop). It is no coincidence that on measures of student satisfaction with campus services during orientation, students rate advising and registration as the best part of the experience.

The First-Year Program: The Cornerstone of the First Year

The mission of TAMU-CC's first-year program, also referred to as the university core curriculum program (UCCP), is clear. According to Provost Harper, the mission of the first-year program is "to immerse students into an active learning environment that provides an integrated curricular context in which to develop skills and a sense of academic community" (http://writing.tamucc.edu/uccp/#core).

In developing the new first- and second-year academic environment in the early 1990s, the campus wanted to avoid what one faculty member called a "pigeon-holed curriculum," a menu-driven system of course selection and placement that had been, in essence, a relic from the university's past, based on the requirements of the Texas State Higher Education Board. Extraordinary planning efforts commenced when the Texas legislature first authorized the expansion of TAMU-CC in 1989, involving some 150 university members, multiple visits to other campuses to learn about the first-year structures, and campus visits from national experts. It is evident that this university attempted from the beginning to elevate the first year to a high priority for faculty and staff; it then designed structures to support those efforts. As a result of the planning process, TAMU-CC adopted the learning communities concept as a way to structure and administer the first year. As it exists today, the first-year learning communities program (FYLCP) is the primary thread in the tapestry of programs and structures that comprise TAMU-CC's first-year experience.

The FYLCP is, in effect, the university's signature program with respect to the first year. Its structure supports a philosophy of interdisciplinary integration among the core components of the academic curriculum, and it encourages cross-disciplinary collaboration between faculty from different academic backgrounds. The FYLCP has its own mission statement, a rather rare feature in any aspect of the first year, let alone for a specific program. According to the University's Web site, "The First-Year Learning Communities Program at Texas A&M University-Corpus Christi immerses students in an active learning environment, providing a context to integrate curricular content, to develop skills, and to develop a sense of academic community." The program was born out of necessity in that it was developed with a commitment to help its first-year students, who have a great deal of potential but are not always fully prepared for university life, adjust effectively to the university through involvement in a program engineered for both academic and social success.

Several of the core principles of the FYLCP—important value-based statements that undergird the work of the program—were shared with us during the Open Forum:

- Complexity of community
- Academic-based and interdisciplinary
- Active learning and meta-cognition

- Writing to learn
- Discussion as a way of teaching and learning
- Critical thinking and information literacy
- Technology-rich environments

The FYLCP is built around the concept of triads and tetrads, which are essentially blocks of academic courses that first-year students can choose among to fulfill a learning community requirement (Figures 11.1 and 11.2). The triad concept involves a unit, or cluster, of three courses, including a large core curriculum lecture course, a core curriculum English composition course, and a first-year seminar. The lecture courses enroll from 150 to 200 students, and the composition and first-year seminar courses enroll the same cohort group of twenty-five students, or fewer, on average. The tetrad clusters are structured similarly, but they also include a second large core curriculum lecture course. Within the clusters, careful attention is paid to further linking the courses and providing students with a connection that they would not otherwise receive if they enrolled in the sections as stand-alone courses.

The courses within the triads and tetrads are linked intellectually as well as structurally; that is, emphasis is placed on making intellectual connections between the courses. Course instructors

Figure 11.1. First-Year Learning Community Triad (Individual Cluster)

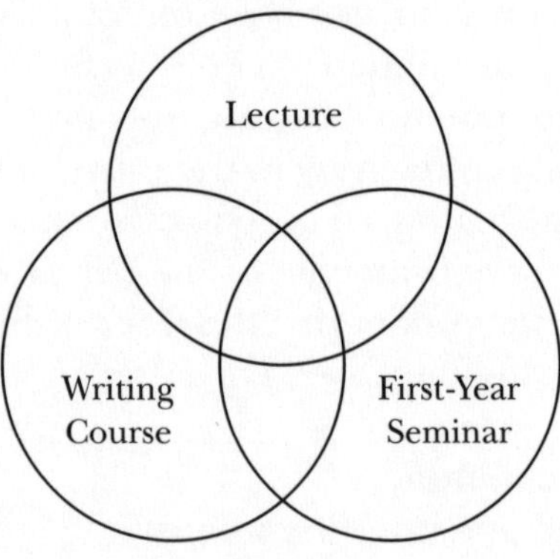

Figure 11.2. First-Year Learning Community Tetrad (Individual Cluster)

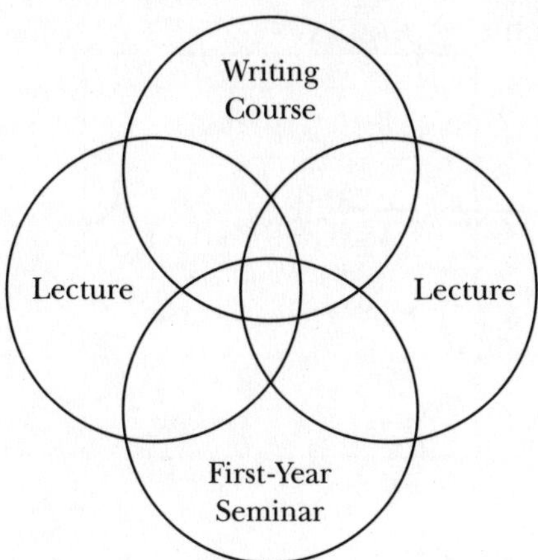

collaborate in an effort to help students integrate their learning experiences. Activities and assignments in the courses are designed intentionally to help students reach across disciplinary boundaries. Taking the same classes within a given triad or tetrad gives students the opportunity to learn together, collaborate on projects, and get to know one another in ways that are more difficult without the presence of the structure.

Another way of describing this unique structure is that each triad has a lecture course comprising eight first-year seminar/first-year writing linked course clusters (the same twenty-five students are in each of the seminar and writing courses), for a total of 200 students. Each tetrad has two lecture courses with eight clusters attending each of the two lecture courses. Using the representation below, consider the structure of the tetrads and triads in Figures 11.3 and 11.4.

Figure 11.3. Triad Lecture Course and All Seminar and Writing Course Clusters

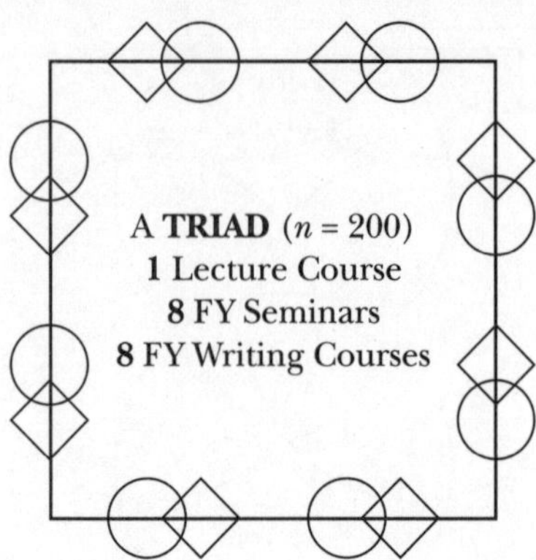

The desired impact of the learning communities on first-year students is systematic, far-reaching, and ambitious. The campus requires all full-time first-year students to enroll in either tetrad or triad learning communities in each of their first two semesters on campus.

There is a significant amount of coordination between the various instructors who teach within the tetrad and triad structures. One faculty member shared a scenario of an unlikely collaboration between an English professor and science professor on campus, exploring the nature of the intellectual connection of their work in the midst of vast differences between their disciplines. Drawing on the differences between the hard sciences and the liberal arts, he acknowledged the difficulty an English professor might experience in helping students prepare suitably for a science class and tying together the English intellectual fare with that of the science course, and vice versa.

Knowing that involvement in learning communities requires faculty to know something about those disciplines with which they are partnered and that there is an ongoing debate about the relative position of each discipline in the academic hierarchy, this arrangement has the potential to create conflict among faculty. As the same faculty member who posed the question about the English-science dichotomy noted, "The English-science relationship

Figure 11.4. Tetrad Lecture Courses and All Seminar and Writing Course Clusters

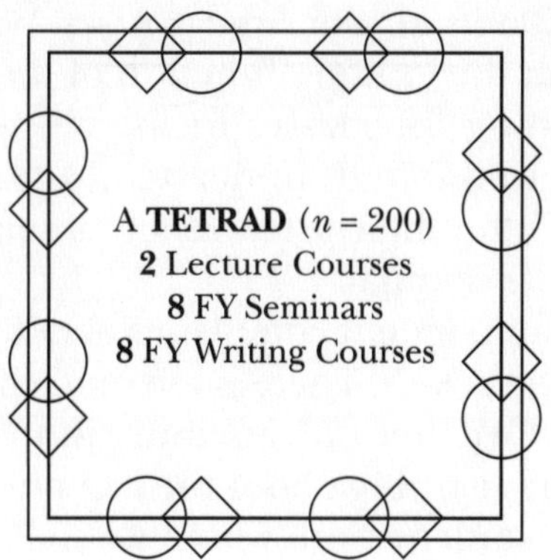

that exists at many institutions has been overcome here." Faculty involved in FYLCP go to extraordinary lengths to ensure that students understand the intellectual and cognitive connections between the courses.

When TAMU-CC welcomed its inaugural class of entering first-year students in 1994, all 400 were coenrolled in multiple sections within a set of tetrads. The program was launched with an intentional commitment to develop programs and structures in the first year that support the success of first-year students. The unique first-year learning communities experience has been in operation as long as first-year students have been on campus.

The First-Year Seminar as Anchor

In the first-year seminar sections, instructors help students understand the material from the lecture courses and relate what they are learning in the various courses within the triad or tetrad. The seminar serves as the anchor for each cluster. At its most successful, the seminar is designed to help students better understand material from their lecture courses; to that end, the seminar takes place in an environment where students can discuss what they are learning in other courses and think more critically about how the unit of courses holds together in a meaningful way.

A particularly striking feature of FYLCP is that seminar instructors, who are adjunct instructors and graduate teaching assistants, attend the tetrad and triad lecture courses with their students and act as teaching assistants for the large courses. Where appropriate, they also assist with the grading function of the discipline-based courses. By attending the classes in the cluster with students, instructors are better able to understand the interconnection between courses within the cluster, which ultimately makes them more effective in the seminar.

We did hear some student complaints about the first-year seminar: "It serves no purpose." "There is too much busy work, and not much substance." "We don't do anything in the class." "It is just basic skills stuff and learning about the campus. I don't need it." But in general the students with whom we spoke understand the role of the first-year seminar in lending meaning to the whole cluster of FYLCP courses. While opinions and attitudes about the relative academic value of the course are varied, students are unequivocally appreciative of the personal value of the course and what it provides to them both personally and socially. It is, in fact, the social glue of the FYLCP structure and the foundation on which students develop their academic and social lives in the first year.

During the semester, the campus regularly collects anonymous feedback from students in the learning communities, asking them questions about the value of their experience and what aspects might be changed. These anonymous reports show that a significant majority of students recognize the value of the seminar and are especially appreciative of the ways their work in seminars helps them in their other learning community classes. In other words, the campus's emphasis on intellectual connections is working.

One point that was stressed repeatedly by many faculty, department chairs, and deans whom we interviewed was the need for the institution to convert the first-year seminar into a more academically rigorous course, a belief shared by Provost Harper. Because the faculty have a strong sense of ownership of the FYLCP, of which the seminar is a major component, this is not surprising. There are also some self-report data from students that speak to their desire to have more academic emphasis in the first-year seminar.

Large lecture classes have become part of the economic reality of the first year at many campuses like TAMU-CC. The university, however, is able to offset the overwhelming nature of the large classroom experience by offering the tetrad and triad structure, which gives students a greater sense of belonging. As one faculty member indicated, students are able to "put energy into the breakout sessions [first-year seminar and English composition] and then bring it back into the big lecture." In a sense, what is given up as a result of the large lecture arrangement is gained as a result of the learning communities, and students feel more comfortable in the large lecture sections because of the intimate nature of the smaller classes. Another way the FYCLP helps students make sense of the cluster of courses in which they are coenrolled is by offering both volunteer and required service-learning experiences to students. These applied learning experiences are embedded in classroom projects and learning components and are evidence of the campus's commitment to its relationship with the external community.

Since 1994, the university has maintained its commitment to growing and expanding the FYLCP, and has done so in an effort to accommodate all entering first-year students. (This is impressive, given that the university enrolls more than 1,200 first-year students per year.) The story of the success of the FYLCP is one of scaling and staging. That is, the goal of the university has been to mainstream more and more students each year into learning communities so that maximum impact can be obtained on a large scale. And the goal has been realized. In 2001, TAMU-CC enrolled all first-year students in a total of eight tetrads and triads.

Striving for Harmony in First-Year Coordination and Implementation

The concept of reaching a critical mass—the idea that desired changes to a system or structure can occur when more and more people are working toward the same goal—is appropriate in describing the work culture at TAMU-CC. The implementation of such a comprehensive first-year program requires a high level of coordination and cooperation among the many units and individuals with responsibility for the first year, and there is palpable harmony among the faculty, staff, and administrators in their work. A campus budget is a reflection of the relative value placed on any particular concept or program, and the university administrators have made it abundantly clear that they support the first year, and do so with both a sizable budget and an effective administrative structure.

Commensurate with the growth of the student population has been an increase in faculty and administrative support for, and involvement in, the first year on campus. Scheduling and staffing the learning communities require a coordination of efforts that is made less onerous by the extraordinary level of support and integration the program enjoys. Involved in this effort are individuals from enrollment management, instructors in the core curriculum, and campus advisers. They work in concert to ensure that students are placed appropriately in the tetrads or triads that best suit their academic, cognitive, and social needs.

There is not only collaboration to make the logistics of the program work, but also a campuswide culture of involvement in the first year. While faculty from the various disciplines teach the core courses and adjunct instructors and graduate students teach the first-year seminar, staff members from student affairs, the library, career development, counseling, and other campus units give presentations to first-year students, typically in the first-year seminar classes, and conduct workshops on issues such as research and study skills and campus diversity.

As a testament to the belief that the success of any first-year program is directly tied to the support of faculty, the First-Year Program at TAMU-CC is coordinated and directed by members of the faculty. This arrangement is vital, given that the FYLCP is an academic structure designed for the delivery of the core curriculum. During the time of our campus visit, the FYLCP was codirected by two faculty members, Andrew Piker from philosophy and Glenn Blalock from the English department. (Blalock was honored in 2002 as one of the nation's Outstanding First-Year Student Advocates by the University of South Carolina's National Resource Center for The First-Year Experience and Students in Transition.)

Piker and Blalock complement each other's styles well and have a common sense of purpose and direction for the program and the first year in general at the university. They are very flexible and honor the changing nature of the academic landscape on campus as the university evolves into a more research-based institution. And they are proactive in their work as well. Blalock shared his motto: "Keep the principles intact, but don't get wedded to the structure." Following that, he provided another guiding principle for the program: "Thou shalt always connect, always find a link." The program, under its current leadership, is flexible and adjustable. In addition, there is a strong desire to experiment with pedagogical approaches and modes of instructional delivery based on feedback and assessment. Blalock indicated the next agenda for the faculty in the First-Year Program, shared by other colleagues as well, is to promote the scholarship of teaching on campus. He is concerned that others on campus—particularly faculty who seem to be averse to the concept of learning communities—see the program as becoming "another college," and he wants to dissuade people from believing that is the extension, and fate, of the FYLCP. He said, "We are *on* an island, but we are *not* an island."

In short, the faculty, staff, and administrators at TAMU-CC take a proactive stance in developing and implementing the first year. In fact, some of the individuals with whom we spoke suggest faculty and others "anticipate a wide range of problems and concerns that potentially occur in the development of programs, creation of schedules, and the delivery of the content and material to the students." One individual said the planners try to find "design blind spots," or areas that are not apparent when setting up the program but might present a fundamental flaw in the design or structure. "The level of integration [in terms of the working relationship of employees and the culture they share] is incredible," said an individual who works in computer science. He indicated that faculty and staff with similar ideas about the role and work of the campus and its service to first-year students find each other on campus. He remarked that individuals "seek out other people who appreciate that culture." In addition, one individual commented that the institution is developing its programs on "good fertile soil," suggesting that the environment, culture, and attitudes of those who work on campus provide a catalyst for growth and development.

Pride Runs Deep: The Lived Experience of First-Year Students

Students are very proud of TAMU-CC, perhaps because the campus is so vastly different from the other large colleges and universities in the state that are euphemistically referred to in casual conversation as "Big State University." The student experience at TAMU-CC is in fact quite different from other nearby campuses—Texas A&M-College Station and the University of Texas, Austin, to name two. Students, faculty, and staff speak frequently about the many ways in which A&M-Corpus Christi is, in their opinion, much better organized to meet the needs of the students enrolled than other campuses they might have attended.

A comparison between what students might experience at "Big State University" versus TAMU-CC was described during a campuswide Open Forum hosted at the beginning of our visit. One of the more powerful examples included the suggestion that students are anonymous at Big State University, whereas students at TAMU-CC have what is called a "mug-shot experience." That is, students' faces are well known. Similarly, students are more likely to have a disjointed academic experience at Big State University, while TAMU-CC offers what they call a "cross-pollinating" classroom experience. That is, students experience a web of classes that are seemingly connected and hold together in a meaningful structure, and there are both formal and informal community-building opportunities provided on campus.

Compared to what their friends at other universities in the state have told them, TAMU-CC students praise many aspects of their relationship with professors, staff, and administrators. One student said, "If you have questions, you can go right up to your instructors afterward; you don't have to go to a TA [teaching assistant] [like students have to do at other schools]." And one student commented on the first-year seminar instructor, saying they "go to the other classes [lecture classes] in the tetrads and triads, and in that sense they are almost like TAs [in that they assist with grading as well as other facets of the tetrads/triads]." Another student shared a story of a friend who visited from another large university and was in awe of the difference between the two institutions in terms of the culture of classroom interaction, the accessibility of the faculty, and the way in which students were treated as individuals. As this student said about TAMU-CC instructors in general, "They made me feel less like a number and more like an individual." (Ironically, the transition issues that new students face are also faced by many new faculty; consider the comment by one faculty member who indicated that he, like many of his students, "did not want to go to 'Big State U' either.")

The transition to college can be challenging for any student, and particularly for those who come from traditionally underrepresented and underserved populations. Whether the challenges relate to the academic or social environment, or both, the first-year program has been highly successful in helping TAMU-CC students make the transition to college life. As one of the student interviewees indicated, "When I came to college, it was tough to meet people, but being in a tetrad really made it easier." Another student echoed the same sentiments: "During the first days on campus, I was nervous and I didn't know anyone. Once you get past the first few weeks, things become routine."

Most of the students made affirming comments about the nature and structure of the learning community clusters and noted their effectiveness in helping students make meaning out of the university academic environment. One student said, "The way tetrads and triads are structured, it is not just like you meet people, but you meet people you can study with," indicating there is a built-in mechanism allowing students to interact on a regular basis, making it easier for them to seek out others for the purpose of developing study groups. Students frequently noted the benefit of having an accessible group of fellow students with whom they can share ideas, study, and discuss their course work. One student commented on the importance of the FYLCP structure: "[The FYLCP] helped a lot with the transition into college. . . . It made it easier to get to know somebody, easier to have [access to] study groups. . . . It made for an easy transition." Following up on these comments, another student suggested the FYLCP not only helped him form study groups but helped him develop good study habits as well.

In our experience, when students feel good about their experience and are treated as though they are valuable—and viable—members of the academic community, they respond in positive ways. And student perceptions about the environment and the faculty and staff with whom they interact on a daily basis are largely positive as well. Talking about her experiences and interactions with faculty and staff on campus, one student indicated that professors and other instructional staff sincerely want students to succeed, and not just academically. "Whether it [relates to] financial problems or personal problems," she said, "they all want you to succeed." In that sense, as another individual put it, many students "find their professors to be like colleagues." This is particularly true for the seminar instructors, who, according to one student, "talk with you about all aspects of first-year life."

Looking Past Disciplinary Boundaries

The deeper hierarchical conceits that exist among the disciplines at many colleges and universities, and the barriers between them that exist as a result, are not major issues at TAMU-CC. When faculty are interviewed for participation in the learning communities—whether they are current or prospective faculty—the line of questioning related to their comfort level with experimentation and working collaboratively with other faculty is a sort of litmus test for their involvement in the program.

There is a culture of sharing and an energy that comes with faculty participation in learning communities. Similarly, there is an experimentation aspect to working in learning communities at TAMU-CC, and it is broadly shared. Not only is there accountability of the faculty, staff, and administration to the students, but there is also accountability "to each other as professionals." For many faculty who have been around the institution for a long time, the advent of the FYLCP was an opportunity, as one said, "to create something from scratch—an opportunity to leave our own stamp on higher education."

The current faculty at TAMU-CC did not inherit a first-year program from other creators and developers, but rather had the opportunity to create one themselves. In that sense, they developed a program in which they would be intellectually invested and willing to participate. As one faculty member and panel presenter at the Open Forum indicated, the first year at TAMU-CC is "faculty designed and faculty owned." As an illustration of the deliberations surrounding the development of the FYLCP, the first-year seminar component started out as an academic concept, but the faculty knew the course needed to include attention to issues of socialization. So both the seminar and the larger learning communities structure, with cohorts of students attending classes and studying together, have become de facto socialization experiences to which students might not have otherwise been exposed.

Within each learning community, professors are essentially given the freedom to develop the tone and theme of the community. That is, the FYLCP structure is a guiding framework that each individual faculty member can use to carve out his or her own niche and focus. They are able to experiment with teaching strategies within the overall framework, and they are ultimately able to discover the most effective method of pedagogy. One faculty member offered a telling comment about the cadre of faculty who are involved in the FYLCP on campus: "This is an active group that pays attention to pedagogy . . . reflective practitioners and scholars in the same skin." Glenn Blalock commented on the desire of faculty to create a sense of community on campus: "This works with real teachers, real students. . . . When it works, it's awesome."

The classroom experience of faculty and students evolves and changes based on the professor's contributions to the courses; one professor's work influences the work of another. In fact, many faculty learn about other instructors' styles by visiting their classes, as evidenced by the first-year seminar instructors' attending the large lecture courses in their tetrad or triad. The process is very "cybernetic" in nature, as one faculty member termed it, and feedback loops (continuous improvement based on continuous feedback) provide an opportunity for professors and their courses to change based on feedback. As one professor at the Open Forum maintained, this arrangement is good for the students, but "it is also a good professional development opportunity for the faculty."

Given the degree to which participation by faculty members in a learning community requires collaboration, a prospect not rewarding to all instructors, we questioned the degree to which faculty have concerns about involvement in the FYLCP. We also wondered if the structure and delivery of learning communities imposed restrictions on faculty and forced them into more social forms of pedagogy at the expense of maintaining a more independent approach to classroom teaching and learning. Many faculty acknowledged that involvement in learning communities is not appropriate for everyone.

Occasionally there is a new faculty member who is particularly concerned with developing a research agenda, is not in favor of collaboration, and would thus not profit from involvement in learning communities. There are also certain faculty who believe that collaboration and academic partnerships require too much work and find it easier to work individually on their pedagogy and scholarship. And this perspective would be true, and perhaps justly so, on any other college or university campus. What sustains the overall approach to the first year at TAMU-CC is the drive and desire of sufficient numbers of like-minded individuals to create, develop, staff, and implement successful programs and structures that require the collaborative efforts of the faculty and staff that are involved.

Faculty impressions of the FYLCP are overwhelmingly positive, at least among the faculty whom we met and interviewed during our visit. There is a high level of support in the administrative ranks for faculty development and involvement in the first-year program. The provost discussed with us the concept of summer teaching institutes, which are designed to educate faculty about first-year students and the structures and methods of teaching that are important in the first year. In addition, faculty are offered course release time for teaching in learning communities. Finally, it should be noted that of the three basic components that comprise the case for tenure and promotion on campus—teaching, research, and service—teaching accounts for 50 percent of the total.

Assessment as Both Teacher and Lever

Texas A&M University-Corpus Christi is engaged in a rigorous and varied assessment program, one that befits an institution aware of its transformational status and desire to improve the campus curriculum and cocurriculum. The assessment regimen is primarily focused on using commercially available national instruments and tools. Several university administrators shared with us findings from the latest campus administration of the National Survey of Student Engagement. Findings were positive in a number of areas. For example, TAMU-CC students scored above the national mean for first-year students on "the frequency with which they integrated ideas from various sources," "prepared multiple drafts of a paper," "gave class presentations," and "had serious conversations with students of a different race or ethnicity."

The above-average score on class presentations was confirmed during our site visit to campus when students described the expectations for class presentations and the frequency with which they were asked to present, either individually or in groups. Many of the students commented that the highly structured design of the learning communities, which brings cohorts of students together for prolonged engagement, gave them the confidence they needed to feel comfortable presenting in front of classes.

Individuals in the Institutional Research Office spoke of the role of assessment on campus and the methods by which assessment is conducted on campus. Paul Orser, the associate vice president for planning and effectiveness, stressed that the university "does not do assessment *to* anyone." Rather, he insisted, assessment is a consultative and collaborative process. Orser conveyed the notion that the university is concerned with meaningful and intentional assessment and avoids "doing assessment for assessment's sake." He added that his office also tries to avoid the "cafeteria approach" to assessment, whereby one randomly selects available and convenient measures and instruments for evaluation. To the contrary, the Institutional Research Office is intentional about developing its own menu of useful assessment resources. For instance, first-year seminar students were asked to assess their individual development with respect to ten common skills and abilities such as note taking, reading retention, writing ability, and critical thinking. On this pre- and posttest survey, students overall reported improvement in all ten areas. In addition, first-year students scored above the national mean on a wide variety of items on the Noel-Levitz Student Satisfaction Inventory (SSI), which focuses, for example, on student perceptions of their own intellectual growth, the quality of instruction they receive, the sense of belonging they feel on campus, the extent to which faculty care about them, and the extent to which they enjoy being a student at the university.

There is an evident open attitude about assessment: TAMU-CC is very public about its desire for evaluation and assessment, and it has a strong commitment to improving by virtue of a culture of evidence. Faculty and staff do not feel assessment is punishment or a means by which the university can arbitrarily hold a person or program up to unfair scrutiny; rather, most people on campus think of assessment as a tool and mechanism for improvement and, just as important, a lever for making the case for new structures. The value that TAMU-CC places on assessment stems from what Paul Orser said was an "introspective campus culture." The faculty and staff involved with the first year are not afraid to open their work and practices to assessment.

At the Open Forum, one faculty member reported that student grades are higher in the tetrads and triads than in the freestanding courses, and institutional assessment data that we received prior to our visit confirm the statement. Overall, the institution has been able to document through assessment and evaluation the effectiveness of the FYLCP structure in providing significant learning experiences for students. In a 1997–98 study comparing students in large tetrad lecture courses with students in large, freestanding lecture courses, data showed that course withdrawal was much lower in the tetrad courses than in the freestanding courses. Similarly, students in the tetrad structure were found to have higher grades at a statistically significant level than students in non-tetrad courses. Perhaps more important, given the historical mission of the campus, the course-level retention rates and higher grades were strongest among Hispanic students.

The positive impact of the FYLCP is evident and well documented. First-to-second-year retention rates for the institution are very high compared to peer institutions in Texas. In fact, retention data for Texas, reported in 1998–199, revealed that TAMU-CC had the highest retention rate among state institutions in its Carnegie classification at 72.2 percent. Another remarkable statistic that underscores the institution's mission and its goal to meet the needs of Hispanic students in the local area and beyond shows the retention rates for Hispanic and African American students in the 1999–2000 academic year were more than 3 percent higher than the rate for European American students.

A History of Recognition

The Institutions of Excellence study is not the first project to recognize and reward TAMU-CC, and specifically the FYLCP, for notable achievement and success with first-year students. In 1996, the FYLCP was invited to participate in the National Learning Communities Dissemination Project, under the auspices of the

Washington Center for Improving the Quality of Undergraduate Education, at the Evergreen State College. At the conclusion of the project, the program received glowing praise from the project director, Jean MacGregor. TAMU-CC shared the following correspondence in its five-page narrative application for the Institutions of Excellence project:

> Texas A&M-Corpus Christi continues to be an important leader in this learning community work . . . . Few schools have exhibited as much commitment to team development and meaningful curricular connections as Texas A&M-Corpus Christi has. We are proud to point to Texas A&M-Corpus Christi and the other campuses in this project as models of practice and expertise, and increasingly, beacons to others in a growing national effort to enhance student learning . . . and deepen our collective understanding of what it means to learn in community [J. MacGregor, personal communication, October 3, 2000].

In addition, TAMU-CC was one of five institutions in Texas to be honored in 2001 with the first annual Texas Higher Education Star Awards from the Texas Higher Education Governing Board. Selected from among eighty-eight programs, projects, or activities, the governor honored the FYLCP for its significant efforts to help students make the transition from high school to college. Finally, TAMU-CC was selected in 2003 as one of twenty-four Founding Institutions in the Policy Center on the First Year of College's Foundations of Excellence in the First College Year project. Founding Institutions have undergone extensive study during the 2003–2004 academic year and have assisted in the refinement of an aspirational model for achieving excellence in the first college year.

Conclusion

We were aware during our visit to TAMU-CC of the importance of self-evaluation on campus and the high level of priority assigned to assessment and continuous improvement. The institution is neither afraid to ask important and tough questions nor to invite scrutiny of the manner in which it develops, promotes, and delivers the first year. There is an extraordinary level of public disclosure about strengths and weaknesses on campus; similarly, the institution does not shy away from experimentation with its first-year program and has not rejected or resisted internal critiques about the first year.

Perhaps the broadest statement about TAMU-CC's success is that there is a high degree of intentionality in the development, implementation, and evaluation of the first year. This intentionality ensures that programs, policies, and procedures are implemented in a deliberate way with a great degree of forethought and anticipation. The institution set this tone early in its work with first-year students, developing and supporting a culture of work that has become deeply embedded in the institutional milieu. Structures such as the FYLCP as well as orientation and advising have attracted faculty and staff with like-minded goals and values, and as a result there is a shared sense of responsibility for the success of the first year. This careful attention to planning and implementation has garnered the institution great success in working with first-year students.

Another striking feature of the culture at TAMU-CC is the degree to which experimentation, risk taking, and innovation are valued and honored by the university community. Whether institutional members are engaged in "responsible innovation" or "controlled experimentation," they all have a measured degree of freedom and flexibility to try new ideas, suggest new structures, and build new campus connections and partnerships in an effort to evolve as the institution changes. This freedom of experimentation allows faculty, staff, and administrators the opportunity to discover the most effective modes of instructional delivery and develop structures to support the academic environment. There is an evident spirit of collaboration at TAMU-CC among the faculty, staff, and administration; it follows that there is a high degree of integration among programs and structures, which follows from good communication and a shared sense of purpose about the first year. There appears to be broad acceptance of the goals of the first year, and as a result departments and units work seamlessly together to help the institution attain those goals.

The close personal attention to students on both academic and social levels is vitally important and effective at TAMU-CC. It is neither condescending nor suffocating. Rather, it is alternatively firm and helpful at the same time. The follow scenario—typical on this campus—illustrates the manner in which issues and concerns are typically dealt. One of the academic support staff members with whom we spoke indicated:

> To assist with retention, we track attendance very carefully. We are not looking for excuses to get people withdrawn [from school]; we are trying to [establish] a policy of inclusion rather than exclusion. Consider a young lady [student] who says, "I have not been to any of my math classes because my dad called me—my mom got sick and he wanted me to come back [home] because I'm expected to cook for my brothers and sisters." We have to understand that . . . so when the student returns we are looking for ways to help her.

There is a sense on campus that individuals, particularly faculty who work with first-year programs, desire a collaborative culture and attempt to create the type of small campus atmosphere that promotes the success of first-year students. There is remarkable intentionality in the way the institution approaches the first year, and it is evident in the big picture as well as in the details. Ultimately, the story of the university's success in working with first-year students is one of a committed group of core faculty and staff who have come together to develop a strong and viable first year, methodically recruiting individuals internally and externally who have a strong desire to support the success of first-year students.

Part Five

Case Studies of Four-Year Institutions with 10,000 to 20,000 Students

Chapter Twelve

Appalachian State University

High Standards for the First Year in North Carolina's High Country

John N. Gardner

Betsy O. Barefoot

Of all the thirteen Institutions of Excellence, Appalachian State University is the most geographically isolated. Its location in Boone, North Carolina, is about two hours driving distance (and 3,000 feet up) from the nearest major cities in North Carolina. The university's enrollment of 13,762 students (12,560 undergraduate and 1,202 graduate) is virtually equal to the permanent resident population of Boone, the county seat of Watauga County. Appalachian is one of the three most selective campuses of the sixteen-member University of North Carolina System and has a total applicant pool of around 10,000 for an entering class of approximately 2,300 students. This entering first-year class is primarily traditional-aged, residential, and almost evenly divided between women and men.

The Boone environs are what the locals call "the high country" of western North Carolina, and this location has been both a great advantage and disadvantage for Appalachian over its history. No doubt the campus's beautiful location, in what is also a major tourist destination and ski resort, accounts for some of its appeal to prospective students, but so do its academic offerings and academic reputation, as well as its more liberal culture by the standards of the state and region. And this relative isolation may account for what the institution's chief academic officer describes as a caring family culture that would be difficult, if not impossible, to replicate in a more urban setting.

The recognition of Appalachian State University as an Institution of Excellence in the First College Year is only one of several honors and accolades the university has received for outstanding first-year initiatives. In September 2001, this campus was one of four in the nation selected by *Time* magazine as a College of the Year for its outstanding first-year programs, and in the spring of 2002, Appalachian received the Noel-Levitz retention award for its Freshman Learning Communities in General Studies (FLC) program.

A number of distinctive factors make up the Appalachian story and set this campus apart from most others of its size and type in its ability to launch and maintain outstanding first-year initiatives. Two of those factors that we will return to again and again in this chapter are Appalachian's history and its remarkably stable leadership. The current chancellor is only the fifth chief executive officer in the 103 years of the institution's existence. In fact, the first president, B. B. Dougherty, who in 1899 founded Watauga Academy, the forerunner to the university, established this precedent for extraordinary stability and presidential influence by serving as president for fifty-six years. Chancellor Frank Borkowski, in describing the origins of the university's current emphasis on first-year students, maintains that its location and history are also central to understanding its current achievements:

> This is a community of great pride. In part, this is built on our traditions of facing adversity. For example, our first state funding didn't come until 1903, and it was won by only one vote. When compared to the Research Triangle area of the state of North Carolina, this campus has never quite received its fair share (other western North Carolinians say the same about the whole region). . . . Why, in the late nineteenth century, this area used to be known as the "lost provinces." I have always had a keen sense of the university's sense of its own history, and that of its region, and our pride in adversity . . . the kind that comes from being ignored by people in the middle of the state.

As visitors enter the valley that now encompasses both the town of Boone and the university campus, it is patently obvious that this area is no longer ignored by the outside world. A variety of shopping malls abut a booming, modern, attractive university campus that is nestled into and onto the backs of the surrounding mountains. The region, town, and campus are flourishing as they deal with all the pressures of growth and demand from a number of sources: a thriving and highly respected state higher education system, a local economy being driven by the area's discovery as a retiree haven, a mecca for local artists, a refuge for Florida natives—some of whom escape here for summers only—and in general a safe and secure "drive-to" tourist destination. In spite of recent budget cuts that are capping salaries and reducing numbers of new employees, the campus is dotted with new construction—a result of the $3.1 billion bond referendum passed in 2000 by North Carolina citizens for the benefit of its higher education system.

Mission and History

Appalachian's mission statement along with its eighteen goals for the baccalaureate degree take up more space than do similar mission statements in many college catalogues. This mission statement, quoted in part below, is inextricable from its history:

> Appalachian State University is a comprehensive university, offering a broad range of undergraduate programs and select graduate programs. Undergraduates receive a well-rounded liberal education and the opportunity to pursue a special field of inquiry in preparation for advanced study or a specific career. . . . Although the campus is largely residential in character and its students are predominately of traditional college age, the University seeks to serve a diverse student body.
>
> With instruction as its primary mission, the University is committed to excellence in teaching and the fostering of scholarship. As an academic community, it takes pride in its tradition of faculty commitment to students both inside and outside the classroom. Mindful of the relationship between the curricular and extracurricular, Appalachian seeks to promote the intellectual, cultural, and personal development of its students. . . . At Appalachian, scholarship and service are complementary to the instructional mission. The major purposes of scholarship, including research,

> writing, and other creative activities, are threefold: to serve as a basis for instruction, to ensure a vital and intellectually engaged faculty, and to contribute to the advancement of knowledge [University Undergraduate Bulletin, 2001—2003, p. 3].

The catalogue then continues for two pages to trace "A History of Service to Students" in five distinct eras, each era coterminous with its five presidents. This level of appreciation, respect, and understanding for its past is something that the university intentionally seeks to inculcate in new students. As part of Appalachian's first-year seminar, students walk through the university cemetery and learn about the lives of noted university citizens for whom many of the buildings are named. For instance, Wey Hall was named for the third university leader, Herbert Wey, who was so interested in innovation (which ultimately led to many of the first-year initiatives) that he appointed a dean for innovation and change, an action that led to an inside joke that the university also needed a "dean of the status quo."

But it was also Herbert Wey, whose title was changed to chancellor in 1971, who saw the importance of the national movement of student unrest and civil disobedience and ordered his subordinates to make a study of the residential college model as a means to better integrate faculty, administration, and students with the overall goal of increasing trust among all members of the university community. At Appalachian, the key structure for innovation, experimentation, and change was Watauga College, which was founded in 1972 as a residential college.

Importance of Senior Leadership

A common theme that emerged from each of the thirteen site visits was the important role of senior leaders in maintaining a focus on the first year. Appalachian is a classic example of this theme.

The Chancellor and the Appalachian Way

The critical connection between Appalachian's mission, history, and leadership is put into perspective by the chancellor, Francis Borkowski, who is keenly aware of this history-leader interface and the call of that history to suggest appropriate means to continue the institution's service mission. (Since this site visit was conducted in fall 2002, Francis Borkowski has been succeeded by Kenneth E. Peacock as Appalachian's chancellor.) Borkowski spoke of "the need to establish a vision for the University based on its history. . . . Our University founder, B. B. Dougherty, in 1899, when he established Watauga Academy, was committed to preparing young people for the twentieth century—I believe that my role now is to prepare students for the twenty-first century." Speaking of the original mission to serve the region, he stated:

> I stress service to the region. . . . But what really makes us what we are is not being a publish-or-perish institution. . . . I wanted to develop a model learning environment. Thus the goal now is to become the best comprehensive university in the country with this model learning environment characterized by very close relationships between faculty and students. . . . Plus we need to have the latest up-to-date technology, plus the ability for students to learn in a state-of-the-art environment without students losing the sense of tradition of why the university was founded in 1899. We are the only university in the state that requires its faculty to post ten hours a week of office hours. In surveys done by the University of North Carolina System Administration, we ranked number one in accessibility to faculty, advising, academic quality, and the quality of food! We have tried to nurture this learning environment so the first-year learning experience would fit into this. It is all about a sense of community, and getting to know others, having fun, coming to know the university, writing about one's experiences. We have nearly 10,000 applications for 2,400 slots, but if students are from this region and have some characteristics of disadvantage—yet also have the potential—then the university as part of its historic mission will take these students.

This sense of intentionality about history and mission and about creating a sense of community are indeed the core values that came through in all interactions between us as the research team and interviewees. This culture is also known as the Appalachian Way—a set of ideals that are even taught in the new department chairs' training sessions. This way was described by one faculty member and chair as "an emphasis on face-to-face interchange, knowing people across faculty and staff lines, and building networks."

The chancellor's own commitment to the first year is evidenced by his personal investment of time and energy in coteaching a section of the first-year seminar. He reflected on his own symbolic behavior as follows: "Due to the budget crisis and our seventy-five position vacancies and impending reductions, I did not want to lay off anyone. So we are not filling vacancies. And I wanted to relieve some of the increased pressure on faculty and demonstrate the symbolic importance of teaching. So I urged administrators to teach, and I had to model that. The response has been good."

We visited Borkowski's first-year seminar class and observed his interactions with twenty-two new students. He drew on the lessons he learned in 1970 from dealing with campus unrest and a town-gown controversy at Ohio University, and he applied them to the contemporary American campus and Appalachian in particular. A student queried the chancellor about his views of a recent town-gown disturbance following a surprise football victory. Specifically, the student asked Borkowski his opinion about a postgame celebration that spilled over the campus boundaries and drew criticism from some local residents. Borkowski responded, "I have complete confidence in Appalachian students." And Appalachian students seem to have the same sentiment about the chancellor. When queried about the basis for the high level of student satisfaction on campus, a student stated, "It's all due to Frank." To which we responded, "Frank . . . ?" and the same student replied, "Frank Borkowski, the chancellor," as if to say, "Who else could I be talking about?"

The Provost and Executive Vice Chancellor

In other research conducted by the Policy Center, we have determined that a key player in any institution's ability to achieve its mission is the chief academic officer. At the time of our study, Appalachian's provost and executive vice chancellor, Harvey Durham, was another study in institutional loyalty, stability, longevity, and keen awareness of institutional history and mission. In addition, he was intentional about maintaining the campus culture, history, and traditions, and he expressed passion about the importance of serving first-year students. In 2002, this vice chancellor was in his thirty-eighth year of service to Appalachian. He had served as vice chancellor since 1979 under two chancellors and prior to that time had also served as associate vice chancellor and department chair. He was sixty-four years old, a mathematician whose first academic position after graduate school was as an assistant professor at Appalachian. (Since this site visit was conducted in fall 2002, Durham has been succeeded by Stanley R. Aeschleman, who is serving as interim provost and vice chancellor for academic affairs.)

Before campus interviews began, we had been told repeatedly that the vice chancellor was the single most important long-term key to success of the university's first-year initiatives. Described by faculty and academic line administrators as "a strong, quiet advocate," he frequently weighed in to oppose reorganization proposals that would weaken a successful organizational model known as "enrollment services." This model integrates virtually all support units for first-year students in a seamless structure reporting through academic channels. One old hand put it this way: "The key role supporting innovation here has been Harvey. Harvey likes a good idea. He is really willing to support new ideas; Harvey is a very talented 'people person.'"

Durham himself attributes much of the university's success to the core value of building and maintaining community, even in the face of mounting pressures to increase undergraduate enrollment (due to tremendous demographic changes in the state) and pressures from department chairs and faculty to reduce faculty teaching loads and increase class sizes. The pressure to provide release time is particularly powerful and, in his judgment, one that should be resisted in order to maintain the core mission and history of Appalachian in support of undergraduates. When asked about what his role had been in a thirty-year history of innovation and then resulting accolades, he modestly replied:

> I sit in the position that provides resources. I have directed those resources incrementally along the way. . . . I have beat the drum in trying to recruit new faculty participants [for example, for first-year seminars]. . . . My greatest contribution has been keeping the doors open budgetarily. I do not have to run to the chancellor; I can make my own decisions. All my professional life, I have had

> an interest in freshmen. My first love was always teaching freshmen. Both John Thomas [former chancellor] and Frank [current chancellor] did not need to hold all of the money. I am not a "pass through" provost; I want the deans to make decisions. I did not want to see Appalachian become the Harvard of the Hills! The basic mission is undergraduate teaching. Top priority has always been enough money for freshman classes, and the issue of class size. . . . My successor [this interview was conducted in his last year prior to retirement] will have to pay attention to the class size issue and must not give in on this one in particular by giving out release time. I have learned to be a flexible leader. This has been accepted by the chairs. I did not want this to be Mr. Chips running Appalachian. . . . The provost needs someone who can come in and bang on the table and honestly tell me what I ought to be doing. . . . Dr. Cratis Williams, the dean of the graduate school here who is now deceased, taught me how to get things done by persuasion versus authority and power.

The Appalachian First-Year Experience

We have written at great length to describe the role of history, mission, culture, values, and senior leadership in shaping the foundation for the university's first-year initiatives. Now we illustrate how this all plays out in the design of the specifics of the first year at Appalachian.

The first-year experience at Appalachian State University comprises so many activities and opportunities for students that it is hard to do justice to all of them in a brief written review. What follows is a summary of the major components of the first year, which the university correctly describes as "intentional, comprehensive, and seamless."

Admissions

The Appalachian experience begins with admissions, a process described by one student as "real personal." Printed admissions materials are comprehensive but extremely well organized and easy to follow. The campus view book, first connection orientation planner, and follow-up academic planner provide Web links for additional information, as well as names and telephone numbers of faculty and staff. When prospective students arrive for a campus visit, they start by viewing a three-screen video extravaganza—music and scenes of the campus and surrounding community with absolutely no verbal narration. This visual promotion has taken on a life of its own, and virtually everyone we interviewed asked if we had seen it. Many faculty and staff members watch it repeatedly themselves, and it brings some of them literally to tears. It is very evocative and, we expect, highly effective with today's highly visual generation. All admissions communications, print, verbal, and media, strive to project a common message. As one senior admissions staff member put it: "We want something informal yet elegant. We hit on the collaboration theme, trying to get at both involvement and collaboration. All department chairs get our admissions materials and have the opportunity to update their content within."

Orientation

Although the vast majority of American campuses offer some sort of preterm orientation, Appalachian's version of this experience is novel because it is required of all students, is academic in emphasis, and is the administrative responsibility of both academic affairs and student development units. Preterm orientation is accomplished in two phases. The two-day phase I orientation is administered by academic affairs with the assistance of upper-level "orienteers" and occurs at various times during the summer months. Orientation materials state that this two-day period gives each student "a time to meet your academic advisor, take assessment tests, begin planning your academic career path, adjust your schedule, receive your Summer Reading book and materials, and become comfortable with the campus." Students may also opt for First Ascent, Appalachian's four-day wilderness orientation in which groups of no more than twelve students spend four days backpacking through the Pisgah National Forest.

When students return for the fall semester, they participate in phase II orientation, administered by student development. This phase introduces students to various aspects of campus life. For example, students learn about opportunities for joining and involvement in campus clubs and organizations as well as leadership training and development opportunities. Students also have a "walking class tour of their academic schedule." Phase II extensively uses students as "Appol Corps leaders," some 106 who are selected out of 200 applicants. Appol Corps leaders go to residence halls to gather new students for the first activity rather than waiting for those students to show up at a predetermined location.

Over 100 faculty (out of a total of over 600 full-time and 300 part-time faculty) are also selected to be leaders in two orientation activities. The first is informal sharing of academic expectations and tips for success in the first year. And the second, conducted in over 100 discussion groups, focuses exclusively on a summer reading assignment. In addition to small group, faculty-led discussion, students attend a presentation by the book's author, who visits the campus to meet with both first-year and upperclass students. Previous readings include National Book Award–winning author Tim O'Brien's *The Things They Carried: A Work of Fiction,* North Carolina author Lee Smith's *Oral History,* and Ernest Gaines's *A Lesson Before Dying.* The summer reading program is also connected to the external community using a model borrowed from Seattle and also practiced in Rochester and Buffalo, New York, as well as Greensboro and Asheville, North Carolina. This model, called "If All of Watauga County Read the Same Book," involves the university, public schools, community college, and community libraries.

Residential Living Options

All first-year students—except those who are married, single parents, or live with a parent or guardian in the local community—are required to live on campus. In recent years, Appalachian has experimented with a number of living-learning models, some restricted to first-year students and others open to students at any level. Campus administrators are quick to acknowledge that some of the residential experiments have been more successful than others, but one that has stood the test of time is Watauga College, an interdisciplinary living-learning community that serves as the academic home for residents during the first and second years. Other residential options include theme housing (wellness, international, and "study" halls or floors).

"If the mind is a wilderness to be explored, the students and faculty of Watauga College are always packed and anxious to get going. . . . Watauga College is not for the weak of mind or the faint of heart. No assumption goes unchallenged, no platitude goes unquestioned, no risk goes unnoticed." This is the language that begins the Web site description for this unique residential college environment, founded in 1972, where faculty and students live and work closely together. The Web description continues:

> Watauga College is an interdisciplinary, residential program that expects its students to read, write, think, argue, challenge, ponder, change, struggle, laugh and live together during their first years of college. Watauga College allows incoming Appalachian State University students to fulfill their core requirements for English and history in small, interdisciplinary classes that place a heavy emphasis on creativity, discussion and curiosity. Watauga students develop writing, critical reading, and discussion skills, while exploring intriguing ideas and histories through a challenging and rigorous curriculum, and are well prepared to select any major Appalachian offers. In Fall, 2003, Watauga College moved to the Living and Learning Center, Appalachian's newest and most beautiful residence hall [http://www.ids.appstate.edu/watauga.html].

This new Living and Learning Center, which accommodates 210 Watauga students, is also home to two other learning communities: Teaching Fellows, a learning community for prospective school teachers; and the international learning community. Students had a significant role in planning this new facility, and student and university planners determined that it would be a nonsmoking hall, a position that continues to foster debate on campus.

Freshman Seminars

Appalachian State University first offered freshman seminars in 1987, and in the intervening years the number of sections has increased dramatically, actually doubling over the past three years to its current level of sixty-two sections. The most significant factor that accounts for this increase is the linking of the freshman seminar in 1998 to other first-year classes in a new program, Freshman Learning Communities in General Studies (FLC). Planning for this program began in 1997, but the first options were available in fall 1998. Currently any student who wishes to participate in a general education, major-related, or theme-based learning community will by default take the freshman seminar as one of two or three learning community courses. The director of Freshman Seminar, Professor Rennie Brantz, observes that the seminar is the cornerstone of the FLC program and has a unique role to play in helping students make a successful transition to college. But its rapid growth has posed the familiar problems of classroom space allocation, faculty recruiting and training, and necessary funding. A growing concern for Brantz is the decreasing number of full-time faculty who express interest in teaching the seminar. Currently faculty comprise only about 20 percent of the instructor pool. The bulk of freshman seminar instruction is provided by part-time instructors, administrators, academic advisers, and student development professionals.

While acknowledging that many nonfaculty instructors do a "wonderful job" of teaching, Brantz worries that a reduction in faculty numbers "undermines the academic credibility" of the course. However, in spite of his concerns about external perceptions of the seminar, he reports that the course does a highly credible job of supporting the primary academic goals of the institution, such as writing, critical thinking, and in-depth learning. In describing Brantz, an award-winning faculty member, many student interviewees called him "a really remarkable teacher."

Freshman Learning Communities

Although Appalachian has a long history of targeted learning communities for certain student populations, the institution's attempt to ramp up this educational structure to serve the majority of first-year students dates to fall 1998. Enrollment in learning communities has grown dramatically over this rather short time span and currently represents about 87 percent of the first-year class. The newly implemented FLC program accounts for the greatest percentage of growth, enrolling approximately 68 percent of all first-year students in one of its linked course offerings. The FLC program was created in an effort to increase student retention and serve students not being served by one of the other learning community options open to first-year students (Watauga College, Honors, Teaching Fellows, Student Support Services, or Reserve Officer

Training Corps). The program has shown itself to be an effective retention tool. With only a few exceptions, the FLC options link two courses and include the freshman seminar as the anchor course. We learned that one concern about linking more than two courses was the phenomenon of "too much togetherness—too much cliquishness." A key conceptual approach to winning faculty support for the learning community concept has been to use existing courses taught by current faculty so as not to dilute or reallocate scarce resources.

Other Programs and Structures

Appalachian provides many other programs and structures that support first-year students. Following are brief descriptions of initiatives that link to both the curriculum and cocurriculum.

Academic Advising

All first-year students at Appalachian are advised in the university's Advising Center, which is staffed by a mix of professional and faculty advisers. Advisers are also assigned to work with each learning community, and once a month, they provide group advising within the learning community setting. In their first meeting with students, academic advisers review individual results of the College Student Inventory (CSI), a product of Noel-Levitz, which students complete during phase I orientation. The CSI is designed to identify student characteristics and behaviors that correlate with possible academic difficulty and early dropout. The Academic Advising Center also oversees the collection and dissemination of midterm academic progress reports for all students. These reports, based on student in-class participation and grades at midterm, are supplied by classroom faculty and are available to students and their advisers. Appalachian's first-year advisers participate in highly detailed training modules and are also involved in faculty development for the freshman seminar.

Academic Assistance

All first-year students may receive academic assistance through a combination of the tutoring, Supplemental Instruction, and learning skills courses and workshops. One-to-one tutoring is provided for approximately 1,400 students at any level of academic ability. Supplemental Instruction is linked to first-year courses in biology, chemistry, and history. The campus also offers a variety of learning skills courses designed for all students, plus a wide range of additional services and programs for at-risk subpopulations, including economically disadvantaged students, students with disabilities, and athletes.

Cocurricular Activities

Through the Center for Student Involvement and Leadership (CSIL) in the Division of Student Development, first-year students can choose from a wide array of cocurricular activities that introduce them to the local environs, civic engagement and service, residential options, opportunities for leadership training, and 250 student organizations. Students can participate in a number of wilderness activities, including two summer "Trailhead Academies" for incoming first-year students, one for women and one for both women and men. Each academy has approximately sixteen participants who are chosen from among the strongest applicants in the incoming first-year class. The four-day academies are an opportunity to meet and get to know other new first-year students while learning about a model of leadership and service that will be useful to students in their college careers and beyond. The CSIL director stated, "At Appalachian, the expectation is involvement—not whether you'll be involved, but what you'll be involved in. We stress what we call the 'Appalachian legacy'—what will you leave here when you graduate?"

Breadth and Depth of First-Year Initiatives

Readers knowledgeable about the range of approaches being taken across American higher education to enhance the transition and academic success of first-year students would have to conclude that Appalachian is doing virtually all of the initiatives that have been implemented at other campuses and doing them to great depth (as opposed to a more superficial set of offerings). In addition, the university has achieved a significant level of participation—a critical mass—in such interventions as the freshman seminar and freshman learning communities.

How First-Year Students Experience Appalachian

The 5-to-1 ratio of applications to admissions is testimony to college-bound students' interest in Appalachian. But what do students find when they arrive? In our interviews with upper-level students on the general topic of what it was like to be a first-year student at Appalachian, the consistency of responses was striking, and the language students used to describe the campus culture was remarkably similar to language used by faculty and staff. In recalling their most significant memories of the first year, students mentioned the following: being pushed to get involved; the impact of the rural environment; the importance of community and small group learning experiences; being taught teamwork and leadership skills; the value of linked classes in the learning communities; the personal nature of the culture; positive attitudes toward faculty, especially older members of the professoriate; the notion of the university as home; and the value of service activities.

Students gave a variety of reasons for selecting Appalachian, but most of the reasons related to the institution's size and environment. One student indicated, "I like winter, so Appalachian was my first choice." Another student was even more candid: "I applied to Appalachian because it was the shortest application. Once I got in, I didn't want to fill out other applications." Although the students interviewed were from a variety of majors and had been participants in multiple, but different, special programs, all described the university's success in providing them meaningful small group experiences that helped them make friends and adjust to the new environment (which was hardest for students from urban environments). One student said, "Freshman seminar was my best class . . . it was more like a family. . . . I really loved the group activities, the ropes course, the focus on teamwork, learning the folklore and history of the university." This student, now a sophomore peer leader, continued, "My freshman seminar was so valuable that now I want to help freshmen. . . . I like this role [as peer leader] because it gives me the opportunity to practice leadership skills."

Students had similar praise for the FLC: "I made my two best friends in this class because I went to the same classes every day with my friends." Another said, "These classes meet every day; they include a movie night, going out for dinner as a group; reading the same books for both courses. I established relationships with both of my professors; it gives us a family-type setting."

Several students whom we interviewed came from the university's residential home for innovation and experimentation, Watauga College. One student described her experience as a Wataugan: "We have over 200 students in the same building; we are all taking the same courses; we are like a family. Immediately as a freshman student, I had a family. I immediately had an identity, a sense of security. . . . The classes in Watauga College were the opposite of 'spit it back' classes, which bore me; for me Watauga College was like a godsend."

Another student from Watauga College spoke to the importance of its size: "If Watauga College were larger, it would not be the same; I like the small environment; I don't want it to grow, it's kind of like a community." This student had come to Appalachian as her second choice after being denied admission at a public, urban university in a popular tourist beach location. But upon coming to "App," she described her experience as "real personal. . . . They are so personal here; someone from the university called me personally [from admissions during the admissions process]; no other college would have done that. . . . It is so community-like here, it is comforting." Another student added, "When I come back to campus, I just feel like I'm pulling in the driveway at home."

Students and employees of the institution alike were of the opinion that the university's "small community" culture should not change, and they expressed concerns about the pressures toward continuing growth. No student interviewee wanted any kind of departure from this small group culture within a university environment. One student summed this up perhaps most poignantly when he told us, "ASU has a smallness and cohesiveness; there are lots of small, tightly knit, groups. All students at ASU want to maintain our sense of community." One student did tell us, "This is not a very diverse community."

We found of interest the students' attitudes regarding faculty, particularly as a function of the students' age. Educators often wonder and worry about the generation gap—the differences between teachers' and students' learning styles, preferences, and other characteristics. But these students expressed particular respect for "older" professors who "have a tendency to act younger; one older professor has far more energy than the younger faculty; older faculty seem more excited about their careers here, because they want to be here." A student generalized about all the faculty when she described them as "generally older and possessing a wealth of knowledge." Another student joined the consensus of others in describing the push from faculty to get involved: "A lot of teachers will give you credit if you just get out and get involved with the school, for example, attend a play or Walk for Awareness. . . . The faculty make you get out; it is great for building a sense of community." Another summed up her experience with faculty and introduced to us a new concept that we describe as the "hug test" for the quality of faculty-student relationships: "I get personal attention from my professors and from everyone else. . . . I haven't had one professor I wouldn't be willing to hug. . . . I feel very comfortable sharing personal information with my professors. . . . They all want to see us do well." Several students spoke appreciatively about how they were either required or encouraged by the faculty to get out and experience the local environment, culture, and traditions. All the students whom we interviewed had had some kind of service experience and testified as to its value.

Although we routinely posed the question, "What would you change about Appalachian if you could?" it was virtually impossible to elicit from students any "suggestions for improvement." Other than the familiar complaints about food and parking, the students whom we interviewed seemed overwhelmingly positive about their experience. We also found remarkable congruity between the way institutional officials described the university culture they were trying to create and what the students told us they had experienced. Perhaps this comment from a third-year student summarizes the consistency between intent and actuality when she told one of the researchers: "This is my home. . . . Appalachian will always be my home. This is the place where I grew up and became myself—where I learned who I am and where I learned what I can be. You learn here that you can be so much more."

Administrative Structures That Support First-Year Innovation

We have argued previously that colleges and universities need a designated home for innovation, experimentation, and risk taking. For Appalachian, Watauga College has served that purpose since

1972. Originally Watauga College was part of the General College, a larger centralized unit for change and nontraditional interventions that originated in the 1960s and existed until its founding dean, Omri Kenneth, "O.K," Webb, a key leader for innovation for over two decades, stepped down in the mid-1990s. (O. K. Webb passed away on January 5, 2004.)

This unit, and Dean Webb in particular, can be credited with launching, establishing, institutionalizing, and then spinning off programs that had demonstrated their long-term value to the institution. These include special programs for honors students, interdisciplinary studies, learning assistance, Supplemental Instruction, academic advising, residential living-learning, and TRIO programs. TRIO programs, established under the Higher Education Act of 1965, are designed to help low-income students enter college, graduate, and participate successfully in life after college, including graduate school. Webb brought to his leadership of the General College the perspectives of both a student affairs administrator and faculty member. He began his career at Appalachian as a professor of religion and philosophy; he then applied his self-described pastoral skills to becoming dean of students before he was asked to head the new General College. In our telephone interview with Webb, he expressed only one "professional regret": his decision to eliminate student affairs functions from the General College structure. He recalled, "Years later I tried to put it back together, but I just couldn't sell it to the faculty or the administration."

A number of our interviewees who could be described as midlevel and senior administrators and program directors, all with more than twenty years of service to the institution, gave testimony to getting their start in the former General College and especially in the TRIO programs. TRIO was singled out as a source for innovation and risk taking on behalf of the most disadvantaged students, which in turn produced larger lessons about how to achieve student success for all Appalachian students. Early TRIO administrators progressed to positions of increasing influence in shaping the long-term culture and directions of the institution's approach to student success. A number of these individuals remain at the institution.

A more recent structure for first-year student success at Appalachian is a unique unit known as enrollment services. This model connects and integrates into one organizational unit almost all functions pertaining to the success of first-year students: admissions, registration, general studies, orientation, TRIO, advising, academic progress reports, learning assistance and tutoring, freshman learning communities, and summer reading. This unit reports to the provost. One senior leader attributed much of Appalachian's success with first-year students to this integrated unit, which includes functions that on other campuses often report to student affairs. This senior administrator went on to say, "We have learned in thirty years to emphasize our partnerships and speak with one voice." This concept of enrollment services then provides a "one voice" structure for new students. The provost offered another perspective when he said: "I have long believed that registration and admissions are academic functions. It is tough enough to work with deans and department chairs, let alone have student affairs control registration and admissions. I would have to go and beg them too [in addition to the academic deans and department chairs, for example, for courses and faculty for first-year students] every time I wanted something."

Finally, a unique structural aspect of this institution is what we have chosen to designate as a culture of councils and committees: multiple groups established for communication, evaluation, policy advisement, problem solving, and advocacy. There are no fewer than twelve such councils and committees that meet regularly to discuss their functions as they relate to the welfare of first-year students:

- University Advising Council
- Core Curriculum Council
- Enrollment Services
- Academic Policies and Procedures
- University Orientation Council
- Learning Communities Council
- Diversity Council
- Summer Reading Committee
- Hubbard Center Faculty Development Council
- Freshman Seminar Student Advisory Council
- Faculty/Resident Assistant Exchange Committee
- Learning Communities Institute Team

What was particularly striking was the frequency with which these groups were referenced and how quickly they were called into session after the arrival of each year's new first-year class to debrief the opening of school and to begin planning immediately for the next year. This is a clearly intentional, highly valued, and institutionalized array of communications structures designed to ensure the coherence of the first-year experience and to maintain a sense of community within the institution for those who are charged with creating and maintaining that sense of community for arriving students. This is also a model that is easily replicable.

A facility that supports Appalachian's current levels of excellence is the John E. Thomas Center (named for a past chancellor) and referred by students and employees alike as the JET. This facility houses and integrates admissions, financial aid, registration, career development, student accounts, and housing into a one-stop area "designed to make the bureaucracy simpler." Finally, while many of these structural components are not necessarily unique in and of themselves, it is their combination and integration that makes this aspect of the Appalachian culture so striking.

Contributions of the Division of Student Development

No examination of a university culture so successful in involving students would be complete without consideration of the contributions and philosophy of those individuals and units responsible for student life outside the formal academic curriculum. At Appalachian, the vice chancellor for student development, Gregory Blimling, reports directly to the chancellor, and like many other of the senior officers of this university, his longevity is another example of the larger theme of leadership stability and continuity. The current vice chancellor has served in the role since 1990 and is known in his larger peer group of student affairs professionals as one of the most prominent scholars and writers in that profession. In fact, he serves as the editor of one of its most important scholarly journals, the *Journal of College Student Development.* (In fall 2004 Blimling became vice president for student affairs at Rutgers University.)

Blimling articulated a strong student-centered philosophy. When commenting on Appalachian's unique enrollment services unit that oversees many traditional student affairs activities for first-year students and reports through academic channels, he remarked, "Special efforts for first-year students do not have to be in student affairs. . . . The key question is: Does it work for the students?" He went on to explain that "this campus has become much more student centered. Historically, this was a faculty-centered campus, but there has been a seminal change in this regard. Student affairs has advocated for this and pressed to do these things. . . . We cannot talk about what student affairs needs—we have had to talk about what students need."

The division of student development oversees housing, financial aid, recreation, judicial affairs, health services, counseling, career development, student clubs and organizations, the Center for Student Involvement and Leadership, and finally the unique Center for Student Life and Learning Research. Over recent years, there has been significant new construction to support student development functions and a twelve-year budget increase of nearly fivefold. Like their counterparts on the academic side, student development administrators also exhibit stability and longevity of service at many levels; the associate vice chancellor of the unit has served thirty years and the vice chancellor thirteen years, and the average age of the staff is forty-six years. Blimling summarized his perspective on the Appalachian Way as follows:

> In the typical research university, students are less on the agenda, and the real issues are faculty rewards, reputation, research, grants, etc. In contrast, at ASU, research grants are not a primary part of the conversation. Here, the conversation is much more about the quality of undergraduate student learning. This is like stepping back into the 1950s. ASU has an advantage—we focus on undergraduates. We have made as our objective increased retention. We do this through the freshman seminar plus student-faculty relationships, involvement in student organizations and the residence halls. Students here have a really positive attitude. There is something about the culture here. Students like one another a whole lot. It is all connected to the kind of students who are attracted here—the L. L. Bean Generation, the kinds of traditional-aged college students who are drawn to the outdoors and who often choose colleges and universities in remote, wilderness locations.

From our perspective, one of the things that is so striking about the Appalachian environment is the consistency of language used across campus to describe institutional priorities and culture: Student development administrators use the same language as their colleagues on the academic side of the house. It would appear that one of the characteristics of the Appalachian Way is that all employees seem to share its inherent culture and values.

Appalachian's Approach to Assessment

In surveying the landscape of American higher education, an observer can identify only a handful of institutions in which first-year assessment and research on first-year students as a unique cohort group are part of the institutional fabric. Appalachian State University is one of those institutions. And this focus on research and assessment is a combined effort of the Office of Institutional Research and Planning in the Division of Academic Affairs and the Office of Student Life and Learning Research in the Division of Student Development.

The Office of Institutional Research and Planning conducts routine tracking of student retention and graduation rates as well as academic progress measured by grade point average. These data are not only provided to state and federal overseers; they are also used internally to determine the impact of various programs and interventions such as the freshman seminar and freshman learning communities. In addition, this office studies a variety of general education learning outcomes that are articulated in the campus mission and goals: oral communication, critical thinking, social science reasoning, computing skills, information literacy, writing, and math literacy. This type of assessment is accomplished by evaluating one skill deeply at multiple intervals throughout the undergraduate experience. Baseline data collection with a first-year cohort group takes place during the first week of the first semester. This is followed by assessment of the same students and the same learning outcome at the beginning of the third year and the end of the senior year.

The Office of Institutional Research and Planning also administers state and national instruments that provide comparative data with other peer institutions. These include the National Survey of Student Engagement, the College Student Expectations Questionnaire, and the College Student Experiences Questionnaire, as well as University of North Carolina Freshman, Sophomore, Senior, and Alumni Surveys. Qualitative research methods such as focus groups are used intermittently to achieve a deeper understanding of survey research. A unique feature of Appalachian's assessment efforts is the annual focus day (assessment day) in which all students are required to participate. Student participation rates in focus days are generally in excess of 97 percent; the carrot is early registration for spring classes, and the stick is delayed registration. Assessment also occurs in both on-line and on-campus formats to compare the effects of these methods.

This university-wide commitment to assessment and the willingness of the director and staff of the Office of Institutional Research and Planning to meet the particular assessment needs of departments and programs have provided Appalachian with a wealth of information. But what we find equally striking is the degree to which students understand the purpose of assessment and the way it can improve their educational experience. And most important, assessment results are routinely used to improve instruction and various campus services. A culture of evidence is alive and well at Appalachian.

The Office of Student Life and Learning Research also conducts various types of research and assessment of program outcomes, but the focus is on measures of overall student development. This office conducts an annual in-house freshman survey, which is given to students during phase II orientation. The survey investigates student characteristics and behaviors and in the future will include student identifiers so that results can be used to study pre-post impact of various student development interventions. The office also administers Winston and Miller's Student Developmental Task and Lifestyle Assessment (SDTLA), which investigates student development along Chickering's seven vectors, and tracks student involvement in clubs and organizations through the student developmental record program. Results of both the SDTLA and student development record system can then be correlated with various interventions, including residence life and involvement in learning communities. These student development researchers have also undertaken a number of special research initiatives to investigate Greek life at Appalachian and patterns of behavior of Greek students.

Although a growing number of student affairs divisions are including a research arm, intensive research on student development is still somewhat rare in American higher education, especially at colleges and universities that are not considered research institutions. The very existence of the Office of Student Life and Learning Research and the creative license its staff has to pursue various areas of research are again testimony to the belief that research and assessment yield important information that can improve the university and its service to students.

The Future of the First Year: Issues of Concern

A critical question that has to be asked of an institution being recognized as excellent in the first college year is, "What's next?" What will be the institution's new directions, and what are the concerns and challenges in considering these directions? In fall 2002 when these site visits were conducted, Appalachian was facing many changes imposed by the looming retirement of its most long-term first-year advocate, Provost Harvey Durham, and economic recession. But with that as a context, what came as a surprise was the lack of a specific vision for where to take the institution next to build on its current level of achievement of excellence in the first year. Instead university officials focused on these core issues:

- *Pressures to increase the size of the university.* Campus administrators, faculty, and students are concerned about possible growth to the extent that Appalachian State will be less likely to maintain the cherished sense of smallness and sense of community that currently seems to thrive. The future of this issue is much more likely to be determined by state policymakers at some more distant level. Nevertheless, university officials seemed resolved to press their opinions and concerns on this issue to those who will ultimately make such determinations.
- *Pressures to increase the size of first-year classes.* These pressures arise not only because of fiscal cutbacks but also because some faculty and departments want reduced teaching loads and more free time to pursue a research-oriented agenda. Less explicitly stated but implied was a concern that younger and newer members of the faculty did not have sufficient buy-in to the Appalachian Way and

its emphasis on community, personal interactions, teaching, and service to this institution and the people of the region. Thus, a research university professorial culture was perceived as a potential threat to this current basis of excellence in the first college year.

- *The uncertain future of the first-year seminar.* Both the provost and chancellor spoke proudly of commitment to expanding the number of freshman seminar sections offered, and the chancellor continues to model his own commitment to the course by personally coteaching a section of it. However, university officials confided that because of pressures on untenured faculty for research productivity, it was becoming increasingly difficult to attract faculty (as opposed to staff and administrators) to teach the seminar. As a result, it was reported that only tenured faculty were now being asked to teach the seminar. The retiring chief academic officer, while speaking proudly of his role in encouraging and sustaining the first-year seminar, nevertheless stated, "I am concerned about the future of the first-year seminar." In contrast, it appeared that the prospects for the future of the FLC program looked brighter. We hypothesized, based on our interviews, that the growth of the FLC program was based on the perception among departments and faculty that these structures enhance teaching and learning across disciplines and create opportunities for new cross-departmental partnerships.
- *Replacing a revered chief academic officer.* Given the enormous respect for the critical role of the current provost and executive vice chancellor, there was considerable concern expressed by subordinate-level administrators about how any successor could carry on the same level of understanding, commitment, and genuine belief in the value of first-year efforts. Of note, this concern was not shared by the chancellor, who seemed confident that the next provost could and would maintain this tradition established by his or her predecessor.
- *Retaining common experiences for all students.* As recently as four years ago, this was a major objective at Appalachian. However, key personnel have realized that this may not be a realistic, achievable, or even appropriate goal. Instead, the university seems to have settled on reaching more than 90 percent of their new students with certain signature experiences. Although we acknowledge that 90 percent of students represents an effective critical mass, we still

maintain that all campuses need to continue asking whether there is any particular experience, activity, course, concept, or belief system that is so important to the achievement of institutional mission that it must be experienced by all students.

- *The importance of first-year teaching.* Several of the most senior unit level administrators—"long marchers" through decades of reform and innovation—spoke about how the changes made in the first year had pointed to the next critical and related challenges: what students are taught and the way they are taught: "The next big challenge is to deal with the curriculum changes that are way overdue. In general education, every department makes constant changes with a narrow view, lacking the bigger picture. Enrollment services has been a big change maker. But it is hard for enrollment services to tell faculty they have to change. It is not just what courses are taken but how students are taught."

We concluded that at Appalachian, there exist simultaneously a strong sense of commitment to a core philosophy and set of practices, a strong sense of confidence in the institution's traditions and abilities to learn from its past, and concerns about constraints and challenges, both internal and external, to this culture and traditions. There was also recognition of future issues, and we sensed a strong inclination not to let the economy and administrative leadership changes deter the university from continuing its exemplary record of achievement.

Chapter Thirteen

The Story of Ball State University

"Everything Students Need"

Randy L. Swing

Marc Cutright

Attention to first-year students is deeply embedded, broadly distributed, and widely embraced at Ball State University (BSU). In fact, we, as the research team, would argue that there are only a handful of other universities in the United States that come close to achieving a comparable range and depth of first-year initiatives. Succinctly capturing the full range of first-year efforts at BSU is supremely challenging, as the institution has developed a large number of programs across the curriculum and cocurriculum to serve all students as well as numerous programs that target special student groups.

The answer to how this unique focus on first-year students came to be can be found in the extraordinary leadership of a core group of formal and informal campus leaders, the institutionalization of services to first-year students by creating and funding formal organizational structures, the partnerships between academic affairs and student affairs, and the institution's ability to embrace teaching as a primary component of the institution's mission. These conditions did not rise spontaneously but rather are the sum of incremental improvements—an evolutionary process that is over two decades in the making.

Institutional History

Ball State began as a private normal school in 1899. The Ball brothers, Muncie industrialists, purchased the institution and in 1918 donated its buildings and land to the state of Indiana to found a state-owned teachers' college. Like most other normal schools in America, the institution slowly expanded beyond a single focus on training teachers. In 1965, following the trend of other former normal schools around the nation, the institution changed its name to Ball State University. While now the institution is clearly far more than a teachers' college, students still report that "everyone will tell you that if you want to be a teacher, Ball State is the place to go. Public schools look for Ball State on your diploma."

Ball State's growth mirrors that of other former normal schools, with dips in enrollment during national wars, rapid growth in the 1960s, and continued growth through the last decades of the twentieth century. Currently, the institution enrolls about 18,000 students, 55 percent of whom are women and about 90 percent of whom are Indiana residents. Most Ball State first-year students are traditional age and live on campus. The current physical plant includes new buildings under construction and evidence of recently remodeled structures, all on 955 acres surrounding the original 1899 campus. The institution's focus on teaching is a proud vestige of its beginnings as a normal school, even though the university awards doctoral degrees as well.

As a state-supported university, Ball State must be examined in the context of the Indiana economic and social setting. Indiana is currently facing a declining economy, which only exacerbates the state's historically low level of financial support for higher education. In the absence of a strong state coordinating board, higher education in the state has traditionally been dominated by Indiana University and Purdue University and their array of regional campuses. Especially in recent years, however, philanthropy from the Lilly Endowment has played a key role in Indiana higher education. Lilly money has seeded a number of first-year initiatives at Ball State University and continues to play a key role. Beverley Pitts, Ball State's provost, maintains that "we are one of the Lilly Endowment's early success stories." In a recent grants competition aimed at increasing retention, Ball State completed its work in three years, rather than the five-year period selected by most other Indiana universities. Because of this success, Lilly offered BSU a second grant even while other campuses had yet to complete their first five-year cycle.

Institutional Mission

Blaine Brownell, president of Ball State University, was clear and unambiguous about the institution's focus: "We are in the teaching business." (In May of 2004, Blaine Brownell stepped down, and Ball State University appointed Jo Ann M. Gora as president.) The primacy of the teaching mission was reported not only by the president, but also by the provost and numerous faculty members indicating that the belief is a widely held, core institutional value. Ball State's serious commitment to teaching can be seen in the track record of promotion and tenure committees, where evidence of teaching capability is both expected and influential in final tenure decisions. Beyond classroom teaching, promotion and tenure committees regularly accept writing textbooks and performing research on pedagogy to be forms of scholarship that are as valued as traditional discipline-linked research. The actions of promotion and tenure committees are congruent with Provost Pitts's observation that Ball State University has "a real handle on the teaching-research split." She sees Ball State as a teaching-centered institution that supports the scholarship of teaching in promotion and tenure decisions. Because so much of the first college year is experienced in the classroom, this focus on teaching has special impact on first-year students.

Careful attention is also given to educational components outside the formal academic program, and the institution provides a multitude of cocurricular experiences, allowing it to live up to the Ball State marketing slogan, "Everything students need." And as President Brownell put it, the current collection of first-year programs is "directly tied to our vision and mission." BSU is purposeful in its first-year design and holistic in its vision of education. Students know Ball State as a friendly place. As one student said, "Everyone is really friendly; you can just say 'hi' to anyone." But the institution is also known as being serious about academics. Another student reflected that "you can tell it is about academics when you come for orientation. You know that they are going to help you."

The Advantage of Stable Leadership

Stable, long-term leadership in senior positions is the norm at Ball State University. Much of the current first year was created during the presidential tenure of John Worthen, who retired in 1999 after serving as president for fifteen years. Worthen was an unusual university president in both the length of his tenure (almost twice the average length of presidents) and background in student affairs administration. Certainly both factors contributed to his interest and success in creating the supporting and challenging first year at Ball State. Both Worthen and former Provost Warren Vander Hill, who served through June 2002, were graduates of highly selective liberal arts institutions. The current vice president of student affairs/enrollment management, Douglas McConkey, also a liberal arts graduate, stated that the prior administration shared a common vision of undergraduate education "to be as much like that [the selective private liberal arts institutions we attended] as we could be without losing our public obligations to serve the people of Indiana." McConkey maintained that this vision contributed to Ball State's success in building the first year.

The current senior leadership team includes McConkey, who has been vice president for student affairs since 1986; Provost Pitts, who is relatively new to her position but has been at the university since 1985; and President Brownell, who is new to both Ball State and the role of president. The current team is an excellent example of careful leadership transition with a mix of internal promotions and new talent brought in from other institutions. Change has been staged over time to ensure smooth transitions. The new team has already advanced the first year by raising first-year tuition for entering students by $1,000 per year because this increased revenue generated by first-year students will be used to continue improving first-year initiatives. In essence, the new leadership team, by establishing a permanent source of revenue for first-year programs, has ensured the continuation and strengthening of programs that were previously funded through grants and other soft monies.

Stable leadership during the development of the current first year has not been limited to the president, provost, and vice president for student affairs. Tom Lowe, associate provost and dean of University College, came to Ball State in 1973 and has some twenty years of experience as a leader of the general education curriculum as well as over ten years as dean of BSU's University College. The director of residence life, Alan Hargrave, has more than twelve years of experience at BSU. Across the campus, it is easy to find faculty who have spent an entire career on the Ball State campus and remain dedicated and enthusiastic about their work with first-year students.

Another Ball State veteran began her twenty-two years at Ball State as an undergraduate student. She expressed to us her unwavering commitment to Ball State students and her desire to help them avoid some of her own first-year history:

> I was academically qualified, an honors student, but I was so out of it on understanding what college was all about. I was terrified. I didn't leave my room, even to eat, the first three days here. I was one of those kids that went to class, and then went back to my room. By the middle of my first term, I told myself, "I don't get it. I don't belong here." I was ready to quit. And then a professor stopped me on campus and said, "I really liked the paper you wrote, how you left the reader wondering at the end." I was really floored. I was a kid who sat in the back of his class and never said anything. That a professor knew my work—and knew my name—was amazing to me. It kept me from dropping out the first time that year.
>
> But I still didn't have a grip on why I was at Ball State until a second saving moment occurred. The concept of hubris came up in an English class. I didn't know it before. Less than a week later, it came up again in a mythology class. All of a sudden, it was, "Oh my God, there's some connection in all of this." It sounds insignificant, but it began to provide some reason for me to be here.
>
> The following term I was out of money, and I was finally convinced that I was going to drop out. But I visited the financial aid office to arrange a payment schedule for what I already owed. The financial aid officer asked me about my grades, which were good, and he asked what I had learned during the year that was most significant. I said, "Hubris," and went on to explain it to him. He told me to

> continue going to class and that he would see what could be worked out. I don't know what he did, if he paid it himself or what; but they came up with some kind of special arrangement, and they let me pay a little here and there as I completed my degree. This is a personal perspective that I see over and over again here at Ball State. We're not perfect, but we're smart enough to see when our bureaucracy is a problem and we need to do something special for someone.

The Power of Grassroots Movements

The Ball State experience gives testimony to the fact that although senior administrative support is necessary to accomplish excellence in the first year, it is not sufficient. While many task forces, committees, and individuals have contributed in building the first year at Ball State, two grassroots groups in particular have had enormous influence. One group lasted formally only a short time, and the other has a long history and continues as an important source of innovation.

The Ad Hoc Committee on the Liberal Arts

Much of Ball State's success in the first year can be traced to an ad hoc committee, or think tank, on the liberal arts, which was created in 1989 by the dean of the College of Science and Humanities. This committee was given the charge to discuss the state of the liberal arts at Ball State University. The group consisted of five professors and three students who met weekly, usually in one of their homes, and the group ultimately produced a white paper on the topic. As one member of the group reported, "The dean thought that somebody should be pondering the liberal arts all the time," and this group was one way to ensure that result. Participants had to apply for one of the committee slots, and membership provided opportunities for those most interested in the liberal arts to identify themselves and their interest in campuswide curriculum efforts. The white paper that the group developed was widely distributed on campus; more important, members of that committee continued on to become key campus administrators.

The committee was made up of Tom Lowe, now dean of University College; Charles Jones, currently the executive director of the Office of Teaching and Learning Advancement; Paul Ranieri, who later became chair of the Department of English and served in the Office of the Dean of the College of Science and Humanities; and Beverley Pitts, who became provost and vice president for academic affairs. These educators who met for the first time as members of the ad hoc study committee on the liberal arts have shaped Ball State University's first year. The importance of the friendships and collegial relationships created in the liberal arts committee established in 1989 cannot be overstated. Whether by foresight or luck, the dean's initiative to ensure that "people are intellectually engaged in talking about the liberal arts" created an opportunity for interdisciplinary thinking that launched individual careers and institutional excellence in the first year.

Freshman Learning Council

One faculty member stated, "Ball State University has a rich history of working across department lines." A clear demonstration of that statement is the freshman learning council (FLC), an ad hoc group of faculty and staff who have direct involvement in the first year. Although not a component of the formal governance system, this council has met regularly since the mid-1980s to discuss issues concerning new students. The FLC, created with the goal of increasing communication between departments and units that serve first-year students, began at the same time that a new core curriculum and the new University College were started.

The FLC has been at the heart of much of the development of the first year at Ball State. As one member said, this is the group that "puts things on the table," meaning it is the place to exchange information and to raise new topics for the institution to consider. Over the years, the FLC, without any formal governance power, has influenced a long list of administrative decisions. For example, the council expressed concerns about Ball State's nearly open-admissions policy, which functioned with little regard to the quality of students entering the institution or their chance of being successful. The policy resulted in a student body that ranged widely from those with the lowest academic skills to those at the high end of academic achievement. Such variation was a problem for both retention and the delivery of high-quality educational services. Actions by the FLC influenced a more intentional set of admissions standards. Ball State continues to enroll a broad range of students but does so with the understanding that it is not in the institution's or students' best interest to enroll those who have little chance of being successful. In 1997, the institution made significant changes in admission requirements, moving from a formula using standardized test scores and high school class rank to the current model, which uses an individually computed academic index that includes only college preparatory and academic high school course work. Standardized test scores are weighed in relation to high school grades in those classes. Academically weaker applicants are encouraged to pursue their first year at a community college.

The council also took a leadership role in Ball State's development of a new policy on academic suspension, advocating for a hard line on expelling students with very low academic performance in the first semester. The group believed, and confirmed with data, that students who end the first semester with less than a 1.0 grade point average are unlikely to recover, no matter how intrusively or intentionally the institution works with them in the second term. So rather than "waste students' time and money," this committee recommended that the university stringently enforce an expulsion policy that requires that students who make less than a 1.0 in their first term take at least two semesters off before returning for academic work at BSU. In practice, this means that first-year students who perform poorly are not allowed to reenroll for the spring or summer term but may return the following fall.

The FLC recognized the need that first-year students have for both challenge and support and therefore advocated for the renewal of a midterm deficiency report plan to accompany the tougher suspension policy. As one faculty member said, the academic suspension policy is just one example of FLC advocacy that supports first-year students without "dumbing down" the first year or inappropriately "coddling" them. Students reported with great pride that Ball State is seen as a campus with "top academic programs in the nation," such as teacher education, journalism, architecture, music engineering technology, and a host of other award-winning majors. As one student said, "It feels like everything is constantly changing and is going up here."

Commitment to FLC is apparent in the attendance at and timing of council meetings. Over thirty people were present at the FLC meeting the morning we visited the campus. Members attend because they want to be present and because their attendance matters. Some have remained on the council since the mid-1980s, but new members join the group as personnel patterns shift over time. The council has become an important staff development unit in that through FLC meetings, new members of the BSU community connect with senior members and the history of first-year initiatives.

The FLC regularly discusses its role as an ad hoc committee in comparison to advantages of being part of the formal governance system. To date, the group has resisted becoming a standing committee in the university's governance structure, opting instead for continued status as an ad hoc group. The informal structure offers an advantage in that members may be added with little difficulty and the organization remains fluid. Minutes are not kept, and members do not cast votes since the council operates more as a group of concerned educators than a formalized power unit.

The FLC is an excellent example of an informal structure at work in the first year of college. Although it has no budget and no line authority, it has tremendous voice in the institution and a long history of advocacy for first-year students. The FLC, comprising mostly midlevel managers and faculty who teach first-year students, has successfully stood the challenge of time to become a keystone of first-year initiatives. Essential elements of the FLC's success include the following:

- A high degree of consensus about the goals of the first year at Ball State and a belief in the combination of support and challenge for first-year students
- A high level of personal investment in first-year students by council members
- Excellent communication among council members as they readily share their thoughts and opinions even when the opinions might not be popular or flattering to the institution
- A willingness of members of the council to speak for themselves, not as official representatives of other structures or units on campus
- An effective system of renewal over time and maintenance of a mix of long-term first-year advocates and those with new roles in the first year

The FLC is a remarkable structure in spite of the fact that it has rarely included students or senior-level administrators in the meetings, characteristics often found to be important variables in such groups. While lacking in formal power, the group's power of advocacy and grassroots strength has established it as a core source of first-year initiatives. Truly this group has touched the lives of thousands of Ball State students and set the stage for many thousands who are on their way.

University College: A Formal Structure Supporting the First Year

Ball State is recognized nationally for excellence in coordination of general education, including academic advising and assessment, and that recognition is well deserved. A range of policies, practices, and structures undergird campus efforts, and many of these are implemented through the University College.

University College, established in 1985, is an administrative division of academic affairs. Although it was begun with the limited mission of providing services to at-risk populations, the unit quickly moved to a more central role in the academic life of the campus. Currently, University College, under the leadership of Dean and Associate Provost Tom Lowe, includes a number of critical academic components. The first to be developed was a professionally staffed academic advising initiative that focused on all first-year students and second-year students who had not yet decided on a major. University College administers a learning center that provides tutoring and Supplemental Instruction; the Office of Teaching and Learning Advancement, a faculty development center that advocates for outstanding teaching practices including teaching with technology; and a summer reading program for first-year students. University College also oversees a collection of related programs for special populations or single point-in-time programs such as an early start program, and collaborates with new student orientation and first-year learning communities. Finally, it monitors the core curriculum in collaboration with academic departments. The core is composed of forty-one credit hours of course work in general education that are required of all Ball State students.

Academic advising was the first function of the University College. It is based on the recognition that the needs of first-year students are substantially different from those of upperclass students; therefore, a team of professional advisers (about twenty-four in number) provides advising to the approximately 3,500 first-year students.

The advising process begins during orientation. To serve all students well during this intensive advising time, the professional advisers are joined by a number of faculty and peer advisers. Students meet in groups and individually with academic advisers to plan a fall schedule. Each student is assigned to one of the twenty-four professional academic advisers for continued service through the fall and spring or until the student has declared a major. Students with declared majors are assigned to faculty within an academic unit for continued advising. To support those students and the faculty advisers, the advising center operates six "branch" advising offices around the campus so that a professional academic adviser is located near faculty offices should faculty advisers need help.

We found the students to be overwhelmingly satisfied with academic advising. Their only complaint about first-year advisers is that it can be difficult to arrange an appointment because advisers are in such high demand. In a focus group we scheduled during the site visit, students offered the following comments:

> My freshman adviser was really helpful when I was changing major. She helped me make sure it was a good decision.
>
> I talk to my adviser all the time she is so helpful.
>
> My adviser is great. I came in late, and she called up the professor and asked if I could join the class so I would be with the same people in my Learning Connections English class.
>
> I don't think the advisers get all the credit they deserve because they work so hard over the summer in orientation and all year long.

Advising at BSU is a combination of personal attention and a computer-generated report, the degree analysis progress report (DAPR), created every term for each student and his or her adviser. The DAPR provides students a comprehensive review of the courses they have completed or are currently taking and compares those courses with the requirements of their intended major. Students can monitor their progress toward a degree and use the analysis to determine future course schedules. Students call the DAPR "great" and "very helpful." One student said it has "everything you would ever want to know" to plan your schedule and graduate on time. While the multipage report is dense with information and somewhat daunting at first review, students report that advisers are excellent at helping them understand the report and become familiar with its structure.

Like many other administrators at Ball State, the director of academic advising and associate dean of University College, Michael Haynes, is a twenty-year veteran of the institution. Haynes trains advisers to understand that first-year advising is distinct in that first-year students have unique needs during this period of transition. His belief is that academic advising must not only be built on accurate information but also must have equal emphasis on the relationship between the adviser and the student. The mix of facts and relationships was acknowledged by an adviser who described a fall advising appointment as a time for students to talk about "their dreams, plans, majors of interest, and schedule for the next term."

We, as the research team, believe that the University College structure is a primary reason for the successful development of first-year programs at Ball State University. Through stable leadership by the dean and now associate provost and the wide-ranging series of administrative functions, University College is central to the lives of first-year students. The unit's impact also extends beyond the Ball State campus. Staff members of University College have been instrumental leaders in the Association of General and Liberal Studies, Association of Deans and Directors of University Colleges, the National Academic Advising Association, the National Association for Developmental Education, and other national organizations that support first-year initiatives. Ball State leaders have borrowed ideas from other institutions, but they have also frequently contributed nationally to the advancement of first-year educational practices.

An Array of Additional Services

In this chapter, it is impossible to name every aspect of the full network of services extended to first-year students at Ball State University. Instead, we provide a sampling of other first-year services, some designed for all students and others for selected students, but each contributing to the overall success of Ball State's first year.

Excellence in Leadership

This is a four-year, four-phase cocurricular leadership program. During phase 1, first-year students attend workshops on topics such as diverse leadership skills and conflict resolution. Participants are assigned a faculty or student mentor who supports their work during this phase of the leadership program. The program continues through the sophomore and junior years and culminates in the senior year with an individual leadership project. The individual leadership projects are supported by participation in an individual leadership project seminar. Students who successfully complete the core requirements for each phase are provided with a leadership transcript that documents their involvement in leadership activities.

Excel Summer Program

This summer program aims to jump-start the first college year. The Excel Summer Program is a three-day summer event designed for American-born minority students. The program is coordinated by the Office of Multicultural Affairs and helps participating students gain early exposure to the university and to the broader community. This program has proven helpful in connecting students to each other, to the Ball State campus, and to the Muncie area.

Cardinal Leadership and Service Seminar

This preenrollment program provides students an intensive three-day opportunity to learn about leadership. The program is limited to 100 participants who work together through a series of outdoor initiatives to discover their own strengths and limitations. Students participate in a community-based project and spend time reflecting on various aspects of leadership. Each student must develop a set of written personal goals and share them with other members of the group.

Welcome Week

Separate from the summer orientation session, Welcome Week is a planned, systematic set of activities that helps students settle into their residence hall and quickly connect with campus support structures. Upperclass students, known as "Red Squad Leaders," greet new students and help them move into the halls. Floor meetings and special meetings for parents comprise each day's activities. Faculty members also have major roles in Welcome Week, including individual sessions with students and parents. A key event is a mandatory convocation, including a procession of the faculty in academic regalia and speeches by the university president and student affairs officers. New students attend convocation with their residence hall assistants.

Summer Reading Program

The summer reading program introduces students to the institution's academic mission. In fall 2002, students read *A Woman in Amber: Healing the Trauma of War and Exile* by Agate Nesaule. Nesaule's memoir concerns her long, nightmarish childhood in Latvia, victim first of the Nazis and then of Russian troops. Ball State personalizes the summer reading program by giving each student a special edition of the selected book printed just for that entering class. The first page of the Fall 2002 book, emblazoned with the Ball State logo, opened with:

> Welcome, Class of 2006, to Ball State University. In your hands you have the first academic assignment of your university career. When you arrive for classes in August, faculty and fellow students—particularly those involved with the Freshman Connections community—will expect you to have read this book and be ready to share your ideas about it. . . . Write questions you have in the book. Maybe even consider what you would ask the author when you meet her in September.

The opening message went on to explain how, after long deliberations, Ball State came to select the book and why the council thought it might have special meaning for 3,500 first-year students and more than 100 faculty, academic advisers, and residence hall staff who would be leading group discussions of the work. Even before they arrived on campus, students were invited to visit a special Ball State Web site to read comments entered by other members of the Class of '06 and to leave their own. In conclusion, the committee acknowledged that the reading is sometimes difficult and brutal, but they also asked students to consider, "in this post-September 11th climate . . . how the power of the human spirit can overcome even the most devastating of experiences."

Students express positive reactions to the summer reading experience. One student said, "They pick some really good books—students actually want to go to see the author speak." Students told us how "cool" it was to see that the university took the time to order special editions of the selected book. It was our impression that the students got the message that they were entering an academic community where support and challenge would be the norm.

The Office of Teaching and Learning Advancement (OTLA)

This office extends the focus on the first year by supporting the faculty who teach general education courses. The OTLA began as a Lilly Endowment–funded project and now continues with institutional funding. In addition to providing workshops on teaching issues, the office houses computers and a variety of software that instructors may use to develop technology-enhanced courses and also sponsors a series of faculty awards that highlight excellence in teaching on the Ball State campus.

Core Curriculum

Ball State's core curriculum, consisting of forty-one credits, spans most of the first and second years. Students must complete a two-course English sequence, Western history, mathematics, and public speaking. These five courses comprise the fifteen hours known as the foundation courses. In addition and prior to graduation, students must complete an additional twenty-six hours in distribution electives: six hours in physical, earth, and life sciences; six hours in social and behavioral sciences; six hours in fine arts and humanities; three hours in international/global studies; two hours of physical education, fitness, and wellness; and one other three-hour course from selected core curriculum electives. Although the core curriculum does ensure that all students complete at least some courses in common, the distribution requirements allow students considerable latitude within each category.

Freshman Connections

The Freshman Connections program, established in 2002, is one of the newest first-year initiatives on the Ball State Campus. Freshman Connections is a residentially based learning community that ensures that students living in a particular residence hall are also coenrolled in two or more first-year courses. Freshman Connections has been supported by grant funds from the Lumina Foundation for Education but will be a major beneficiary of a new increase in tuition for first-year students.

When first proposed, Freshman Connections was to be offered as a pilot program for about 400 students. But because the effort was well designed and based on research showing that learning communities improve retention and increase learning outcomes, the university president said, in effect, that there was no reason to move slowly in providing this program to all Ball State students. The decision was made to move directly to full-scale implementation for all students in 1997. As one faculty member summarized the decision, "We believed it would be good for students and even better if delivered to all." This program is relatively new and so has not developed the same amount of assessment evidence as is true for most other BSU first-year initiatives. Students, however, are very clear that they like Freshman Connections and the special registration assistance they receive, and that the residential-learning link enables them to make new friends easily. As Vice President for Student Affairs and Enrollment Management McConkey said, the program is aimed at improving retention but goes far beyond that: "It is about learning, it is about involvement, it is about connecting faculty and students. It is a work in progress."

Freshman Connections builds on one aspect of Ball State that is already attractive to students: a strong sense of community. A first-year student, in responding to our question of why she chose Ball State, echoed sentiments expressed by others: "It is because of the people . . . the people were very welcoming . . . it felt more like home . . . like you could find your place within this campus. Any time you talk to administrators, they are glad you are here, and they care about you as opposed to your being just another number here, another source of revenue."

Residence Life: A Vehicle for Student Affairs and Academic Affairs Partnerships

Vice President of Student Affairs and Enrollment Management Douglas McConkey reports that in the past, Ball State University "had a party school image." That image was inconsistent with former President Worthen's vision for the institution, and under McConkey's leadership, Ball State's Student Affairs Division, and especially residence life units, have built extraordinary academic affairs–student affairs partnerships. Conversations about the role of student affairs in encouraging student academic achievement are common across all areas of student affairs now, but, according to McConkey, achieving that goal required "substantially changing some of the roles and missions of some student affairs units to bring them into the mainstream of thinking of the faculty and administration. If a provost and student affairs vice president are not on the same page, it becomes very difficult. But we have essentially been on the same page since I've been here."

McConkey's comments were repeatedly confirmed through observed actions and interviews with student affairs staff and faculty. Residence hall staff members and faculty are active participants of the learning teams associated with each of the Freshman Connections residential learning communities. Members of each team work together to help students make the first semester a particularly successful experience. One faculty member said, "I found that I learned a lot from the residence hall directors such as theories of student development, the cycles of campus life, and issues of student transition from high school to college."

Several faculty members described holding review sessions in the residence halls, contacting resident assistants for help with students who were falling into academic difficulty, and involving student affairs officers in interventions. Another faculty member who reported that she frequently makes presentations in the residence halls stated that although she teaches large classes, "students tend to speak up more in classes" after they have attended one of the sessions she holds in the residence hall. She pointed out that "entering their space" and interacting with students outside the formal classroom "establishes a dynamic which is very difficult to develop in a big lecture class." Yet another faculty member gave considerable credit to the residence hall staff for their impact on the learning communities program. He referred to the residence life contribution to learning communities as "the real glue" that holds the program together, thereby signaling the faculty's respect for their colleagues in student affairs.

Student affairs practitioners have not hesitated to advocate for greater student involvement in the academic life of the campus. We found one residence hall engaged in a week-long game that was designed to create interaction among hall members. While the game itself was about having fun and building community, the residence director (RD) had written into the rules that "any student who misses a class will immediately be removed from the game." In this example, the residence director had purposely used a fun activity to signal his values that academics come first. By involving all the residents, he established a community that encouraged each member to attend class, even when distractions abound.

Many other initiatives can be cited to show how residence life has embraced an academic mission. The establishment of "green floors," campus residence halls that embrace environmentally sensitive practices, is purposefully marketed to first-year students majoring in environmental studies. The green-floor living space includes energy-efficient lights, low-flow showers, and an active recycling program so that students can apply lessons learned in the classroom in their daily lives. Connections between academic majors and residence halls continue even into the evening hours as hall programs often focus on environmental issues.

Another residence hall initiative aimed at improving academic performance is playfully named, "Take your butt to class." This program provides free cold cereals and other breakfast items in residence hall lobbies to encourage students to grab breakfast on the way to early morning class. Each evening, leaders of the initiative go through the residence halls knocking on doors and seeking a promise from fellow students that they will get up and go to their first class the next day. Mornings become a group effort to get everyone up and off to class on time with the added incentive of a free and convenient breakfast.

As active partners in the academic mission, residence life staff receive assessment data about students on their floors and also midterm deficiency reports as part of an early warning system designed to ensure multiple and early interventions with first-term students who are not performing well academically. Undergraduate resident assistants (RAs) and RDs contact students receiving midterm deficiencies to counsel and refer students to other sources of help. One RA said these reports "are a real wake-up call for freshmen. I've seen students really get in gear after being told they were failing at midterm." When a student violates hall policies or abuses alcohol, residence directors report that they regularly ask, "How did this incident affect your classes?" In this way, the RD purposefully encourages students to connect the consequences of personal decisions to their academic performance.

In addition to traditional residence hall staff, each hall housing a Freshman Connections learning community also has one Freshman Connections assistant. In 2002, there were fifteen of these upper-level students who served as resources for the hall directors and the faculty. These students plan programs in the residence halls, help build community among the learning community students, occasionally attend classes with first-year students, and always know the syllabus and class assignments of the linked courses. The Freshman Connections assistants are carefully selected and paid for their services to the learning community.

One residence life professional reported, "We used to be really busy doing programs, programs, and more programs—whether they really mattered or not." The emphasis on number of programs did not encourage high quality or academically focused events. But the new model based on clearly defined learning goals encourages student affairs staff to seek partnerships with faculty in the creation of residentially based educational experiences that are aligned with intentional learning outcomes. To accomplish these goals, residence life staff report taking the initiative to invite faculty into the residence halls and to assist those who wish to provide programming or to use residence hall facilities for study groups.

Most students appear to appreciate the level of concern and care they receive in the residence hall, although a minority of students reject the level of intrusion as being "too much in my business." The residence life teams, while being respectful of individual student privacy, seem to prefer to err on the side of too much, rather than too little, engagement with students.

University Assessment

Ball State University was one of the first institutions in the country to embrace assessment of the undergraduate experience. An office of academic assessment was established in the mid 1980s under the leadership of Beverley Pitts, serving as the founding director of assessment. Pitts was one of the original members of the ad hoc committee on the liberal arts and is now Ball State provost. She recalls that BSU approached the Indiana legislature with a plan for the development of an institution-wide assessment program; the institution was the first to be funded by the state for assessment. Those funds and the leadership of a strong assessment team led to the development of the Making Achievement Possible (MAP) instrument and an array of assessment efforts that explored how students improved in writing, mathematics, and other learning outcomes. The detailed work on this project originated in academic advising and quickly led to cooperative efforts among advising, student housing, and the office of academic assessment. These efforts gave Ball State an early leadership role in the country's assessment movement and have served as model approaches for other institutions to emulate.

The locally developed MAP survey, a central component of the assessment effort at Ball State that evaluates the skills, abilities, and attitudes of entering students, is administered during new student orientation. Each year, about 80 percent of Ball State first-year students complete the survey, which contains questions about attitudes and interests, motivation, time management, anxiety, concentration, information processing, selecting main ideas, study aids, self testing, and test-taking strategies.

A key to the success of the MAP instrument is the feedback process, which returns results to student participants and decision makers. The data are processed immediately following collection of the surveys, and within a day or two, students receive individualized printouts of their own answers. The printouts compare each individual student's responses with aggregate data for all other first-year students and also provide advice about the meaning of the data. A particularly powerful aspect of MAP is comparative data showing how the prior year's class of first-year students performed. These data are presented so that students can "predict" their own end-of-first-year outcomes by comparing their survey responses to both responses and actual outcomes of the previous year's first-year class.

Assessment results are disaggregated and distributed to key decision makers across the campus. For example, residence hall directors receive aggregated MAP data for students residing in their residence halls. Each director also receives individual reports on each student in the residence hall. Academic advisers receive both aggregate and individual reports for students in their advising caseload. In addition to providing an early warning alert, the information is used all year long when hall directors or advisers meet with students for academic advising or to deal with students who exhibit behaviors indicating that they are at risk of failure or dropout. MAP serves many important purposes, including reminding students that their own actions and study patterns matter. It also serves as tangible evidence that the institution listens to students and uses assessment results both to support individual student success and to improve the institution.

Key Actions Affecting the First Year of College

Ball State University's first-year approach is the product of an extended evolutionary period; however, a number of significant decisions and actions in recent years have shaped the current first year:

- The university decided to hire a team of professional advisers who are the initial advising contact for new students. The advising center is a key element of and foundation for a University College, serving as a central coordinating structure for a number of first-year curricular programs.

• The institution made a strategic decision to raise its admission standards by enrolling fewer weak students. That decision led to an initial drop in enrollment, but the increased student quality has subsequently led to increased enrollments and higher-performing students.

• With increased enrollment and higher-quality students, the institution initiated a strict academic eligibility policy. Students who earn a grade point average of less than 1.0 in the first semester are immediately suspended for as many as two additional semesters. The message given to students is that they are held accountable for their academic performance and are not allowed to build a weak academic base at BSU.

• Ball State University has largely financed improvements in its approach to the first year through new monies, not redistribution of existing funds. The majority of funds have come through grants from external donors such as the Eli Lilly and Company Endowment. More recently, Lumina Foundation for Education has provided new monies for experimentation and establishment of new programs. However, the institution's decision to move from grant-funded to perpetually funded programs through a $1,000 increase in tuition charged to first-year students and earmarked for first-year initiatives will ensure the long-term institutionalization of the innovations created over the past two decades.

• Stable leadership of the president, provost, and vice president of student affairs has contributed to Ball State's successful creation of a first year of excellence. While two of those senior leaders have retired and successors appointed, there appears to be no regression in the focus on the first year at BSU. In fact, the current provost was instrumental as a faculty member and as director of assessment in the establishment of many of the first-year structures before taking on the role of chief academic administrator.

• The collaboration between student affairs and academic affairs at Ball State University is extraordinary. The similar educational backgrounds of senior administrators provided a common vision for the first year at Ball State and helped them achieve their shared vision.

• Ball State University has played an active leadership role in a number of national educational organizations. This role in the Association for General and Liberal Studies, the National Association for Developmental Education, and the National Academic Advising Association is an example of ways in which Ball State has both added to the national conversation and gained from exposure to a wide range of new ideas.

• Faculty development has not been left to chance. The Office of Teaching and Learning Advancement ensures that faculty are engaged in conversations about the needs of first-year students and pedagogies that are engaging.

• Ball State University is truly a unique institution. While it rose from being a normal school, it has managed to obtain Carnegie research-intensive status while continuing to focus on the undergraduate experience.

Coming Challenges

The first year at Ball State evolved over time rather than springing forth fully formed. As with any other evolutionary process, change is continuous, so it is not a surprise that there are challenges for the institution as it moves forward in improving the first year or maintaining the current overall level of excellence. Among the challenges that Ball State faces are these:

• The facilities at BSU do not always support the kinds of student-faculty and student-student interaction that many faculty and student affairs professionals wish to design for students. For example, the lack of quiet study spaces and faculty parking near the residence halls deter rather than encourage faculty presence in residence halls.

• Increases in tuition for first-year students were enacted with the promise to deliver even better quality services to students. As one person said, "Now we had better be able to put up!" Ball State has raised expectations and must now meet those expectations.

• Enrollment growth is not likely in the near future, so the institution will not see new money from enrollment growth.

• Because most first-year students at BSU live on campus and eat in the campus dining halls, that component of the first year could better support other aspects of residential life and learning communities. Currently, food services reports to business affairs, and as one person said, they see food services as simply "deciding how many mashed potatoes to put on the food line" rather than as a partner in the educational experiences of students.

- Ball State wants to integrate international students more effectively on campus and to have more students participating in study-aboard programs. It is not clear that the role of the first year in encouraging these goals has been well developed. At least one plan in the works is to recruit more Asian students. If that plan becomes a reality, there will be new challenges for housing, food services, language classes, the international student center, and more.
- BSU faces challenges in providing opportunities for students to experience diversity. A group of students reported that the institution tries to be supportive of diversity, but as one said, "You have to remember we are out in the middle of a big corn field here! A lot of students come from small towns, you know, white Christian Indiana; some are not very accepting of diversity. Ball State does a really good job of getting students to consider other views." Students were glad that the institution sponsors a number of programs to feature and honor minority populations on campus, but at least one minority student pointed out that she is often the only minority student in a class or group.

Conclusion

Ball State is doing so much that is right that the major challenge is simply to continue the status quo. Students said that they came to BSU because of the "size and friendly people." One student decided to attend BSU while visiting the campus on a middle school field trip, another during a precollege summer program, and another said, "In the back of my mind, I always knew I would go to Ball State. Both of my parents graduated from here and my brother and sister. They always told me how special the place is." Students like the compact campus and report that "you always see people raking leaves or planting flowers or working to keep the place beautiful." There is much to love about this place. But once students arrive, they discover the real reason to attend BSU: the personal attention and array of services virtually ensure that no student falls between the cracks. It is hard to be anonymous in a true learning community.

Part Six

Case Studies of Four-Year Institutions with More Than 20,000 Students

Chapter Fourteen

Indiana University-Purdue University Indianapolis

Success and the City

Marc Cutright

Michael J. Siegel

In 2003, after only five years in NCAA Division I, the men's basketball team at Indiana University-Purdue University Indianapolis, the Jaguars, made the championship tournament.

IUPUI, with a relatively modest 20–13 record, got into the tournament as the champion of the Mid-Continent conference. Its assignment, as the 16—bottom—seed in the Midwest Region, was to take on perennial basketball monolith Kentucky. *Sports Illustrated,* running down the four regional brackets and giving their assessment of each team's chances in ten words or fewer, summarized IUPUI's chances: "IU might. Purdue might. But Jags? No way."

As it turns out, IUPUI did not advance to the second round. In fact, no 16 seed ever has. But IUPUI's mere presence in the tournament after only five years in Division I is a bit of a metaphor for its rapid emergence as a leader in first-year education. While it may be a while before the Jaguars are contenders for the championship, no fan of progressive, innovative, and effective institutional efforts on behalf of first-year students is surprised to see IUPUI cited as a leader.

IUPUI came into being in 1969, a joining together of Indiana University's and Purdue University's extension programs in Indiana's capital city. Large graduate and professional units from the two universities, such as Indiana University's medical school, were brought under the same umbrella. The new campus did not, and still does not, issue its own degrees. Rather, individual schools, programs, and degree recipients are formally associated with either Purdue or Indiana. Indiana University holds primary administrative oversight of the institution.

Some thirty-five years of existence have seen the campus established as a physical entity bringing together scattered locations, although the campus still feathers into the surrounding city at its boundaries. Progress has been substantial on many fronts. The campus attracts more than $400 million a year in contract and grant support in the medical units and elsewhere. Enrollment has grown to more than 29,000 students, 8,000 of them in graduate and professional schools. Some twenty different schools offer 180 programs of study.

And yet the reputation of the undergraduate units falls behind that of the state's two flagship campuses. Part of this springs from the fact that IUPUI was at one time virtually open enrollment, to compensate for Indiana's lack, until recently, of a community college system. Students who could not qualify for admission to the Bloomington campus of Indiana University or the West Lafayette campus of Purdue University would begin at IUPUI with the full intention of leaving at the earliest opportunity for their true target institution. And some would return to IUPUI after leaving Purdue or IU—voluntarily or not.

IUPUI has always been an attractive option to students who are place-bound to Indianapolis—those with jobs and families, for example—or those of more modest means who could not afford to live away from parents or other family. In a state that ranks close to the bottom of all fifty states in the proportion of adults over twenty-five with college degrees ("Educational Attainment of Adults, 2000," 2003), IUPUI has always embraced this mission of outreach to the community of Indianapolis and the region. But acceptance of this charge has meant that it serves a student population with many risk factors. Only half of its students qualify for full-time classification. More than 80 percent work the equivalent of four full workdays a week off campus. Many students come to IUPUI underprepared for college-level work; 60 percent are admitted conditionally, not having met minimum regular-admission requirements. Reflecting the state's historically low level of college completion, nearly two of every three enrollees are first-generation college students. Although the university is constructing some campus housing, only 1 percent of students now live on campus. In fact, IUPUI's students, almost all commuters, sometimes refer to themselves as "PCP students," reflective of their "parking lot/classroom/parking lot" pattern of daily mobility.

Conversations with students revealed that IUPUI's somewhat limited image historically, at odds with its substantial successes, is an irony that many have personally experienced. When we asked students in focus groups, "Why did you come to IUPUI?" the typical initial reaction was laughter and head shaking of an experienced, self-deprecating sort. It turns out that many students came to IUPUI because they were "short": short on money to go out of state; short on academic credentials to get into IU or Purdue; short on the quality of their transcripts after getting to IU or Purdue and partying their way out. And their intentions were short too; many wanted to bootstrap as quickly as possible to Bloomington or West Lafayette. But these same students offered insights into why, for example, twice as many students eventually transfer to IUPUI from Bloomington as make the reverse journey.

"I figured I could come to IUPUI and get a Purdue degree with a minimum of effort, just slide by," confessed one student. "It wasn't that way at all. I've had a great academic experience." In fact, the student represented IUPUI on the Academic Bowl team, which defeated both Purdue and IU and went on to the national finals.

Another undergraduate student reflected on his more limited ambitions as an entering student and contrasted it with his experience: "I can get to my physics professors. In fact, I've done some research with them, and have been listed as a coauthor on a publication. And I've gotten to mentor other students, which I really enjoy. My friends at other universities just aren't having that kind of experience."

IUPUI's conditions are not those that typically prove fertile ground for success. And while the urban university may be "the future of higher education in this country," as one member of the executive staff put it, the unique or acute challenges that have arisen in these contexts have relatively few solutions that benefit from a long history and evidence of success. It is, in "university years," a young place, and every mechanism for improvement of its educational services is relatively recent. "We had no background, no support structure" for attacking the challenges, the same executive said. "We've had to solve every messy, sleazy problem ourselves." It is a challenge that those at IUPUI seem to relish.

While other institutions may resign themselves to less accomplishment, IUPUI is driven not only by the beliefs that its students can and will succeed and that the university is accountable to them for that success, but also the realization that Indianapolis itself will not reach its full potential without IUPUI's success in meeting its challenges. "A vision that has proven compelling for us," said Chancellor Gerald Bepko "is that Indianapolis is a city of the future. An important part of our mission is to help make this city successful." (Since this site visit was conducted in fall 2002, Gerald Bepko has been succeeded by Charles Bantz as IUPUI's chancellor.) For that reason, IUPUI has little interest in becoming more selective, in "importing students that meet our requirements," as one individual said; rather, the institution is dedicated to the students it has.

The focus on and dedication to student success, particularly first-year student success, has yielded results. In fall 2002, one-year retention rates for first-time, full-time students had risen to 65 percent, up five points from 1997. Fall-to-spring first-year retention rate percentages are in the mid-80s. Student satisfaction rates, as indicated through surveys, have risen fairly steadily; in 2001, 85 percent indicated satisfaction with their overall academic experience, and more than 80 percent positively evaluated several dimensions of instruction. Learning communities that include gateway courses—those that are introductory to disciplinary study but often suffer high rates of failure and dropout—have completion rates of 84 percent, compared to conventional, nonlinked sections of gateway courses with completion rates that are 15 percent lower. Students who enroll in the university's summer bridge program have grade point averages that are a half letter grade better than their peers, despite referral to the program due to at-risk characteristics.

These accomplishments have been recognized several times in the recent past by various national organizations. The creation of the Gateway Group, a faculty-led effort to improve student learning and retention in first-year gateway courses, was commended in the 2002 TIAA Hesburgh competition. In 2000, the Association of American Colleges and Universities (AAC&U) included IUPUI in its competitive Greater Expectations project, focused on the development and dissemination of models for student learning in a liberal arts context. In 1997, IUPUI was one of three urban universities selected to participate in the RUSS (Restructuring for Urban Student Success) Project, funded by The Pew Charitable Trusts. This project, designed to nurture a dialogue about learning communities, culminated in 1999 with an evaluation by a national panel of "critical friends." This panel characterized the university's learning communities program as "an impressive effort, one which we will commend to colleagues elsewhere in the country seeking a model."

Most of the institutional efforts described in this book have come to fruition from years of hard, consistent work and incremental but steady movement toward the improvement of student learning. If there is a single element that distinguishes IUPUI's efforts from most other institutional efforts that have produced impressive results, it is the remarkable speed by which many ambitious goals have been developed and largely accomplished. While many of IUPUI's efforts have historic roots, most of the current successful initiatives are less than a decade old.

While this may reasonably give heart to institutions that desire substantial improvement of first-year enhancement in a compressed time frame, it is important to note that IUPUI's efforts have not been one-shot, minimal efforts. Rather, they reflect institution-wide creativity, hard work, partnership, critical self-analysis, and resource commitment.

University College

Absolutely central and essential to IUPUI's rapid progress in becoming an exemplar of first-year programming has been the establishment and support of its University College, the port of entry for all new students at the university. In some respects, it is the only IUPUI academic unit, since all other schools and degree programs are formally affiliated with either Purdue or Indiana University. While the roots of University College extend to at least 1989, with the formation of the Council on Undergraduate Learning and the appointment of Herman Blake as vice chancellor for undergraduate learning, progress on that front was fairly incremental in nature until the founding of University College.

University College was established in 1997, with the mission to serve as a welcoming and supportive portal of entry for all entering students through the coordination of existing university resources and the development of new initiatives to promote academic excellence and enhance student persistence. University College provides preentry orientation services, extended orientation and campus connection through learning communities and first-year seminars, intensive first-year advising designed to help students transfer to their eventual degree program homes, and academic support in general education. Some $2 million is devoted each year to the college's programs and their development, signaling strong institutional commitment to the centrality of undergraduate achievement and continued investment in initiatives that have proven successful or promising.

University College, both philosophically and in practice, is much more than a remedial education center, much more than a place where students are "fixed" before being dispatched to "regular" college work. For one thing, it is the home not only to supplemental and developmental education, but to the university's honors program. It is a place where educational paths, inclinations, and skills are deliberately shaped, not only to the institution's advantage through retention, but to the individual's advantage through the foundation of an educational experience more substantial than the student might have imagined on university entry.

A Deliberate and Explicit Educational Agenda

An early objective of University College was the development of an educational philosophy and intended outcomes. After all, as a wag has observed, if you do not know where you are going, any road will do. Discussions that had been ongoing for several years took on a new life and urgency and in 1998 resulted in adoption by the Faculty Council of the Principles of Undergraduate Learning:

- Core Communication and Quantitative Skills: The ability of students to write, read, speak and listen, perform quantitative analysis, and use information resources and technology—the foundation skills necessary for all IUPUI students to succeed

- Critical Thinking: The ability of students to analyze carefully and logically information and ideas from multiple perspectives
- Integration and Application of Knowledge: The ability of students to use information and concepts from studies in multiple disciplines in their intellectual, professional, and community lives
- Intellectual Depth, Breadth, and Adaptiveness: The ability of students to examine and organize disciplinary ways of knowing and to apply them to specific issues and problems
- Understanding Society and Culture: The ability of students to recognize their own cultural traditions and to understand and appreciate the diversity of the human experience, both within the United States and internationally
- Values and Ethics: The ability of students to make judgments with respect to individual conduct, citizenship, and aesthetics [http://clas.iupui.edu/undergraduatelearning.html]

The institutional articulation of these principles, printed, displayed, and showcased in a variety of formats, goes on to give examples of outcomes that would be associated with these principles and their definitions. All undergraduate students are deliberately and systematically exposed to these values early in their IUPUI careers, so that ambiguity over larger educational objectives is resolved and so that students might reach toward higher accomplishment consistent with the principles.

Faculty are asked to determine which of the principles will be taught and assessed in each of their classes. Faculty of disciplines and areas of study are asked to determine what their specific graduates will know and be able to do within the framework of the principles.

Strong Orientation and Transition Programs

IUPUI designs exemplary preterm orientation programs for students and for their families. While students are going through their own, more traditional orientation, parents and families meet with university representatives and get their own welcome and acclimation to IUPUI. The fifty-page *Parents' Handbook* moves from the most frequently asked questions and common circumstances—how to drop and add classes, for example—to detailed descriptions of the support programs available to students, such as learning communities and technology assistance. A special section of the handbook and orientation deals with other issues of college entry, a time in the family and student's life that "is both exciting and frightening, a period of joy, pain, discovery and disappointment." Parents are both cautioned and encouraged: "Like it or not, you are entering this period with your son or daughter. You'll experience the same exhilaration and dejection as your son or daughter, perhaps from a distance, but often as vividly or achingly." Following that are some key nuggets of advice, such as, "Ask questions—but not too many," or "Common statements your student might make." The handbook contains not just office descriptions but specific names and personal telephone numbers for everyone employed by University College. Families every year are asked to evaluate the handbook and program, which are modified the next year to reflect that input.

The preterm orientation programs for students at IUPUI have broken from more traditional fun-and-games approaches and have a decidedly academic focus, with clear enunciation of expectations, standards, the character of particular majors, and support services. Each of IUPUI's undergraduate schools is represented in the orientation program, and each has a thirty-minute time period to talk about the school and its organizations, why majors within the school should be of interest, the support services offered by the school (such as special learning communities and co-op programs), student organizations, and school- and major-specific academic issues, such as special admission, probation, and attendance standards. University College has a complementary block of time to talk about its unique circumstances ("You do not receive a degree from University College"), the purposes and structure of general education, the purposes and structures of academic advising, and such opportunities as learning communities. IUPUI understands that an undergraduate experience well begun is more likely to be successful.

Centralization of Basic and Support Services

Our first day at IUPUI was a crisp, fall morning, and we began it in the University College, a large building in the center of the campus. On our way to an early morning appointment, we came across a first-year seminar class meeting in an open, multifunctional room rather than a regular classroom. Laptop computers had been distributed to the twenty or so students who sat in small clusters. A wireless Internet connection and the instructor's guidance had them all on the same IUPUI Web page, where they were registering for spring classes. Student peer leaders circulated, taking individual questions and giving advice. When the peer leader felt that a question or a scheduling idea might be helpful to the whole group, the peer leader repeated it to the group; individual students exercised that option as well. As the hour-long session wound down, students would hit the final Send button, shut down the computer, and return it to a central cart. Students with more lingering issues would be counseled and assisted until everyone had completed the task.

This method of registering students is a definite contrast to the way class registrations are often handled elsewhere: by a student working alone, using a base of obtuse printed material, folklore, and guesses. IUPUI knows, by contrast, that crafting an individual schedule is a foundation of student success and a responsibility held jointly by student and institution; therefore, time, resources, and expertise are devoted to it, as they are to student advising and academic assistance in general.

This centralized approach is typical of University College, which is designed to provide students essential services in a convenient and accessible location. One of the most important components of the college is the Bepko Learning Center, named in honor of the chancellor when he retired from that position. The center has three primary student-centered functions. The first of these is Supplemental Instruction (SI). Students with academic difficulties work together with an upper-level SI leader and a group of other students. The SI leader attends assigned class lectures, takes notes, and conducts weekly collaborative learning sessions throughout the semester. The University College Web Site offers the following description of SI:

> Active student participation in these sessions is voluntary, but highly suggested, and the sessions are held several times weekly to be as accessible as possible to all students. The collaborative learning sessions are meetings in which students gather to discuss the reading

> or lecture material from a particular course. These sessions provide students with the opportunity to become involved in the course material in a non-judgmental and supportive environment. Collaborative learning helps students build learning communities themselves and share learning strategies while reviewing the course material [http://www.universitycollege.iupui.edu/learningcenter].

A central selling point of SI to students is the finding at IUPUI that participants have typically experienced a one-half to full grade average advantage over similar students who did not accept SI assistance.

While SI is voluntary for students, a similar program, structured learning assistance (SLA), an idea borrowed from Ferris State University, is a mandatory one-hour-per-week class attached to certain high-risk-for-failure gateway courses. The SLA sessions themselves are content centered and depend typically on directed study and practice. IUPUI's decision to mandate SLA for certain courses was made because voluntary participation rates were low. The belief was that SLA participation was being negatively affected by the same factor that contributes to undesirable outcomes in high-risk courses: inadequate time investment in class work as compared to off-campus jobs and activities. While this strategy is optional to departments where the high-risk courses are offered, buy-in to the concept is strong and expanding. This is attributable not only to the positive impact the SLA courses are having, but to the fact that the intervention strategy was developed and endorsed by the faculty themselves.

The Resource Center within the Bepko Learning Center might be viewed as a glue for all of the other programs and activities of the learning center, both the more established and the situational. The resource center is an active intake point for student concerns, issues, problems, and questions, a "one-stop shopping" place for students. It supports the SI and SLA programs and mentors, as well as special programs for athletes and members of learning communities. Referrals are an important part of its functioning, with guidance to such offices and services as tutoring, the writing center, and the "speaker's lab." Resource mentors in the resource center do individual tracking of and follow up with students who get assistance to make sure that they successfully accessed services and information appropriate to their individual needs.

Faculty Involvement and Development

University College is substantially more than an administrative unit. It is also a faculty who are carefully selected and contribute fundamentally to the shaping of University College beyond the individual instruction they offer. The faculty of University College are about forty in number and are carefully selected, lending to the association a prestige and panache that might be associated with graduate faculty in some institutions.

Nancy Van Note Chism, associate dean of the faculties and associate vice chancellor for professional development, N. Douglas Lees, chair of the Department of Biology, and Scott Evenbeck, dean of University College, described the development of faculty for University College, and in many respects the development of University College itself, in the summer 2002 issue of *Liberal Education,* the quarterly publication of the Association of American Colleges and Universities. They describe a model of "reflective practice" that is the norm within University College. This model involves selecting new practices, experimenting with them, collecting information on the learning that resulted, and reflecting on the practice, its results, and its desirability for more long-term change (Chism, Lees, & Evenbeck, 2002). Even the authors' collaboration is itself suggestive of the cross-functional cooperation that marks first-year education at IUPUI

The reflective practice model has played out at IUPUI through the cooperative efforts of University College and the Center for Teaching and Learning, bringing together many long-term and serious, but scattered, conversations about the improvement of teaching and learning. These conversations began in the early 1990s when a town meeting was called, focused on the poor first-year-student retention rate. Faculty, students, and administrators gathered to hear what the institution knew from ongoing assessment about the issues of retention at IUPUI and peer institutions. All the participants had the opportunity, which they seized, to voice their perspectives and to pledge cooperative effort.

A series of "Dialogues on First-Year Student Success" followed, bringing together first-year-student faculty to discuss fundamental course design issues and teaching strategies that had proven effective. The exchanges yielded "tip sheets" and the beginning of codified, institutional knowledge about effective practice. A particular concern was the high rate of student dropout and failure in gateway courses.

In 2000, a team of faculty and administrators, calling themselves the Gateway Group, attended a summer institute sponsored by the American Association for Higher Education. According to a special Gateway Web link, the group proposed the formation of a coordinating body that would "foster communication across courses that enroll many first-time, first-year students." The functions of the Gateway Group include:

- Disseminating information on best practices for promoting learning in these courses, obtained either through campus experimentation and research or findings from other campuses
- Seeking funding and other resources to foster innovation and improvement
- Promoting existing resources available through University College, the Center for Teaching and Learning, and other campus units
- Fostering best organizational and administrative practices to support student success
- Identifying work that needs to be done in connection with the improvement of gateway courses and early student success and funding task groups to accomplish this work
- Reporting on progress with respect to student achievement in gateway courses and organizational changes that have occurred to better support these courses [http://opd.iupui.edu/special/Gateway/index.htm].

The Gateway Group was and continues to be composed of faculty from schools with large undergraduate populations, professional faculty development staff, institutional leaders, and students. It has used faculty forums, departmental meetings, and a grants program as mechanisms for advancing conversations and implementing new strategies. Faculty forums have tackled such highly charged issues as attendance policies. Regular meetings have been scheduled as well at the departmental and other levels, focused on discussing and evaluating effective practices and policies for first-year and general undergraduate learning. An institutional grants program is giving financial support to special initiatives such as new course development, dissemination of effective practices, and the integration of proven methods across course sections. Teams, rather than individuals, are favored in the grants competitions. An example of supported projects is a program in which writing faculty work collaboratively to set standards for assessing student portfolios.

Another notable faculty development activity is the institutional fostering of "communities of practice," groups of eight or so faculty who work, often across disciplines, on issues and concerns in effective learning, such as the use and implications of instructional technology. The communities of practice are expanding in number as the institution learns from its efforts.

Learning Communities

IUPUI is making strong and expanding use of learning communities—the linkage of two or more classes by common enrollment, faculty consultation, and cooperation—and is using opportunities to connect content across courses. The intentions of learning communities include a more holistic approach to knowledge and the development of supportive relationships among students. The outcomes are typically better classroom performance and enhanced retention (Shapiro & Levine, 1999).

The simplest and least structured of learning community formats is basically a matter of coscheduling of students and hoping for a kind of serendipity: student connections to one another, formation of study groups, and similar student-based support. At the most sophisticated levels, learning communities are thematic, courses are purposefully linked through overarching educational purposes, and faculty work closely together to coordinate content and learning objectives (Shapiro & Levine, 1999). IUPUI's approach is an exemplar of this latter type.

IUPUI's commitment to learning communities is one of its older initiatives, with internal sources dating it to a 1992 visit to IUPUI by John Gardner and his focus on the approach. The planted seeds resulted in learning communities that were piloted in 1995. Beginning in 1997, IUPUI began requiring beginning students and transfers with fewer than seventeen hours of semester credit to enroll in learning communities.

Now, more than 100 learning communities are offered each fall semester for entering students. The core is a first-year seminar linked to a discipline course. Second semester communities involve Critical Inquiry, a one-to-two-credit-hour course that is attached to a particular disciplinary course and concentrates on helping students learn how to read and understand dense text material within that discipline. Skills intended for acquisition in Critical Inquiry include the critical evaluation of materials, strategies for learning in the discipline, and communication of disciplinary knowledge in written and oral forms. Collaborative strategies are commonly employed. Critical Inquiry is not remedial in nature; is appropriate as well, for example, for students who intend to excel in highly competitive majors.

First-Year Seminars

A central component of each first semester learning community is the first-year seminar. While first-year seminars are among the most adopted and used of first-year student success strategies across the nation (National Resource Center for The First-Year Experience and Students in Transition, 2002), the IUPUI version of the strategy is notable in the comprehensiveness of its philosophy, precision in its objectives, and integration into the institution's larger academic mission. While some schools of the university have developed their own versions of the first-year seminar with the intention of including discipline-specific materials and learning objectives, the faculty of University College worked collaboratively to develop a template for first-year seminars that all sponsoring units use as a standard.

Foremost among the foundations of IUPUI's first-year seminars are eight learning outcomes as listed in an internal document, *A Template for First-Year Seminars at IUPUI.* The learning outcomes state that as a result of successful completion of an IUPUI first-year seminar, students should:

- Develop a comprehensive perspective on higher education
- Experience a safe, supportive and positive university learning experience, which includes the establishment of a network of staff, faculty, and other students

- Understand and begin to practice basic communication skills appropriate to the academic setting
- Begin the process of understanding critical thinking in the university context
- Acquire a basic understanding of the fundamentals of scholarly inquiry, including the identification and use of academic library resources
- Understand and apply campus resources for information technology in support of academic work and campus connections
- Begin to develop a knowledge of their own abilities, skills and life demands so that they can develop these more effectively in pursuit of their academic goals
- Make full utilization of IUPUI resources and services that support their learning [excerpted from http://uc.iupui.edu/LC/2002template_yr1seminar.pdf].

Each of these learning outcomes includes more specific skills and knowledge relevant to the larger outcome. Under the first outcome of developing a comprehensive perspective on higher education, for example, students are expected to be able to understand and appreciate the open exchange of ideas and knowledge; respect diversity; see relationships among academic disciplines; understand the larger dialogue of society in which scholarship is a part of religious, cultural, and economic interests; understand academic integrity; demonstrate appropriate academic behavior; and be familiar with IUPUI's Principles of Undergraduate Education.

While many of those objectives are ambitious and foundational to ongoing intellectual and personal development beyond the first year, other specific elements of the eight learning outcomes are more utilitarian. Use of campus resources, for example, includes specifically the abilities to (1) identify the purpose and location of significant campus services such as career counseling and financial aid, (2) use IUPUI documents such as the schedule of classes and the student manual, and (3) meet with academic advisers to develop a plan of study.

These eight first-year seminar learning objectives are supported by detailed pedagogical strategies and required curriculum components. These too were developed by the faculty and staff of University

College. The pedagogical strategies consider the composition of the instructional teams, maximum class size (25 students), the central role of faculty in shaping the seminar and student mentorship, the use of collaborative and active learning strategies, assignments that require active connection between the student and the campus, syllabi that provide rich and appropriate details, and the use of assessment by students of the class and its instruction.

While latitude is available to seminar planners to include introductory material on particular majors, specialized skills, or components addressing the needs and aptitudes of particular groups of students, all first-year seminars are required to include some basic components. These include an orientation to the culture and context of the university, an introduction to critical thinking skills and dispositions necessary to success in higher education, advancement of each student's skills with technology, facility with library resources, practice with a range of communication skills, knowledge about university resources, meetings with academic advisors, and emphasis on IUPUI's Principles of Undergraduate Education.

Some sixteen schools of the university (all schools serving undergraduate students) are involved in offering learning communities and the larger concept, learning blocks, that include the first-year seminar. Some of the learning community courses are also supported by SLA and Supplemental Instruction. Beyond the learning outcomes and instructional strategies that support each community, each is managed by a team that includes the instructors, an academic adviser, a student mentor or peer leader, and a librarian. Examples of learning blocks include the University College's own Exploratory block, which includes courses in English, psychology, and math, along with a first-year seminar course and a math critical inquiry offering.

Faculty Perspectives

During site visits at IUPUI, we had the opportunity to meet with several groups of faculty involved in learning communities, often teaching both the first-year seminar and a discipline-based course. While instructors in learning communities at IUPUI have all volunteered for the effort, we were concerned that the instructors chosen for group interviews might have been selected on the basis of the most positive dispositions toward the learning communities rather than as a more balanced representation of the involved instructors. And even if the hosts intended to put forth groups truly representative of faculty opinion and experience within learning communities, we also feared that there might be a correlation between those faculty who were most vocal about the learning communities and those whose experiences were most positive. Finally, there was a concern about groupthink, the subtle suppression of contrary perception carried along on a wave of optimism.

And so early questions we put to all such groups were designed to tease out and validate dissent:

> I'm a faculty member. If I was approached about participation in a learning community, I'd have three concerns. First, the time investment for coordination is substantial; who's got it? Second, cooperating with two or more other instructors opens my classroom and my teaching to yet another level of external evaluation; who needs it? Finally, meshing my course with another, apparently unrelated course means that I have to water down my content to worry about connections; who can afford it?

Every faculty member, at every opportunity, on every point, refuted the scenario and its premises. "It's why I got into teaching," was the bottom line offered by more than one faculty member. Others noted that the opportunities, the focus, and the cross-disciplinary conversations were converting faculty attitudes about teaching at IUPUI. It was once, one faculty member asserted to knowing nods around the table, a place where you took a job on your way to a university you really wanted to be. Now it's more of a destination itself rather than a way-station.

Asked to offer metaphors for their learning community experiences, some faculty members used examples of family. "We're that aunt or uncle who is really concerned about the student but who gives hard advice too," said one. "We make it clear: you only get out of your education what you put in. You don't get by on seat time."

Another faculty got strong agreement with his metaphor of the learning community experience as a good cup of coffee. "It's stimulating. It's something you start with. It can be addictive; students come back to us all the time to reconnect. We, faculty or faculty with students, sit around a table and talk and enjoy it. And it comes in all kinds of flavors."

The creativity that learning communities engender and empower among faculty is typified by the first-year seminar conducted by Drew Appleby specifically for student athletes; it is in a learning block composed of a psychology course (which Appleby also teaches), an English composition course, a math course, and an SLA offering for the math content. "I found out early that a difficulty they commonly had was that they couldn't cook. Many were away from home for the first time, and they could no longer count on their mothers to cook for them. So we began a project to compile a cookbook. Everybody had to contribute a recipe that was nutritious, easy, and inexpensive."

The fact that the project was about personal planning, life adjustment, composition, and identifying life support strategies has been secondary to the fact that it has been fun and highly successful too. "I send the cookbooks to my students' parents at the end of the semester (along with a picture of the class I take on the last day) to let them see what their children are doing. I get notes back all the time, saying, 'I didn't know there would be someone there who really cared about my child.' That's important. Parents are an important but frequently unrecognized part of student success, and you have to use that resource."

A Dedication to Unvarnished Assessment and Evaluation

When University College was established, the search for a dean was conducted nationwide. The qualifications for this position were so advanced and multifaceted that it seemed unlikely that anyone could qualify. Among other things, IUPUI sought an individual who had an outstanding record in undergraduate learning, extensive administrative experience, a talent for working across disciplines, an understanding of the curricular and cocurricular elements of student support, and the energy and drive to establish a new college from scratch. Knowledge of Indiana, IUPUI, and the universities in West Lafayette and Bloomington was also thought to be desirable.

Scott Evenbeck was named dean as a result of the search. He was an IUPUI insider, having come to the university as a faculty member in psychology and having held several administrative posts, including, immediately prior to his appointment as dean, associate vice chancellor for undergraduate education and director of the Undergraduate Education Center. The appointment was very well received on campus. But among his first requests of the institution was that University College—and he—be reviewed for performance after three years rather than the customary five at IUPUI.

That review was done in 2001–2002, upon a highly detailed charge from Chancellor Bepko. The ten questions about the college and the six questions about Dean Evenbeck that the chancellor wanted investigated included, for example, "University College seeks to establish a unique model in having the leadership of full-time tenured faculty in context of collaborative governance. How well is this concept succeeding?" The evaluation process involved a committee of nearly twenty administrators, students, and particularly faculty. The effort included extensive document review, a faculty survey, and more than two dozen individual interviews. The final report was thirty-four single-spaced pages, plus appendixes. Its findings, in summary, were that University College and Dean Evenbeck were exceeding expectations. A common concern, however, was that the college and the dean moved quickly, and it was difficult to keep up. While the report affirmed University College's directions and progress and was consistent with an independent external review that the college had commissioned earlier, its notation here is as demonstration of the dedication of IUPUI and University College to meaningful, ongoing, ever more probing public assessment and evaluation.

The university's commitment to assessment predates the University College, with the recruitment of nationally noted assessment scholar and practitioner Trudy Banta to the executive staff, her recruitment in turn of Vic Borden (also a nationally recognized scholar and practitioner) to lead institutional research, and his recruitment in turn of an institutional research staff highly qualified in both quantitative and qualitative methods and analyses.

Assessment data are not digested privately and released in bits and pieces publicly for PR benefit as might be the case elsewhere. Rather, the data environment is rich and public at IUPUI. The university's Web presence, for example, continues page after page with detailed information on university goals for itself and its students, with plenty of multiple-year trend charts and comparative data.

While the university notes with pride the areas of campus life where it has largely or substantially accomplished target goals, it also notes and highlights where its performance has been unacceptable or where means to measure progress have not been adequately developed and agreed on.

IUPUI's unique challenges as an urban university and its student population have meant that many conventional benchmarks have not been as helpful as one might hope. The standard six-year graduation rate, for example, tells only part of the story when a substantial number of students are part time, older, and employed virtually full time. Ten-year graduation rates tell a stronger story of accomplishment and are further indicative of the institution's commitment, for the long haul, to student success.

Institutional research staff indicated great professional satisfaction in working in a collegiate environment where assessment is built into program design, where people want to dig deeper and deeper into analyses, and where qualitative and quantitative analyses are seen as being mutually supportive. As with others at the university and within University College particularly, however, they saw the pace of change as a challenge and sometimes a limitation. "Sometimes it will be announced that we're expanding a program or making changes even while we're finishing the evaluation of that program." But the criticism is offered in the spirit that one might caution a prodigy to move more carefully and deliberately. Within this function, as seems to be true across University College, people are enjoying the unusual experience in higher education of a movement that is progressing so quickly and successfully in positive directions that hanging on and keeping up is a central issue and a required talent.

Strong Commitment from Institutional Leadership

Scott Evenbeck and many others at IUPUI have demonstrated the qualities of leadership that contribute to substantial institutional change and improvement over the long term, including empowerment of others, an active search for new ideas, a respect for and use of conventional sources of authority and power, and a dogged commitment to staying on message and advancing a few primary goals. Evenbeck, for example, related that the initial plans for the redevelopment of the building that is now University College's physical home did not include a highly desired feature, an interior walkway connection from that building to the university library. It was important, he believed, to have this literal connection to the university's core, not just for practical reasons but for highly important symbolic reasons as well. The connection did not make it past the budget process. And so between that time and the final building plans, Evenbeck attended a holiday party and relentlessly buttonholed a key decision maker on the importance of the connection. He got a bit of a reprimand from another university officer about the breach of conventional protocol. Evenbeck related the story, half apologetically for his unbridled enthusiasm, as we walked from the University College building to the library using the walkway and as students passed us each way.

Such leadership is critical to sustained evolutionary change. But revolutionary change is sometimes necessary as well, the great leap forward that is more push than nudge. Chancellor Gerald Bepko and Executive Vice Chancellor and Dean of the Faculties William M. Plater have provided such revolutionary leadership at critical moments.

Through the years, IUPUI has sent teams to several AAHE-sponsored multiple-day retreats and planning institutes, and both men attended one such event together in the mid-1990s. The presence of individuals of either rank at such retreats is somewhat unusual, and having both there proved critical. "We came away from that institute realizing that despite our progress on first-year learning, we really needed to establish a University College. And we intended to do it—in one year," the chancellor recalled.

Dean Plater recalls his plan of action on returning to the campus: "I haven't told this before, but here's what I did. I visited each dean of each school in his or her office. I closed the door. And I told them, we're going to create this new college. This is why. We're going to do it next year. You can tell me why it won't work, and if those are good reasons, we'll address them before moving. But if I can answer those concerns, it will happen."

Either out of deep personal commitment to the improvement of undergraduate education or because of this strong statement of leadership priority, the university quickly coalesced around the university college concept. And it was established in one year.

While Bepko and Plater may have empowered revolutionary change, they are "long marchers" in IUPUI's existence and progress. Gerald Bepko became chancellor of IUPUI in 1986, after his deanship of the Indiana University School of Law-Indianapolis, an IUPUI component. He also held the title of Indiana University vice president for long-range planning before being named interim president of Indiana University in late 2002. He continues to hold that post at this writing, after which he will retire. His legacy at IUPUI includes not only the establishment of University College, but a capital campaign that had a $700 million goal by summer 2004. By the end of 2003, that campaign had already crossed the $900 million mark. William Plater, an English scholar by background, became executive vice chancellor in 1988. Before that, he was dean of the IUPUI School of Liberal Arts, starting in 1983.

Plater and Bepko were regularly mentioned to us as leaders who were key to making University College and the entire first-year movement at the university a reality. Occasionally, some irony was noted in the fact that both were well along in their careers and might have had a personal interest in maintenance of the status quo. But both invested their prestige, credibility, and influence in the rapid and revolutionary changes that have occurred in the past few years. A closer inspection might reveal that progress toward the current model was steady and more incremental for many years. Under their terms, for example, Herman Blake was recruited to IUPUI as vice chancellor for undergraduate education. Blake, who served in that role from 1989 to 1997, came to IUPUI after being president of Tougaloo College and academic appointments at Swarthmore College and the University of California at Santa Cruz. He left IUPUI to become a professor of sociology at Iowa State University and founding director of Iowa State's interdisciplinary African-American Studies Program. Likewise, Plater and Bepko were at the helm when Trudy Banta was recruited to IUPUI to lead assessment efforts. Banta is a nationally and internationally recognized authority on assessment, and her publications include *Building a Scholarship of Assessment* (2002).

The kind of steady, purposeful progress for which these appointments are examples came to a point of critical mass eventually, a golden moment when it was possible to move forward much more rapidly. Perhaps that is a characteristic of strong leadership in first-year programming and university leadership in general: knowing when to maintain a consistent, steady hand on the helm, but knowing too when to unfurl all the sails and hit full speed.

Leadership at IUPUI is not just top-down and formal. It is empowering too and has developed in the absence of a zero-sum mentality. In other words, there is little or no sense of finite possibilities and capacity for invention, no sense of a circumstance in which there will be winners and losers in some sort of balance. Stories abound at IUPUI and in University College of individuals having an idea, becoming its champion, gathering the support and evidence requisite to institutional commitment and resource allocation, and moving ahead. "It's a place where you believe that you can make things happen," said a faculty member.

A Steady, Outward Gaze

There is no evidence at IUPUI of the "not invented here" syndrome, the notion that an idea not originated at IUPUI cannot be relevant to its environment, students, or challenges. Instead, IUPUI's efforts are remarkable for their grounding in an ongoing search for best practices, construction of benchmarking data, and interest in evaluations by outsiders. When the university realized that its first-year-student efforts and results were short of its aspirations, it turned to AAHE for assistance and the ability to network with other institutions facing similar challenges. When it considers new programs or tackles new problems, it scans the college and university world for examples of institutions that have tackled similar issues with good results and has adapted programs from Ferris State University, Brooklyn College, and other institutions. IUPUI's University College has convened reviews of its operations by outside critical friends, not so that it can meet minimal standards of internal evaluation or accreditation agency mandates but so that it can simply do better work.

A notable example of such initiations is the RUSS project—Restructuring for Student Success—sponsored by The Pew Charitable Trusts. Starting in 1997, IUPUI worked with Temple University and Portland State University to examine and maximize the effectiveness of learning communities and other strategies in the context of an urban university serving many first-generation college students. Data and strategies were generously and publicly shared with the intention and result of improving and fine-tuning the effectiveness of the learning communities. More recently, IUPUI was a central participant in the AAC&U's Greater Expectations project to critically examine the role and improvement of liberal education, and IUPUI is a founding institution, through its membership in the American Association of State Colleges and Universities, in the Policy Center on the First Year of College's Foundations of Excellence project. AASCU members were competitively selected to establish the standards and practices by which an institution might be judged to provide exemplary education for first-year students.

This exposure to external review has its risks but also its rewards. National recognition in the TIAA-CREF awards competition and numerous other commendations from higher education groups have affirmed IUPUI's strategic directions and results. This institution that was once defined mostly as not Indiana, not Purdue, has emerged as a model to which all sectors of higher education might look in their enhancement of first-year student success.

Chapter Fifteen

University of South Carolina

Creator and Standard-Bearer for the First-Year Experience

Libby V. Morris

Marc Cutright

The story of American higher education is one of growth, diversification, and specialization. Since the founding of Harvard College in 1636, more than 4,000 colleges and universities have enlisted faculty, professed knowledge, and opened their doors to students far and wide. Across these four centuries, only a handful of institutions have emerged as trailblazers and leaders in the development of higher education. The University of South Carolina is one of those and is destined to go down in the history of the undergraduate experience in America as the birthplace of the seminar course, University 101, that launched the national and international movement known as the first-year experience. Central to this story are University 101, its legacy of innovation, dissemination, and assessment, and how the University of South Carolina—a large, public research university—created and sustained a student-centered focus across more than thirty years, six presidents, and seven provosts to be named an Institution of Excellence in the First College Year.

Institutional Context

The University of South Carolina (USC) was chartered in 1801 in Columbia, South Carolina. In its earliest years, it achieved distinction for excellence in the classical tradition and was known as a well-endowed and distinguished U.S. college. Today, the institution is rich in academic programs, committed campus constituents, and a meaningful and relevant educational philosophy. As the outgrowth of its third and last reorganization in 1906, the university became an institution dedicated to "the education of the state's diverse citizens through teaching, research, creative activity, and service" (University of South Carolina, 2001, p. 3).

The University of South Carolina includes the original Columbia campus, located in the heart of the state capital; three four-year campuses in Aiken, Beaufort, and Spartanburg; and four regional campuses across the state. The Columbia campus provides a comprehensive range of undergraduate, master's, and doctoral-level programs combined with research and public service. This campus, hereafter referred to as USC, is a pedestrian-friendly campus located between the popular city areas of Five Points and the Vista.

The mission statement of USC, approved by the board of trustees in April 1998, reads in part:

> Committed to becoming one of the finest universities in America, USC Columbia is dedicated to nationally recognized excellence in its student population, faculty, academic programs, living and learning environment, technological infrastructure, library resources, research and scholarship, public and private support and endowment. . . . As a relatively selective institution, USC Columbia seeks to attract inquisitive students who have demonstrated academic ability, who are committed to learning, who are capable of self discipline, and who wish to benefit from the variety of experiences provided by a major university with students, faculty, and staff drawn from throughout South Carolina, the nation, and the world. The University strives to educate graduates who are capable of excelling in their chosen fields, who are dedicated to learning throughout their lives, and who are responsible citizens in a complex society requiring difficult ethical and value-related decisions.

Although written in 1998, this statement captures the longstanding commitment of university faculty and administrators to serve students; students are named first in the list of constituents and are discussed at length in subsequent paragraphs of the statement. In many ways, this statement reads like the mission statement of a small liberal arts college, yet USC enrolls approximately 16,000 undergraduates and 10,000 graduate and professional students each year and offers over 300 degree programs. Annually, approximately 3,300 enter as first-year, full-time students at the Columbia campus. Approximately 83 percent of incoming students matriculate from high schools in South Carolina, reflecting the university's dedication to educating the citizens of the state; 25 percent are minority students. In addition, thirty foreign countries are represented in the student body. Attesting to the strength of the university's commitment to diversity, USC was ranked eighth among Division I public universities for graduation of minority students according to the *Journal of Blacks in Higher Education* (http://president.sc.edu/highlights.html, 2004).

The diversity in the student body extends beyond racial and ethnic diversity as the university enrolls first-generation college students, valedictorians, economically disadvantaged students, world travelers, out-of-state and international students, and those who are multiple generation "gamecocks," so named for the University's mascot. The campus echoes with the philosophy of President William Davis Melton expressed in 1925: "Education is not a special privilege to be enjoyed by a special few" (University of South Carolina, 2001, p. 2). Carolina's first-year programs are central to the success and retention of the large, diverse, first-year student body.

Origins of the First-Year Experience

USC's first-year experience began in 1972 with a first-year seminar that has since given rise to a complex array of living and learning communities, core course initiatives, blended academic and student life services, targeted programs for special populations, and the National Resource Center for The First-Year Experience and Students in Transition. Perhaps it is a result of these programs and first-year enhancements that students applying to USC are academically stronger than ever before. In 2001, the incoming class averaged over 1100 on the SAT, and first-to-second-year retention averaged over 80 percent. Interestingly, USC's first-year programs did not emerge from a rational model of planning and deliberation. Rather, the USC first-year seminar was born out of crisis.

The University of California, Berkeley, and Kent State University are campuses closely tied to images of unrest in the 1960s and 1970s, but in fact hundreds of other higher education institutions experienced protest and shutdowns of varying degrees during those decades. The University of South Carolina was no exception. During 1969–70, student unrest became pronounced as various dissident groups and individual protesters were in regular conflict and skirmishes with the administration. In the spring of 1970, the conflict came to a head when approximately 1,000 students turned out to protest the U.S. invasion of Cambodia in addition to other state and campus issues that had been brewing for months. The governor called out the National Guard, and although no shots were fired, the students responded by storming the office of President Thomas Jones and holding him a virtual prisoner for hours. This activist behavior shocked President Jones, a native Mississippian, a graduate of MIT, and a former dean of engineering at Purdue.

President Jones had arrived at USC in 1962 with ideas of transforming a rather quiet regional university into a major national research institution, and in the fall of 1968, his desire to establish a "premier research university was undiminished" (Watt, 1999, p. 151). Yet the ongoing tension between students and the status quo fueled President Jones's interest in balancing the needs of a research university and holistic student development; consequently, at one point, he ordered and distributed several copies of a 1960s Hazen Foundation study that concluded the freshman year should be a "breathing-spell of orientation" rather than intensive academic study (Watt, 1999).

In May 1970, Jones experienced a complete transformation in his thinking about collegiate life brought about by external forces that profoundly affected him and the future of the University of South Carolina. As described by John Gardner, the founder of the first-year experience concept at USC, the student unrest and sit-in were seminal events that transformed Jones from an innovative electrical engineer to a social engineer. Following the sit-in and the tensions that erupted in the days that followed, Jones pronounced that the university had failed its students in some fundamental way, and it was incumbent on the institution to do a better job of assimilating students into university life, specifically USC's history, purposes, and traditions.

As Jones reflected on the causes of the riot and the university's response, he ultimately came to believe that USC could affect the success of students through affecting group dynamics, through a more deliberate process of student assimilation as done in other large social organizations, and through influencing the perspectives and roles of faculty in relationship to its students. In the early 1970s, Jones became involved in activities of the National Training Laboratories (NTL) for Applied Behavioral Science. He attended several of the NTL summer sessions in Maine and became a student of group dynamics and human behavior. He believed that group dynamics would be critically important to the first-year experience.

After that fateful day in May, Jones formed a faculty committee to discuss the changes necessary to respond to the turbulence of the times. As is often common for faculty committees, the months wore on, the study of the riot and responses continued, and Jones grew impatient; consequently, he developed his own agenda and proposed to the committee a course that would be offered as a pilot for one year called University 101. The course would not be tied to any specific discipline and would educate the whole student through small group interaction, thus, in Jones's view, eliminating the need for students to riot. "Faculty would teach persons as well as disciplines" (Watt, 1999, p. 238). In the spring of 1972 the faculty senate approved University 101 as an elective course for beginning students.

Jones's leadership did not end with course approval, however. He used money from a discretionary fund, provided by the Ford Foundation, to assemble twenty-four faculty and student affairs professionals to engage in professional development while creating the new course—its objectives, pedagogies, and activities. The student affairs profession was just beginning to emerge on college campuses, and Jones was forward thinking to include student affairs professionals in the development of this academic course. His decision laid the groundwork for continuing collaboration across student and academic affairs.

John Gardner, a twenty-eight-year-old untenured assistant professor, was invited to join this group. Gardner terms this group experience as "life altering"; members met for three hours every afternoon for three weeks—a total of forty-five hours of development. He recalls that President Jones was "hands-on" with the group, attending every session. At the end of the workshop, Gardner was one of seventeen participants invited to teach the University 101 course. Following the first round of course offerings in fall 1972, the president asked for a report from each of the seventeen faculty members. At this point, Gardner distinguished himself with his involvement and commitment to the process; he submitted a journal containing his analyses and reflections on each class, student involvement and learning, and important issues to be considered. Journaling was not an activity followed by many faculty members then, nor is it now. But Gardner had captured the vision of University 101, and he was invited to meet and discuss his reflections with the president.

In the spring of 1974, following his creation of numerous curricular and cocurricular innovations, Jones lost a vote of confidence with the university's board of trustees, and he resigned. As a last act of his presidency, he decided to name a permanent faculty director for University 101. Two senior professors with the clout and campus presence to give credibility to the project were approached about heading it, and they summarily turned it down, believing that the course would be doomed under new presidential leadership. The position of director soon fell to John Gardner. In the days that followed, the provost of thirty years became the new president. His first act was to announce his intention to review all so-called innovations of his predecessor, and, as the story goes, there were quite a few. Much to Gardner's dismay, the president announced in his initial speech to the faculty senate that University 101 would be the first candidate for evaluation.

In retrospect, Gardner acknowledges that this occurrence set the stage for future success, as evaluation became a standard, ongoing part of University 101 and all subsequent first-year activities. At the time of the initial review, however, three criteria were deemed important for identifying someone to conduct the evaluation: (1) no personal involvement in University 101, (2) appropriate research skills in the social sciences and human behavior, and (3) intellectual credibility and personal integrity that would command respect for the findings. Paul Fidler, an esteemed faculty member in the College of Education, was selected to conduct the first University 101 study. Following an exhaustive study, his findings were widely disseminated, and after much analysis and discussion the faculty senate voted to continue the course as long as there was faculty and student interest. The course, and therefore Gardner, reported to the chief academic officer. Consequently, from the outset, University 101 was viewed as an academic course that was university owned and not the province of any single department. These ingredients are now viewed as keys to its long-term success.

Under John Gardner's firm guidance, clear vision, and interpersonal skills, University 101 prospered, and it became the prototype for emulation and dissemination across colleges and universities nationwide and abroad. And for many in undergraduate education, a trip to the University of South Carolina is a pilgrimage to learn about University 101 and the first-year experience.

First-Year Seminar: University 101

As stated in *Transitions,* the internally produced University 101 handbook, the essential mission of University 101 is "to maximize the student's potential to achieve academic success and to adjust responsibly to the individual and interpersonal challenges presented by collegiate life" (University 101, 2002, p. 2). University 101 is a three-hour-credit seminar, now open to both first-year and transfer students during their first semester at USC. In 2002, *US News and World Report* ranked University 101 as number one nationally for the first-year experience among "Programs That Really Work" ("America's Best Colleges," 2002).

Approximately 80 percent of USC's first-year students enroll in University 101, where they are introduced to the culture of higher education. Course goals include building academic and personal life skills; developing an understanding of the services, facilities, and resources of USC; and learning the traditions and values important to life at "Carolina" as codified in a campuswide code of ethical behavior known as the Carolinian Creed. University 101 is organized around a peer support group of twenty to twenty-five students and a faculty or administrative mentor. Students are required to purchase the University 101 handbook, *Transitions,* in its eleventh edition in fall 2002.

Not surprisingly, over the years University 101 has evolved to meet the ever-changing needs of incoming students, and in tandem the faculty senate has adjusted academic policies governing the course. For example, in 1992 the faculty senate approved letter grading for University 101, recognizing both the course's academic rigor and the initiation of discipline-specific sections in partnership with several of USC's colleges. College and program-specific University 101 sections now exist in liberal arts, engineering, business, journalism, premedicine, prelaw, education, exercise science/public health, and science and mathematics. In addition, the College of Science and Math sponsors Frontiers Night for its discipline-specific sections of University 101. After a pizza party, the students convene for faculty presentations and small group sessions on career opportunities, research opportunities for undergraduates, and other campus-based resources.

A distinctive but not unique feature of the University 101 program at USC is the use of undergraduate peer leaders. Since 1993, junior and senior students, approximately seventy in 2002–2003, have cotaught University 101 with the instructor of record. Peer leaders are selected through a competitive application process, and they must have a minimum 3.0 grade point average in addition to a demonstrated record of campus leadership. In the spring, prospective peer leaders apply, or are nominated, for the position. After peer leaders are selected, they participate in a two-day training workshop to prepare them for their roles. Following the workshop, they meet instructors at an informal matching reception. When instructor–peer leader teams have been determined, peer leaders and instructors participate in a team-building workshop. During the coteaching experience, peer leaders enroll in a three-credit-hour academic course, The Teacher as Manager, where reflective writing assignments on the teaching experience are a course requirement.

Over the years, the University 101 program has collected end-of-term reflections from peer leaders. Many of those reflections are shared with aspiring peer leaders. The experienced leaders make sure that novices know the importance and challenges of the duties they wish to assume. "You can't go into it treating it as just another extracurricular activity or a résumé booster," said one. "If you can't provide the necessary time and commitment, it's not for you. Deadbeat peer leaders are unacceptable." Another talked about the skills and investment necessary for success: "Being a peer leader means being responsible, hard working, confident, and organized. It requires a good deal of work and preparation, and your communication skills need to be sharp." Another peer leader described disappointments and on-the-job learning: "There will always be downfalls and moments of pure amazement. If someone told you they never had a bad experience in a class, they would be lying."

But over and over, the expressions by peer leaders were ones of deep fulfillment and service: "It's been the best experience I have had at USC. It made me appreciate what professors do for us. It gave me a chance to help mold incoming freshmen into outstanding students. It has helped strengthen my confidence in myself. I know I can make a difference, and I was able to through the peer leader program."

University 101 was termed "a great program" and an "awesome program" in focus groups we convened with students. The first-year students did, however, express some concern about the variability among sections, as faculty leaders are free to mold the course to their own expertise and interests while still covering the basics.

The vice president for student services and dean of students, Dennis Pruitt, is a long-term integral partner in the USC first-year experience. He described the benefit of University 101 as follows:

> They [students] have the opportunity to explore all the virtues of a university and all the things they can do to augment their learning; all the things they can do to supplement their classroom experiences through everything from community service, service-learning to the use of a library that's ranked thirty-eighth in the country. But the other thing they have had an opportunity to do is explore the vices of collegiate life that many might experience even if they were not in college.
>
> Many of them are lifestyle and life management issues. We face it straight on. . . . We have done [programs on] everything from harassment to domestic violence to campus sexual assault to alcoholism. And the list goes on. . . . University 101 makes them feel included in the scholar guild. University 101 really breaks it down into first this little niche of other peers who are going through the same thing developmentally and a faculty member who is central to and responsive to their particular needs. It creates this gathering place where all kind of things can be explored and discussed.

In spring 2001, a Hewlett Foundation grant supported the USC Honors College and the University 101 program in the development of University 201, a course for sophomores, second-semester first-year students, and junior-level transfers that emphasizes discipline-based inquiry and research-based learning. In fall 2001, a partnership with residence life resulted in scheduling approximately half of all University 101 sections in residence hall classrooms to emphasize and strengthen the academic presence in residence life. In that year, more than 2,650 students enrolled in University 101, the highest enrollment ever enjoyed by a single course on the Columbia campus.

As required from the beginning, faculty development continues to be an overarching goal of University 101. Since 1972, University 101 has offered more than sixty instructor training workshops for the university's eight campuses, serving an estimated 2,000 faculty and staff interested in teaching the course; typically, there is a waiting list for participation. Similarly, more than fifteen undergraduate peer leader workshops and nine graduate student workshops have trained approximately 500 upperclass students and 200 graduate students as assistants for these sections. The 2003 version of University 101 is certainly more than President Jones imagined in 1970. But in this story is the clear example of how presidential leadership, faculty involvement, and ongoing assessment turned a university challenge into an opportunity for the education of first-year students.

National Resource Center for The First-Year Experience and Students in Transition

In 1982, sufficient national interest and practice in first-year seminars had developed to the point that Gardner and his USC associates convened a national meeting in Columbia on the freshman seminar concept that drew 175 participants. At the urging of attendees, a second meeting ensued in 1983 having the entire first year of college as its concern; this meeting was appropriately titled the First Annual Conference on The Freshman Year Experience. In 1987, in response to the growing interest in the first year of college and under John Gardner's leadership, the university launched the National Center for The Study of the Freshman Year Experience with an initial seed grant from the South Carolina Commission on Higher Education. This funding allowed the center to launch publications and formalize its de facto role as the nation's resource center for information on the first year of college. According to Gardner, the center was not only a national resource for dissemination of information through publications and conferences but also served as an internal, developmental resource for the University of South Carolina, providing publications, workshops, and cutting-edge ideas and practices to campus faculty, staff, and administrators.

In 1998, an expanded mission resulted in a new name for the center, the National Resource Center for The First-Year Experience and Students in Transition. This name change was implemented to recognize a broadening of the Center's focus to include conferences and publications on the transition experience of transfer students and departing seniors. Today, the center hosts annual conferences and teleconferences, both national and international. It continues its publication of a refereed journal, the *Journal of the First-Year Experience and Students in Transition,* as well as a newsletter, a monograph series, and other items of original research.

Administratively, the National Resource Center and University 101 are combined into a single academic unit with a mission "to build and sustain a vibrant campus-based and international educational community committed to the success of first-year-college students and all students in transition." As in the early years, the center and University 101 continue to report to the Office of the Executive Vice President for Academic Affairs and Provost. The unit therefore has access to and support from the highest level of administration.

When Gardner retired from the University of South Carolina in 1999 after more than thirty years of service to the university, his responsibilities to University 101 and the National Resource Center were divided between two successors. Mary Stuart Hunter, the center's long-time codirector, assumed leadership of the National Resource Center. Her involvement in first-year education at USC goes back to 1978, the year she earned a graduate degree from the institution and began teaching University 101. Clearly, with her experience and knowledge base, the center remains strong.

Reflecting expanded scope for both the National Resource Center and University 101, faculty member Dan Berman, who had served as codirector for University 101 since 1989, was named director, with responsibilities for selection, training, and supervision of seminar instructors. Berman is also responsible for University 401, a senior-level capstone seminar, and University 290, the residential college seminar, both of which have gained faculty senate approval.

Meanwhile, Gardner continues his life-long commitment to the first year of college and to the University of South Carolina by serving as a senior fellow with the National Resource Center. Today, he is also the founding executive director of the Policy Center on the First Year of College, a research center located in Brevard, North Carolina, focused on the assessment of first-year efforts and the development of standards for first-year excellence.

The Carolinian Creed: Creating a Model for Behavior

In the late 1980s, the campus and its constituents were again cast into turmoil. The president at that time enjoyed spectacular success in developing the physical campus, and he lured an impressive roster of visitors, including Pope John Paul II, to Columbia. But a series of financial problems and other excesses led to his downfall and brought his presidency to an end in 1989. Because of the widespread negative public attention, many felt that the reputation of the University of South Carolina suffered during this period. A marketing study commissioned by the university stated that it might take twenty years for the institution's image to recover. This was not a time line that President John Palms, inaugurated in 1991, was prepared to accept.

"He said we were going to do two things," noted an administrator speaking of President Palms during our on-campus interviews. "The first was, we were going to have a student-centered learning environment. And the second was, we were going to create a civil and humane environment." A peg on which Palms hung his hope as a symbol and a guide was the Carolinian Creed, a statement based on both the university motto and the Golden Rule. Developed in 1989 by USC faculty, administrators, students, and staff, under the leadership of Dennis Pruitt, vice president for student services, the creed predated Palms, but "it was his endorsement that gave it real power and meaning. And he didn't just endorse it," the administrator noted, "He cited it every day. He said, 'We're going to reestablish this as a civil place, where everyone's treated with dignity.'" The Carolinian Creed appeared on every one of the holiday cards sent from the president's office for over ten years, as well as being featured in other prominent displays.

Palms also championed the idea of an opening convocation for new students at which he routinely presided. He envisioned the convocation as a means by which to induct first-year students ceremonially into the USC community of scholars. A key moment in the convocation is the acceptance of the creed by a first-year student on behalf of the first-year class. The sense on campus is that the creed is widely known, is taken seriously, and is a touchstone for all that is Carolina. The text of the creed follows:

> The Community of Scholars at the University of South Carolina is dedicated to personal and academic excellence. Choosing to join the community obligates each member to a code of civilized behavior. As a Carolinian . . .
>
> - I will practice personal and academic integrity.
> - I will respect the dignity of all persons.
> - I will respect the rights and property of others.
> - I will discourage bigotry, striving to learn from differences in people, ideas, and opinions.
> - I will demonstrate concern for others, their feelings and their need for conditions which support their work and development.
>
> Allegiance to these ideals obligates each student to refrain from and discourage behaviors which threaten the freedom and respect all USC community members deserve [http://www.sa.sc.edu/creed].

The Carolinian Creed is foundational to the programs, services, and activities of USC's first-year experience and beyond. It is also a philosophy of behavior that guides the actions of students, faculty, and staff. It is part of the discussion of University 101; of living and learning communities, academic courses, and advising; and is typically agreed to and signed by first-year students on the first day of University 101 classes. The Carolinian Creed was described in more generic terms when Provost Jerry Odom spoke about faculty and student relationships:

> And we have those people in the University who really care about the student and about whether they have the kind of experience that they ought to have; understanding that the freshman year is such a time of transition that you get students who, for the first time in many cases, are experiencing the kind of freedom that they've never had before. They're experiencing the kind of intellectual challenge that they've never experienced before, and they're experiencing the diversity that many of them have never experienced before. And all of that brought together is a time of real turbulence, I think, for a student. So, we need to show them that we care about them . . . that we want them to be here; we want them to learn; we want them to have experiences outside the classroom that are good.

(In August of 2004, Jerry Odom was succeeded by Mark P. Becker as executive vice president for academic affairs and provost.)

In the fall, the Carolina Student Judicial Council promotes Creed Week, a week-long series of activities that focus community-wide dialogue on the Carolinian Creed. In recognition of this significant campus activity, in 2002 the National Association of Student Personnel Administrators (NASPA) named Creed Week as one of ten exemplary programs nationwide in its Bridging to Student Success program. This unique USC program was termed "innovative and effective" and was highlighted by NASPA as an example of fulfilling the mission of higher education. The Carolinian Creed serves not only as a guidepost for behavior but also as a symbol of Carolina community that transcends differences in class, race, status, and position; its effectiveness is in the unity it brings to the diversity, a mantra that signifies membership in the community.

First-Year Reading Experience

The University of South Carolina's first-year reading program was launched in 1994 by Associate Provost and Dean for Undergraduate Affairs Don Greiner, when he discovered with great dismay that Greek rush was the primary introductory activity for students coming to Carolina. (Karl Heider, professor of anthropology assumed the position of associate provost of undergraduate affairs upon Don Greiner's retirement in June 2004.) As the Carolina Distinguished Professor of English and a tenured faculty member, Greiner said, "No more." Since that year, a summer first-year reading program has become a hallmark. During the summer, hundreds of books are distributed to incoming first-year students as well as to faculty and administrators who serve as discussion leaders. Then on a Monday morning in late summer, following move-in day on Saturday and New Student Convocation on Sunday, more than 700 students (about 25 percent of the first-year class) and seventy discussion leaders assemble to launch the academic life at Carolina around the common reading in University 101 groups. This experience is limited to this smaller cohort for reasons of quality control, space, and logistical considerations. However, the university has announced that it plans to expand this opportunity to the entire first-year class in fall 2005. Participants enjoy a continental breakfast, a sponsored lunch, and opportunities to see thematic explorations of the book in multiple exhibits around campus. For example, a library collection of primary sources is developed around the author and events of the author's life and period. A Web site is created, and a poster contest is launched to promote the reading, with the posters exhibited in the campus museum.

Each year, the book's author or other literary experts are present to discuss the selection and to inspire the students to a life of learning and reading. When illness kept Ray Bradbury away from a scheduled appearance on campus, USC sent a video team to his home in California and captured the moment for students on video. Books are carefully selected, and a host of activities throughout the year are spin-offs from the book, the author, or the streams of literary thought represented by the selection. The Office of the Provost, Honors College, University 101, Thomas Cooper Library, and the Department of English jointly administer and underwrite the first-year reading experience.

First-Year English Programs

While many large research universities struggle with teaching effectiveness in multiple sections of core courses taught year after year, the English Department at USC has integrated undergraduate composition requirements and graduate education in a unique program of first-year instruction and "preparing future faculty." Because English 101 and 102 reach virtually every first-year student, a deliberate effort has been made to create meaningful and effective instruction in these core courses. At the beginning of the course, each student is given a comprehensive guide to the first-year English programs, *Writers and Writing at Carolina: A First-Year English Companion,* which addresses a wide range of topics, such as attendance, academic resources, plagiarism, and grading.

As a prerequisite for teaching, all new graduate teaching assistants are required to take a six-credit-hour, in-service training sequence, English 701A and 701B, during their first year of instruction. As part of these courses, teaching assistants are introduced to instructional strategies, their classes are observed, and their grading proficiency is evaluated. In addition, first-year students complete evaluations of each instructor, and the evaluations are reviewed by the program's director. At the end of the term, a student from each section taught by a new graduate student is invited to a focus group with other students and teaching assistants to discuss the course, its materials, activities, and effectiveness. The entire English Department—faculty, staff, and students—participates in offering and evaluating the first-year courses.

In recent years, the provost's office has provided additional support for these core courses through a second reading experience that takes place in the fall semester. The Common Reading Experience, administered by the English Department, is an initiative through which all students taking English 101 read and study the same book. In most years, the book's author or a well-known literary scholar comes to campus to speak to the students. Beginning in 2002, as part of a state-funded Sustainable Universities Initiative, first-year students were also given the option to enroll in special sections of English 101 that focus on writing about the environment and include a special service-learning component.

While competency in writing for first-year students is the primary goal of this program, the program director, Professor William Rivers, is equally proud of the faculty development and training opportunities given to graduate students. He reports that the graduate students in this program are frequently invited to other departments to talk about their experiences and frequently are the recipients of university teaching awards.

University Housing: Designing Communities for Living and Learning

Living and learning centers for first-year students represent another of USC's structural and organizational responses to creating excellence in the first year of college. Eight residence halls are designated as first-year centers to accommodate and support academic goals for students and to assist them in making a successful transition to the university. Only first-year students live in these specially designated residence halls, and programs and services are guided by professional staff who are full-time residence life coordinators. More than two thousand first-year students participate in the living and learning communities on the USC campus.

The university administration and the Office of the Provost are central to the support of the first-year living and learning communities. In an interview, current President Andrew Sorensen noted that the future for undergraduate education is "a fusion of living and learning," and his cabinet meetings, which include the chief academic and student affairs administrators, encourage discussions around this topic. Of primary importance in the living and learning initiatives are the Student Success Initiative, the Center for Academic Excellence, Preston Residential College, and other special-purpose residences.

Student Success Initiative

The Student Success Initiative (SSI), started in 1998, is the umbrella program for USC's first-year residential communities and is staffed by a ratio of one resident adviser (RA) to twenty students, much lower than the national ratio of one to forty. In combination with University 101, the SSI strengthens engagement of the student in the first year of college by building an intentional relationship between the student and the RA. According to the associate director for residence Life, the components of the SSI program include the following:

- Facilitating a proactive discussion with roommates using a written contract
- Developing strong, intentional communities among students
- Providing easily accessible academic support and information to first-year students
- Devoting staff resources to developing strong relationships between students and staff

At the core of activities of the SSI is the development of a roommate contract. The RAs at the beginning of fall semester facilitate development of a contract between roommates. The contract is aimed at building communication between roommates and the RAs. Items for discussion include student academic goals, use of personal property, visitation, room cleanliness, and general behavior. As a living document, the contract may be revised throughout the year, and it encourages relationship development as well as attention to the process of communication, goal setting, and negotiation.

To facilitate proactive relationships between the RAs and students and to enhance student success in the first year, University Housing developed the SSI Discussion Guide, which provides RAs with a purposeful and intentional document for leading one-on-one academic discussions with first-year students. The guide takes RAs and students through a series of four structured interactions; two are held each semester.

Goals for the first session include orienting the student to the campus, promoting involvement, and helping the student with academic success. The second meeting centers on assessing student progress in social and academic adjustment and involvement. During the second semester, issues of academics and involvement continue, and students are introduced to the Career Center. At a final meeting, students are assisted with making the transition to the sophomore year. From the outset, the Carolinian Creed is a deliberate part of this student-RA dialogue and serves as a guide for discussions.

To gauge the success of the SSI program and make improvements, students complete the SSI exit survey at the end of the spring semester. In the most recent assessment, 46 percent reported that meetings with the RA had been "greatly" or "very much" helpful. Only 15 percent believed that these interactions were of "little" or "no" help.

Building on the collaboration between housing and academics, university housing implemented an academic intervention initiative. Each spring, students who have low grade point averages from fall term and may need academic intervention are referred to housing professional staff for assistance and referral. At the other end of the academic spectrum, university housing also implemented the academic excellence reception to honor students who have excelled academically during the year. Through partnering with academic and other student life units, university housing attempts to create a first-year culture that views residence life as an extension of the academic community.

An RA captured the goal of holistic student development as follows: "Even though it's a large university, we almost make it seem like a smaller university. I think that's very beneficial to making sure that students don't feel like they're just a number or lost in the crowd."

In commenting on the first-year experience, one student said:

> I really like the fact that I feel like I fit in. . . . You know, like when something happens to one of us, like more than just your group of friends finds out, and everyone cares. So much, that you can just get involved easily. And you know that you have this great support group, that's also your academic place, and the place where you live. It is really awesome I have no problem calling this place home.

Former President Jones would be pleased.

Academic Center for Excellence

The Academic Center for Excellence (ACE) is an example of a successful collaboration between academic and student affairs to support the growth and development of first-year students. Established in 1995, ACE is a collaboration among university housing, the English Department's Writing Center, and the Mathematics Department to bring academic support into first-year residence halls. ACE partners with the writing and math centers to make tutorial and other academic services available in the early evenings in or close to the first-year halls.

University Housing Classroom Project

In another effort to connect living and learning, the University Housing Classroom Project converted bedroom and other available space to create multimedia classrooms in ten residence halls. As several administrators noted, this conversion was done at considerable current and future expense to housing's bottom line; yet the director of student development and university housing, Gene Luna, is in the forefront of blending student services to support the academic mission of the university. As he said at the campus forum on the first-year experience, "academics and student learning must come first" in a university, thereby creating a win-win situation for everyone.

Housing also supports the first-year experience by providing classroom space to University 101. In 2002, more than half of all 101 sections were taught in the residence halls. Overall, more than seventy sections of various courses are taught throughout the residence facilities. Through the incorporation of classrooms in the residence halls, the opportunity to collaborate with faculty has increased, and the connection between residence life and academics has been strengthened.

Preston Residential College and Special Interest Housing

In addition to overall programming for first-year students in the residence halls, university housing provides several special-interest living arrangements. The premier example is Preston Residential College, which focuses on the development of skills, knowledge, and attitudes of a liberal arts education. Opened in 1995 after extensive planning and collaboration by Associate Provost Don Greiner and Director of Student Development and University Housing Gene Luna, Preston College combines a live-in faculty principal, a dining hall for shared evening meals, and forty faculty mentors for 240 students, one-third of whom are in their first year. Greiner went on to say "The director of housing met me halfway. It couldn't have worked without him. He had to commit to it."

Faculty mentors for Preston apply for the position and agree at the beginning of the year to dine with students one evening each week and to serve as volunteer mentors. Special programs are arranged by and for this student population throughout the year. Graduate degree candidates serve as resident tutors in Preston Hall. The first-to-second-year retention rate for students living in Preston Hall (84.9 percent) is about three percentage points higher than the rate for the university as a whole.

University housing also designates halls for students with special academic interests. For example, Maxcy College houses the South Carolina Honors College first-year students and provides classes, study groups, and upper-division honors students as mentors. An engineering learning community is located in Bates House, and Moore Hall, in partnership with the Office of Pre-professional Advising and the Provost's Office, provides living and learning for pre-med students. In cooperation with the College of Education, Moore and Patterson Halls also host the Teaching Fellows, a state-funded scholarship program that attracts outstanding students to secondary teaching. First-year fellows also share a University 101 section. Through these special residence hall living-learning collaborations, first-year students (and beyond) can access academic support, interact with faculty and teaching fellows in their respective fields, and participate in specially designed academic programs reflecting their interests.

Targeted Programs

In addition to broad-based and discipline-specific programs for first-year students, USC offers programs for specifically targeted subpopulations. We highlight the First-Year Scholars Program, Minority Assistance Peer Program, and the Pre-professional Advising Program here.

First-Year Scholars Program

Through the Office of Fellowships and Scholar Programs, USC brings in academically superior first-year students each year through two special programs: the Carolina Scholars program for in-state students begun in 1969 and the McNair Scholars program for out-of-state students begun in 1998. The McNair Scholars program was endowed by a $20 million gift from alumnus Robert McNair and his wife, Janice. Each year about twenty students are selected for each scholarship program. Illustrating student input into program improvement, Associate Provost Greiner related a story of an exit interview with a graduating senior who suggested that the greatest improvement for the scholars program would come from the assignment of faculty mentors. Now, every student has a faculty mentor, not adviser, with whom he or she meets regularly.

Faculty members are eager to mentor these outstanding students and are asked to do so by invitation from the associate provost. The participants in this program may share dinners, attendance at special events, and research—all funded by the provost's office. At the end of each year, the experience is assessed from the student and mentor's point of view. Following the program, the associate provost writes a letter to the appropriate department chair or college dean commending the instructor's participation in this teaching (not service) mission of the institution. This approach to rewarding faculty involvement in extracurricular programs was noted not only by Associate Provost Greiner but also by other upper-level administrators.

Minority Assistance Peer Program

The Office of Multicultural Affairs coordinates the Minority Assistance Peer Program (MAPP), which connects students of color with junior or senior peer counselors during the first year in order to ease their social, cultural, and academic adjustment. MAPP students and peers are matched based on special interests or majors. Students are mentored by their peers, and they participate in social events, tutoring, and special workshops. As noted earlier, based on the high percentage of students of color graduating from USC, this program and other first-year programs are clearly important to the success of minority students.

Preprofessional Advising Program

The Office of Pre-Professional Advising reports to the associate provost and dean for undergraduate affairs and was created to provide undergraduate students with advice concerning the professions of law, medicine, and other health-related careers. This office guides students through the courses they need to take, provides opportunities for them to experience the career as undergraduates, and assists them in the professional school application process.

To launch the premedical advising process, incoming first-year students are invited to a Pre-Medical Academic and Career Exploration Series (PACES) summer residential program, a week-long program focused on the academic skills and interests important to study in medicine. University 101 continues the focused advising emphasis with designated sections for participating PACES students. The integration of residential life and career goals is reflected in a forty-person living and learning community for premed students.

Students in prelaw, prehealth, and premedicine are also assisted in understanding these professions through participation in established networks of volunteer opportunities and shadowing placements. The director of the Pre-Professional Advising Office described the health and law shadowing and volunteering opportunities as a "real eye opener for the freshmen." Clearly the process is working; in the past four years for which data are available, USC graduates have exceeded the national average in acceptance to medical school by more than 10 percentage points.

Leadership: Champions of the First Year

For many years, the recognized leader of USC's first-year experience was John Gardner. Many administrators on the USC campus have a "John Gardner story"—an episode of his active intervention on behalf of first-year students and their interests. Originally, the concept for Preston College, the USC residential college, included no first-year students. "John buttonholed me on that one, and in five minutes convinced me I was wrong," said Associate Provost Donald Greiner, one of the concept's founders. Preston College opened admitting twenty-five Honors College first-year students and twenty-five regular new students out of a population of 240. Now, about 100 of those 240 are first-year students.

Another academic administrator told of a period when a particular college was not assigning its "first-team" faculty to University 101. By the end of Gardner's persistence on the issue, the college had not only agreed to the assignment of more senior and noted teachers to the course but also helped design a discipline-specific

101 course that became a high-demand offering in the college and served as a model for other academic units. That is the kind of dogged, unwavering championship from which first-year programs often benefit.

At USC, another recognized champion of the first-year student is Don Greiner, associate provost and dean for undergraduate affairs. A well-published scholar of contemporary American literature and an award-winning teacher, Greiner commanded respect among the faculty when he advocated improvement of undergraduate education, and that is why the provost asked him to take the job. "I agreed to do it for nine months," Greiner said, and a decade later, he was still in the job.

Greiner was the leading advocate for the First-Year Reading Experience and the primary administrative champion of Preston Residential College. For the latter project, he sent a team to the University of Virginia and told them, "Ask anything you want, but you've got to ask two questions: What did Virginia do right, and what did Virginia do wrong?" From such inquiries, consultation with others on campus, and his own vision of what Preston was to accomplish, he worked on realization of the project for several years—repeatedly "bumping against others' priorities or ideas." The board of trustees proposed putting the residential college in a remote campus location. "I told them that their location was closer to the Georgia border than it was to the Horseshoe [the campus core]." The remark earned a laugh, but Greiner's research and insistence earned a location in the center of campus contiguous to prime Horseshoe property.

The importance of dedication and commitment to making things work was stated clearly by the provost, Jerry Odom: "You have to have the right people. . . . If you don't have the right people to really do this, then I don't think it'll work. And that started with John Gardner a long time ago. And we have continued to draw the kind of person who is just so dedicated."

When asked about how a large research university balances the rewards of teaching and research, President Sorensen noted that there is no tug of war between the first year and good research, and he reminded us of South Carolina's roots in the liberal arts tradition. He reported that he frequently interacts with students; for instance, he tries to go to the campus dining halls at least once each week to talk with students. He states that doing research in and of itself is not enough for promotion. The faculty member must be a capable and productive researcher and dedicated teacher. In his own words, "Good teaching and a passion for students can be enhanced by research. More and more research grants are calling for undergraduates to be involved with research programs. The future is a fusion of living and learning."

Central Role of Assessment: Commitment to Continuous Improvement

Despite diverse programs and substantial investment and improvement over time, USC is unwilling to rest on its laurels. There is a culture of assessment, a sense of self-critical analysis, an interest in national benchmarking, and the search for particular components of the first-year approach to examine and improve. The culture is facilitated and empowered by a number of elements. These include an ongoing effort to make data available and widely accessible through an open-access database where data may be linked about programs, student surveys, and institutional activities. The Office of Institutional Planning and Assessment is central to the efforts of assessment and accountability campuswide, and it has strong support from the provost to accomplish its mission.

Assessment is a long-standing and continuous activity at USC. University 101 has been evaluated annually since 1972, and this dedication to evaluation and evidence-based change has been central in keeping this elective first-year seminar relevant to first-year students. Even before University 101, however, in 1966 USC participated in the first administration of the UCLA Higher Education Research Institute's Freshman Survey, commonly known as the Cooperative Institutional Research Program (CIRP) survey. This instrument, which profiles the nation's entering college students, has been used continuously by USC, and thus the institution mines a rich longitudinal database for changes in students over time and for comparisons with other institutions.

The Division of Student Affairs in collaboration with the Office of Institutional Planning and Assessment provides campuswide leadership in assessing student development experiences and their impact on student growth and satisfaction. For example, USC administers the College Student Experience Questionnaire (CSEQ) every other year and provides the faculty and administration with insights into the college experience of students at all academic levels, including the first year. USC also participated in piloting and currently administers the National Survey of Student Engagement's (NSSE) *College Student Report* and the Higher Education Research Institute's end-of-first-year survey, Your First College Year. Reflecting sensitivity to cost and time required for student participation, USC faculty are now investigating the feasibility and value added from this combination of instruments.

Even more impressive than the ongoing use of national standardized instruments is the institution's commitment to data accessibility and data use. For example, at the Office of Institutional Planning and Assessment's Web site, a simple query pulls up the institution's NSSE data from 2001 with charts showing USC responses as compared to national data. Also on-line are national CIRP data, CSEQ data, and a range of alumni surveys. This interactive Web site hosts an impressive array of information and data that can be queried, aggregated, and analyzed for assessment purposes. The office staff described the openness toward data as follows: "These are our data, and if we're embarrassed by them, then we need to change something. We're not hiding from anybody. This gets down to the, you know, you don't hide the thermometer on a really hot day. Everybody knows it's hot. Until somebody pulls the plug on us we're going to continue to let anybody look at this."

USC also has built a comprehensive program of qualitative and quantitative assessments for specific uses. In fall 2001, the university retention committee collaborated with the registrar to add an open-ended survey to the Web-based student withdrawal process. Using this qualitative approach, the committee has gleaned additional insight into why students leave the university. The committee also conducts telephone interviews with first-year students who do not return for their sophomore year.

The Office of Institutional Planning and Assessment assists units with specific institutional studies. As an example, the director described a higher education myth that the impact of living on campus applies only to the first year; consequently, in collaboration with university housing, IR staff investigated the relationship of living on-campus and found that students are 1.7 times more likely to return to college each year, even through the senior year, if they live on campus.

The Office of Institutional Planning and Assessment has been given extensive responsibility by the provost to coordinate degree program assessments and the approval process for assessment plans. Each year, every program unit must submit to the provost a strategic plan, and in recent years an accompanying assessment plan. If the assessment plan is not approved, the strategic plan is not eligible for budget consideration. Tying funding to planning and assessment provides real leverage for evaluation.

As evidenced in the process and organization described, the reliance on assessment data goes right to the top at USC. As the provost noted concerning budget cuts that are endemic throughout higher education, "One of the things I really like about our operation is the assessment that we do. We are continually assessing what the outcomes are. . . . When somebody says, 'Well, why didn't you cut this area?' I've got what I need to back that up, and that's very important to me." Clearly, through assessment, USC closes the loop on program improvement and change.

Seamless Connections: Linking Academic and Student Affairs

Another key to USC's success in the first year is the collaborative and cooperative relationship between student affairs and academic affairs. This collaboration can be seen in the academic intervention initiatives, the creation of academic space in residence halls, the design and implementation of Preston Residential College, the creation of the Academic Centers for Excellence, and the presence of faculty mentors and tutors in residence hall settings.

During the site visit to the University of South Carolina, we were constantly struck by the cross-campus collaborations and the frequency with which staff and faculty referenced other units in planning or implementing a project or idea. Associate Provost Greiner stated USC's approach to the first year best by using the analogy of a puzzle (paraphrased): USC is not offering a series of unconnected programs for various groups of students. Rather, the university is creating an elaborate and dynamic puzzle, where every piece fits and interacts with other pieces to create a whole. This requires the involvement of multiple units—academic, administrative, and student.

Conclusion

The University of South Carolina is an institution of excellence because the first-year experience is mission and purpose driven; because multiple activities cut across the lines of student and academic affairs to put students first; because there has been and is significant leadership at the top and broad-based ownership throughout of the first-year experience; because virtually every first-year student is touched in a meaningful way by one or more carefully constructed curricular or cocurricular activities; and because assessment is ongoing, shared, and used in decision making.

The University of South Carolina continues the original quest of President Jones to create an academic culture within a major research university that nurtures and engages first-year students while supporting the goals of scholarship and research. Across the past four decades, the University of South Carolina has excelled in the integration of student centeredness and an ethos of research. And along the way, the institution, through the work of John Gardner and the National Resource Center for The First-Year Experience and Students in Transition, has been a national and international leader in creating a needed dialogue and focusing the academy on the experience of the first-year student.

Part Seven

Conclusion

Chapter Sixteen

Findings and Recommendations

This study was designed to select and describe thirteen colleges and universities in the United States that have achieved excellence in the way they structure and implement the first year. The case study chapters have explored in rich detail the particular mix of campus history, culture, leadership, curricular and cocurricular initiatives, and means of assessment that enabled each institution to achieve this recognition. We trust that these thirteen case studies have provided not only interesting reading, but also new ideas and insights about how the first year can challenge and support students and establish for them a solid foundation for the undergraduate experience. We also hope that these case studies either have served to confirm the merits of your institution's approach to the first year and or have inspired you to consider adapting some of these initiatives to your own campus.

The most powerful results of case study research come not from a single example but from findings that are consistent across multiple situations (Yin, 1994). Our final task as a research team therefore was to collaborate on this concluding chapter by reflecting together on our findings and identifying those that are common to most, if not all, of the thirteen institutions. The chapter ends with recommendations for ways to move beyond a study and analysis of other institutional best practices toward an action agenda designed to improve the first year on your campus.

A Word of Caution

In a book of this type, any summing up brings with it the danger of oversimplification, the temptation to imply or infer—either intentionally or unintentionally—that the achievements of the thirteen colleges and universities cited in the text can be achieved quickly and easily by following the actions or implementing the programs of the thirteen. The reality is that excellence achieved on these campuses, and for that matter on any other campus, results not only from intentional decisions and actions but also from a broader set of factors that include institutional history, culture, and values. For instance, "the late 1960s intersection of people and time" that engendered a spirit of social activism still alive and well at LaGuardia Community College would be difficult to replicate in today's political environment. The student riot that inspired the president of the University of South Carolina to begin a long-term institutional commitment to the first year is unlikely to occur on other campuses any time soon. The generosity of the Lilly Endowment to Indiana higher education that enabled first-year improvements at Ball State University and Indiana University Purdue University Indianapolis (IUPUI) is not available outside that state. But accidents of fate or serendipity notwithstanding, all these thirteen institutions have capitalized on their circumstances and have used them to their own advantage and to the advantage of first-year students.

In spite of this caution, there is much to learn in these institutional stories about effective ways to structure the academic and social experiences of new students. Perhaps one of the most consistent findings of this research is that reaching high standards of educational excellence requires persistence over many years and willingness to continually scan the horizon for best practices that can be adapted with care to particular institutional contexts and cultures.

Study Findings

As we designed the research protocol to conduct the thirteen site visits, we concluded that certain components of campus life would likely have a significant impact on the first year, and we acknowledge that to some extent our expectations structured our investigation. For instance, we agreed that an institution's explicit rationale for its first-year approach, its leadership, and particular campus history would be important. Therefore, we studied those elements in addition to exploring the specifics of each campus's approach to the first year and the students' self-reported experiences.

From the very beginning of the research project, we also developed and made public certain selection criteria. These criteria undoubtedly determined which institutions were nominated; for example, the criterion that first-year efforts should be institutionalized and durable over time essentially precluded the nomination of campuses just beginning their first-year efforts. The criteria also had obvious influence on the way each institution prepared nomination materials and what we sought to investigate more intensively during the site visits. These thirteen campuses not only achieved, but in many cases also surpassed, the criteria that we set forth; in addition, their stories reveal unanticipated and sometimes surprising information.

Therefore, some of our findings were indeed what we were looking for. But we could not have anticipated much of what we found, and overall what we learned from the inside stories of these campuses vastly exceeded our expectations for institutional resourcefulness, commitment, and creativity.

1. *Institutions that achieve first-year excellence place a high priority on the first year among competing institutional priorities and accept a significant share of the responsibility for first-year student achievement.* This statement is both a finding and our deeply held conviction. Although many U.S. campuses today would likely claim such commitment, our investigation enabled us to see what happens when colleges and universities actually walk their talk. Historically, the dominant culture of higher education has been to hold students primarily, if not exclusively, responsible for sinking or swimming. Hence, this acceptance by institutions of a portion of the responsibility for the fate of first year students is truly exceptional.

An intentional focus on first-year students requires a substantial share of existing campus resources—both human and financial. IUPUI could decide to focus primarily on its research mission rather than undergraduate education. But this campus has a deep sense of responsibility to its students and to economic growth in central Indiana, and so it tries to do both. The fiscal resources and human talent that IUPUI has applied to the first year have reaped benefits for student learning beyond anyone's expectations. As a highly selective institution, Kalamazoo College could rely on its students to create for themselves a meaningful first year. But Kalamazoo recognizes that even the best students need support and has designed an intentional array of structures that help students achieve more than they, or the institution, ever imagined. At the U.S. Military Academy, the entire chain of command, from the superintendent down to the "yearlings" (second-year students), assumes responsibility for the success of each plebe, and at both Elon and Drury universities, responsibility for student success is inculcated in the process of hiring and orienting new faculty and staff.

2. *Leadership, operating on multiple levels, is essential to the achievement of excellence.* On these thirteen campuses, leadership is not a zero-sum game; it is multidirectional: top-down, bottom-up, and lateral. In some cases, it has grown out of the vision of a president or chief academic officer who has gained the trust of many stakeholders. On other campuses, first-year excellence has sprung from the seeds sown by faculty or staff members who have been willing to invest professional and personal capital in improving the first year. Although we visited campuses where strong and committed leaders essentially fell from the sky, at all the thirteen institutions leadership was also nurtured and developed from within.

Several of the campuses have a history of strong leadership. There is no doubt that the Community College of Denver owes much to its former president, Byron McClenney, who set this fledgling institution on a course of excellence. The same was true at LaGuardia Community College, where faculty and staff still speak reverentially about the first president, Joe Shenker, and his role in making the campus what it is today. At both institutions, current leaders, Christine Johnson and Gail Mellow, respectively, have continued as committed guardians of the campuses' mission and heritage. At Drury University, a leadership team of President John Moore and Vice President Stephen Good rescued the campus from financial exigency in the early 1980s, and in their twenty years together they were the collective driving force behind first-year improvement. President Donald Eastman of Eckerd College and former president James Jones of Kalamazoo College view themselves as the guardians of traditions involving the mission of the college. While they know that implementation of the mission will change over time, their chief task is to maintain its preeminence.

In contrast, first-year leadership at Lehman College came primarily from Steven Wyckoff, an English professor who, with the support of senior administrators, assumed responsibility for a required year-long, first-year learning community and also wrote the original grant that funded that effort. At Elon University, credit for the sustainability of Elon 101 often goes to Lela Faye Rich, a long-serving academic adviser and director of the academic advising center, who is one of the institution's most effective informal leaders and student advocates. Ball State University acknowledges the important role of Tom Lowe, dean of University College, as well as two ad hoc groups, the Freshman Learning Council and the Ad Hoc Committee on the Liberal Arts, in providing the leadership necessary to create and sustain first-year efforts. And at the University of South Carolina, John Gardner for twenty-five years used his formal and informal influence as a faculty member and senior administrator to mold and maintain not only University 101 but also a national center dedicated to disseminating research and information focused on the first year.

3. *Excellence flourishes in a culture that encourages idea generation, pilot projects, and experimentation.* What allows the will to change to take hold on some campuses and not on others? The knowledge base supporting programmatic change is readily available, and leadership is not usually a monopoly held by a handful of institutions. What appears to make the difference is the culture itself. Campus culture may be likened to soil—either soft and pliant or hard and stony. In the former, ideas take hold and yield abundant harvests; in the latter, no matter what the effort is, the field is barren. In addition, some campuses have developed not just a tolerance for risk but a taste for it.

Each of the thirteen campuses can be characterized as a place where the overriding culture not only accepts innovation as part of the status quo but also rewards risk takers. Two corollaries are important components of the willingness to take risks. The first is that trying something new does not mean that the institution will have to live with it forever. If it works, it becomes institutionalized.

If it fails, it is scrapped. The second is that those who try out the new venture will be held blameless for failure. How can an institution encourage innovation if it punishes the innovator?

On several campuses, innovations seemed to originate in one or more discrete units before spreading to the entire campus. For instance, the learning communities, first-year seminars, and system of advising at Appalachian State University were nurtured in either the former General College or in Watauga College, a residential living-learning unit created in the 1980s and still flourishing. A former chancellor of Appalachian who served in the 1960s and 1970s even appointed a dean for innovation and change who served during this chief executive's tenure. At the University of South Carolina, University 101 was an innovation conceived in the early 1970s by the university president himself. But other faculty and staff leaders nurtured the course, and it thrives today, in significant part because of the university's willingness to subject the course to annual, systematic evaluation. Texas A&M-Corpus Christi had the advantage of a clean slate: it had no first-year students or programs until the year 1994. It borrowed an innovative idea from other institutions—the learning community—and adapted it in novel ways to its present system of clustering courses into groups of three (triads) or four (tetrads). And even the U.S. Military Academy, known for its discipline and traditions, has experienced in recent years what senior administrators termed "a fundamental paradigm shift" from a model of expected attrition to one that develops the potential of each cadet. The academy believes that students can be taught how to achieve both success in college and strong leadership abilities. At LaGuardia Community College, innovation knows no bounds. Hardly a semester goes by when a faculty member or administrator does not try something new—an idea learned at a conference or created from scratch. To borrow a notion from our Penn State University colleague, Pat Terenzini (personal communication, March 14, 2003), LaGuardia, through its pattern of continuous innovation, may quite unintentionally be "institutionalizing the Hawthorne effect."

4. *Excellence in the first year is achieved through efforts designed for all or for a critical mass of first-year students.* An unresolved debate among college and university educators revolves around whether certain first-year courses or programs should be required or

optional, and in this group of thirteen institutions, excellence has been achieved through both means. At Eckerd College, the signature approach to the first year is the core curriculum that begins in late August in a three-week autumn term and continues throughout the year. No student is exempt from the core. Lehman College, Drury University, and Texas A&M-Corpus Christi also have year-long efforts—first-year seminars or learning communities, or both—in which every first-year student must participate. Appalachian State University, Elon University, and the University of South Carolina do not require all students to enroll in their versions of the first-year seminar. But all three institutions have achieved a critical mass of participants: over 80 percent of students at each institution take the first-year seminar as an elective.

At many colleges and universities across the United States, first-year efforts are targeted exclusively to students designated as at risk for academic failure or dropout. These thirteen campuses, in contrast, attempt to meet the needs of students at all levels of academic preparation. LaGuardia Community College, IUPUI, Ball State University, the Community College of Denver, and others have a menu of offerings from which students can pick and choose—services to at-risk and honors populations and all those in between. Thus, what distinguishes these thirteen institutions is their attention to all first-year students.

5. *Assessment is an essential component of moving toward and sustaining excellence.* Termed "a steady inward gaze" by two of our chapter authors, continuous assessment is absolutely fundamental to a claim of excellence in the first year, and each of the thirteen institutions described has a solid record of not only conducting but, more important, using assessment findings for institutional improvement. Furthermore, assessment findings go far beyond the simple measure of retention rates from the first to the second year. These colleges and universities are investigating student achievement of core learning objectives that are linked to institutional mission and purpose. Excellence requires that a steady inward gaze be an ongoing process. To quote an IUPUI administrator, "If we ever stop changing because we've 'got it right,' that's when we're wrong, because students are changing all the time."

Ball State University has a long record of national leadership in the country's assessment movement. Its survey of first-year students called Making Achievement Possible, coupled with a feedback process, enables students to predict their own first-year outcomes by comparing their survey responses to those from members of the previous year's first-year class. At Appalachian, first-year assessment is a shared activity between the Office of Institutional Research and Planning in the Division of Academic Affairs and the Office of Student Life and Learning Research in the Division of Student Development. Findings from both units provide a comprehensive picture of holistic student achievement and development. The assessment committee at Kalamazoo College encourages the use of both in-house and external assessment measures. Kalamazoo's assessment process begins with the foundations essay written prior to matriculation. This essay becomes the baseline against which further writing in each student's electronic portfolio is measured. Kalamazoo also routinely shares data about incoming students with faculty who participate in first-year teaching workshops. At the U.S. Military Academy, assessment is a high-stakes activity that is part of the fabric of institutional life. The academy is accountable to its trustees, the U.S. Army, and the Congress for implementing constant improvement of future military leaders.

6. *Of the campuses that achieve first-year excellence, a common characteristic is clarity of institutional identity and mission and a concomitant respect for students.* Within this group of thirteen institutions, only four—Community College of Denver, LaGuardia Community College, Kalamazoo College, and Eckerd College—provide undergraduate education exclusively. At all the others, graduate education and research productivity comprise significant, and in some situations growing, components of the institutional mission. But all of these campuses, even the three Carnegie research universities, are clear about and accepting of their mission to improve both undergraduate and first-year education for all students who actually attend—not just some mythical group of "better" students. On the whole, they are not part of what David Riesman, writing in 1956, termed the "academic snake," the procession of institutions aping the characteristics of those perceived to be in the lead.

In these thirteen, clarity of mission is also coupled with what we found to be a high level of respect for first-year students, whether they are traditional eighteen-year-olds or older students dealing with the pressures that come with juggling competing priorities.

This culture of positive regard includes a respect for even the most at-risk students and a belief in the merits of and need for developmental education. There is a level of dignity accorded this mission to respect and serve first-year students that sets these institutions apart. These thirteen colleges and universities are well grounded in the reality of the here and now—the changing characteristics of college students that result in a highly diverse, and often unevenly prepared, student population. They therefore spend their time learning to serve these diverse students rather than bemoaning the absence of a formerly homogeneous student body. Valuing the students they have, they demonstrate respect for and realistic acceptance of these students and meet them where they are while holding students to high levels of performance. No institution among these thirteen can rightly be accused of "dumbing down" the curriculum or setting low expectations for student performance.

Faculty who teach at LaGuardia Community College, many of whom could choose to teach at more prestigious four-year institutions, speak of their students as "heroic." Faculty expectations for student achievement are high, and students respond by surpassing those expectations. The same can be said for faculty at the Community College of Denver. By believing in its students and setting high institutional goals coupled with support, this campus has seen equal levels of high achievement for students, regardless of their racial or ethnic identity. At IUPUI and Lehman College, institutions that draw heavily from surrounding urban neighborhoods, first-year classes are structured to provide connection and relevance to students' lives beyond campus. Administrators and faculty in IUPUI's University College realize that for their students who commute and work off campus, involvement in campus life must be tightly linked to course expectations. Therefore, this campus has created a number of ingenious ways to link first-year courses to opportunities for faculty-student and student-student interaction. Lehman's clustered curriculum, the First-Year Initiative, intentionally connects content across courses but also connects course work to students' external lives and day-to-day experiences.

7. *Excellence in the first year relies on the direct involvement of an institution's faculty.* While we recognize the important role that all other constituent groups, especially student affairs professionals,

play in implementing a successful first year, the experience of these thirteen campuses would argue that involvement of faculty is a must. By this we do not mean to imply that every faculty member at an institution must commit to teaching a first-year course or interacting with first-year students out of class. That would be an unrealistic and perhaps illogical goal. But without the support of a meaningful number of faculty, first-year efforts will inevitably suffer a kind of second-class citizenship in the academy. Among these thirteen campuses, we discovered that the key to faculty support is faculty ownership. First-year initiatives in which faculty members have had a major role at the point of conception and initial implementation are more likely to be sustained.

Drury University's Global Perspectives 21 curriculum and its keystone ALPHA Seminar are examples of faculty ownership, as is Eckerd College's structure of five academic collegia and its history of offering a three-week opening autumn term in which every faculty member is expected to participate on a rotating basis. At Eckerd, faculty mentors teach in the autumn term and are students' first and primary link to the institution, and mentors continue as the linchpin between the student and the institution throughout the first year. At Kalamazoo College, twenty-two faculty members from a variety of disciplines teach the required first-year seminar. But other faculty become involved as coadvisers for first-year students. Every section of the seminar offers students access not only to the adviser who teaches the class, but also to one or two coadvisers who are more familiar with the demands of the curriculum. At the University of South Carolina and Appalachian State University, faculty live in residence in traditional residential colleges, and other faculty are directly involved in various living-learning activities. At Elon University, LaGuardia Community College, the University of South Carolina, Appalachian State University, Drury University, Ball State University, Kalamazoo College, and the U.S. Military Academy, faculty interact with students often during orientation to study, discuss, and reflect on a common reading. At both Kalamazoo and LaGuardia, faculty also work closely with students in the creation of electronic portfolios that serve as a means of assessing student learning and encouraging their creativity and personal expression.

8. *Excellence in the first year requires attention to pedagogy in first-year courses.* As we stated in the first chapter, a central goal of this

research project and therefore this book was to identify institutions that had successfully moved the first year from the periphery to the center of the collegiate experience. The classroom is that center. Without a focus on the way first-year courses are structured, organized, and taught, all other efforts may serve as mere antidotes to the core academic experience of new students.

In 2000, the Community College of Denver (CCD) won a Hesburgh award for its Teaching/Learning Center, which offers approximately 100 workshops a year on various topics, including technology, diversity, and learning strategies. The center also has developed alternative pedagogies to meet first-year students' multiple learning styles. All the institutions, including CCD, offer targeted faculty development activities to prepare faculty to teach in special first-year programs such as learning communities and first-year seminars. During its thirty-year history of offering University 101 faculty training workshops, the University of South Carolina has opened those workshops to any faculty member including, but not limited to, faculty teaching the University 101 course. To date, over 2,000 faculty from across the university's eight campuses have taken part in one or more of these workshops. At IUPUI, faculty teaching first-year gateway courses collaborate on the development of innovative pedagogy. Their sharing of ideas and experiences in a first-year community of practice has helped students achieve higher levels of academic performance in courses that previously were "more barrier than gateway" to entry into the university's majors. At Elon College, Global Studies faculty from across the disciplines meet weekly for lunches sponsored by the administration to discuss instructional strategies, resources, and links to other activities, such as study abroad and service-learning.

9. *First-year excellence necessitates both creative acquisition and judicious use of financial resources.* Achieving and maintaining excellence often means finding resources to support new first-year efforts, and many of the initiatives detailed here were generated with new money rather than a reallocation of existing institutional resources. The sources for this funding were federal, state, local, and private grants. Federal Title III and Title V monies have supported efforts at Texas A&M Corpus Christi, CCD, LaGuardia Community College, Lehman College, and Appalachian State University. Funds made available by the Lilly Endowment and Lumina Foundation

for Education have provided a needed boost for first-year services at Ball State University and IUPUI. The Mellon Foundation has been a benefactor to first-year changes at Kalamazoo College, and the University 101 faculty training workshop at the University of South Carolina was initiated with a seed grant from the Ford Foundation. At LaGuardia Community College, students themselves have contributed student fees to the common reading program, mentoring activities, and study-abroad opportunities.

But soft money does not last forever, and institutions must find a way to continue support for programs they value and believe to be important. CCD maintains the standard practice of moving program support from 100 percent grant funding in the first year to approximately 20 percent in the grant's last year. The college is then better able to absorb the cost of successful programs into regular budgets. Ball State University and IUPUI have recently implemented a $1,000 per student increase in tuition. Monies received from first-year students will cover the various retention programs previously funded by grants.

10. *A central component of excellence is a steady outward gaze—the willingness to learn from and share with others.* Our collective experience is that first-year excellence rarely flourishes in isolation. And we found that each of these thirteen institutions is both a provider and receiver of myriad good ideas from other colleges and universities. Faculty and administrators are recognized leaders in national organizations such as the American Association for Higher Education, the Association of American Colleges and Universities, the Association for General and Liberal Studies, the National Academic Advising Association, and the National Association for Developmental Education. Institutional leaders make frequent use of external consultants and participate in national conferences such as the Annual Conferences on The First-Year Experience. They search for external benchmarks against which to measure their own achievements through occasional visits to and frequent interaction with other campuses, and they follow through on their professional responsibility by disseminating to national audiences their own policies and practices, thereby also holding them up to scrutiny and critical examination.

As a group, these institutions are proud of their achievements and are willing to be measured against other campuses to determine their comparative level of excellence. Each of the thirteen campuses has received awards for educational excellence at the state or national level. While space does not allow the listing of every award, following are some examples. Appalachian State University has a floor-to-ceiling wall space contiguous to its admissions office displaying a number of awards, including its recognition in 2001 as one of *Time* magazine's featured four "Colleges of the Year" for the first-year experience. In its 2002 college rankings issue, *US News & World Report* named the University of South Carolina number one and Appalachian State University number three in implementing a successful first-year experience ("America's Best Colleges," 2002). The Community College of Denver is a 2000 Hesburgh award winner for faculty development and was recognized as a Vanguard Learning College by the League for Innovation. Texas A&M-Corpus Christi has played a major role in the National Learning Communities Dissemination Project and was one of only five institutions in Texas to win a Star award in 2001 for educational excellence. Elon University has been consistently cited in national media for its high levels of student engagement as measured by the National Survey of Student Engagement.

11. *Excellence rests on an intentional first-year curriculum and on supportive curricular structures.* Determining what and how students should learn in the first year is a central focus for all the institutions of excellence. Whether defined as a core curriculum or general education distribution requirements, these campuses as a group have focused on desired learning objectives in the first year that are realized through specific courses. At each of these thirteen institutions, the academic mission is preeminent, and the curriculum, supported by the cocurriculum, enables the achievement of the mission

Of the thirteen institutions, ten employ some version of the first-year seminar, sometimes as a stand-alone course, but more often as one of several linked courses in a learning community. Seven of the thirteen campuses are implementing learning communities in various specific formats, including Ball State's residentially linked learning community program.

The learning community, while seen as valuable at all institutions, is especially useful at institutions with large numbers of commuting students. At IUPUI, Lehman College, Texas A&M-Corpus

Christi, LaGuardia Community College, and CCD, learning communities are providing students needed connections with each other that substitute for out-of-class interactions that occur more easily in a traditional residential campus.

12. *Excellence thrives in an environment where divisional walls are down.* Our collective experience in higher education alerts us to the difficulty of achieving true cross-divisional collaboration at many, if not most, college and university campuses. But we have also learned that the first year provides a unique opportunity to bring together various campus constituent groups, all with an important role to play in entering student success.

While the existence of such partnerships was an initial criterion for selection, these campuses once again surpassed our expectations for the variety and quality of their collaborative efforts. The autumn term at Eckerd College depends on the involvement of faculty and student affairs professionals to deliver both the academic and the social dimensions of this unique experience. Jim Annarelli, Eckerd's dean of students, spoke of the autumn term as an opportunity to "dismantle the invisible wall" that had grown up slowly between these campus divisions.

At Kalamazoo College, student life professionals are committed to helping students adjust to academics as much as to the residential side of the first-year experience. But Kalamazoo faculty also recognize their need to learn more about student development, and many faculty development activities focus intentionally and directly on students. Kalamazoo's early alert committee is a cross-divisional structure that depends on both the input of faculty to provide names of students who are struggling with academic work and the actions of advisers and other administrators who intervene with those students as appropriate.

At Elon University, the Elon Experiences are designed by faculty but administered by the Division of Student Life, and at Ball State University, residence life is described as the vehicle for student affairs–academic affairs partnerships. Ball State's Freshman Connections residential learning communities are administered by learning teams comprising both faculty and residence life staff. LaGuardia Community College has mandated that faculty and student affairs professionals accompany each other to academic conferences. This time away from campus has been the fertile environment where academic and student life professionals working together have conceived and planned a number of LaGuardia's most successful interventions.

We could certainly extend this list of findings to include other common elements of success, such as the extensive use of student peer leaders or mentors and the important roles of academic support units on each of the campuses. The ingredients that go into a recipe for excellence are many. But we believe these twelve core findings are most central, most essential in creating and sustaining an exemplary first year.

Conclusions and Recommendations

As authors, we have pursued a dual mission for this book. On the one hand, we trust that this book will be a substantial contribution to the research and literature base on the first year. On the other hand, we admit to a strong, practical bias for what we hope will be the book's ultimate uses. We designed this book as a contribution to the literature and, more important, as a work that will be useful to practitioners on campuses of every type either to confirm existing practices in the first year or to encourage and then assist in the process of achieving significant educational improvement.

Although the book focuses on thirteen individual campuses, they are representative of a twenty-year evolution—some would say revolution—in the way American higher education has structured the first year. Although the reasons for this evolution have been as varied as the programs themselves, the primary motivation for most institutions has been enhancing the retention of students.

While we fully recognize the importance of retention as an appropriate public policy and institutional goal, we do not believe that this focus—perhaps obsession—has been sufficiently engaging, educationally and intellectually, to capture both the attention and involvement of many members of the academy, especially the faculty. It is our firm belief that only by securing faculty engagement will students become more successful learners and graduate in greater numbers.

This work's focus on excellence in the first year is intended to stimulate a more intellectually productive conversation than a focus on retention per se. Such a conversation will help move us to a serious consideration of what constitutes excellence in the foundation year of the college or university experience—the time period when admittedly retention is the hardest to achieve—and how such excellence might be achieved. We recommend that campuses consider these options for using this book:

- Conduct a major self-study of the first year as a single unit of analysis using a campuswide task force. This book can be a framework for appropriate conversations about your institution's response to its new students. A model for convening such a task force that was developed in the Policy Center's Foundations of Excellence project is described in the Epilogue. The task force is an ideal mechanism for convening campus stakeholders to conduct an intellectually engaging self-study of current approaches to the first college year. These stakeholders include faculty, representatives from the office of academic affairs, other academic administrators, student affairs professionals, institutional research and assessment experts, and students.
- Use the five basic criteria of the Institutions of Excellence study to illuminate your campus's current first-year practices. These criteria could provide a template for consideration and action by policymakers, practitioners, and assessment personnel on your campus. In your conversations, do not hesitate to add criteria if you feel they will advance your thinking. In fact, if you believe we have omitted something important, please share your thinking with us and others in higher education.
- Use Table 1.2 to enumerate the components of your own institution's first year. Comparing your table with Table 1.2 will serve as a conversation starter with colleagues. It will enable you to note the strengths of your current first-year activities in relation to those of these thirteen campuses and to determine how your strengths can be used as a basis for moving to the next level of excellence in the first year.
- Review the findings presented in this chapter. Which ones provide insight into your campus? What judgments and conclusions do you draw?

• Create a discussion group built around this book. Chapters could be assigned to group members for presentation and discussion; the process would unfold naturally according to the culture and needs of your own campus.

• Consider the first year as a focus for reaffirmation of accreditation. In recent years, the six regional accrediting associations have taken a more flexible approach to self-study. Many campuses are now free to choose an area for concentrated study in order to demonstrate continuous improvement of student learning outcomes. We would argue that because the first year is the foundation of all learning outcomes, it can be effectively used as a focus for reaffirmation of accreditation.

A Final Suggestion

No matter which of the above processes you choose as the means for analyzing your own campus, we encourage you not to confine yourself to consideration of institutional types that are the same as your own. Private institutions have much to learn from their state-supported counterparts and vice versa. In particular, we urge you not to ignore the two community colleges described in this volume if you are in the baccalaureate sector, for many of the initiatives at LaGuardia Community College and the Community College of Denver are both applicable to and replicable at four-year institutions, especially if your own campus is urban, not highly selective, serving minority students, and offering any developmental education.

The case studies reported in this book are based on in-depth portraits, taken in the year 2002, of thirteen outstanding institutions. Like the photographs collected in any album, these portraits represent the past, the way things were. We remind you that these institutions are dynamic places; what they are now is not exactly what they were when we visited them and learned their stories. Thus, if you have an interest in a particular campus or campuses, we urge you to communicate directly with campus officials to determine how these institutions have evolved in their approach to the first year since the time of this research. We are confident that ongoing change is a given at all of these campuses. So visit their Web sites, review their catalogues, and communicate with those responsible for the first year in their respective settings.

As always, we encourage you to give us feedback—both on the text itself and on your experience using it. We are eager to learn more about your path to excellence. The first year of college, too long considered the stepchild of higher education, is, after all, the foundational year, the year in which we acculturate new students to the values of higher education and of our particular institutions. As we look back over the past twenty years of first-year reform, we recognize the emergence of a grand scheme, an aspirational model for the first year. Let us all take advantage of the opportunity we now have to bring together the many fragments of which our first years are composed and form them into the solid base on which we and our students will achieve excellence.

Epilogue: Foundations of Excellence® in the First College Year

This book tells the stories of thirteen colleges and universities in the United States that model excellence in their approach to the first year. These institutions merit our recognition and emulation. While we hope that this book will influence readers to consider first-year efforts on their campuses in comparison to these thirteen Institutions of Excellence, we acknowledge that true first-year improvement in American colleges and universities will require more than the study of a few exemplary institutions.

In January 2003, to meet what we believe is both a need and desire for a valid model of first-year excellence that could be used by any college or university, the Policy Center on the First Year of College undertook a project entitled Foundations of Excellence in the First College Year. This project has been supported by funding from The Atlantic Philanthropies and Lumina Foundation for Education. Project partners included the American Association of State Colleges and Universities (AASCU), the Council of Independent Colleges (CIC), Patrick Terenzini and Robert Reason of the Penn State Center for the Study of Higher Education, Edward Zlotkowski of Campus Compact and Bentley College, and George Kuh of Indiana University's National Center for Postsecondary Research.

Project Details

While the Foundations of Excellence project builds on the Institutions of Excellence recognition process, Foundations of Excellence was designed as a collaborative venture of researchers and campus-based practitioners to develop and vet a set of mutually agreed-on standards for the first year—standards that could be used as both an aspirational model and a means of measuring a campus's level of first-year excellence. The project began with an open invitation to more than 900 chief academic officers at regional public and small private institutions. These institutions were members of either the American Association of State Colleges and Universities (AASCU) or the Council of Independent Colleges (CIC). AASCU and CIC member institutions were invited by their respective association leaders to join the Policy Center staff in the collaborative development of first-year standards that we termed Foundational Dimensions, or "dimensions" for short. Two hundred nineteen member institutions of both organizations agreed to participate in the project by forming campuswide task forces to react to an initial list of six dimensions developed by the Policy Center staff and our external research partners. Dimension statements were designed to be defining characteristics of an institution's effectiveness in supporting the learning and success of every first-year student.

We asked each campus task force to review and edit the six dimensions, delete any that were judged to be irrelevant, and suggest additional dimensions statements. The collective work of the 219 task forces resulted in a number of changes to the initial dimensions and the creation of additional dimensions statements. Ultimately, AASCU and CIC campuses developed eight dimensions that were common to both cohort groups and additional cohort-specific dimensions as listed in Table E.1.

In the second phase of the project beginning in summer 2003, the Policy Center selected twelve AASCU and twelve CIC campuses to participate in an intensive eighteen-month effort to use the

Exhibit E.1. Foundational Dimensions for AASCU and CIC

1. Foundations Institutions approach the first year in ways that are intentional and based on a philosophy/rationale of the first year that informs relevant institutional policies and practices.
2. Foundations Institutions create organizational structures and policies that provide a comprehensive, integrated, and coordinated approach to the first year.

3. Foundations Institutions facilitate appropriate recruitment, admissions, and student transitions through policies and practices that are intentional and aligned with institutional mission.
4. Foundations Institutions elevate the first year to a high priority for faculty.
5. Foundations Institutions serve all first-year students according to their varied needs.
6. Foundations Institutions engage students both in and out of the classroom in order to develop attitudes, behaviors, and skills consistent with the desired outcomes of higher education and the institution's philosophy and mission.
7. Foundations Institutions ensure that all first-year students experience diverse ideas, worldviews, and peoples as a means of enhancing their learning and preparing them to become members of pluralistic communities.
8. Foundations Institutions conduct assessment and maintain associations with other institutions and relevant professional organizations in order to achieve ongoing first-year improvement.

Dimension for AASCU Institutions Only

1. Foundations Institutions promote student understanding of the various roles and purposes of higher education, both for the individual and for society, and support the development of relevant personal goals.

Dimensions for CIC Institutions Only

1. Foundations Institutions begin a process by which students gain an understanding of what it means to be an educated person according to institution mission and values.
2. Foundations Institutions build commitment of first-year students to the institution through a clear articulation of its identity and ethos.
3. Foundations Institutions involve all students in an exploration of life purpose through instructional content and reflections on life experiences.

While AASCU (regional public) and CIC (small private) institutions agreed on eight common Foundational Dimensions, they also developed these unique dimensions that reflect differences between these cohort groups in institutional mission, ethos, and desired first-year outcomes.

dimensions as a means for evaluating the first year. This group of twenty-four was later joined by a larger group of seventy institutions that volunteered to use the Foundational Dimensions to conduct evaluation independently, without on-campus assistance from Policy Center staff. These twenty-four Founding Institutions and seventy Affiliates used three data sources to assess their campus's achievement of each dimension. The first data source was the existing evidence related to each dimension collected by task force members that enabled them to make a collective judgment about the institution's level of performance. Second were results from surveys of faculty and senior administrators that were developed by Penn State University's Center for the Study of Higher Education and administered on each of the twenty-four campuses. The third source was first-year student responses to the National Survey of Student Engagement (NSSE). Findings from all three data sources were analyzed collectively and were used either to confirm current institutional practice or suggest the need for improvement.

Taken together, the Foundational Dimensions are not only a tool for evaluation, but they also constitute an aspirational model, articulated at a high level of generality, for a purposeful and effective first year. The model enables each institution to design its own first-year approach with its particularities in mind. And in the future, this model can be used as the basis for an external certification that would confer on an institution an imprimatur of excellence.

The Special Role of the Task Force

The engine of this process has been the institutional task force, and project participants have provided consistent feedback to the Policy Center about the value of the task force as a meaningful structure for undertaking broad, campuswide first-year evaluation. In our initial communications with each campus, we suggested that task force participants on each campus include faculty, student affairs professionals, academic administrators (ideally the chief academic officer), institutional research or assessment officers, and students—individuals who rarely sit together in the same room for any length of time to focus on the first year. We also suggested that as a first step in the analysis, each task force undergo a discovery and professional development process related to the institution's first year. We provided a template for investigation, the Current Practices Inventory (CPI), which provides a structure for gathering information about (1) existing first-year policies and programs, (2) the campus-specific definition of "first-year student," (3) student demographic characteristics, and (4) existing campus studies about first-year students. For many campuses, this inventory represented the first and only comprehensive review of the first year ever undertaken by the campus.

What the Foundations Project Adds to Existing Assessment of the First Year

While a number of survey instruments exist to examine "input characteristics" and "outcomes" for first-year students, the Foundations of Excellence project adds the all-important study of the environment: what institutions do intentionally to structure and enhance first-year students' learning experiences. While we agree that the characteristics of entering students have a profound impact on their first-year experience, we would concur with Alexander Astin (1990) that an analysis of outcomes is incomplete without a thorough examination of environmental variables.

The Future of the Foundations Project

Campuses involved in the pilot process of creating and then using the Foundational Dimensions as a mechanism for self-study and assessment of the first year have found this process to be extremely valuable in the larger process of campus improvement; in fact, for some, it has been transformative. And while this process was tested only with ninety-four small private and regional public institutions, feedback from interested colleagues in other sectors indicates an unmet need for this type of first-year evaluation in all institutional types.

As we plan the future of this project, we are exploring multiple avenues for future foundations work that will enable other campuses to undertake this evaluation independently or with external assistance, that will potentially link the Foundational Dimensions with reaccreditation activities, and that will give appropriate credit and recognition to the institutions that confirm a high level of commitment to achieving the foundational dimensions.

Appendix A: All Participants in the Institutions of Excellence Study (N = 130)

Abilene Christian University, Texas
Albion College, Michigan
Appalachian State University, North Carolina
Arcadia University, Pennsylvania
Arizona State University
Baker University, Kansas
Ball State University, Indiana
Barnard College, New York
Bethel College, Kansas
Birmingham Southern College, Alabama
Bowling Green State University, Ohio
Bridgewater State College, Massachusetts
Brooklyn College, New York
California State University, Fullerton
California State University, Long Beach
Charleston Southern University, South Carolina
Clemson University, South Carolina
Columbia College, South Carolina
Community College of Denver, Colorado
Concordia University, Wisconsin
Cumberland College, Kentucky

DePauw University, Indiana
Dickinson College, Pennsylvania
Drury University, Missouri
Dyersburg State Community College, Tennessee
East Tennessee State University
Eckerd College, Florida
Elon University, North Carolina
Georgia College and State University
Georgia State University
Greenville College, Illinois
Grinnell College, Iowa
Gustavus Adolphus College, Minnesota
Hampton University, Virginia
Idaho State University
Indiana University Purdue University Indianapolis
Iowa State University
Iowa Wesleyan College
Ivy Tech State College, Indiana
Kalamazoo College, Michigan
Kean University, New Jersey
Kennesaw State University, Georgia
Keuka College, New York
LaGuardia Community College, New York
Lake Michigan College, Michigan
Lee University, Tennessee
Lehman College, New York
Lewis and Clark College, Oregon
Longwood College, Virginia
Maryville College, Tennessee
Mesa Community College, Arizona
Middlesex Community College, Massachusetts

Minnesota State University, Mankato
Muhlenberg College, Pennsylvania
New Mexico Tech
North Carolina Central University
North Carolina State University
Northern Kentucky University
Northern Michigan University
Palm Beach Community College, Florida
Peace College, North Carolina
Penn State Lehigh Valley
Pennsylvania State University
Point Park College, Pennsylvania
Purchase College, State University of New York
Purdue University, Indiana
Radford University, Virginia
Richland College, Texas
Rochester Institute of Technology, New York
Saint Francis University, Pennsylvania
Saint John Fisher College, New York
Saint Lawrence University, New York
Saint Leo University, Florida
Saint Xavier University, Illinois
Seton Hall University, New Jersey
Slippery Rock University, Pennsylvania
Sonoma State University, California
Southeast Missouri State University
Southern Polytechnic State University of Georgia
SUNY College at Old Westbury
SUNY, College of Environmental Sciences and Forestry
SUNY, Geneseo
Tabor College, Kansas

Texas A&M University-Corpus Christi
Texas Christian University
Texas Tech University
Tomball College, Texas
Towson University, Maryland
Trinity College, Connecticut
Tri-State University, Indiana
U.S. Coast Guard Academy, Connecticut
Union University, Tennessee
United States Military Academy, New York
University of Akron, Ohio
University of Arizona
University of Arkansas-Fort Smith
University of California, Berkeley
University of Central Arkansas
University of Central Florida
University of Charleston, West Virginia
University of Denver, Colorado
University of Hartford, Connecticut
University of Houston, Texas
University of Illinois at Urbana-Champaign
University of Massachusetts Amherst
University of Minnesota
University of Nebraska at Omaha
University of New Orleans, Louisiana
University of North Carolina at Charlotte
University of Oklahoma
University of Portland, Oregon
University of South Carolina-Columbia
University of Southern California
University of the Pacific, California

University of Texas at El Paso
Ursinus College, Pennsylvania
Ursuline College, Ohio
Valdosta State University, Georgia
Valencia Community College, Florida
Villanova University, Pennsylvania
Volunteer State Community College, Tennessee
Wagner College, New York
Waynesburg College, Pennsylvania
Weber State University, Utah
Western Maryland College
Westminster College, Missouri
Westminster College, Pennsylvania
Wheeling Jesuit University, West Virginia
William Jewell College, Missouri
Worcester Polytechnic Institute, Massachusetts

Appendix B: Initial Letter of Invitation to Participate in the Institutions of Excellence Project

This letter was forwarded by e-mail in early February 2002 to chief academic officers at approximately 2,400 institutions.

Dear Colleague,

As one of its projects funded by The Pew Charitable Trusts and The Atlantic Philanthropies, the Policy Center on the First Year of College is engaging in a national study to identify "Institutions of Excellence in the First College Year." These colleges and universities are those that exemplify **comprehensive "best practice" in their approach to the first year supported by assessment.** We invite nominations of institutions from all sectors of American higher education to be considered for inclusion in this study. From nominations received, we will ultimately select approximately twelve colleges and universities that will become the subject of in-depth case studies to be published as a major book and disseminated via the Policy Center Web site. Policy Center staff members will undertake these case studies in calendar year 2002 by means of campus visits and off-site interviews and review of materials.

Nomination Process-First Stage

To nominate your institution, complete the short form located at http://www.brevard.edu/fyc/form.pdf. Print this form and fax (828–883–4093) or mail it, along with a two-page narrative description of the institution's first-year initiatives, to the Policy Center at the address below.

Betsy Barefoot, Co-Director

Policy Center on the First Year of College

400 N. Broad St.

Brevard, NC 28712

We would also request that **an electronic copy of the narrative description only** be sent to the following e-mail address: mailto:barefoot@brevard.edu

Please Note

1. The nomination form must be signed by either the institution's president or chief academic officer. Send this form in hard copy, either by fax or mail. This PDF form was constructed using Adobe 3.0. If you have difficulty opening or printing this form, please direct an e-mail message to barefoot@brevard.edu with your fax number. We will fax a form to you immediately.
2. The accompanying narrative description must be no more than two pages in length (1,000 words). Send this description in hard copy with the nomination form. Please also send an electronic version of this narrative, either as an e-mail message, an e-mail attachment, or on computer disk if necessary.
3. The primary criteria for selection will be evidence of **(a) an intentional, comprehensive approach to improving the first year that is appropriate to an institution's type (i.e., two-year or four-year, residential or non-residential, etc.) and mission; and (b) assessment of the various initiatives that constitute this approach.** Additional criteria are the following:

- Evidence of broad impact on significant numbers of first-year students, including, but not limited to, special student subpopulations.
- Strong administrative support for first-year initiatives, evidence of institutionalization and durability over time
- Involvement of a wide range of faculty, student affairs professionals, academic administrators, and other constituent groups

4. Nominations must be received by the Policy Center no later than **March 15, 2002.**

Nomination Process-Second Stage

1. Nominations will be reviewed by an external panel, and semi-finalists will be invited to submit a more comprehensive narrative description (approximately five pages) and relevant supporting materials. Names and program descriptions of all institutions in the semi-final category will be posted on the Policy Center Web site. Institutions will be notified of their selection to semi-final status no later than May 1, 2002.
2. Selection of twelve institutions to be scheduled for intensive follow-up and site visits will be made by June 15, 2002.
3. The Policy Center will name the institutions selected for inclusion in the book on best first-year practices during Fall 2002.

If you have questions about this study or selection process, please contact me directly. In consideration of other listserv subscribers, please do not respond directly to the list.

Thank you,

Betsy Barefoot, EdD
Co-Director, Policy Center on the First Year of College
Brevard, NC 28712
Phone: 828–966–5310
FAX: 828–883–4093

Institutions of Excellence in the First College Year Nomination Form

Name of Institution

____

Address

____

Name of Primary Contact Person

____

Title ______________________________________

Telephone Number ______________________________

E-mail address __________________________________

Signature of Senior Campus Official

____

Date __________________________

(President or Chief Academic Officer)

Please attach a narrative description—maximum of two pages (1,000 words)—describing your institution's approach to the first college year. This narrative should include:

- Rationale for institution's approach to the first year
- Description of program(s), policies, strategies, etc.
- Evidence of effectiveness

Criteria for Selection. These criteria are not all-inclusive, but are representative of the ways in which an institution's approach to the first year will be comparatively evaluated:

- Evidence of an intentional, comprehensive approach to improving the first year that is appropriate to an institution's type (i.e., two-year or four-year, residential or non-residential, etc.) and mission
- Evidence of assessment of the various initiatives that constitute this approach
- Evidence of broad impact on significant numbers of first-year students, including, but not limited to, special student subpopulations
- Strong administrative support for first-year initiatives, evidence of institutionalization and durability over time
- Involvement of a wide range of faculty, student affairs professionals, academic administrators, and other constituent groups

Mail or fax this form to the Policy Center. **Deadline for receipt: March 15, 2002**

Appendix C: Semifinalists

Community Colleges

Community College of Denver
Dyersburg State Community College
LaGuardia Community College
Mesa Community College
Middlesex Community College
Richland College
Valencia Community College

Four-Year Colleges and Universities, Under 2,000

Albion College
Eckerd College
Grinnell College
Iowa Wesleyan College
Kalamazoo College
St. Lawrence University
U.S. Coast Guard Academy
University of Charleston (West Virginia)
William Jewell College

Four-Year Colleges and Universities, 2,000–5,000

DePauw University
Drury University

Elon University
Muhlenberg College
Purchase College, State University of New York
Saint Francis University
St. John Fisher College
U.S. Military Academy
University of Portland
Wagner College
Western Maryland College

Four-Year Colleges and Universities, 5,000–10,000

Hampton University
Lehman College of the City University of New York
Northern Michigan University
Radford University
Southeast Missouri State University
State University of New York, Geneseo
Texas A&M University-Corpus Christi
University of Arkansas-Fort Smith
University of Central Arkansas
University of Denver
University of Hartford

Four-Year Universities, 10,000–20,000

Appalachian State University
Ball State University
Bowling Green State University
Kennesaw State University
Northern Kentucky University
University of Texas at El Paso

Four-Year Universities, Over 20,000 Students

Georgia State University
Iowa State University
Indiana University Purdue University Indianapolis
University of Minnesota
North Carolina State University
Purdue University
University of Akron
University of Arizona
University of Oklahoma
University of South Carolina

Appendix D: Letter to Semifinalists

May 2, 2002

Dear ____________ :

We are pleased to report that the University of _________ has been selected as a semifinalist in the selection process to identify "Institutions of Excellence in the First College Year." We commend you for both the outstanding initiatives you are undertaking on behalf of first-year students and your commitment to evaluation. Overall, we received 130 nomination narratives, and 54 have progressed to the semi-final category. A list of semifinalists is enclosed.

We would like to obtain your permission to post on the Policy Center Web site the two-page nomination narrative, which you have already forwarded to us. The narratives from all semifinalists will be placed on a Web page, and institutions will be identified as those that model best first-year practice in American higher education. If you would like to make any revisions or corrections to the narrative you submitted, you may do so; however, we would need a revised narrative no later than **May 15, 2002. If you have not already done so, please respond to this letter via an e-mail message (barefoot@brevard.edu), by fax (828–883–4093), or by letter to me at the address below indicating your permission for the Policy Center to post your institution's narrative and notifying us if you would like to make any revisions.**

Following review of additional materials from your campus, as described below, twelve finalists will be selected and notified approximately August 1, 2002. Shortly thereafter, we will work with the designated contact person at each institution to formalize plans for additional review of materials as needed, interviews, campus visits, etc.

Next Steps

We would like to request that you forward to us **by June 15, 2002** more detailed information about your first-year initiatives and assessment thereof. You can use the two-page narrative as a base and expand your discussion of each component. However, we encourage you to describe additional initiatives or assessment methodologies. We would request that the second narrative be limited to five pages (2,500 words); however, the narrative may be supplemented by relevant program materials. Please do not send electronic materials (e.g., videos, CD-ROMs, etc.), as we do not have the ability to duplicate these for external review. The five-page narrative may be submitted **electronically, by regular mail to the Policy Center address below, or by fax to 828–883–4093.**

In selecting the final twelve Institutions of Excellence in the First College Year, it is our intent to identify those institutions that have a high level of commitment to (a) improving the learning and success of first-year students and (b) assessing those efforts. In the first round of nominations, we found that many campuses wrote interesting and compelling narratives that gave detailed descriptions of programs and other initiatives. However, many of these narratives were lacking any discussion of how these initiatives are being evaluated and to what end—how assessment is being used to enable continuous improvement in the first year.

We draw your attention to the five selection criteria as provided on the original nomination form:

1. **Evidence of an intentional, comprehensive approach to improving the first year that is appropriate to an institution's type (i.e., two-year or four-year, residential or non-residential, etc.) and mission.** Institutions of Excellence are characterized by an approach to the first year that spans the curriculum and co-curriculum. This approach is central and systemic rather than "appended" or patched on to the core institutional mission.

2. **Evidence of assessment of the various initiatives that constitute this approach.** Institutions of Excellence are committed to an assessment process that results in data-driven continuous improvement in the first year. They should be able to report what was studied, how assessment was conducted, and how results were used.

3. **Evidence of broad impact on significant numbers of first-year students, including, but not limited to, special student subpopulations.** Institutions of Excellence understand their responsibility and demonstrate their responsiveness to all first-year students. First-year initiatives are characterized by high expectations and essential support for students at all levels of academic ability.

4. **Strong administrative support for first-year initiatives, evidence of institutionalization, and durability over time.** Institutions of Excellence have a demonstrable track record of support for first-year initiatives. First-year programs and policies enjoy high status and receive an equitable share of fiscal and personnel resources.

5. **Involvement of a wide range of faculty, student affairs professionals, academic administrators, and other constituent groups.** Institutions of Excellence involve all campus constituent groups in the design, implementation, and maintenance of first-year initiatives. These institutions are characterized by "partnerships" in support of the first year across divisional lines.

As you prepare your more detailed narrative, please feel free to call upon any member of the Policy Center staff for assistance. Again, we congratulate you for your accomplishments on behalf of first-year students, and we look forward to reading the next round of nomination portfolios.

Sincerely,

Betsy O. Barefoot, Co-Director
John N. Gardner, Executive Director

Appendix E: Announcement Letter to Thirteen Institutions of Excellence

August 28, 2002

Dear ____________ :

Congratulations! On behalf of the Policy Center on the First Year of College, funded by The Pew Charitable Trusts and The Atlantic Philanthropies, it gives me great pleasure to inform you that ________________ University has been selected as an Institution of Excellence in the First College Year. The narrative description of your first-year initiatives and supplementary materials that you submitted have been reviewed by three external reviewers and members of the Policy Center staff, and _____________ University is one of the final thirteen institutions selected for this honor from 130 nominees.

As you know, this process will result in the publication of a major book. Your institutional story as it relates to your achievement of this honor will be a significant part of this work.

Our next step is to ask that either the chief executive officer or chief academic officer confirm, in writing, your institution's acceptance of this award and willingness for two members of the Policy Center staff to visit your institution. During this site visit, we would like to talk with a range of individuals and groups, including students, and gather the rich descriptions, history, and rationale that can only come from face-to-face interviews and observations. Satisfactory completion of the on-site visit is the final step in our selection of your campus as an Institution of Excellence in the First

College Year and identification as such in our subsequent publishing. It is our intent during the visit to confirm the merits of your selection and to gather additional evidence and insights to adequately portray your accomplishments. The Policy Center reserves the right to withdraw any institution's selection in the highly unlikely event that we were to determine during the site visit that such selection would be inappropriate, given our stated criteria for this process.

We anticipate that site visits will be one and a half to two days in duration and we would like to conduct them during this fall term. The enclosed document describes the site visit process and protocol. There will be no expenses incurred by institutions for the site visits; the Policy Center will cover all travel and accommodations costs for staff researchers. However, we will need your involvement in arranging the various meetings as detailed on the enclosed sheet.

Within the next two weeks, a member of the Policy Center staff will contact you to schedule this visit. In the meantime, please forward confirmation that your institution accepts this honor and would be willing to host a site visit from the research team. You may e-mail confirmation to Betsy Barefoot, barefoot@brevard.edu; fax to 828–883–4093; or mail a response to the address below. We need to receive this confirmation of your institution's acceptance no later than **September 16, 2002.**

As the site visit will involve interviews of administrators, faculty, and students, your institution may require approval from an Institutional Review Board (IRB or human subjects research committee). Additional information about this process is included on the enclosed sheet. Please let us know if you have questions at this time about IRB matters.

If you choose, you may announce your selection immediately to both internal and external audiences. We have prepared boilerplate language that you may use for a press release, if you so desire. Please let us know if you would like us to forward this information. The Policy Center, however, will not release names of the thirteen campuses selected until confirmation of acceptance has been received from all institutions.

Again, we congratulate you for your commitment to the first-year students on your campus, and we look forward to learning more about what makes your campus an Institution of Excellence in the First College Year. If you have questions at this time or need additional information, you may call or e-mail either of us using the information provided below.

Sincerely,
Betsy O. Barefoot
Co-Director and Principal Investigator
barefoot@brevard.edu
828–966–5310

John N. Gardner
Executive Director
gardner@brevard.edu
828–966–5309

cc: President
Vice President of Academic Affairs

Enclosure: Important Step-by-Step Instructions and Information for Institutions of Excellence

Appendix F: Research Subject Information and Consent Form

TITLE: Site Visits Institutions of Excellence in the First College Year

PROTOCOL NO.: WIRB 20021551

SPONSOR: Policy Center on the First Year of College, Brevard, NC 28712

INVESTIGATOR: Betsy O. Barefoot, MEd, EdD
Policy Center on the First Year of College
400 North Broad Street, Duplex One
Brevard, NC 28712
(828) 966–5310
(828) 862–8005 (24 hours)

SITE LOCATION: This consent form may contain words that you do not understand. Please ask the investigator or the study staff to explain any words or information that you do not clearly understand. You may take home an unsigned copy of this consent form to think about or discuss with family or friends before making your decision.

You are invited to participate in a national research study conducted by the Policy Center on the First Year of College. The purpose of this consent form is to (1) provide basic information about the study, (2) describe the rights of participants, and (3) obtain consent from subjects to participate in the study.

PURPOSE: The purpose of this study is to provide in-depth case studies of thirteen colleges and universities that have been preliminarily identified and selected as "Institutions of Excellence in the First College Year." These institutions, selected from among 130 nominees, demonstrate comprehensive "best practice" in their approach to the first year as supported by assessment. The Policy Center is conducting site visits with each institution to gather and collect data on the first year of college and learn about the delivery of first-year curricular programs and services.

PROCEDURES: Research will be conducted primarily by interviews (individual as well as group), document analysis, and observation. Individual interviews and group interviews will be conducted at various points during a one and a half- to two-day campus visit, and will last approximately one hour in length. Various administrators, faculty, staff, and students have been invited to participate in either an individual or group interview conducted by a member of the research team. To facilitate accurate information gathering, interviews and focus groups may be tape-recorded by mutual consent. The audio-tapes and data gathered from the study will be securely stored and accessible only to the research team.

RISKS: The risk of participating in this study is the possible risk of loss of confidentiality. You do not have to answer any questions that you do not want to.

BENEFITS: Your participation will not directly benefit you. The investigator expects to learn more about institutions with successful first year programs.

ALTERNATIVES: Your alternative is not to participate in this study.

CONFIDENTIALITY: Information from this study will be given to the sponsor. "Sponsor" includes any persons or companies which are contracted by the sponsor to have access to the research information during and after the study.

The consent form signed by you will be looked at and/or copied for research or regulatory purposes by:

- the sponsor;

and may be looked at and/or copied for research or regulatory purposes by:

- the Western Institutional Review Board (WIRB).

Absolute confidentiality cannot be guaranteed because of the need to give information to these parties. Work titles and responsibilities of institutional subjects may be identified in future publications and conference presentations. Student subjects will not be identified by name. Other subjects will be identified by title.

SOURCE OF FUNDING: Funding for this research study will be provided by Policy Center on the First Year of College.

VOLUNTARY PARTICIPATION/WITHDRAWAL: Your participation in this study is voluntary, and you may decline to participate. If you decide to participate, you may withdraw from the study at any time without penalty. If you withdraw from the study before information collection is completed, information you have provided will not be used in the study. Your decision will not affect your standing or status in the institution.

Your participation in this study may be stopped at any time by the investigator or the sponsor without your consent.

QUESTIONS: If you have questions at any time about the study or the procedures, contact the investigator, *Dr.* Betsy O. Barefoot, at:

Dr. Betsy O. Barefoot, Co-Director
Policy Center on the First Year of College
400 North Broad Street, Duplex One
Brevard, NC 28712
(828) 966–5310
FAX: (828) 877–4093; E-mail: barefoot@brevard.edu.

If you feel you have not been treated according to the descriptions in this consent form, or your rights as a subject in this research have not been honored during the course of this study, you may contact:

Western Institutional Review Board (WIRB)
3535 Seventh Avenue, SW
Olympia, Washington, USA 98508–2029
Telephone: 1–800–562–4789.

WIRB is a group of people who perform independent review of research.

Do not sign this consent form unless you have had a chance to ask questions and have received satisfactory answers to all of your questions.

You will receive a signed and dated copy of this consent form for your records.

CONSENT: I have read the information in this consent form. All my questions about the study and my participation in it have been answered. I agree to participate in the research study.

I authorize the release of my research records, including audiotapes, for research or regulatory purposes to the sponsor and WIRB.

By signing this consent form, I have not waived any of the legal rights which I otherwise would have as a subject in a research study.

Subject Signature and Title	Printed Name
	Date
Signature of Person Conducting	Date
Informed Consent Discussion	
Signature of Principal Investigator (if different from above)	Date

References

American College Testing Program. (1999). *National dropout rates.* Iowa City: Author.

America's best colleges. (2002, September 23). *US News & World Report,* 60–112.

Astin, A. (1990). *Assessment for excellence: The philosophy and practice of assessment and evaluation in higher education.* Old Tappan, NJ: Macmillan.

Banta, T. (2002). *Building a scholarship of assessment.* San Francisco: Jossey-Bass.

Barefoot, B. (2000, January-February). The first-year experience: Are we making it any better? *About Campus,* 12–18.

Brunello, A. (2000). *General education: First-year program assessment report.* St. Petersburg, FL: Eckerd College.

Chapin, L. W. (2000). The core curriculum at Eckerd College. In M. Nelson (Ed.), *Alive at the core: Exemplary approaches to general education in the humanities* (pp. 96–122). San Francisco: Jossey-Bass.

Chism, N., Lees, N. D., & Evenbeck, S. E. (2002). Faculty development for teaching innovation. *Liberal Education 88*(3), 34–41.

Educational attainment of adults, 2000. (2003). *Chronicle of Higher Education Almanac Issue, 2003–4.*

El-Khawas, E. (1987). *Campus trends.* Washington, DC: American Council on Education.

Goetz, J. P., & LeCompte, M. D. (1984). *Ethnography and qualitative design in educational research.* Orlando FL: Academic Press.

Kalamazoo College. (n.d.). *Kalamazoo College/A fellowship in learning.* Internal document.

Kalamazoo College. (2003). *Self-study report outline and chapter drafts for upcoming North Central Association visit in the spring of 2003.* Internal document.

Kuh, G., Schuh, J., Whitt, E., & Associates. (1991). *Involving colleges: Successful approaches to fostering student learning and development outside the classroom.* San Francisco: Jossey-Bass.

Lincoln, Y. S., & Guba, E. G. (1985). *Naturalistic inquiry.* Thousand Oaks, CA: Sage.

Marshall, C., & Rossman, G. (1999). *Designing qualitative research* (3rd ed.). Thousand Oaks, CA: Sage.

McCracken, G. (1988). *The long interview.* Thousand Oaks, CA: Sage.

Merriam, S. B. (1988). *Case study research in education: A qualitative approach.* San Francisco: Jossey-Bass.

National Resource Center for The First-Year Experience and Students in Transition. (2002). *The 2000 national survey of first-year seminar programs.* Columbia, SC: University of South Carolina, Author.

Policy Center on the First Year of College. (2002). *2002 National Survey of First-Year Academic Practices.* http://www.brevard.edu/fyc/Survey2002/index.htm.

Ramirez, G. E. (2002). *Learning communities in action: A case study of the programmatic experiences of faculty and students in the first year program at Texas A&M University-Corpus Christi.* Unpublished doctoral dissertation, Texas A&M University-Corpus Christi.

Riesman, D. (1956). *Constraint and variety in higher education.* Lincoln: University of Nebraska Press.

Roueche, J. E., Ely, E. E., & Roueche, S. D. (2001). *In pursuit of excellence: The Community College of Denver.* Washington, DC: Community College Press.

Shapiro, N. S., & Levine, J. H. (1999). *Creating learning communities: A practical guide to winning support, organizing for change, and implementing programs.* San Francisco: Jossey-Bass.

Tagg, J. (2003). *The learning paradigm college.* Bolton, MA: Anker.

Trudeau, G. B. (1976). *Doonesbury.* New York: Universal Press Syndicate.

United States Military Academy. (2002). *Cadet leader development system,* USMA Circular 1-101. West Point, NY: Author.

University of South Carolina. (2001). *2001–02 Mini fact book.* Columbia, SC: Author.

University 101. (2002). *Transitions: A University 101 handbook.* Columbia, SC: University of South Carolina, University 101 Program.

Upcraft, M. L., & Gardner, J. N. (1989). *The freshman year experience: Helping students survive and succeed in college.* San Francisco: Jossey-Bass.

Upcraft, M. L., Gardner, J. N., & Barefoot, B. O. (2005). *Challenging and supporting the first-year student: A handbook for improving the first college year.* San Francisco: Jossey-Bass.

USC highlights. (2004). Retrieved February 18, 2004, from http://president.sc.edu/highlights.html.

Watt, E. (1999). *The freshman year experience, 1962–1990: An experiment in humanistic higher education.* Unpublished doctoral dissertation, Queen's University, Kingston, Ontario, Canada.

Yin, R. K. (1994). *Case study research: Design and methods* (2nd ed.). Thousand Oaks, CA: Sage.

Index

M

R

S

T